Progress in Laser Accelerator and Future Prospects

Progress in Laser Accelerator and Future Prospects

Editors

Toshiki Tajima
Pisin Chen

MDPI • Basel • Beijing • Wuhan • Barcelona • Belgrade • Manchester • Tokyo • Cluj • Tianjin

Editors
Toshiki Tajima
University of California
USA

Pisin Chen
National Taiwan University
Taiwan

Editorial Office
MDPI
St. Alban-Anlage 66
4052 Basel, Switzerland

This is a reprint of articles from the Special Issue published online in the open access journal *Photonics* (ISSN 2304-6732) (available at: https://www.mdpi.com/journal/photonics/special_issues/Laser_Accelerator).

For citation purposes, cite each article independently as indicated on the article page online and as indicated below:

LastName, A.A.; LastName, B.B.; LastName, C.C. Article Title. *Journal Name* **Year**, *Volume Number*, Page Range.

ISBN 978-3-0365-7472-1 (Hbk)
ISBN 978-3-0365-7473-8 (PDF)

Cover image courtesy of Keiichi Makino/Ayumi Shima (posted at Kids Museum of Photon, QST, Kyoto)

© 2023 by the authors. Articles in this book are Open Access and distributed under the Creative Commons Attribution (CC BY) license, which allows users to download, copy and build upon published articles, as long as the author and publisher are properly credited, which ensures maximum dissemination and a wider impact of our publications.
The book as a whole is distributed by MDPI under the terms and conditions of the Creative Commons license CC BY-NC-ND.

Contents

About the Editors vii

Toshiki Tajima and Pisin Chen
Preface for Special Issue: Progress in Laser Accelerator and Future Prospects
Reprinted from: *Photonics* 2023, 10, 292, doi:10.3390/photonics10030292 1

Weijian Sha, Jean-Christophe Chanteloup and Gérard Mourou
Ultrafast Fiber Technologies for Compact Laser Wake Field in Medical Application
Reprinted from: *Photonics* 2022, 9, 423, doi:10.3390/photonics9060423 5

Jonathan Wheeler, Gabriel Petrişor Bleotu, Andrei Naziru, Riccardo Fabbri, Masruri Masruri, Radu Secareanu, et al.
Compressing High Energy Lasers through Optical Polymer Films
Reprinted from: *Photonics* 2022, 9, 715, doi:10.3390/photonics9100715 19

Dongyu Li, Tang Yang, Minjian Wu, Zhusong Mei, Kedong Wang, Chunyang Lu, et al.
Introduction of Research Work on Laser Proton Acceleration and Its Application Carried out on Compact Laser–Plasma Accelerator at Peking University
Reprinted from: *Photonics* 2023, 10, 132, doi:10.3390/photonics10020132 31

Bjorn Manuel Hegelich, Lance Labun and Ou Z. Labun
Revisiting Experimental Signatures of the Ponderomotive Force
Reprinted from: *Photonics* 2023, 10, 226, doi:10.3390/photonics10020226 53

Martin Matys, Jan Psikal, Katsunobu Nishihara, Ondrej Klimo, Martin Jirka, Petr Valenta and Sergei V. Bulanov
High-Quality Laser-Accelerated Ion Beams from Structured Targets
Reprinted from: *Photonics* 2023, 10, 61, doi:10.3390/photonics10010061 73

Bernhard Hidding, Ralph Assmann, Michael Bussmann, David Campbell, Yen-Yu Chang, Sébastien Corde, et al.
Progress in Hybrid Plasma Wakefield Acceleration
Reprinted from: *Photonics* 2023, 10, 99, doi:10.3390/photonics10020099 93

Kangnan Jiang, Wentao Wang, Ke Feng and Ruxin Li
Review of Quality Optimization of Electron Beam Based on Laser Wakefield Acceleration
Reprinted from: *Photonics* 2022, 9, 511, doi:10.3390/photonics9080511 107

Ernesto Barraza-Valdez, Toshiki Tajima, Donna Strickland and Dante E. Roa
Laser Beat-Wave Acceleration near Critical Density
Reprinted from: *Photonics* 2022, 9, 476, doi:10.3390/photonics9070476 119

Ales Necas, Toshiki Tajima, Gerard Mourou and Karoly Osvay
Laser Ion Acceleration in a Near Critical Density Trap
Reprinted from: *Photonics* 2022, 9, 453, doi:10.3390/photonics9070453 129

Vasyl I. Maslov, Denys S. Bondar and Ivan N. Onishchenko
Investigation of the Way of Phase Synchronization of a Self-Injected Bunch and an Accelerating Wakefield in Solid-State Plasma
Reprinted from: *Photonics* 2022, 9, 174, doi:10.3390/photonics9030174 141

Dante Roa, Jeffrey Kuo, Harry Moyses, Peter Taborek, Toshiki Tajima, Gerard Mourou and Fuyuhiko Tamanoi
Fiber-Optic Based Laser Wakefield Accelerated Electron Beams and Potential Applications in Radiotherapy Cancer Treatments
Reprinted from: *Photonics* **2022**, *9*, 403, doi:10.3390/photonics9060403 . . . . **149**

Daniel Papp, Ales Necas, Nasr Hafz, Toshiki Tajima, Sydney Gales, Gerard Mourou, et al.
Laser Wakefield Photoneutron Generation with Few-Cycle High-Repetition-Rate Laser Systems
Reprinted from: *Photonics* **2022**, *9*, 826, doi:10.3390/photonics9110826 . . . . **159**

Masaki Kando, Alexander S. Pirozhkov, James K. Koga, Timur Zh. Esirkepov and Sergei V. Bulanov
Prospects of Relativistic Flying Mirrors for Ultra-High-Field Science
Reprinted from: *Photonics* **2022**, *9*, 862, doi:10.3390/photonics9110862 . . . . **173**

Pisin Chen, Gerard Mourou, Marc Besancon, Yuji Fukuda, Jean-Francois Glicenstein, Jiwoo Nam, et al.
AnaBHEL (Analog Black Hole Evaporation via Lasers) Experiment:Concept, Design, and Status
Reprinted from: *Photonics* **2022**, *9*, 1003, doi:10.3390/photonics9121003 . . . . **185**

About the Editors

Toshiki Tajima

Toshiki Tajima is the Norman Rostoker Chair Professor at the University of California at Irvine. He invented Laser Wakefield Acceleration with John Dawson in 1979. He served as Chair of APS Subdivision of Plasma Astrophysics and ICUIL, and as a member of NAS USLC/IUPAP. He was previously Director General of Kansai Photon Science Institute and the Jane and Roland Blumberg Professor at Univ. of Texas at Austin. He is the recipient of the Wilson Prize, Alfven Prize, Chandrasekhar Prize, Fermi Prize, Nishina Prize, Townes Award, etc.

Pisin Chen

Pisin Chen is the Chee-Chun Leung Distinguished Chair Professor of Cosmology at the National Taiwan University. He invented Plasma Wakefield Acceleration (PWFA) with John Dawson et al. in 1985, and discovered charged particle beam self-induced plasma focusing in 1987. In 2000, he initiated and helped establish the Chen Institute for Particle Astrophysics and Cosmology (later renamed the Kavli Insitute) at Stanford University. In 2007, he founded the NTU Leung Center for Cosmology and Particle Astrophysics (LeCosPA). He is a recipient of the 2018 Blaise Pascal Chair, and the 2023 Alfven Prize.

Editorial

Preface for Special Issue: Progress in Laser Accelerator and Future Prospects

Toshiki Tajima [1,2,*] and Pisin Chen [3,4,*]

1. Department of Physics and Astronomy, University of California, Irvine, CA 92697, USA
2. International Center for Zetta–Exawatt Science and Technology (IZEST), Ecole Polytechnique, F-91128 Paris, France
3. Leung Center for Cosmology and Particle Astrophysics, National Taiwan University, Taipei 10617, Taiwan
4. Department of Physics, National Taiwan University, Taipei 10617, Taiwan
* Correspondence: ttajima@uci.edu (T.T.); pisinchen@phys.ntu.edu.tw (P.C.)

In early 2022, one of the authors (Professor T. Tajima) was invited to edit a Special Issue of the journal *Photonics* under the title of "Progress in Laser Accelerator and Future Prospects". Since this topic is one of the most vigorously pursued and rapidly advanced in the field of photonics, T.T. decided to take up the challenge. T.T. then suggested *Photonics* to invite Professor Pisin Chen as a co-Editor to join the project. Together, we formed the editorship of this Special Issue. We then invited about 15 of the world's authorities on this subject to outline the current status and the future prospect of the field. Nearly all these invited authors accepted our invitations.

As we are motivated to cover theoretical, experimental, and technological advancements from fundamental science to societal applications of Laser Wakefield Accelerator (LWFA), we design the content of this Special Issue as follows.

I. Introduction;
II. Laser Technology;
III. Review of Experimental Status;
IV. Energy Frontier of Laser Wakefield Accelerators;
V. High Density Laser Wakefield Accelerators and Medical Applications;
VI. Fundamental Physics using Wakefields.

Section II consists of two papers, one by Sha et al. [1] and the other by Wheeler et al. [2], where the former reviewed the laser technology of the ultrafast fiber lasers and the fiber delivery of such pulses, and the latter described the thin-film compression technique to increase the pulse intensity in PW-class lasers. These are at the very forefront of state-of-the-art laser technology.

Section III reviews experimental progresses in laser acceleration in Asia, Europe, and the U.S. Li et al. [3] reported on the progress of the Compact Laser Plasma Accelerator (CLAPA) at Peking University, where high quality proton beams have been routinely produced. Hegelich et al. [4] revisited the experimental signatures of the ponderomotive force with fresh insights, while Matys et al. [5] reviewed how high-quality laser-accelerated ion beams can be attained by invoking structured targets where the relativistic instability induced can be utilized to produce highly collimated and quasi-monoenergetic ion beams.

Section IV deals with issues relating to the energy frontier of LWFA. In particular, Hidding et al. [6] reviewed the concept of the Hybrid Laser Plasma Wakefield Accelerator, which attempts to combine the LWFA scheme with that of the charged particle beam-driven Plasma Wakefield Accelerator (PWFA) so as to take advantage of both schemes to address the technical challenge of reaching high energies. Another critical challenge is the production of high-quality electron beams in laser acceleration, whose optimization scheme was nicely examined by Jiang et al. [7].

The next topic in this Issue (Section V) regards the high-density regime of LWFA and its medical applications. Here, we have collected as many as five papers by top experts from both the laser-plasma science and medicine industries. These include the excitation of Wakefields via laser beat-waves in the near-critical regime by Barraza-Valdez et al. [8], the slow phase velocity laser acceleration of ions at the near-critical density by Necas et al. [9], and the investigation of electron acceleration using phase synchronization through nanomaterials density inhomogeneity by Maslov et al. [10]. Roa et al. [11] focused on potential applications of fiber-optic-based laser Wakefield accelerated electron beams for radiotherapy cancer treatment, while Papp et al. [12] introduced the idea of LWFA-driven photoneutron generation aspired by high-impact societal applications. These directions all have a high potential in societal applications.

This Special Issue ends with Section VI that connects LWFA with fundamental physics. The paper by Kando et al. [13] reviewed the theoretical and experimental progress of the relativistic flying mirror (RFM) concept, which is a realization of the relativistic regime of LWFA, for the application to probing the Schwinger critical field limit in strong field science. The other paper, by Chen et al. [14], reports on the concept, design, and status of the AnaBHEL (Analog Black Hole Evaporation via Lasers) experiment. This is an attempt to accelerate ultra-intense LWFA-induced RFM with pre-designed trajectories as analog black holes to investigate the fundamental physics of black hole Hawking radiation.

We see that through the efforts of these world-leading experts and their outstanding coauthors, this Special Issue presents a broad and exciting landscape of the current status and the future prospects of LWFA. It is our sincere hope that this Special Issue provides a timely perspective as well as a future roadmap in the developments of laser Wakefield acceleration not only to the practitioners of this field, especially the younger generation of scientists, but also to those who work in other, albeit related, fields such as high energy physics, black hole physics, high-field science, and medicine. We are very grateful to all authors who contribute to this meaningful endeavor. Our gratuity also goes out to *Photonics* for initiating this Special Issue and the journal's staff for their tireless efforts, without which this Volume would not have been in such a wonderful shape. Last but not least, we deeply appreciate the administrative assistance of Maria Gaytan throughout the preparation of this Special Issue.

Conflicts of Interest: The authors declare no conflict of interest.

References

1. Sha, W.; Chanteloup, J.; Mourou, G. Ultrafast Fiber Technologies for Compact Laser Wake Field in Medical Application. *Photonics* **2022**, *9*, 423. [CrossRef]
2. Wheeler, J.; Bleotu, G.; Naziru, A.; Fabbri, R.; Masruri, M.; Secareanu, R.; Farinella, D.; Cojocaru, G.; Ungureanu, R.; Baynard, E.; et al. Compressing High Energy Lasers through Optical Polymer Films. *Photonics* **2022**, *9*, 715. [CrossRef]
3. Li, D.; Yang, T.; Wu, M.; Mei, Z.; Wang, K.; Lu, C.; Zhao, Y.; Ma, W.; Zhu, K.; Geng, Y.; et al. Introduction of Research Work on Laser Proton Acceleration and Its Application Carried out on Compact Laser–Plasma Accelerator at Peking University. *Photonics* **2023**, *10*, 132. [CrossRef]
4. Hegelich, B.M.; Labun, L.; Labun, O.Z. Revisiting Experimental Signatures of the Ponderomotive Force. *Photonics* **2023**, *10*, 226. [CrossRef]
5. Matys, M.; Psikal, J.; Nishihara, K.; Klimo, O.; Jirka, M.; Valenta, P.; Bulanov, S. High-Quality Laser-Accelerated Ion Beams from Structured Targets. *Photonics* **2023**, *10*, 61. [CrossRef]
6. Hidding, B.; Assmann, R.; Bussmann, M.; Campbell, D.; Chang, Y.; Corde, S.; Cabadağ, J.; Debus, A.; Döpp, A.; Gilljohann, M.; et al. Progress in Hybrid Plasma Wakefield Acceleration. *Photonics* **2023**, *10*, 99. [CrossRef]
7. Jiang, K.; Wang, W.; Feng, K.; Li, R. Review of Quality Optimization of Electron Beam Based on Laser Wakefield Acceleration. *Photonics* **2022**, *9*, 511. [CrossRef]
8. Barraza-Valdez, E.; Tajima, T.; Strickland, D.; Roa, D. Laser Beat-Wave Acceleration near Critical Density. *Photonics* **2022**, *9*, 476. [CrossRef]
9. Necas, A.; Tajima, T.; Mourou, G.; Osvay, K. Laser Ion Acceleration in a Near Critical Density Trap. *Photonics* **2022**, *9*, 453. [CrossRef]
10. Maslov, V.; Bondar, D.; Onishchenko, I. Investigation of the Way of Phase Synchronization of a Self-Injected Bunch and an Accelerating Wakefield in Solid-State Plasma. *Photonics* **2022**, *9*, 174. [CrossRef]

11. Roa, D.; Kuo, J.; Moyses, H.; Taborek, P.; Tajima, T.; Mourou, G.; Tamanoi, F. Fiber-Optic Based Laser Wakefield Accelerated Electron Beams and Potential Applications in Radiotherapy Cancer Treatments. *Photonics* **2022**, *9*, 403. [CrossRef]
12. Papp, D.; Necas, A.; Hafz, N.; Tajima, T.; Gales, S.; Mourou, G.; Szabo, G.; Kamperidis, C. Laser Wakefield Photoneutron Generation with Few-Cycle High-Repetition-Rate Laser Systems. *Photonics* **2022**, *9*, 826. [CrossRef]
13. Kando, M.; Pirozhkov, A.; Koga, J.; Esirkepov, T.; Bulanov, S. Prospects of Relativistic Flying Mirrors for Ultra-High-Field Science. *Photonics* **2022**, *9*, 862. [CrossRef]
14. Chen, P.; Mourou, G.; Besancon, M.; Fukuda, Y.; Glicenstein, J.; Nam, J.; Lin, C.; Lin, K.; Liu, S.; Liu, Y.; et al. AnaBHEL (Analog Black Hole Evaporation via Lasers) Experiment: Concept, Design, and Status. *Photonics* **2022**, *9*, 1003. [CrossRef]

Disclaimer/Publisher's Note: The statements, opinions and data contained in all publications are solely those of the individual author(s) and contributor(s) and not of MDPI and/or the editor(s). MDPI and/or the editor(s) disclaim responsibility for any injury to people or property resulting from any ideas, methods, instructions or products referred to in the content.

Review

Ultrafast Fiber Technologies for Compact Laser Wake Field in Medical Application

Weijian Sha [1,*], Jean-Christophe Chanteloup [2] and Gérard Mourou [3]

[1] CommScope Access Technologies Advanced Research, 2500 Walsh Ave, Santa Clara, CA 95051, USA
[2] LULI, CNRS, Ecole Polytechnique, CEA, Sorbonne Université, Institut Polytechnique de Paris, 91120 Palaiseau, France; jean-christophe.chanteloup@polytechnique.edu
[3] Ecole Polytechnique, Institut Polytechnique de Paris, 91120 Palaiseau, France; gerard.mourou@polytechnique.edu
* Correspondence: weijian.sha@commscope.com

Abstract: Technologies, performances and maturity of ultrafast fiber lasers and fiber delivery of ultrafast pulses are discussed for the medical deployment of laser-wake-field acceleration (LWFA). The compact ultrafast fiber lasers produce intense laser pulses with flexible hollow-core fiber delivery to facilitate electron acceleration in the laser-stimulated wake field near treatment site, empowering endoscopic LWFA brachytherapy. With coherent beam combination of multiple fiber amplifiers, the advantages of ultrafast fiber lasers are further extended to bring in more capabilities in compact LWFA applications.

Keywords: fiber laser; LWFA; brachytherapy; coherent beam combination

1. Introduction

Progresses of laser-wake-field acceleration (LWFA) are presented in this special volume of Photonics. Over the last few decades, LWFA has advanced to become an alternative form of particle acceleration [1,2]. Energy of accelerated electrons by LWFA has reached beyond 10 GeV. LWFA produces electric field gradient at GeV/cm; acceleration length is on a scale of centimeters. Laser accelerators are seen as the space- and cost-efficient alternatives to conventional GeV accelerators such as synchrotron of large building size or linear accelerator scaled at kilometer. A typical petawatt-peak-power (10^{15} W) laser system that drives the LWFA occupies laboratory space of several hundred square meters in comparison, representing a large reduction in accelerator size and cost.

Electrons obtained from conventional accelerators have been used in radiation therapy. Even at the low energy levels the apparatus still occupies a very large room. The inherent advantage of LWFA, exemplified in the reduction factor above, has the potential to reduce the footprint of lower-energy accelerator proportionally or even more [3]. One promising avenue of cancer treatment is brachytherapy, in which a source of radiation is brought inside the body close to the tissues requiring treatment [4,5]. For endoscopic and intraoperative brachytherapy at the local treatment site electron radiation from few tens to few hundreds of keV are sufficient as treatment radiation needs not to traverse healthy tissues. Electron radiation is emitted from LWFA cell near the local treatment site by laser pulses from the flexible delivery system. Simulation studies in the high-density domain of LWFA have shown electron radiation at these energies can be produced using novel nanomaterials [6,7] at relatively low peak power and intensity of the drive laser. At these intensity levels laser sources can be devised in compact and reliable forms and formulated for field use.

In this paper we shall discuss the enabling technologies in ultrafast fiber lasers and subsequent flexible delivery for the compact electron accelerator for medical applications such as cancer treatment. Ultrafast fiber laser systems are now capable of generating the intense light pulses for medical LWFA in compact and portable manner. This technology is further advanced by the Coherent Beam Combining (CBC) lasers. Advents in hollow-core fibers are enabling flexible light delivery of the intense pulses to the locations that cannot be reached with conventional free-space optics. These technologies are coming out from laboratories to the application fields.

2. Lasers for LWFA

LWFA transforms light energy from the high-peak-power laser pulses into the kinetic energy of accelerated electrons. There are excellent review papers on laser plasma acceleration (LPA) and the necessary lasers to drive the LPA [8,9]. From the perspective of this paper, we divide high peak-power laser systems into two categories, the ultra-intense (sub-terawatt, terawatt, and petawatt) and the intense (gigawatt and sub-gigawatt). This only reflects a laser construction point of view as we shall see below. Our main focus is the intense lasers (in fact, they are very intense) considered for LWFA applications yielding tens or hundreds of keV electron energy in medical applications.

Terawatt (TW, 10^{12} watt) lasers [10] use table-top solid-state lasers. Enabled by chirped pulse amplification [11,12], these systems attain TW peak power at various combinations of pulse energy and pulse duration (for example, 1 TW is 1 J/1 ps or 100 mJ/100 fs). Beam diameter in propagation insider the amplifier is expanded to about a centimeter [10]. TW lasers reach focused light intensity of 10^{18} W/cm^2, at the starting point for high-field plasma physics (laser peak intensity at 10^{18} W/cm^2 has the electric field strength that drives plasma electrons into relativistic quiver motion). Free-space optical elements (mirrors, lenses, spatial filters, stretcher and compressor, etc.) allow beam expansion for energy extraction, beam and pulse conditioning without damage. These elements need mechanics for mounting, stabilization and alignment. The laser system often has several amplification stages, stationed on top of floating optical table(s) for vibration isolation.

Petawatt (PW, 10^{15} watt) or tens of PW class lasers are the pinnacles of ultra-intense laser achievements [13,14]. One would only need to imagine that PW systems will have laser beams sized proportionally.

Lasers for LWFA in the lower energy regime of tens to hundreds of keV for oncology application require focused intensity from 10^{14} W/cm^2 and up [7]. For a moderate focal diameter of 20 µm, the corresponding laser peak power is about 1 gigawatt (GW, 10^9 watt). LWFA laser parameters, either 1 mJ and 1 ps or 100 µJ and 100 fs, involve GW peak power from a laser system. Ultrafast solid-state lasers based on free-space optics can certainly produce the peak power and the intensity. Our focus here is ultrafast fiber lasers, constructed from wave-guiding optical fibers. Bulk optics is eliminated from most parts in the system and the compactness aids or necessitates portable field application. For endoscopic LWFA, the other key element is the flexible delivery pathway for the laser pulses. Kinetic electrons are emitted in the LWFA cell at the end of the light delivery cable near the treatment site.

We shall review the advances in fiber lasers and specialty delivery fibers that are capable or close to be capable to generate and deliver gigawatt laser pulses. These technological advances are empowering as we promote the "miniature" LWFA scheme for medical applications.

3. Compact Electron Accelerator

Perspectives of LWFA applications to brachytherapy are discussed in detail medically and technologically [3,5]. In endoscopic approach, LWFA adopts the use of solid-state carbon nanotubes (CNTs) excited by the laser pulses [6,7].

A brief illustration of the laser acceleration mechanism in CNT is given in Figure 1. The wake-field excited by the laser is in the high-density regime of LWFA (the classical LWFA is in the low-density regime) and accelerates electrons to energies to the range from a few tens to a few hundreds of keV, which are sufficient to damage cancer cells locally but low enough not to cause collateral damage to healthy tissues.

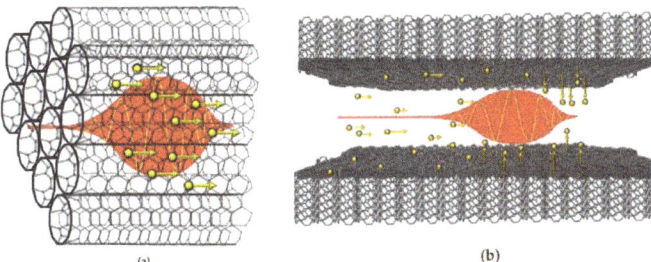

Figure 1. Illustration for CNT to emulate high density plasma. A laser pulse, shown in red, interacts with sheets of CNT, shown in grey. The laser permeates the nanotubes, extracting and accelerating electrons, shown in yellow. (**a**) CNTs arranged parallel to the laser propagation direction, and (**b**) CNTs arranged perpendicularly. Reprinted from Ref. [6].

LWFA transforms light energy from the high-peak-power laser pulse into the kinetic energy of accelerated electrons. The large gradients produced by the transverse laser intensity profile at focus and by the longitudinal temporal profile produce strong pondermotive forces, resulting in laser plasma wake-fields which accelerate electrons. The strength of laser wake field is determined by the driving laser's peak intensity, defined by the peak power of the ultrashort pulses (temporal) and the focal profile (spatial). Laser intensity for electron acceleration in the high-density LWFA regime to attain electron energies from a few tens to a few hundreds of keV for endoscopic applications needs to be 10^{14} W/cm^2 and higher [7].

The field of compact Electron Accelerator is rich and full of creativity. Other approaches exist among which the dielectric laser accelerator (DLA) [15] where an incident laser pulse is focused onto a nanofabricated accelerating structure, exciting traveling near-field modes. Electrons, propagating in close proximity to the structure, are accelerated when their velocity matches the phase velocity of one of the traveling modes, and they are injected into these fields at a particular time.

The dose (total electrons in treatment duration, e.g., seconds) required for each point of treatment is related to the average power of the excitation laser. With good efficiency in high-density LWFA, we expect that several watts of average power are sufficient. This power is readily available and thus our focus of the technology is on peak-power generation and delivery.

4. Fiber Laser Technology

It is interesting to note that our laser goal in this paper for the compact LWFA scheme, gigawatt, is the power level that the very first Chirp Pulse Amplification (CPA) demonstrated [12]. Since then, CPA has propelled laser amplification to unprecedented level, and it is the technology used for all levels of LWFA today. We shall discuss the compact version of CPA system with fiber lasers reduced from the table-top lasers, much like table-top CPA lasers downsized the much larger laser systems otherwise.

This compactization comes from the progress in research and industry to the condensed forms of fiber lasers and diode lasers. Fiber laser takes a thin strand of optical fiber, active or passive, and a diode laser is built on a tiny yet powerful light-emitting semiconductor junction. Ultrafast fiber oscillators have been developed while amplification in fiber rely on the use of CPA. Advances of these "compressed" lasers are not only shown in academic research but also in rapid commercialization. We can see where the technologies are going, and they hold the promise leading to compact LWFA scheme for medical applications.

4.1. Fiber Laser Advantages and Characteristics

Fiber lasers have gain media confined within the core of an active optical fiber. Core diameter (more precisely mode-field diameter, or MFD) ranges from several μm to tens and hundreds of μm. Single-transverse mode MFD can be up to 100 μm. Pump laser diodes have emitters each sized from under an μm to several μm, with outputs coupled into the gain fiber. Pump intensity in the small cross-section of the fiber produces high inversion. Signal and pump in fiber propagate as guided wave permitting long interaction length in meters, yielding high conversion efficiency (more details in Section 4.3). Fiber is flexible with typical bending radius of 20 cm or less, allowing fiber spooling in compact assembly. Heat dissipation is much more efficient compared to solid-state laser crystal due to the high surface-to-volume ratio of fiber and the distributed heat load along the length of the fiber. Besides, active fibers and passive fiber components and pump diodes can all be made from cost- effective scalable manufacturing.

There are two predominant fiber laser wavelengths in the industry, one is based on Ytterbium (Yb)- doped fiber operating slightly above 1 μm and the other Erbium (Er)-doped centered at 1.55 μm. Many Yb fiber lasers, operating in continuous-wave (CW) or Q-switch are used in metal cutting and welding and semiconductor processing. Ultrafast lasers utilize both Yb and Er doped fibers.

Fiber lasers with large cores (hundreds of μm) in multi-mode (MM) are used to produce kilowatt and higher power in CW. Beam quality is not optimal and M^2 is large but adequate for metal cutting and welding which do not require tight focusing. For diffraction-limited focusing, single-mode (SM) waveguiding is required permitting only the fundamental mode. Pump guiding is often in a double-clad configuration, allowing a larger guided pump core (which serves as inner cladding for signal) while the amplified signal light is in the smaller inner core. This results in brightness conversion from the pump to the laser. More details regarding the double-clad technology are discussed in Section 4.3. Fiber lasers have the main advantages in producing high average power and high efficiency due to the fiber geometry of small cross-section and long interaction length. On the other hand, high peak-power lasers suffer detrimental nonlinear effects for the same reason. There are remarkable advances in making large-core (up to 100 μm) single-mode fibers to enable high peak-power amplification. The innate average-power advantage of fiber allows for high repetition rate of the amplified pulses.

We will, in this paper, only examine the peak power aspect of fiber systems for compact LWFA medical application. Available average power from fiber lasers typically exceeds requirement; for example, several watts of average optical power is abundant for endoscopic LWFA.

4.2. Efficient, Compact and Reliable Laser Diode Pumps

The overall high wall-plug efficiency and the compactness in fiber lasers are also attributed to semiconductor laser technology. An active laser diode emitter of a few μm wide and less than 1 μm thick can produce for example 10 watts of power, for example Quantum-well design of direct band-gap semiconductor laser diode and the choice of material systems (III-V and II-VI, each has subsets) cover emission wavelengths essentially across the visible and near infrared spectrum. Diodes from 920 nm to 980 nm are used for pumping Yb or Er-Yb fibers; 980 nm or 1480 nm pumping Er fibers. Diode pumps have electrical to optical efficiency from 50% to 70% in literature [16] for example and in product catalogs from commercial diode manufacturers [17–19] including the loss after assembled into fiber-coupled packages in research literature and also in commercially available products.

The research and industry have achieved extraordinary reliability over the years, from the first lab diode laser that lasted for milliseconds to those used in submarine fiber-optic link today with millions of hours of mean-time-between-failures. These are all remarkable that current density in the diode junction and optical facet power density are at the levels of 10 kA/cm^2 and 100 MW/cm^2. Today, a typical single emitter at 10 W is rated for tens of thousands of hours. Lifetime can be prolonged at de-rated power levels.

4.3. Double-Clad Fiber as Brightness Convertor

Double-clad fiber technology enables high power and high efficiency in fiber laser operation. Light to be amplified is in the inner core while pump light is guided in the larger pump core. The middle portion in turn serves as the cladding of the signal. Pump is confined by the outer cladding. Design of the double-clad structure introduces features to allow sufficient crossing of pump in the signal core. See Figure 2 for illustrations. Meters-long interaction length allows for a high pump absorption efficiency of 90%. Fiber conversion efficiency from pump power is in the range from 50% to 70% in commercially available double-clad fiber products [20–23] depending on pump wavelength which determines quantum efficiency.

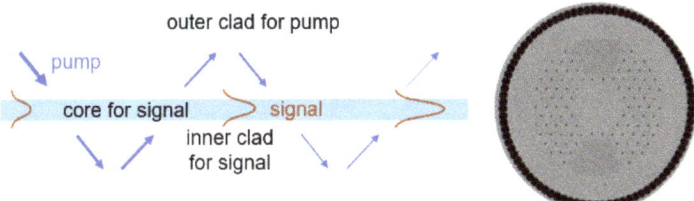

Figure 2. (**Left**) Illustration of double-clad fiber with step index profile. Center core for signal has highest index; inner cladding for the signal also guides the pump; outer cladding for the pump has the lowest index. (**Right**) Cross section of an advance large-mode-area photonic crystal fiber using air-holes in the low index regions. The center solid portion is the core for signal and the outer ring of air holes serves as the clad of the pump which guides pump in the fiber structure. It is designed for large-mode-area single-mode and polarization maintaining amplification, reprinted from Ref. [24]. See more about this technology in Sections 5.2 and 7.1.

The larger pump guide is substantial in gathering pump power from broad-area MM laser diodes. Thus, double clad fiber is seen as a brightness up-converter from the lower intensity of pump light to higher intensity of the laser light in the inner core. Several pump modules can be combined in a fiber combiner for more pump power while maintaining each pump module at moderate power for long-term reliability.

A more advanced double-clad fiber design utilizes an air clad as the outer clad for the pump (Figure 2). The low index of air holes provides much higher index contrast, facilitating high numeric apertures (0.4 to 0.6) to couple in even more divergent pump light.

4.4. CW and Nanosecond Fiber Lasers

Fiber laser and laser diode industries have seen unprecedented progress in the last few decades. For example, fiber lasers of refrigerator size (mostly electrical and cooling), can deliver tens of kilowatts of CW power while keeping component damage under control. These fiber lasers are expanding the capabilities of other lasers, with the sheer light power to convert to high heat. Beam quality is often far from diffraction limit. Because of this, kW CW lasers typically have moderate focused intensity (Table 1 below).

Nanosecond fiber lasers from Q-switched operation can be used in semiconductor wafer and chip processing. There are designs in SM or MM, depending on the needed spatial precision. These lasers have nanosecond pulse duration boosting laser peak power and intensity (Table 1) which can be viewed as the intermediates between CW and ultrafast fiber lasers in peak power and intensity.

Table 1. Some applications of CW, nanosecond and ultrafast fiber lasers. Representative orders of average power, peak power and intensity levels are listed.

Application	Average Power	Pulse Width	Peak Power	Spatial Mode	Focused Intensity
Metal cutting (heat)	1 to 100 kW	Continuous	same as average	MM [1]	10^7 W/cm^2 (CW)
Semiconductor Processing	10 to 1000 W	1 to 100 ns	MW (10^6 W)	MM/SM [2]	10^9 W/cm^2 (peak)
Glass cutting (cold ablation)	>10 W	≤0.5 ps	Hundreds of MW	SM	10^{13} W/cm^2 (peak)
Portable LWFA (>10 keV electrons)	1 to 10 W	≤1 ps	≥ GW (10^9 W)	SM	≥ 10^{14} W/cm^2 (peak)

[1] MM: multi-mode (spatial); [2] SM: single mode.

5. Ultrafast Fiber Lasers and Amplifiers

Ultrafast fiber lasers soon followed the advent of mode-locked femtosecond dye lasers in 1980s and have seen rapid expansion in R&D and commercialization. As of 2020, there have been 5000 publications on ultrafast fiber lasers [25].

Having 100 µJ pulse energy with sub-picosecond width delivers hundreds of megawatts peak power (Table 1 above). Focused pulses have light intensity which corresponds to electric field strength greater than molecular bonding force. At several hundred femtoseconds, a laser pulse is shorter than phonon scatter time in solids; thus, there is no heat transferred from the laser. Such conditions create cold ablation or photoionization [26]. Micromachining applications are enabled where hard materials—such as glass or sapphire—can be cut with superior quality; for example, in fabricating smart-phone screens.

Our application, laser-wake-field acceleration in endoscopic oncology, acquires tens of keV electron energy from laser pulses at intensity starting from 10^{14} W/cm^2 [7]. This intensity can be produced by focusing a gigawatt laser (Table 1 above) to a moderate focal diameter such as 20 µm. We now discuss the technologies leading to gigawatt fiber lasers.

Most ultrafast fiber system (or in general high peak-power lasers) are configured in a master-oscillator-power-amplifier (MOPA) architecture. An ultrafast fiber oscillator provides stable seed pulses of femtoseconds or picoseconds. Prior to amplification, the pulse repetition rate is often reduced. Power amplifier(s) then concentrate laser energy to the fewer selected pulses and increase peak power by many orders.

5.1. Ultrafast Fiber Laser Oscillator

Nature has offered mechanisms of organizing broad spectral bandwidth in laser media into ultrashort pulses in time. In the early 1980s, colliding pulse mode-locking was discovered in dye lasers [27,28] using saturable absorbers. The first-ever femtosecond pulses were generated, opening the ultrafast time scale. Kerr-lens mode-locking in Ti:Sapphire lasers were later revealed and developed [29]. Around the same time, mode-locked femtosecond fiber lasers were reported [30]. Mode-lock mechanisms shaping laser light into ultrashort pulses are based on one type or another of nonlinear optical processes.

Advances in ultrafast fibers are reviewed by a number of excellent papers for example [25,31,32]. Many ultrafast fiber oscillators are mode-locked or aided (start action and stabilization) by saturable absorption and the mechanisms alike. Saturable absorption is a nonlinear process in which the lower intensity of a pulse's pedestals or wings is absorbed to a greater extent than the peak. Repetitive laser action shapes random waveform into pulse of short duration supported by laser gain bandwidth. Semiconductor, carbon nanotube [33] and other materials can be made of this function. Semiconductor saturable absorber mirror (SESAM) [34] is often used in mode-locking ultrafast lasers. Other effective saturable mechanisms—such as nonlinear polarization evolution (NPE) and nonlinear amplifying loop mirror (NALM) [30,35]—also function very well.

Ultrafast fiber lasers also have to deal with large amounts in nonlinearity and group velocity dispersion (GVD) due to small mode area and long propagation length. These factors can either benefit pulse shaping or have detrimental effects. Silica fiber has normal GVD at 1 μm (Yb gain region) and is anomalous at 1.5 μm (Er region). A laser cavity can be configured in a net dispersion of either way. Soliton lasers take advantage of the soliton mechanism in balancing self-phase modulation (SPM) and anomalous dispersion [36,37]. Pulse energy in soliton fiber lasers is typically low. In the normal dispersion regime, similariton is effective in producing higher energy pulses, where the interplay of dispersion, SPM, and gain renders an input pulse of arbitrary shape evolving asymptotically into an amplified, linearly chirped pulse. The pulse grows in duration, spectral width, and peak power in a self-similar manner to that the temporal profile and the chirp rate remains unchanged [25,38,39]. Chirp can be externally compressed. Additional techniques—such as spectral filtering and polarization control—can also be useful to assist the mode-locking [40].

Robustness of well-designed femtosecond fiber lasers has been established. For example, in the SLAC National Accelerator Laboratory's Linac Coherent Light Source, the injector ultrafast laser system has an Yb ultrafast fiber laser as its source. Up-converted UV pulses from this femtosecond laser system emit photoelectrons in the injector photocathode. Synchronized electrons are accelerated by the linear accelerator to generate femtosecond X-rays in the free-electron laser section [41].

5.2. Ultrafast Fiber Amplifiers

Packing a gigawatt laser into a fiber laser system has many challenges. Intensity of short pulses in fiber is inherently high. Nonlinear (non-recoverable) phase accumulation can quickly deteriorate the spectral and temporal profiles as the pulse propagates. When the pulse gains intensity above the material damage threshold, it damages or vaporizes the fiber.

Two major technologies are the key enablers to overcome the obstacles: chirped-pulse amplification (CPA) helps to boost amplifier output peak power by 3 to 4 orders, while large mode area (LMA) fibers increase by another 2 to 3 orders.

5.2.1. Chirped-Pulse Amplification

CPA proceeds in three steps: (1) an ultra-short laser pulse is stretched in time by several orders of magnitude, so that its peak power is correspondingly reduced, (2) it is amplified in a laser material without damaging it, (3) it is compressed in time back to its original duration, resulting in very high peak power [11].

Light amplification by stimulated emission preserves the optical phase. Pulse stretched into a linear chirp prior to amplifier is a reservable process by the corresponding compression after amplification.

5.2.2. Large Mode Area Fiber

Increasing the mode-field diameter (MFD) in the amplifying fiber is another key to mitigate the peak power problem [39,42]. In doing so, single mode must be maintained. Modal dispersion in multi-mode propagation obliterates temporal profile of the pulses. Furthermore, the fundamental mode allows diffraction-limited focusing for the targeted intensity. SM fiber designs with step-index or graded-index profiles are limited due to the small index contrast and the simple spatial profile. Breakthrough in photonic crystal fibers (PCF) makes large-mode-area single-mode fiber design possible and enables much higher peak power in ultrafast fiber amplifiers, in conjunction with CPA.

PCF guiding employs periodic index modulation with air holes to achieve high index contrast. Preferential design in the cladding discriminates high-order modes allowing single mode with larger core sizes (see Section 7.1). Commercial PCF fibers with MFD over 30 μm are now available. As evident in Figure 3, fiber amplifier output peak power level goes hand-in-hand with mode-field area. In the fiber system producing 4 GW, the final amplifier stage employed a PCF Yb gain fiber with 105 μm MFD [43].

5.3. Towards Gigawatt

In Figure 3, a survey of high-power ultrafast fiber laser research in last 15 years is presented. Even with this limited survey we can see the extraordinary advances in laser peak power from tens or hundreds of megawatts to gigawatts. As remarked earlier, the first CPA gigawatt system was based on table-top solid-state lasers with free-space optics. Now gigawatt can be condensed to a fiber laser system. Gigawatt fiber lasers enable compact, portable LWFA medical applications.

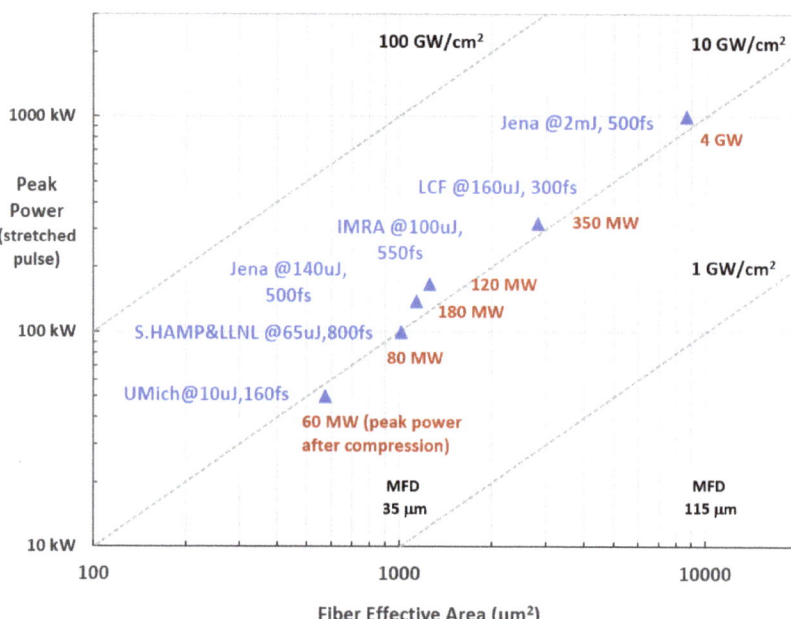

Figure 3. Survey of research work in CPA ultrafast fiber amplifiers from a number of publications in this limited survey. Triangle data points mark reduced peak power of stretched pulse (stretch ratio up to 4000) in fiber amplifiers. Blue notations are the resulted output pulse energy and pulse width after compression and the corresponding output peak power is marked in red. Output peak power up to 4 GW is seen increasing with fiber effective area. The ratio of instantaneous power (stretched) in the vertical axis over fiber area in horizontal axis is light intensity in fiber. Blue triangle data points are seen following along the intensity line of 10 GW/cm², indicative of the limit imposed by nonlinear phase accumulation as discussed below.

5.3.1. Limitation due to Fiber Nonlinearity

Over the length L in fiber, nonlinear phase φ_{nl} is accumulated from the small but existent nonlinearity index n_2 (3×10^{-16} m²/W in silica),

$$\varphi_{nl} = \frac{2\pi n_2}{\lambda} \frac{P}{A} L$$

where A is effective mode-field-area. P is the peak power of the pulse averaged over the fiber length, already reduced by the stretch ratio from CPA. L is typically of meters. φ_{nl} can be also viewed as proportional to the light intensity P/A in fiber.

As a rule-of-thumb estimate, acceptable φ_{nl} (or B integral) is about 2π. Above this level, non-correctable detrimental effects are seen on temporal and spectral quality of the pulse. This obstacle is seen at lower intensity levels in fiber amplifiers, compared to solid-state lasers.

Note that the blue triangle data points in Figure 3 are "pushed" along the intensity line of 10 GW/cm^2, indicative of the limit imposed by nonlinear phase accumulation. Further increasing the fiber mode area is becoming more difficult. MFD of 100 µm is already 100 times that of the laser wavelength. With large core diameters, single-mode guiding becomes highly sensitive to fiber bending. In fact, some of the large-core fibers are the rod-type fibers.

5.3.2. Summary

Gigawatt ultrafast amplifier systems are empowered by the two key technologies:

- CPA reduces P by 3 to 4 orders by stretching the seed pulse prior to amplification.
- Large-mode-area fibers increase mode area A, thus reducing light intensity P/A by 2 to 3 orders.

As efforts continue to drive fiber lasers to higher peak power, coherent combination of many ultrafast fiber lasers is seen as the next frontier [44,45]. Progresses and highlights are reported in the next section. The state-of-the-art takes fiber lasers beyond gigawatt and open a new array of capabilities in bringing on "digital laser" applications.

6. Coherent Beam Combining (CBC) Lasers

Coherent beam combining (CBC) introduces a paradigm shift in laser architecture offering major opportunities for laser design and consequently for applications. CBC can be seen as the space domain equivalent to what CPA allows in time domain: spreading the energy prior to amplification to mitigate limitations such as B integral. CBC consists indeed in the spatial splitting of an initial laser beam into N small aperture sub-beams followed by subsequent recombination of the amplified beams. The above-mentioned limitations (Section 5.3) remain valid at each individual fiber level but are overcome at a global scale if the N amplifying channels are ultimately successfully coherently combined. Gigawatt ultrafast fiber systems can then be empowered by a third key technology (from Section 5.3.2):

- CBC improves amplification by a factor η N (η being the combining efficiency).

Figure 4 illustrates Ecole Polytechnique/Thales N = 61 channel XCAN CBC prototype (with η experimentally ranging from 40% to 50%) [46].

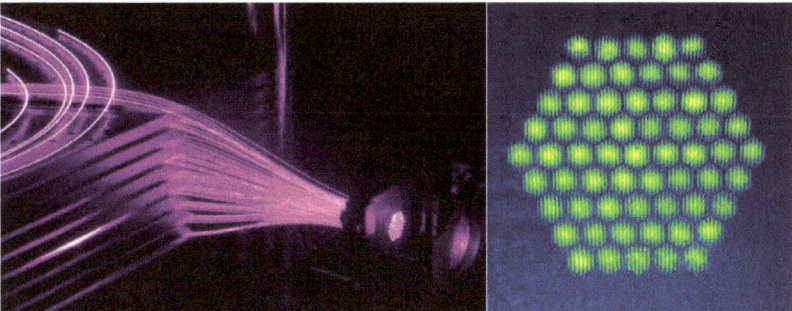

Figure 4. XCAN 61 channel CBC laser. The bundle of 61 YB doped 30 µm MFD amplifying fiber can be seen fluorescing. The fibers are arranged in the laser head in a honeycomb distribution and subsequently collectively collimated through a lenslet array (far right of the **left** image). Collective phase delays recording through interference pattern (**right**). Adapted from Ref. [47].

XCAN relies on far field CBC (also described as tiled-aperture CBC), a combining approach inherently limiting the efficiency to η = 65% theoretical value but offering two experimental key advantages: absence of a final optic dealing with the full combined peak and average power (see Figure 5) and near field access to individual control of phase, amplitude and polarization for digital laser applications [47,48].

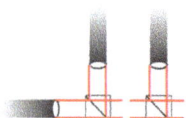 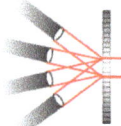 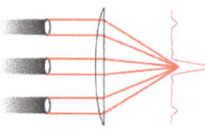

Figure 5. Near field/filled-aperture CBC architecture with combining polarizing cubes (**left**) or diffractive optical plate (**center**). Far field/tiled-aperture CBC through a lens as on XCAN setup (**right**).

Alternative architectures falling into the near field combining category (also described as filled-aperture CBC) does not face such an efficiency limit with experimental η only limited by optics quality (generally above 90%). Recently, 81 beams have recently been combined with a diffractive combiner [49] whereas 16 amplifying channels were combined with beam splitters [50]. More recently, the same group achieved a similar channel number coherent addition within a single multicore fiber [51], paving the way for even more compact (even though the involved fiber was not flexible) laser system. Each core has a diameter of 19 µm with a pitch of 55 µm between the core centers.

7. Photonic Bandgap Fiber (Hollow-Core Fiber) for Pulse Delivery

Fiber amplifiers capable of producing gigawatt peak power are proven, further enhanced by coherent beam combining lasers that push beyond gigawatts and are capable of shaping user-desired wavefronts. Compact fiber laser sources are here for LWFA medical applications. In endoscopic applications, laser pulses need to be delivered with flexible channel to the LWFA cell near the treatment site. We look to the hollow-core fiber technology for carrying the intense gigawatt peak-power laser pulses. Light propagation is mostly in the hollow core made of air. In this way, material damage is avoided; nonlinearity and dispersion can be drastically reduced.

Hollow-core fiber stems from the advents of photonic crystal fiber (PCF) technology. PCF technology pushes fiber design well beyond what conventional step-index fibers can do. It branches into two distinct mechanisms: high-index guiding and low-index guiding. Large-mode- area fibers enabling ultrafast fiber lasers are based on high-index guiding PCFs and hollow-core fiber belongs to low-index guiding.

7.1. High-Index Guiding PCFs

Conventional step-index fibers utilize total internal reflection (TIR) to guide light rays, having higher optical index in the core than in the cladding. This index contrasts (with converging power) shapes collective wave-guiding by balancing natural light diffraction in the fiber. Proper single-mode fiber design is to have only the fundamental mode. PCFs greatly broaden the limited design capabilities with step-index fiber design.

PCFs have a sophisticated microstructure of different refractive indexes [24,52]. They are typically glass fibers fabricated by pulling from a preform in a furnace—like conventional fibers—and they maintain bending flexibility. The background material is often undoped silica and low index regions are typically air voids. Air has the lowest optical index, thus producing very high index contrasts. Stronger guiding results from this modified total internal reflection (M-TIR) [52]. Locations of air-hole networks can be arranged according to desired function, such as mode-guiding differentiation, dispersion, and cut-off wavelength (or the absence of it).

PCFs allow a new range of novel properties. The large-mode-area (LMA) PCF is an essential element in ultrafast fiber amplifiers for reducing intensity. In a commercial offering of an Yb-doped fiber, for example, using precise control of airhole diameter and spacing and induced birefringence yields a single mode polarizing fiber with diffraction-limited beam quality at 40 µm diameter core size (see Figure 2, the shape on the right).

Another example of PCF having the opposite function of large-mode-area fibers is the highly nonlinear fiber for supercontinuum generation. The small-core (1 or 2 µm) fiber sharply increases the light intensity, and the near-zero-dispersion design allows long interaction length without dispersing the femtosecond pulses. The resultant supercontinuum spans over an octave wide in frequency, allowing f-to-2f interferometry for carrier-envelop-phase stabilization in the laser oscillator. The accomplished system generates phase-synchronized frequency comb in high-precision metrology applications [53].

7.2. Hollow-Core Fiber (Low-Index Guiding) for Ultrafast Pulse Delivery

Low-index-guiding PCFs uses photonic bandgap (PBG) effect to guide light. The guiding mechanism in PBG fiber is fundamentally different from high-index guiding in M-TIR. The light is typically confined to the empty core such as air while the surrounding microstructure region as the cladding displays a photonic bandgap [54]. Much like electron waves in a crystal where a band of electron wavevectors is forbidden, optical waves of certain wavelengths in the photonic bandgap cannot propagate. Therefore, light is trapped and propagates only in the hollow core surrounded by the anti-resonant (being reflective) microstructure. Only the edge of the transverse profile (less than a few percent of the light power) sees the glass material.

PBG fiber is a new paradigm in fiber design. Nature has existing examples of the PBG effect; for example, the color of a butterfly is the result of anti-resonant nano-cavities at the reflecting wavelength. Dispersion of PBG fibers can be tailored as it is mostly determined by the microstructure. PBG fiber design is sophisticated, which requires full vectorial calculation from Maxwell Equations. Mechanically PBG fibers are also flexible.

With light being guided in the hollow core of air, vacuum, or gas, the high-intensity ultrafast laser pulses do not experience nonlinearity (and damage) as in the solid core fibers—facilitating fiber delivery applications with ultrafast pulses. For example, high-harmonics generation (UV) from laser pulses can be generated at the end of the delivery fiber as UV light darkens fiber. Ophthalmology surgery can be performed with the laser delivered by the hollow-core fiber. This is also what is needed in endoscopic LWFA.

Capabilities of hollow-core fibers are given in a couple of demonstrated results. In the first result [55], 70 W of average power of picosecond pulses are transmitted over the hollow-core fibers with only a few percent power loss after 5-10 meters. Diffraction-limited beams in MFD of 8 µm, 13 µm, and 22 µm fibers are delivered while bending radii are kept at 8 cm. Another demonstrated result [56] is the hollow-core fiber with a MFD of 40 µm. It has the capacity to carry 500 fs pulses of 500 µJ energy. This amounts to 1 GW of peak power. The bending radius of the fiber is about 25 cm. Ultimately, hollow-core fibers are limited due to damage of the glass structure at the edge of the laser intensity profile.

7.3. Additional Delivery Capability

The limit of hollow-core fiber transmission is affected by damage at the edge of the intense laser mode profile. To further increase delivery capability, we may anticipate the coming of a multi-hollow-core fiber. There are multi-core fibers existent today based on step-index solid materials. This type of design has multiple cores with a common outer wall, protection coating, enforcement, etc. It has been developed as a compact form for space-division multiplexing in optical communication to multiply the data-carrying bandwidth. Similarly, we may boost throughput of laser pulses with multiple hollow cores in a common fiber structure. Laser channels in the close spatial vicinity help to facilitate a common focal point with the use of a lenslet array for collimation prior to a common focusing lens. It is similar to CBC lasers (see Section 6) in spatially combining beams, but without phase locking. Power addition is not coherent thus intensity distribution varies from shot-to-shot within the focal boundary. Effectiveness of such a laser field in LWFA requires further study.

8. Applying Ultrafast Fiber Technologies to Endoscopic LWFA

One promising avenue of cancer treatment is brachytherapy, in which a source of radiation is brought inside the body close to the tissues requiring treatment. For endoscopic and intraoperative brachytherapy at the local treatment site, electron radiation from few tens to few hundreds of keV can be effective (see brief introductions in see Sections 1 and 6). Laser intensity for electron acceleration in the high-density LWFA regime for endoscopic applications needs to be 10^{14} W/cm^2 and higher. In this paper, we have brought forth ultrafast fiber technologies for this application: ultrafast fiber lasers (single-fiber system or coherent-beam-combining lasers) which are capable of generating gigawatts and above as the light source, and hollow-core fibers for delivering these intense laser pulses endoscopically.

Laser pulses are delivered flexibly to the LWFA cell and ready to focus on to the target material to generate and accelerate electrons. Engineering design must be mindful of damage in the delivery optics due to the nature of the intense laser pulses. For such the laser beam after exiting the hollow-core fiber should be expanded to encounter optics based on solid material. Furthermore, the expanded beam is necessary for the proper beam size to optimize diffraction-limited focusing to the target. The choice of focusing design also depends on the Rayleigh range needed for LWFA. At a modest 20 µm focal diameter, Rayleigh range is about 300 µm for laser wavelength of 1 µm; 1 gigawatt peak power will yield 3×10^{14} W/cm^2, in range for target LWFA laser intensity.

An effective scheme of LWFA utilizing the relatively low laser intensity of 10^{14} W/cm^2 is the plasma beat-wave accelerator (PBWA) [7,57]. The scheme uses two co-propagating laser pulses with two optical frequencies—ω_1 and ω_2—and the beat gives a modulated laser amplitude for the resonant excitation of a plasma wave at $\omega_p = \omega_1 - \omega_2$ where ω_p is the plasma frequency. The modulated laser intensity profile which is resonant with plasma wave gives in-phase pondermotive kicks to accelerate the electrons. The advantage of PBWA is that lower peak power and longer laser pulses from the fiber lasers can be used. We may choose two common fiber laser wavelengths of 1.03 µm and 1.56 µm respectively for the two laser frequencies of ω_1 and ω_2. Reference [7] has more discussion and data about electron energy spectrum, plasma frequency related to this setup and application.

Since hollow-core fiber is anti-resonant design to specific wavelength (or to the specific photonic bandgap), a single hollow-core may not support the transmission of both wavelengths for the generation of the plasma beat wave. In that case, two hollow-core fibers for the respective wavelengths can be employed and are brought together at a common focus for the PBWA.

9. Summary

The ultrafast fiber lasers discussed in this paper may be used or combined into a system of fiber lasers, together with hollow-core fiber delivery as a converged technology to be applied in the use of high-density LWFA and its applications to endoscopic cancer therapy. Ultrafast fiber laser technology of today is capable of generating gigawatt peak-power for the compact LWFA and is further enhanced by coherent-beam-combining of multiple fiber lasers. Hollow-core fibers make it possible to flexibly deliver the intense pulses that conventional fibers cannot. These technologies pave the way in realizing the potential of compact and practical laser wake-field applications to oncology.

Funding: This review paper received no external funding.

Data Availability Statement: Data presented and referenced are available in publicly accessible repositories.

Acknowledgments: Author (WS) is grateful to comments and feedbacks from T. Tajima.

Conflicts of Interest: The authors declare no conflict of interest.

References

1. Tajima, T.; Dawson, J.M. Laser electron accelerator. *Phys. Rev. Lett.* **1979**, *43*, 267–270. [CrossRef]
2. Hooker, S.M. Developments in laser-driven plasma accelerators. *Nat. Photonics* **2013**, *7*, 775. [CrossRef]
3. Roa, D.; Moyses, M.; Barraza, E.; Tajima, T.; Necas, A.; Strickland, D. LWFA-Based Brachytherapy, A Vision of the Future. *Photonics* **2022**. in preparation for the same Special Issue "Progress in Laser Accelerator and Future Prospects".
4. Nicks, B.S.; Tajima, T.; Roa, D.; Necas, A.; Mourou, G. Laser-wakefield application to oncology. *Int. J. Mod. Phys. A* **2019**, *34*, 1943016. [CrossRef]
5. Roa, D.; Kuo, J.; Moyses, H.; Taborek, P.; Tajima, T.; Mourou, G.; Tamanoi, F. Fiber-Optic Based Laser Wakefield Accelerated Electron Beams and Potential Applications in Radiotherapy Cancer Treatments. *Photonics* **2022**, *9*, 403. [CrossRef]
6. Nicks, B.; Barraza-Valdez, E.; Hakimi, S.; Chesnut, K.; DeGrandchamp, G.; Gage, K.; Housley, D.; Huxtable, G.; Lawler, G.; Lin, D.; et al. High-Density Dynamics of Laser Wakefield Acceleration from Gas Plasmas to Nanotubes. *Photonics* **2021**, *8*, 216. [CrossRef]
7. Barraza-Valdez, E.; Tajima, T.; Strickland, D.; Roa, D. Laser Beat Wave Acceleration near Critical Density. *Photonics* **2022**, in preparation for the same Special Issue "Progress in Laser Accelerator and Future Prospects".
8. Leemans, W.; Esarey, E. Laser-driven plasma-wave electron accelerators. *Phys. Today* **2009**, *62*, 44–49. [CrossRef]
9. Tajima, T.; Nakajima, K.; Mourou, G. Laser Acceleration. *Riv. Del Nuovo Cim.* **2017**, *40*, 33.
10. Maine, P.; Strickland, D.; Bado, P.; Pessot, M.; Mourou, G. Generation of ultrahigh peak power pulses by chirped pulse amplification. *IEEE J. Quantum Electron.* **1988**, *24*, 398. [CrossRef]
11. About Chirped Pulse Amplification, See Scientific Background on the Nobel Prize in Physics. 2018. Available online: https://www.nobelprize.org/uploads/2018/10/advanced-physicsprize2018.pdf (accessed on 10 June 2022).
12. Strickland, D.; Mourou, G.A. Compression of amplified chirped optical pulses. *Opt. Comm.* **1985**, *55*, 447–449. [CrossRef]
13. Danson, C.; Haefner, C.; Bromage, J.; Butcher, T.; Chanteloup, J.-C.; Chowdhury, E.; Galvanauskas, A.; Gizzi, L.; Hein, J.; Hillier, D.; et al. Petawatt and exawatt class lasers worldwide. *High Power Laser Sci. Eng.* **2019**, *7*, e54. [CrossRef]
14. Perry, M.; Pennington, D.; Stuart, B.; Tietbohl, G.; Britten, J.; Brown, S.; Herman, S.; Golick, B.; Kartz, M.; Miller, J.; et al. Petawatt laser pulses. *Opt. Lett.* **1999**, *24*, 160–162. [CrossRef] [PubMed]
15. Yousefi, P.; Schönenberger, N.; Mcneur, J.; Kozák, M.; Niedermayer, U.; Hommelhoff, P. Dielectric laser electron acceleration in a dual pillar grating with a distributed Bragg reflector. *Opt. Lett.* **2019**, *44*, 1520–1525. [CrossRef] [PubMed]
16. Kanskar, M.; Earles, T.; Goodnough, T.J.; Stiers, E.; Botez, D.; Mawst, L.J. 73% CW power conversion efficiency at 50 W from 970 nm diode laser bars. *Electron. Lett.* **2005**, *41*, 245. [CrossRef]
17. Diode Laser Product Catalog, Coherent Inc. Available online: https://www.coherent.com/components-accessories/diode-lasers (accessed on 10 June 2022).
18. Diode Laser Product Catalog, II-VI Photonics. Available online: https://ii-vi.com/laser-components/ (accessed on 10 June 2022).
19. Diode laser product catalog, Lumentum. Available online: https://www.lumentum.com/en/diode-lasers/products (accessed on 10 June 2022).
20. Specialty Optical Fiber Product Catalog, Fibercore. Available online: https://fibercore.humaneticsgroup.com/products/passive-cladding-pumped-fiber (accessed on 10 June 2022).
21. Specialty Optical Fiber Product Catalog, iXblue Photonics. Available online: https://www.ixblue.com/north-america/photonics-space/passive-fibers/ (accessed on 10 June 2022).
22. Specialty Optical Fiber Product Catalog, NKT Photonics. Available online: https://www.nktphotonics.com/products/optical-fibers-and-modules/ytterbium-doped-double-clad-fibers/ (accessed on 10 June 2022).
23. Specialty Optical Fiber Product Catalog, OFS Optics. Available online: https://fiber-optic-catalog.ofsoptics.com/Products/Fiber-Laser-Components-and-Amplifiers/Optical-Fiber-Components/Active-Optical-Fibers-3100100891 (accessed on 10 June 2022).
24. NKT Photonics Application Note, "MODAL PROPERTIES OF THE DC-200/40-PZ-YB LMA FIBER". Available online: https://www.nktphotonics.com/wp-content/uploads/2022/01/modal-properties-of-dc-200-40-pz-yb-updated.pdf (accessed on 10 June 2022).
25. Chang, G.; Wei, Z. Ultrafast Fiber Lasers: An Expanding Versatile Toolbox. *iScience* **2020**, *23*, 101101. [CrossRef]
26. Du, D.; Liu, X.; Korn, G.; Squier, J.; Mourou, G. Laser-induced breakdown by impact ionization in SiO_2 with pulse widths from 7 ns to 150 fs. *Appl. Phys. Lett.* **1994**, *64*, 3071–3073. [CrossRef]
27. Fork, R.L.; Greene, B.I.; Shank, C.V. Generation of optical pulses shorter than 0.1 psec by colliding pulse mode locking. *Appl. Phys. Lett.* **1981**, *38*, 671. [CrossRef]
28. Norris, T.; Sizer, T.; Mourou, G. Generation of 85-fsec pulses by synchronous pumping of a colliding-pulse mode-locked dye laser. *J. Opt. Soc. Am. B* **1985**, *2*, 613–615. [CrossRef]
29. Spence, D.E.; Kean, P.N.; Sibbett, W. 60-fsec pulse generation from a self-mode-locked Ti:sapphire laser. *Opt. Lett.* **1991**, *16*, 42–44. [CrossRef]
30. Fermann, M.E.; Haberl, F.; Hofer, M.; Hochreiter, H. Nonlinear amplifying loop mirror. *Opt. Lett.* **1990**, *15*, 752–754. [CrossRef] [PubMed]
31. Wise, F.W.; Chong, A.; Renninger, W.H. High-energy femtosecond fiber lasers based on pulse propagation at normal dispersion. *Laser Photonics Rev.* **2008**, *2*, 58–73. [CrossRef]
32. Fermann, M.E.; Hartl, I. Ultrafast fiber laser technology. *IEEE J. Sel. Top. Quantum Electron.* **2009**, *15*, 191–206. [CrossRef]

33. Set, S.; Yaguchi, H.; Tanaka, Y.; Jablonski, M. Laser mode locking using a saturable absorber incorporating carbon nanotubes. *J. Lightwave Technol.* **2004**, *22*, 51. [CrossRef]
34. Keller, U.; Weingarten, K.; Kartner, F.; Kopf, D.; Braun, B.; Jung, I.; Fluck, R.; Honninger, C.; Matuschek, N.; der Au, J.A. Semiconductor saturable absorber mirrors (SESAM's) for femtosecond to nanosecond pulse generation in solid-state lasers. *IEEE J. Sel. Top. Quantum Electron.* **1996**, *2*, 435–453. [CrossRef]
35. Tamura, K.; Doerr, C.R.; Nelson, L.E.; Haus, H.A.; Ippen, E.P. Technique for obtaining high-energy ultrashort pulses from an additive-pulse mode-locked erbium-doped fiber ring laser. *Optics Letters* **1994**, *19*, 46–48. [CrossRef]
36. Kafka, J.D.; Hall, D.W.; Baer, T. Mode-locked erbium-doped fiber laser with soliton pulse shaping. *Opt. Lett.* **1989**, *14*, 1269. [CrossRef]
37. Duling, N., III. All-fiber ring soliton laser mode locked with a nonlinear mirror. *Opt. Lett.* **1991**, *16*, 539. [CrossRef]
38. Oktem, B.; Ülgüdür, C.; Ilday, F. Soliton–similariton fibre laser. *Nat. Photonics* **2010**, *4*, 307–311. [CrossRef]
39. Lefrancois, S.; Liu, C.; Stock, M.; Sosnowski, T.; Galvanauskas, A.; Wise, F. High-energy similariton fiber laser using chirally coupled core fiber. *Opt. Lett.* **2013**, *38*. [CrossRef]
40. Kieu, K.; Wise, F.W. All-fiber normal-dispersion femtosecond laser. *Opt. Express* **2008**, *16*, 11453. [CrossRef] [PubMed]
41. Gilevich, S.; Alverson, S.; Carbajo, S.; Droste, S.; Edstrom, S.; Fry, A.; Greenberg, M.; Lemons, R.; Miahnahri, A.; Polzin, W.; et al. The LCLS-II Photo-Injector Drive Laser System. In Proceedings of the CLEO: Science and Innovations 2020, Washington, DC, USA, 10–15 May 2020. paper SW3E.3.
42. Limpert, J.; Stutzki, F.; Jansen, F.; Otto, H.J.; Eidam, T.; Jauregui, C.; Tünnermann, A. Yb-doped large-pitch fibres: Effective single-mode operation based on higher-order mode delocalization. *Light Sci. Appl.* **2012**, *1*, e8. [CrossRef]
43. Eidam, T.; Rothhardt, J.; Stutzki, F.; Jansen, F.; Hädrich, S.; Carstens, H.; Jauregui, C.; Limpert, J.; Tünnermann, A. Fiber chirped-pulse amplification system emitting 3.8 GW peak power. *Opt. Express* **2011**, *19*, 255–260. [CrossRef] [PubMed]
44. Mourou, G.; Brocklesby, W.; Tajima, T.; Limpert, J. The future is fibre accelerators. *Nat. Photonics* **2013**, *7*, 258. [CrossRef]
45. Daniault, L.; Bellanger, S.; Le Dortz, J.; Bourderionnet, J.; Lallier, E.; Larat, C.; Antier-Murgey, M.; Chanteloup, J.C.; Brignon, A.; Simon-Boisson, C.; et al. XCAN—A coherent amplification network of femtosecond fiber chirped-pulse amplifiers. *Eur. Phys. J. Spec. Top.* **2015**, *224*, 2609–2613. [CrossRef]
46. Fsaifes, I.; Daniault, L.; Bellanger, S.; Veinhard, M.; Bourderionnet, J.; Larat, C.; Lallier, E.; Durand, E.; Brignon, A.; Chanteloup, J.C. Coherent beam combining of 61 femtosecond fiber amplifiers. *Opt. Express* **2020**, *28*, 20152–20161. [CrossRef]
47. Chanteloup, J.-C.; Bellanger, S.; Daniault, L.; Fsaifes, I.; Veinhard, M.; Bourderionnet, J.; Larat, C.; Brignon, A. Shaping the Light: The Advent of Digital Lasers. Laser Focus World 2021. Available online: https://www.laserfocusworld.com/lasers-sources/article/14201008/shaping-the-light-the-advent-of-digital-lasers (accessed on 1 June 2021).
48. Veinhard, M.; Bellanger, S.; Daniault, L.; Fsaifes, I.; Bourderionnet, J.; Larat, C.; Lallier, E.; Brignon, A.; Chanteloup, J.-C. Orbital angular momentum beams generation from 61 channels coherent beam combining femtosecond digital laser. *Opt. Lett.* **2021**, *46*, 25–28. [CrossRef]
49. Du, Q.; Wang, D.; Zhou, T.; Li, D.; Wilcox, R. 81-beam coherent combination using a programmable array generator. *Opt. Express* **2021**, *29*, 5407–5418. [CrossRef]
50. Müller, M.; Klenke, A.; Stark, H.; Buldt, J.; Gottschall, T.; Tünnermann, A.; Limpert, J. 1.8-kW 16-channel ultrafast fiber laser system. In Proceedings of the SPIE 10512, Fiber Lasers XV: Technology and Systems, San Francisco, CA, USA, 27 January–1 February 2018; p. 1051208. [CrossRef]
51. Klenke, A.; Müller, M.; Stark, H.; Stutzki, F.; Hupel, C.; Schreiber, T.; Tunnermann, A.; Limpert, J. Coherently combined 16-channel multicore fiber laser system. *Opt. Lett.* **2018**, *43*, 1519–1522. [CrossRef]
52. Russell, P. Photonic crystal fibers. *Science* **2003**, *299*, 358–362. [CrossRef]
53. Cundiff, S.T.; Ye, J. Femtosecond optical frequency combs. *Rev. Mod. Phys.* **2003**, *75*, 325–342. [CrossRef]
54. Yablonovitch, E. Photonic Band-gap structures. *Opt. Soc. Am. B* **1993**, *10*, 283–295. [CrossRef]
55. Michieletto, M.; Lyngsø, J.K.; Jakobsen, C.; Lægsgaard, J.; Bang, O.; Alkeskjold, T.T. Hollow-core fibers for high power pulse delivery. *Opt. Express* **2016**, *24*, 7103–7119. [CrossRef] [PubMed]
56. Wedel, B.; Funck, M. Industrial fiber beam delivery enhances ultrafast laser machining. *Ind. Laser Solut.* **2016**, *31*, 28–30.
57. Clayton, C.E.; Marsh, K.A.; Dyson, A.; Everett, M.; Lal, A.; Leemans, W.P.; Williams, R.; Joshi, C. Ultrahigh-gradient acceleration of injected electrons by laser-excited relativistic electron plasma waves. *Phys. Rev. Lett.* **1993**, *70*, 37–40. [CrossRef]

Article

Compressing High Energy Lasers through Optical Polymer Films

Jonathan Wheeler [1,*,†], Gabriel Petrișor Bleotu [2,3,4], Andrei Naziru [2,4], Riccardo Fabbri [2], Masruri Masruri [2], Radu Secareanu [2], Deano M. Farinella [5], Gabriel Cojocaru [2,6], Razvan Ungureanu [6], Elsa Baynard [7], Julien Demailly [7], Moana Pittman [7], Razvan Dabu [2], Ioan Dancus [2], Daniel Ursescu [2,4], David Ros [7], Toshiki Tajima [5] and Gerard Mourou [1]

[1] DER-IZEST, Ecole Polytechnique, Route de Saclay, 91128 Palaiseau, France
[2] Extreme Light Infrastructure-Nuclear Physics, National Institute for R&D in Physics and Nuclear Engineering (IFIN-HH), 30 Reactorului, 077125 Magurele, Romania
[3] LULI-CNRS, CEA, Institut Polytechnique de Paris, Universite Sorbonne, Ecole Polytechnique, 91128 Palaiseau CEDEX, France
[4] Department of Physics, University of Bucharest, 077125 Magurele, Romania
[5] Department of Physics and Astronomy, University of California, Irvine, CA 92697, USA
[6] Center for Advanced Laser Technologies (CETAL), National Institute for Laser, Plasma and Radiation Physics (INFLPR), 409 Atomistilor, 077125 Magurele, Romania
[7] Laboratoire de Physique des 2 Infinis Irène Joliot-Curie—IJCLab, UMR9012—CNRS/Université Paris-Saclay/Université de Paris, 91405 Orsay CEDEX, France
* Correspondence: jonathan.wheeler@auspexphotonics.com
† Current address: Independent Researcher, 92340 Bourg-la-Reine, France.

Abstract: The thin-film post-compression technique has the ability to reduce the pulse duration in PW-class lasers, increasing the peak power. Here, the nonlinear response of an increasingly available optical thermoplastic demonstrates enhanced spectral broadening, with corresponding shorter pulse duration compared to fused silica glass. The thermoplastic can be used close to its damage threshold when refreshed using a roller mechanism, and the total amount of material can be varied by folding the film. As a proof-of-principle demonstration scalable to 10-PW, a roller mechanism capable of up to 6 passes through a sub-millimeter thermoplastic film is used in vacuum to produce two-fold post-compression of the pulse. The compact design makes it an ideal method to further boost ultrahigh laser pulse intensities with benefits to many areas, including driving high energy acceleration.

Keywords: pulse compression; ultrashort lasers; ultrafast nonlinear optics; high power lasers

Citation: Wheeler, J.; Bleotu, G.P.; Naziru, A.; Fabbri, R.; Masruri, M.; Secareanu, R.; Farinella, D.M.; Cojocaru, G.; Ungureanu, R.; Baynard, E.; et al. Compressing High Energy Lasers through Optical Polymer Films. *Photonics* **2022**, *9*, 715. https://doi.org/10.3390/photonics9100715

Received: 21 June 2022
Accepted: 27 September 2022
Published: 30 September 2022

Publisher's Note: MDPI stays neutral with regard to jurisdictional claims in published maps and institutional affiliations.

Copyright: © 2022 by the authors. Licensee MDPI, Basel, Switzerland. This article is an open access article distributed under the terms and conditions of the Creative Commons Attribution (CC BY) license (https://creativecommons.org/licenses/by/4.0/).

1. Introduction

High power laser facilities produce energies of tens to hundreds of Joules contained within pulse durations of tens of femtoseconds (10^{-15} s) thus reaching the class of Petawatt (PW: 10^{15} W). PW-class laser systems based on Chirped Pulse Amplification (CPA) [1] and Optical Parametric Chirped Pulse Amplification (OPCPA) [2] technologies are becoming more and more common all over the world. These laser facilities, such as LASERIX [3], HPLS at ELI-NP [4,5], CETAL-PW [6], Apollon [7,8], BELLA [9], CoReLS [10], SULF [11], etc. are operating at various repetition rates and reaching ever-increasing peak intensities. Such systems deliver laser pulses with duration in the range of 25 fs at a central wavelength of $\lambda_o \sim 800$ nm, corresponding to ~10 optical cycles for the single-cycle period of $T_o \sim 2.5$ fs.

Post-compressing these pulses while preserving their energy, economically increases the achievable peak intensity of the pulse for experiments that use extreme fields. In addition, reducing the number of optical cycles in the pulse helps in the elimination of cycle-averaging in the investigation of physical processes that occur at this timescale, such as X-ray generation [12–15] and ion acceleration [16,17]. Studies predict achieving high energy, single or few-cycle laser pulses leads to improved conversion efficiency in these laser-driven processes, in addition to boosting the intensity. These gains open a path for ascending toward Exawatt (EW) class lasers with benefits for the next stage of high field scientific investigation of processes such as QED studies, as drivers for particle acceleration, in relativistic compression to attosecond pulses, and X-ray crystal wakefield accelerators [18,19].

The post-compression of TW scale (10^{12} W) table-top mJ laser systems with Gaussian beam profiles is already a mature technique applied in many laboratories around the world [20] relying on designs involving gas-filled, hollow-core capillaries [21,22], multiple plate post-compression [23], or multipass Harriott cells [24,25]. These current compression techniques prove difficult to apply to Joule-level lasers, primarily due to the high intensity creating unstable plasma effects within the nonlinear materials at the focus of the beam. However, during the beam transport in PW-class, short pulse laser systems, the beam propagates at sufficient intensities to drive nonlinear processes in the near field that modify the initial pulse spectrum if the pulse is transmitted through a material. If the material thickness is properly controlled across the flat-top mode of the large aperture beam of high energy laser systems, the nonlinear optical processes can lead to significant spectral broadening while avoiding significant degradation of the profile. Several methods of employing a thin nonlinear element for pulse compression have been suggested [26].

Here, the emphasis is placed on self-phase modulation (SPM) within a thin (sub-millimeter) film, where the broadening of the spectrum is proportional to the nonlinear response due to the time-dependent change in intensity. The subsequent broadened, but chirped, pulse spectrum requires correction of the second order phase, or Group Delay Dispersion (GDD), due to the SPM process as well as the material dispersion in order to attain the new transform limited pulse duration [27]. This is typically managed by balancing the number of reflections from negative-dispersion mirrors, often referred to as chirped mirrors, along with any subsequent transmission through optical materials contributing additional positive dispersion, as shown in Figure 1. This configuration is referred to as a Thin Film Compressor (TFC), or the Compression AFter Compressor Approach (CAFCA) [28–30]. The primary impact on pulse energy due to the TFC is incurred by reflection losses at the thin film surfaces, typically no more than 5%. Minimizing these losses implies an efficiency of the pulse compression process that permits implementation of one or more TFC assemblies to extend the capability of existing laser infrastructures toward their fundamental limit of a single optical cycle.

Studies of high energy pulse post-compression has considered the nonlinear interaction with thin wafers made of crystal [31], glass [32,33], or plastic [29,34]. To date, the most powerful implementations employ glass plates and have shown the capability of producing with 14 J, 22 fs pulses spectra supporting sub-10 fs [35], compression of a 3.24 J pulse from 24 to 13 fs [36], compression of a 17 J pulse from 70 to 17 fs [37], an 18 J pulse compressed from 64 to 11 fs [38], and compression to sub-10 fs of a 2.5 J, 23 fs pulse [39]. Despite the many demonstrations using glasses, these plates often show thickness variations due to the manufacture process that cannot be polished over large apertures. The implementation with polymers is expected to prove more economical in producing the uniformity over the large film areas required to accommodate the beam sizes (often ∼0.5 m) of multi-PW laser systems.

In this paper, a novel plastic film, specifically cyclic olefin polymer (COP, brandname ZeonorFilm™) is first tested [40]. COP is used in the economical production of optical components such as lenses, but its nonlinear response is not widely reported.

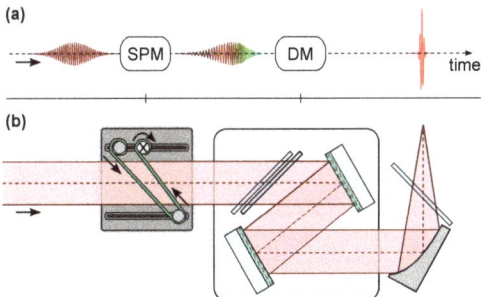

Figure 1. The conceptual steps from initial to post-compressed pulse of the TFC technique are shown in (**a**) that correspond to the laboratory configuration in (**b**). Relying on the uniform intensity profile of the beam, the femtosecond pulse passes through enough thin film material to induce sufficient SPM. The resultant chirped pulse achieves the optimized duration by the dispersion management (DM), which includes fixed negative GDD elements (i.e., chirped mirrors) balanced with the GDD of any additional optical elements (e.g., thin plates, turning mirrors, off-axis paraboloid or debris shield).

New classes of thin, high-quality optical films are becoming available on the market, intended primarily for new screen technologies in the electronics industry. The index of refraction n for COP is 1.53; its GDD value is 70.219 fs^2/mm at 800 nm. COP is known to be resistant to changes in its birefringence under stress; this offers an ideal alternative to plastic materials such as PMMA whose birefringence is known to vary with tension. This type of optical film is chosen also because it can be attained in rolls of a format $(100(l) \times 1(w))$ m^2 of 100–180 μm thick films) that economically accommodates the large beam sizes of 0.5 m diameter expected for 10 PW laser systems. The rolls can be sliced to appropriate widths for the beam diameter during the manufacturing process. The principle is to employ a roller mechanism which allows continual replacement of the material if it should degrade. Such a design is shown in Figure 1 where the thin film is held in a roller assembly that folds the long film to pass several times in the beam, so that the beam transits sufficient material for the desired spectral modification. By using a series of 100 μm thick films rather than a single bulk substrate, the amount of material interacting with the pulse can be optimized to the minimal required at the given initial pulse intensity and minimizes contributions to the B-integral and dispersion from excess material.

In this paper, the nonlinear properties of thin COP sample are measured to compare its effectiveness as an SPM material relative to typical fused silica wafers. A small-scale prototype of a Film Roller Mechanism (FRM) has been built, and experimental results using the TFC technique and the FRM within a vacuum environment are presented from measurements performed at the LASERIX laser platform [41] using a COP sample, and a 45 fs pulse with variable energy up to 500 mJ within an 18 mm diameter beam. The resulting pulse duration reduction is compared to simulations. Because the FRM prototype design is intended to be scaled to multi-centimeter beam sizes typical at Petawatt laser facilities, the requirements for TFC to be performed at the multi-PW level are presented based on the measured nonlinear properties of COP.

2. Experiment Setup

Figure 2 shows perspective views of the FRM, panel (a), and the layout of the configuration used in the experiment, panel (b).

The pulse interacts with the target film within a vacuum chamber immediately following the laser compressor. A variable attenuator (VA) consisting of a waveplate/polarizer combination is placed before the compressor in order to vary the energy of the pulse incident on the thin film. The FRM holding the COP film is placed in the experimental vacuum chamber immediately after the compressor. After interacting with the film, the pulse is attenuated by partial reflection (PR1) from two uncoated fused silica mirror substrates for an expected reflectivity of 8% each. This attenuation prevents further SPM or damage to subsequent optics during the propagation of the pulse to the diagnostics bench, outside the vacuum chamber. The vacuum window is 5.1 mm thick and made of MgF_2 to minimize the additional dispersion introduced by traversing this optical component to +100 fs^2. A beamsplitter (PR2) transmits 2% of the beam energy towards a lens of focal length f = 300 mm used for the imaging diagnostics (IM box) of the near and far fields (NF and FF, respectively) thus allowing for qualitative monitoring of the collimated and focused beam mode profiles. PR2 has a reflectivity of 98%, so that 0.6% of the original interaction energy is directed through the dispersion management (DM box) toward the pulse diagnostics (DG box). The DM begins with an adjustable aperture that reduces the beam diameter to the input size of the pulse diagnostics (≤5 mm), and permits, by a slight variation in the angle of incidence on the first mirror, to vary the number of passes through a pair of chirped mirrors to provide 2, 4, or 6 bounces (typically 4 bounces). The chirped mirrors (CM; Ultrafast Innovations, HD58) provide a GDD of −250 fs^2 per bounce. As the CM overcompensate the initial pulse chirp, combinations of glass windows (W) made of fused silica or magnesium fluoride are inserted within the beam for control of the final measured pulse duration. Two temporal diagnostics (Light Conversion TIPA Single-shot Autocorrelator—AC; FastLite WIZZLER—WZ) record the pulse duration in parallel in order to verify the accuracy of the measurement. The WIZZLER is capable of retrieving the spectral phase of the pulse, which allows for the optimization in the final pulse compression. A fiber spectrometer (SP; Ocean Optics USB2000) also records the spectrum of the pulse for comparison with that recovered from the other diagnostics.

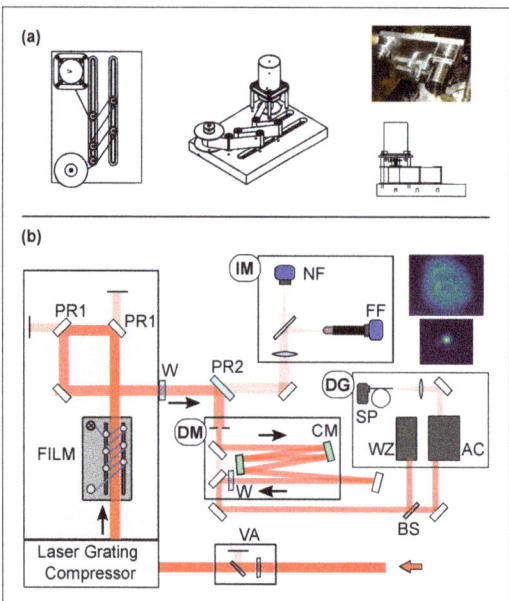

Figure 2. Perspective views and in situ photograph of the FRM prototype are shown in (**a**). The layout of the experiment as described in the text is pictured in (**b**).

In addition to the investigation performed with 0.1 mm thick COP film in the roller mechanism, measurements with a single fused silica window (University Wafers) of 0.5 mm thickness and 50 mm diameter act as a reference measurement for comparison to a material with known value of the nonlinear component of the refractive index n_2. The fused silica plate is mounted under vacuum at the same location as the FRM prototype, with sufficient translation for the samples to be moved in and out of the beam path without breaking vacuum. The COP films are mounted near to Brewster's angle with respect to the incoming beam, resulting in an effective thickness of 0.69 mm for a 6-pass configuration.

3. Results

3.1. Nonlinear Material Response

The nonlinear intensity-dependence of the refraction index of materials $n(t) = n_o + n_2 \cdot I(\mathbf{x}, t)$ depends on the time-dependent pulse intensity I and gives rise to SPM as it propagates over an interaction length Δz within a material due to the rapid change in the pulse intensity over the pulse duration. In the case of a flat-top beam profile, where the spatial variation in the pulse intensity is minimized, the induced spectral shift $\delta \omega_{rel}$ relative to the fundamental frequency ω_o is expected to be uniform across the pulse profile and is derived from the definition of the instantaneous angular frequency, $\omega(t) = \omega_o + \delta \omega_{rel}(t)$. The spectral shift is thus expected to be proportional to $\frac{\partial I}{\partial t}$ by the definition of $\omega(t) = \frac{d\phi}{dt}$, where $\phi = \omega_o t - kz$ for the wave vector $k = k_o\, n(t)$, or

$$\delta \omega_{rel}(t) = \omega(t) - \omega_0 = \frac{d\phi}{dt} - \omega_0 = k_0 n_2 \frac{dI(t)}{dt} \Delta z \,. \qquad (1)$$

As the intensity of the pulse retains a Gaussian temporal envelope, the time variation of the pulse intensity profile is expected to vary as $\frac{dI(t)}{dt} \sim I_o / \tau_p$, where the peak intensity is estimated by the input pulse energy E_p, pulse duration τ_p and the effective area of the pulse A_p by the relation $I_o \propto E_p / (\tau_p \cdot A_p)$ [42]. An estimate to the extent of the bandwidth after spectral broadening can then be estimated from Equation (1) in terms of readily measured beam quantities,

$$\delta \omega_{rel} = k_0 n_2 z \left. \frac{dI(t)}{dt} \right|_{max} \propto \frac{k_0 n_2}{\tau_p^2 A_p} (E_p \cdot \Delta z) \,. \qquad (2)$$

The COP response is investigated, keeping the amount of film constant at six passes and varying the pulse energy in order to see the response to the changing laser intensity. For each energy value, several shots (from five to ten) are performed. The pulse spectral amplitude (red) and phase (green) as measured with the WIZZLER are presented in Figure 3a as a function of the input energy. When available, the reference spectrum is superimposed in gray color. The latter was measured with the FRM removed from the beam line; only two energy points ($E_p = 78.7$ mJ and $E_p = 157.9$ mJ) are available, with pulse energy values similar to the ones used with COP films. The phases for the reference spectra are flat as the compressor was adjusted during the experiment to deliver the optimized pulse duration.

The curves correspond to the mean values of the respective laser shots. The shaded band indicates the uncertainty estimated as half of the maximum deviation between the measurements.

The pulse bandwidth and duration values are given in Table 1 as function of the input energy E_p. For each shot measurement, the pulse bandwidth is calculated as the RMS of spectrum $\Delta \nu_\sigma$. For each energy point, the mean value is then calculated, and its uncertainty estimated as half of the maximum deviation. A Gaussian fit is superimposed on the reconstructed pulse duration, and the extracted FWHM along with its fit uncertainty is used to estimate the pulse duration τ_p. The pulse parameters are also presented as a function of the scaling variable $\xi \equiv E_p \cdot \Delta z$, Δz being the target thickness in millimeters. The expected increase (decrease) is seen in the trend for the bandwidth (pulse duration) as a function of increasing input pulse energy with a fixed amount of material.

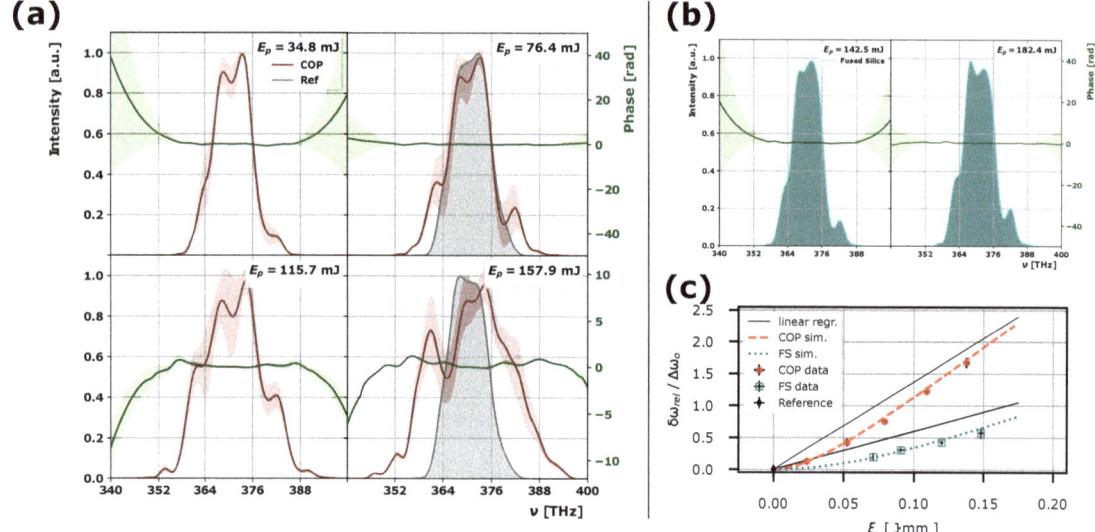

Figure 3. The measured spectra and phase response of the pulse passing through six layers of COP film are shown in (**a**). The pulse energy increases from top left to bottom right, corresponding to 35 mJ, 76 mJ, 116 mJ and 158 mJ, respectively. Superimposed in gray are the original spectra measured with no material present. In (**b**), the spectra and phase measured using a fused silica (FS) plate are shown. The measured response of the COP film is compared with FS in (**c**). The induced bandwidth ($\delta\omega_{rel}$) relative to the original reference bandwidth $\Delta\omega_0$ of the input pulse is shown vs. the parameter ζ. A linear regression performed on the two data-sets is superimposed on the measurements (solid line), as well as the results obtained from simulations (dashed lines).

Table 1. Measured pulse parameters for reference pulse with no film installed (NA), 6× COP with total effective thickness of 0.69 mm, and fused silica (FS) wafers.

Film	E_p [mJ]	ζ [J·mm]	$\Delta\nu_\sigma$ [±0.4, THz]	$\Delta\lambda_{FWHM}$ [±2, nm]	τ_p [fs]
NA	all	–	4.1	21	45.5
COP	35	0.025	4.6	24	43.3
COP	76	0.054	5.9	30	32.6
COP	116	0.081	7.2	37	29.4
COP	158	0.112	9.2	47	23.4
FS	143	0.071	4.9	25	39.8
FS	182	0.091	5.4	28	36.3
FS	240	0.120	5.9	30	31.9
FS	296	0.148	6.4	33	29.0

The resulting pulse duration of 23 fs is half the original pulse duration of 45 fs in the highest energy case, with little adverse modification in the beam.

In order to better simulate the SPM response for the COP material, it is necessary to extract the nonlinear response n_2 of the material from the data, as there is limited information provided for this material within the femtosecond regime around 800 nm in the literature at this time. In considering the extent of the bandwidth shift after spectral broadening ($\delta\omega_{rel}$), Equation (2) gives the expected response. The majority of these parameters ($f(k_0, \tau_p, A_p)$) depend on the laser conditions and remain constant throughout the experiment, except for the varied input pulse energy E_p and the interaction distance Δz due to the thickness of the material. This simplifies the multivariate dependence on spectral broadening of Equation (1) by studying the spectral broadening as a function of the variable $\zeta = E_p \cdot \Delta z$,

$$\delta\omega_{rel} \propto \frac{k_0}{\tau_p^2 A_p} \cdot n_2 \cdot (E_p \cdot z) \equiv C_L \cdot n_2 \cdot \zeta. \tag{3}$$

From the simplified Equation (3), a linear dependence of the shift of the frequency relative to ζ is expected from the assumed approximation. The slope can be separated into two factors, the material-dependant n_2 and the constant factor C_L that depends on the laser pulse geometry, $m = C_L \cdot n_2$. This demonstrates that the spectral broadening measured for a specific material should fit a straight line with respect to the variable ζ. The slope m of the linear regression to the data is thus proportional to the n_2 for a given material. The unknown parameter n_2 of COP can be then estimated by comparing the extracted fit slope m of COP response to that of the well known material Fused Silica (FS), $m_{COP}/m_{FS} = n_2^{COP}/n_2^{FS}$. The spectrum and phase were thus measured using a single 0.5 mm thick fused silica plate at normal incidence; two example spectra are shown in Figure 3b for different values of pulse energy, and the measured parameters are also presented in Table 1.

The relative maximum spectral shift due to SPM ($\delta\omega_{rel}$) is approximated from the experiment by subtracting the initial reference bandwidth ($\Delta\omega_0$) from the bandwidth measured after SPM ($\Delta\omega_{spm}$): $\delta\omega_{rel} \sim \Delta\omega_{spm} - \Delta\omega_0$. The comparison of measured relative spectral shift for six passes of COP at a thickness of 0.1 mm (6× COP) with a Fused Silica plate at normal incidence is presented in Figure 3c. The response of the COP film is significantly larger than the fused silica. A linear regression is performed on the two data-sets and superimposed to the measurements as black lines in Figure 3c. The ratio of the slopes extracted from the linear fits of the COP to fused silica data ($m_{COP}/m_{FS} = 2.3 \pm 0.1$) gives access to n_2^{COP} using the known value for fused silica, $n_2^{FS} = 2.4 \times 10^{-4}$ cm^2/TW. [43] Therefore, the value n_2 for COP at 800 nm can be estimated to be $n_2^{COP} = (2.3 \pm 0.2)\, n_2^{FS}$,

$$n_2^{COP} = (5.5 \pm 0.6) \times 10^{-20} \text{ m}^2/\text{W}.$$

The simplified estimate used for the relative spectral broadening is a linear function of ζ and is shown in Figure 3c by the solid black lines with the extracted slope to not fit the data well. The estimated value of n_2^{COP} is then used in the simulations based on the Python nonlinear optics package pyNLO [44], and overlaid on the experimental data in Figure 3c as dashed lines. The simulation is able to better demonstrate the observed behavior by using the respective values for n_2 and taking into account the reflection loss at each surface due to the angle of incidence (θ_i) with each film. The transmission for a surface is calculated using the typical Fresnel equations for p-polarized light $\left(T(\theta_i) = 1 - R_p(\theta_i)\right)$. The first five COP films were measured with $\theta_i = 50^\circ$ (T = 0.99/surface) while due to space constraints the final film was reduced so that $\theta_i = 23^\circ$ (T = 0.93/surface). The entire stack of six films should then result in a total transmission, $T_{tot} = (0.99)^{10} \times (0.93)^2 = 0.78$. In general, each film has a total transmission of 98% and if the final film had been at a similar θ_i then the $T_{tot} = (0.99)^{12} = 0.89$ for the series of six films. For the single FS film at normal incidence, the $T_{tot} = 0.96$.

3.2. Beam Profile

With the camera monitoring the near-field to detect damage in the thin film, the ability to characterize the development of the multi-filamentation process due to modulation instabilities (MI) in the beam must be considered. In the modulation instability gain theory based on steady-state waves, the characteristic size, d, should rise exponentially during propagation until reaching the exit of the material, or the laser-induced damage threshold (LIDT) of the material. When the peak power of the pulse exceeds the critical power $P_{cr} = 3.79\lambda_0^2/(8\pi n_0 n_2)$ (~1.2 MW for COP at 810 nm), intense pulses with super-gaussian modes are susceptible to multi-filamentation through the modulation instability initiated by noise in the beam profile [45,46]. The characteristic size for maximum MI gain is given by the parameter $d \approx \left(\frac{2\pi P_{cr}}{I_0}\right)^{1/2}$ which in the case of COP at $I_0 \approx 1.4 \times 10^{12}$ W/cm^2 gives an approximate feature size of $d \approx 23$ µm [47], which is smaller than the near-field system is capable of resolving (46 µm with two pixels). The profile imaging will need to be further developed to better capture the crucial feature sizes relative to the earliest stages of damage. In Figure 4a, the discrete change in material with additional passes of the film ranges from a reference with no film, a single 0.1 mm thick film, 4× 0.1 mm thick films, and 6× 0.1 mm thick films are compared showing the increasing development in the modulation noise with increasing material interaction. If the beam modulations reached the point that material damage or discoloration occurred, it appeared in the final pass of the film so that partial shifts of the material are sufficient to refresh the film. Improved optimization in the number of passes, i.e., five, could also maximize the spectral broadening while minimizing any degradation in the spatial mode.

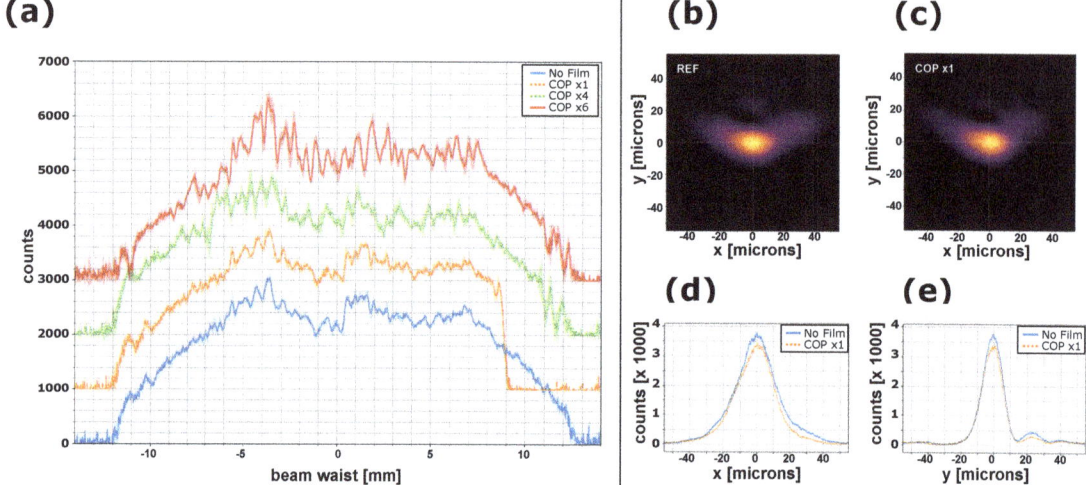

Figure 4. Beam profile with COP film. In (**a**) central line outs from near field images are compared with increasing number of film passes from bottom to top: reference beam (no film); a single 0.1 mm film (showing hard cut in beam due to mounting); 4× 0.1 mm; and 6× 0.1 mm, respectively. The input energy is kept at 160 mJ. In (**b**) the REF focus is shown without a film in place while (**c**) shows the focus after the 1× COP [0.1 mm] film is placed in the beam. In (**d**), the comparison with/ without the film in place of the horizontal line out is shown while (**e**) compares the same along the vertical axis.

Because the multipass spectral study was performed with a lower optical quality grade of COP, the focus from the single high quality COP film is also considered in order to demonstrate the effect on the beam's focusability. Typical focus images with no film (Ref) and with a single film (COP ×1) are shown in (b) and (c) of Figure 4, respectively. The line outs comparing the horizontal and vertical directions are given in (d) and (e) of Figure 4. The focus is not optimized even before the film is introduced, but there is no significant change in the structure of the focus with the inclusion of the film. The details of the profiles should be clarified by further studies implementing a deformable mirror for an improved initial focus, higher quality optical films, and an intentional imaging assembly for spatial characterization of the beam with better resolution.

4. Discussion

The results of these studies, measuring the compression from 45 fs down to 23 fs at a pulse fluence similar to the PW lasers at ELI-NP, point to achieving compression by at least a factor of two for high peak power pulses containing Joules of energy. This will extend the capabilities of this new generation of high energy laser technology by compressing the current pulses of 25 fs by a similar factor [48]. The scalability of the COP film up to an aperture of 1 m makes this material suitable for implementation at normal incidence, or even Brewster's angle, for the large beam apertures of 10 PW-class systems, e.g., the 55 cm beam diameter at the HPLS 10 PW output. The simulations of the resulting increase in bandwidth for a 25 fs pulse at appropriate fluences for the 10 PW HPLS laser facility of ELI-NP are presented in Figure 5. As the pulse begins at 25 fs rather than the 45 fs of these experiments at LASERIX, less material is required. The simulation indicates that passing once or twice through films of thickness of 0.10 mm or 0.18 mm (labelled in the figure as COP 0.10 mm, COP 0.18 mm, COP 2× 0.10 mm, COP 2× 0.18 mm, respectively) is expected to achieve a significant spectral broadening, even enough to support a sub-10 fs pulse.

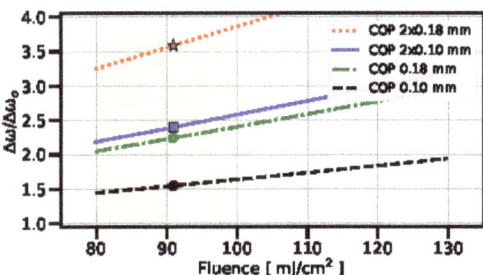

Figure 5. Simulated response of the COP film obtained from a 1-D simulation in PyNLO for initial pulse duration of 25 fs. The induced increase in bandwidth ($\Delta\omega$) relative to the original reference bandwidth $\Delta\omega_0$ of the input pulse is shown relative to pulse fluence for examples of a single film and two films. The shaded region highlights the values that correspond to the relevant pulse fluences of 80–100 mJ/cm². The points correspond to bandwidths supporting ftl pulse durations of 17.75 (•), 12.75 (○), 12.0 (■), 8.25 (⋆) fs.

As an example of an optimized design for a COP compressor, a pulse of 25 fs interacting with two passes of a 0.18 mm thick film of COP at Brewster's angle produces a bandwidth that supports a pulse of duration below 9 fs with a small compensation of only -70 fs² in GDD. This value reduces the challenges for the chirped mirror production, and also suggests the possibility to replace them with more conventional broadband mirrors with negative residual GDD. Another possibility is to use a second thin plate with thickness on the order of the wavelength in reflection [48]. Because the design consists of only two passes, the total transmission is expected to be $T_{tot} = (0.99)^4 = 0.96$. Such implementations would enable pulses with peak power in excess of 20 PW.

5. Conclusions

Optical-grade extruded thermoplastic films, such as COP, demonstrate great promise for nonlinear manipulation of high energy beams of large diameter aperture. The polymer shows greater uniformity in thickness for the cost than many glasses, or other rigid materials, at these dimensions. In addition, the larger n_2 value of the COP film concentrates the nonlinear B-integral contribution to the film rather than any additional elements made of glasses, e.g., debris shield, or thin plates for fine tuning the GDD with positive dispersion. Rolls of the film can be mounted using an FRM device for long-term use in the case when eventual degradation requires the material to be refreshed. An up-scaled version of the set-up can be demonstrated with existing technology and, in combination with adequate, less constrained dispersion management, it can provide practical access to pulses with peak power in excess of 20 PW. This is an efficient alternative, alongside the nonlinear amplification [49] and coherent combination methods, to generate Exawatt class lasers. The compact design makes it an ideal method to further boost ultrahigh laser pulse intensities for driving high energy acceleration.

Author Contributions: Conceptualization, J.W., A.N., T.T. and G.M.; software, R.F., J.D.; formal analysis, J.W., G.P.B., R.F., M.M., D.M.F., and R.U.; investigation, J.W., A.N., R.F., M.M., R.S., D.M.F., G.C., R.U., E.B., J.D. and M.P.; methodology, J.W., A.N. and M.P.; resources, J.W., A.N., E.B., J.D. and M.P.; writing—original draft preparation, J.W.; writing—review and editing, J.W., G.P.B., R.F., M.P. and D.U.; supervision, J.W., M.P., R.D., I.D., D.U., D.R., T.T. and G.M.; project administration, J.W.; funding acquisition, J.W., R.D., G.C., D.U. and G.M. All authors have read and agreed to the published version of the manuscript.

Funding: The authors wish to acknowledge support for this work through Laserlab-Europe (EU-H2020 654148). The authors are thankful for the financial support from the Romanian National Nucleu Program (PN 19060105), Project ELI-RO 16/2020 SBUF funded by Institute for Atomic Physics (IFA) and from the European Union's Horizon 2020 research and innovation programme under grant agreement No 871161 (IMPULSE). G. Cojocaru acknowledges the support by a grant of the Ministry of Education and Research, CNCS-UEFISCDI (project no. PN-III-P1-1.1-PD-2019- contract no. 84/2020).

Institutional Review Board Statement: Not applicable.

Informed Consent Statement: Not applicable.

Data Availability Statement: Data underlying the results presented in this paper may be obtained from the authors upon reasonable request.

Acknowledgments: The authors wish to acknowledge many discussions with S. Mironov and E. Khazanov of the Institute of Applied Physics at the Russian Academy of Science, Nizhny Novgorod.

Conflicts of Interest: The authors declare no conflict of interest.

References

1. Strickland, D.; Mourou, G. Compression of amplified chirped optical pulses. *Opt. Commun.* **1985**, *56*, 219–221. [CrossRef]
2. Dubietis, A.; Jonušauskas, G.; Piskarskas, A. Powerful femtosecond pulse generation by chirped and stretched pulse parametric amplification in BBO crystal. *Opt. Commun.* **1992**, *88*, 437–440. [CrossRef]
3. Ple, F.; Pittman, M.; Jamelot, G.; Chambaret, J.P. Design and demonstration of a high-energy booster amplifier for a high-repetition rate petawatt class laser system. *Opt. Lett.* **2007**, *32*, 238. [CrossRef]
4. Lureau, F.; Matras, G.; Chalus, O.; Derycke, C.; Morbieu, T.; Radier, C.; Casagrande, O.; Laux, S.; Ricaud, S.; Rey, G.; et al. High-energy hybrid femtosecond laser system demonstrating 2 ∗ 10 PW capability. *High Power Laser Sci. Eng.* **2020**, *8*, e43. [CrossRef]
5. Gales, S.; Tanaka, K.A.; Balabanski, D.L.; Negoita, F.; Stutman, D.; Tesileanu, O.; Ur, C.A.; Ursescu, D.; Andrei, I.; Ataman, S.; et al. The extreme light infrastructure—Nuclear physics (ELI-NP) facility: New horizons in physics with 10 PW ultra-intense lasers and 20 MeV brilliant gamma beams. *Rep. Prog. Phys.* **2018**, *81*, 094301. [CrossRef]
6. Matras, G.; Lureau, F.; Laux, S.; Casagrande, O.; Radier, C.; Chalus, O.; Caradec, F.; Boudjemaa, L.; Simon-Boisson, C.; Dabu, R.; et al. First sub-25fs PetaWatt laser system. In Proceedings of the CLEO: 2013, San Jose, CA, USA, 11–13 June 2013; Paper CTh5C.5; OSA: Washington, DC, USA, 2013. [CrossRef]
7. Zou, J.; Le Blanc, C.; Papadopoulos, D.; Chériaux, G.; Georges, P.; Mennerat, G.; Druon, F.; Lecherbourg, L.; Pellegrina, A.; Ramirez, P.; et al. Design and current progress of the Apollon 10 PW project. *High Power Laser Sci. Eng.* **2015**, *3*, e2. [CrossRef]
8. Le Garrec, B.; Papadopoulos, D.N.; Le Blanc, C.; Zou, J.P.; Chériaux, G.; Georges, P.; Druon, F.; Martin, L.; Fréneaux, L.; Beluze, A.; et al. Design update and recent results of the Apollon 10 PW facility. In Proceedings of the SPIE 10238, High-Power, High-Energy, and High-Intensity Laser Technology III, Prague, Czech Republic, 26–27 April 2017; Hein, J., Ed.; International Society for Optics and Photonics: Bellingham, WA, USA, 2017; Volume 10238. [CrossRef]
9. Nakamura, K.; Mao, H.S.; Gonsalves, A.J.; Vincenti, H.; Mittelberger, D.E.; Daniels, J.; Magana, A.; Toth, C.; Leemans, W.P. Diagnostics, Control and Performance Parameters for the BELLA High Repetition Rate Petawatt Class Laser. *IEEE J. Quantum Electron.* **2017**, *53*, 1–21. [CrossRef]
10. Yoon, J.W.; Kim, Y.G.; Choi, I.W.; Sung, J.H.; Lee, H.W.; Lee, S.K.; Nam, C.H. Realization of laser intensity over 10^{23} W/cm^2. *Optica* **2021**, *8*, 630. [CrossRef]
11. Cartlidge, E. The light fantastic. *Science* **2018**, *359*, 382–385. [CrossRef] [PubMed]
12. Naumova, N.M.; Nees, J.A.; Sokolov, I.V.; Hou, B.; Mourou, G.A. Relativistic Generation of Isolated Attosecond Pulses in a λ^3 Focal Volume. *Phys. Rev. Lett.* **2004**, *92*, 063902. [CrossRef]
13. Naumova, N.M.; Nees, J.A.; Mourou, G.A. Relativistic attosecond physics. *Phys. Plasmas* **2005**, *12*, 056707. [CrossRef]

14. Ma, G.; Dallari, W.; Borot, A.; Krausz, F.; Yu, W.; Tsakiris, G.D.; Veisz, L. Intense isolated attosecond pulse generation from relativistic laser plasmas using few-cycle laser pulses. *Phys. Plasmas* **2015**, *22*, 033105. [CrossRef]
15. Zhang, Y.X.; Qiao, B.; Xu, X.R.; Chang, H.X.; Yu, M.Y.; Zhong, C.L.; Zhou, C.T.; Zhu, S.P.; He, X.T. Intense single attosecond pulse generation from near-critical-density plasmas irradiated by a few-cycle laser pulse. *Phys. Plasmas* **2018**, *25*, 023302. [CrossRef]
16. Zhou, M.L.; Yan, X.Q.; Mourou, G.; Wheeler, J.A.; Bin, J.H.; Schreiber, J.; Tajima, T. Proton acceleration by single-cycle laser pulses offers a novel monoenergetic and stable operating regime. *Phys. Plasmas* **2016**, *23*, 043112. [CrossRef]
17. Wu, X.Z.; Gong, Z.; Shou, Y.R.; Tang, Y.H.; Yu, J.Q.; Mourou, G.; Yan, X.Q. Efficiency enhancement of ion acceleration from thin target irradiated by multi-PW few-cycle laser pulses. *Phys. Plasmas* **2021**, *28*, 023102. doi: 10.1063/5.0029171. [CrossRef]
18. Wheeler, J.A.; Mourou, G.; Tajima, T. Science of High Energy, Single-Cycled Lasers. *Rev. Accel. Sci. Technol.* **2019**, *10*, 227–244. [CrossRef]
19. Tajima, T. Laser acceleration in novel media. *Eur. Phys. J. Spec. Top.* **2014**, *223*, 1037–1044. [CrossRef]
20. Mével, E.; Tcherbakoff, O.; Salin, F.; Constant, E. Extracavity compression technique for high-energy femtosecond pulses. *J. Opt. Soc. Am. B* **2003**, *20*, 105. [CrossRef]
21. Brabec, T.; Krausz, F. Intense few-cycle laser fields: Frontiers of nonlinear optics. *Rev. Mod. Phys.* **2000**, *72*, 545–591. [CrossRef]
22. Goulielmakis, E.; Schultze, M.; Hofstetter, M.; Yakovlev, V.S.; Gagnon, J.; Uiberacker, M.; Aquila, A.L.; Gullikson, E.M.; Attwood, D.T.; Kienberger, R.; et al. Single-cycle nonlinear optics. *Science* **2008**, *320*, 1614–1617. [CrossRef] [PubMed]
23. Cheng, Y.C.; Lu, C.H.; Lin, Y.Y.; Kung, A.H. Supercontinuum generation in a multi-plate medium. *Opt. Express* **2016**, *24*, 7224. [CrossRef] [PubMed]
24. Ueffing, M.; Reiger, S.; Kaumanns, M.; Pervak, V.; Trubetskov, M.; Nubbemeyer, T.; Krausz, F. Nonlinear pulse compression in a gas-filled multipass cell. *Opt. Lett.* **2018**, *43*, 2070. [CrossRef]
25. Lavenu, L.; Natile, M.; Guichard, F.; Zaouter, Y.; Delen, X.; Hanna, M.; Mottay, E.; Georges, P. Nonlinear pulse compression based on a gas-filled multipass cell. *Opt. Lett.* **2018**, *43*, 2252. [CrossRef]
26. Mironov, S.Y.; Wheeler, J.; Gonin, R.; Cojocaru, G.; Ungureanu, R.; Banici, R.; Serbanescu, M.; Dabu, R.; Mourou, G.; Khazanov, E.A. 100 J-level pulse compression for peak power enhancement. *Quantum Electron.* **2017**, *47*, 173–178. [CrossRef]
27. Fisher, R.A.; Kelley, P.L.; Gustafson, T.K. Subpicosecond Pulse Generation Using The Optical Kerr Effect. *Appl. Phys. Lett.* **1969**, *14*, 140–143. [CrossRef]
28. Mourou, G.; Cheriaux, G.; Radier, C. Device for Generating a Short Duration Laser Pulse. U.S. Patent Application US20110299152A1, 8 December 2011.
29. Mourou, G.; Mironov, S.; Khazanov, E.; Sergeev, A. Single cycle thin film compressor opening the door to Zeptosecond-Exawatt physics. *Eur. Phys. J. Spec. Top.* **2014**, *223*, 1181–1188. [CrossRef]
30. Khazanov, E.; Mironov, S.Y.; Mourou, G. Nonlinear compression of high-power laser pulses: Compression after compressor approach. *Uspekhi Fiz. Nauk* **2019**, *189*, 1173–1200. [CrossRef]
31. Mironov, S.Y.; Ginzburg, V.N.; Lozhkarev, V.V.; Luchinin, G.A.; Kirsanov, A.V.; Yakovlev, I.V.; Khazanov, E.A.; Shaykin, A.A. Highly efficient second-harmonic generation of intense femtosecond pulses with a significant effect of cubic nonlinearity. *Quantum Electron.* **2011**, *41*, 963–967. [CrossRef]
32. Voronin, A.A.; Zheltikov, A.M.; Ditmire, T.; Rus, B.; Korn, G. Subexawatt few-cycle lightwave generation via multipetawatt pulse compression. *Opt. Commun.* **2013**, *291*, 299–303. [CrossRef]
33. Mironov, S.; Lassonde, P.; Kieffer, J.C.; Khazanov, E.; Mourou, G. Spatially-uniform temporal recompression of intense femtosecond optical pulses. *Eur. Phys. J. Spec. Top.* **2014**, *223*, 1175–1180. [CrossRef]
34. Mironov, S.Y.; Ginzburg, V.N.; Yakovlev, I.V.; Kochetkov, A.A.; Shaykin, A.A.; Khazanov, E.A.; Mourou, G.A. Using self-phase modulation for temporal compression of intense femtosecond laser pulses. *Quantum Electron.* **2017**, *47*, 614–619. [CrossRef]
35. Bleotu, P.G.; Wheeler, J.; Papadopoulos, D.; Chabanis, M.; Prudent, J.; Frotin, M.; Martin, L.; Lebas, N.; Freneaux, A.; Beluze, A.; et al. Spectral broadening for multi-Joule pulse compression in the APOLLON Long Focal Area facility. *High Power Laser Sci. Eng.* **2022**, *10*, E9. [CrossRef]
36. Mironov, S.Y.; Fourmaux, S.; Lassonde, P.; Ginzburg, V.N.; Payeur, S.; Kieffer, J.C.; Khazanov, E.A.; Mourou, G. Thin plate compression of a sub-petawatt Ti:Sa laser pulses. *Appl. Phys. Lett.* **2020**, *116*, 241101. [CrossRef]
37. Ginzburg, V.; Yakovlev, I.; Zuev, A.; Korobeynikova, A.; Kochetkov, A.; Kuzmin, A.; Mironov, S.; Shaykin, A.; Shaikin, I.; Khazanov, E.; et al. Fivefold compression of 250-TW laser pulses. *Phys. Rev. A* **2020**, *101*, 013829. [CrossRef]
38. Ginzburg, V.; Yakovlev, I.; Kochetkov, A.; Kuzmin, A.; Mironov, S.; Shaikin, I.; Shaykin, A.; Khazanov, E. 11 fs, 15 PW laser with nonlinear pulse compression. *Opt. Express* **2021**, *29*, 28297. [CrossRef] [PubMed]
39. Kim, J.I.; Kim, Y.G.; Yang, J.M.; Yoon, J.W.; Sung, J.H.; Lee, S.K.; Nam, C.H. Sub-10 fs pulse generation by post-compression for peak-power enhancement of a 100-TW Ti:Sapphire laser. *Opt. Express* **2022**, *30*, 8734. [CrossRef]
40. Available online: https://www.zeonex.com/displays-touch-sensors.aspx.html (accessed on 24 February 2017).
41. Laserix. Available online: http://hebergement.u-psud.fr/laserix/en/Laserix (accessed on 12 December 2019).
42. Lassonde, P.; Mironov, S.; Fourmaux, S.; Payeur, S.; Khazanov, E.; Sergeev, A.; Kieffer, J.C.; Mourou, G. High energy femtosecond pulse compression. *Laser Phys. Lett.* **2016**, *13*, 075401. [CrossRef]
43. Taylor, A.J.; Clement, T.S.; Rodriguez, G. Determination of n_2 by direct measurement of the optical phase. *Opt. Lett.* **1996**, *21*, 1812. [CrossRef]

44. Hult, J. A Fourth-Order Runge – Kutta in the Interaction Picture Method for Simulating Supercontinuum Generation in Optical Fibers. *J. Light. Technol.* **2007**, *25*, 3770–3775. [CrossRef]
45. Bespalov, V.; Talanov, V. Filamentary Structure of Light Beams in Nonlinear Liquids. *ZhETF Pisma* **1966**, *3*, 471–476.
46. Rubenchik, A.M.; Turitsyn, S.K.; Fedoruk, M.P. Modulation instability in high power laser amplifiers. *Opt. Express* **2010**, *18*, 1380–1388. [CrossRef] [PubMed]
47. Voronin, A.A.; Zheltikov, A.M. Pulse self-compression to single-cycle pulse widths a few decades above the self-focusing threshold. *Phys. Rev. A* **2016**, *94*, 023824. [CrossRef]
48. Mironov, S.Y.; Wheeler, J.A.; Khazanov, E.A.; Mourou, G.A. Compression of high-power laser pulses using only multiple ultrathin plane plates. *Opt. Lett.* **2021**, *46*, 4570. [CrossRef] [PubMed]
49. Li, Z.; Kato, Y.; Kawanaka, J. Simulating an ultra-broadband concept for Exawatt-class lasers. *Sci. Rep.* **2021**, *11*, 151. [CrossRef] [PubMed]

Article

Introduction of Research Work on Laser Proton Acceleration and Its Application Carried out on Compact Laser–Plasma Accelerator at Peking University

Dongyu Li [1], Tang Yang [1,2], Minjian Wu [1,2], Zhusong Mei [1,2], Kedong Wang [1,2], Chunyang Lu [1], Yanying Zhao [1,2,3], Wenjun Ma [1,2,3], Kun Zhu [1,2,3], Yixing Geng [1,2,3], Gen Yang [1,2], Chijie Xiao [1,2], Jiaer Chen [1], Chen Lin [1,2,3,*], Toshiki Tajima [4] and Xueqing Yan [1,2,3]

[1] State Key Laboratory of Nuclear Physics and Technology & CAPT, Peking University, Beijing 100871, China
[2] Beijing Laser Acceleration Innovation Center, Huairou District, Beijing 101400, China
[3] Institute of Guangdong Laser Plasma Advanced Technology, Guangzhou 510540, China
[4] Department of Physics and Astronomy, UC Irvine, Irvine, CA 92697, USA
* Correspondence: lc0812@pku.edu.cn

Abstract: Laser plasma acceleration has made remarkable progress in the last few decades, but it also faces many challenges. Although the high gradient is a great potential advantage, the beam quality of the laser accelerator has a certain gap, or it is different from that of traditional accelerators. Therefore, it is important to explore and utilize its own features. In this article, some recent research progress on laser proton acceleration and its irradiation application, which was carried out on the compact laser plasma accelerator (CLAPA) platform at Peking University, have been introduced. By combining a TW laser accelerator and a monoenergetic beamline, proton beams with energies of less than 10 MeV, an energy spread of less than 1%, and with several to tens of pC charge, have been stably produced and transported in CLAPA. The beamline is an object–image point analyzing system, which ensures the transmission efficiency and the energy selection accuracy for proton beams with large initial divergence angle and energy spread. A spread-out Bragg peak (SOBP) is produced with high precision beam control, which preliminarily proved the feasibility of the laser accelerator for radiotherapy. Some application experiments based on laser-accelerated proton beams have also been carried out, such as proton radiograph, preparation of graphene on SiC, ultra-high dose FLASH radiation of cancer cells, and ion-beam trace probes for plasma diagnosis. The above applications take advantage of the unique characteristics of laser-driven protons, such as a micron scale point source, an ultra-short pulse duration, a wide energy spectrum, etc. A new laser-driven proton therapy facility (CLAPA II) is being designed and is under construction at Peking University. The 100 MeV proton beams will be produced via laser–plasma interaction by using a 2-PW laser, which may promote the real-world applications of laser accelerators in malignant tumor treatment soon.

Keywords: laser plasma acceleration; beamline; plasma lens; FLASH-radiotherapy; ion irradiation

1. Introduction

A particle accelerator is a device that uses the electromagnetic field to accelerate charged particles to a high energy, which is one of the most important scientific tools to study basic nuclear physics and to explore the deep structure of space and time. In the meantime, the accelerators also play an important role in promoting social development and improving the quality of people's lives. More than 30 thousand accelerators are in operation around the world in the field of medicine (oncology therapy and radioisotope production), national defense, and industrial production (ion implanters). However, due to the restriction of the vacuum breakdown threshold, the acceleration gradient of the conventional accelerators is limited to 100 MV/m. The huge volume and the expensive construction costs have become the bottleneck of the accelerators to higher energy development. Therefore, the new principle of acceleration with lasers, which was first proposed by

Tajima and Dawson in 1979, has been extensively studied during the last few decades in order to offer an alternative [1].

With the continuous development of high-power laser technology [2,3], the intensity of a focused laser pulse can exceed the relativistic optics regime, and even reach 10^{22} W/cm^2. When such an ultra-intense laser pulse interacts with plasma of different parameters, it can either excite the wakefield [4] (accelerating electrons) or the electrostatic sheath field [5] (accelerating ions) at a micron scale, and the acceleration gradient is as high as GV/m to TV/m. Laser plasma acceleration is expected to achieve the miniaturization of accelerators due to the acceleration gradient that exceeds that of the conventional accelerators by three orders of magnitude, and has attracted extensive attention. Up to now, the 8 GeV [6] quasi mono-energetic electron beam and the proton beam with the highest energy of nearly 100 MeV [7] have been successfully demonstrated using laser–plasma acceleration. At present, laser-accelerated protons have initially been applied in the fields of biomedicine, material science, high-energy-density physics, and so on [8]. With the development of high-repetition-rate Petawatt (PW) laser technology [9], we can now envision a new generation of accelerators with many applications [10,11], especially for cancer therapy [12–14], in the near future.

It should be noted that, compared with electron acceleration, it is more challenging for laser ion acceleration to reach a high beam quality, due to the quick diffusion of hot electrons, which work as the energy transfer medium between the lasers and the ions [15,16], as well as the variety of instabilities during the laser–solid target interaction process [17,18]. Except for the maximum energy of the accelerated ions, the major issues are the emittance, the energy spread, the charge, and especially the reliability-availability-maintainability-inspectability (RAMI), which are necessary conditions to raise the laser "acceleration" to "accelerator" for applications. Irradiation research based on this new type of proton beam is also challenging and innovative; on one hand, it is necessary to optimize the beam transmission and control; on the other hand, it is also necessary to explore new irradiation phenomena and to expand the application fields. Here, we introduce some research progresses on laser proton acceleration and its irradiation application at Peking University. Most of the work below was carried out on the compact laser plasma accelerator (CLAPA) platform.

2. Experimental Demonstration of a Laser Proton Accelerator with Accurate Beam Control through Image-Relaying Transport

A compact laser plasma accelerator (CLAPA) that can stably produce and transport protons with different energies of less than 10 MeV, an energy spread of less than 1%, and with several to tens of pC charge, has been demonstrated [19]. The high-current proton beam with a continuous energy spectrum and a large divergence angle [20,21] is generated by using a high-contrast laser and micron thickness solid targets, which is later collected, analyzed, and refocused by an image-relaying beamline by using a combination of quadrupole and bending electromagnets [22,23]. It eliminates the inherent defects of the laser-driven beams, realizes the precise manipulation of the proton beams with reliability, and takes the first step towards applications of this new generation of accelerators.

In the experiment, a p-polarized laser pulse with 1.8 J of energy and 30 fs duration was focused onto a 1.2 µm thickness plastic target by using a f/3.5 off-axis parabola at an incident angle of 30 degrees with respect to the target's normal direction. The on-target intensity was 8×10^{19} W/cm^2. The laser contrast was 10^{-10} at 40 ps before the main pulse, which was achieved by using a cross-polarized wave generation (XPW). The high energy protons were mainly generated by the target normal sheath acceleration (TNSA) mechanism [15,24]. In the TNSA, the hot electrons are driven out of the solid density target due to the ponderomotive force of the laser, forming a sheath field with a gradient of up to TV/m. The ions (mainly protons with the highest charge-to-mass ratio) on the surfaces of the target are accelerated accordingly to high energy within tens of micrometers. Due to the ultra-short transient acceleration process, the proton beam has the characteristics of a high short pulse duration (ps-ns), a high peak current, a large divergence angle (tens of degrees), and an exponential decay energy spectrum.

A Thomson spectrometer was placed 14 cm behind the target in order to measure the energy spectrum of the protons. One typical energy spectrum is shown by the black curve in Figure 1a. During the beamline experiment, this Thomson spectrometer was replaced by a quadrupole triplet lens. Then, an insertable radiochromic film (RCF) stack that was positioned 4 cm behind the target was used to measure the original spatial and energy distribution of the protons [25]. After the ionizing radiation, the active material inside of the RCF undergoes polymerization and changes its color from transparent to opaque, with the degree of color conversion that is proportional to the absorbed dose. Figure 1b shows the typical images of one RCF stack, where three types of RCFs (HD-V2, MD-V3, and EBT-3) were superimposed. The corresponding energy spectrum that was extracted from the RCF stack is shown in Figure 1a (pink dots), which is quite consistent with the Thomson spectrometer measurement.

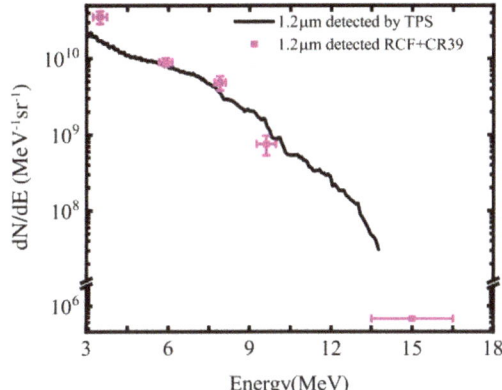

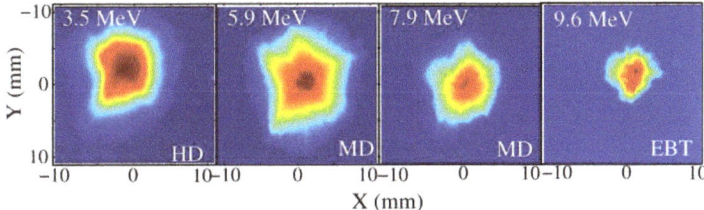

Figure 1. (a) The typical energy spectrum measured by the Thomson spectrometer (black curve) and the RCF stack (pink dots) based on a 1.2 µm plastic target. (b) Images in one RCF stack, where three types of RCFs (HD-V2, MD-V3, and EBT-3) were used.

After detecting the characteristics of the laser-driven proton beams, a magnet lattice consisting of quadruple and bending electromagnets was specially designed, as shown in Figure 2. The protons are first collected and focused by a quadrupole triplet lens that was placed 19 cm behind the target with a collection angle of ±50 mrad [26], then analyzed by a 45° sector magnet, and finally refocused by a quadrupole doublet lens onto the irradiation platform. The beamline incorporated three beam profile detectors (the first two using scintillators and the third using micro-channel plate (MCP)), which were located near the focal plane of the triplet lens as BPD#1, the image point of the sector magnet as BPD #2, and at the irradiation point as BPD#3, respectively. The flexibility of the electromagnets between the slits and the BPDs is crucial in order to enable effective beam diagnostics without impacting the applications.

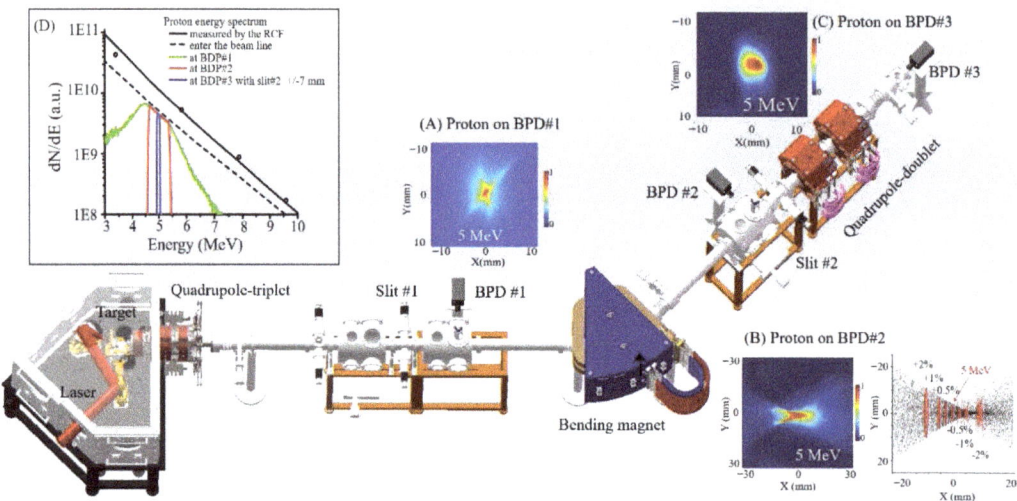

Figure 2. Layout of the acceleration chamber and beamline for CLAPA. The proton beam is accelerated by using a high-contrast laser and micro-thickness foil; it is then focused by a quadrupole triplet lens, analyzed by a bending electromagnet, and refocused by a quadrupole doublet lens with selected energy onto the irradiation platform. The inserted graph (**A**) Experimental result of the 5 MeV proton beam profile at BPD#1 after focusing by the triplet lens. (**B**) Experimental (left) and simulated (right) spatial distributions of the protons at BPD#2. The red dots in the simulated result, from right to left, represent the protons with energy deviated −2%, −1%, −0.5%, 0%, 0.5%, 1%, and 2% from 5 MeV, respectively. (**C**) Proton beam distribution at BPD#3, with a 5 MeV central energy and 1% energy spread. (**D**) Energy spectra of protons at different positions along the beamline. The black solid curve is the original exponentially declining energy spectrum (based on the RCF data shown in Figure 1). The black dashed curve is the actual spectrum entering the beamline within an acceptance angle of ±50 mrad. The green, red, and blue curves are the simulated spectra at the three beam position detectors BPD#1, BPD#2, BPD#3, respectively. The initial beam with a very broad energy spectrum is gradually confined to a 1% energy spread.

Figure 2A shows the experimental result of the proton beam profile on BPD#1 after it was focused by the triplet lens. The focused central energy was set at 5 MeV. The slit#1 was put at the object point of the bending magnet, which could partially screen the unwanted energies, leading to about ±10% energy spread of the beam within a 3 cm^2 transverse area. The beam spot distribution that is shown here has a cross shape with a blurred boundary, due to the chromatic aberration and the large acceptance angle of the initial beam. Following this, a 45° sector magnet was used to select the proton energy, under which the protons from the same object point with the same energy and different angular divergence converge to the same image point at the x axis, while the protons with different energies are separated in the x direction. This object-to-image point transport system can remove the influences of a large divergence angle and a large energy chirp of the initial protons at the image point. Figure 2B shows the simulated (right) and the experimental (left) spatial distributions of the proton beam at BPD#2. They both show a bow tie profile with 5 MeV protons at the knot, which indicates that the chromatic aberration in the y direction, and those with energies that deviated from 5 MeV, were dispersed aside. By controlling the opening width of slit#2, which was installed at the image point of the sector magnet, the energy spread of the protons could be precisely controlled. In the end, a quadrupole doublet lens was used to focus the mono-energetic protons to the irradiation point with a desired spot size. Figure 2C shows the experimental spatial distributions of the proton beam at BPD#3 (5 MeV and ±1% energy spread). The final focused beam profile could be adjusted as required, for the quadruple doublet lens had the advantage of controlling the envelopes independently in the x and y directions.

The energy spectrum evolution of the proton beam through the beamline is presented in Figure 2D, which demonstrates how the initial broadband beam energy was gradually confined to ±1% energy spread after each electromagnet. The black curve is the original energy spectrum that was deconvolved from the RCF data that is shown in Figure 1b. The black dashed curve is the energy spectrum entering the beamline that takes the ±50 mrad acceptance angle into account. The green, red, and blue curves are the simulated spectra at BPD#1, BPD#2, and BPD#3, respectively. In the experiment, by varying the width of slit#2 from 3 to 54 mm, the corresponding energy spread was increased from ±0.5 to ±4%, and the final charge was tuned correspondingly. The beam transmission efficiency has been reduced to less than 30% since the first triplet lens. Combined with the subsequent energy selection, the overall beam loss rate was higher than 95%, which is a great waste of energy. Therefore, the subsequent design of the beamline with achromatic ability is very critical. The proton source can also be modified from the beginning of the acceleration. Apart from TNSA which has a better stability, other acceleration mechanisms, such as radiation pressure acceleration (RPA) [27,28] or guided post-acceleration [29,30], should also be adopted, to modulate the proton energy spectrum being more concentrated in the aimed energy.

3. Emittance Measurement along Transport Beamline for Laser-Driven Protons

The particle emittance quantifies the ability to focus and transport a beam and is one of the most important parameters for a beamline [31]. The laser–plasma accelerated proton beam has been characterized by a micron scale point source and a small emittance of less than 0.004 mm mrad [32], indicating that it should be easier to focus and transmit compared to that of the conventional accelerators. However, due to the broad energy spread and the large divergence, its initial ultralow emittance will increase rapidly in the subsequent transmission process. We have systematically measured the emittance of a proton beam that was produced by ultra-intense laser irradiation on a micron-thick flat solid target along the CLAPA transport beamline [33]. An over 3-fold emittance growth was found for the 5 MeV laser-driven protons with an energy spread of ±2% and a divergence of ±20 mrad after being transported 5.9 m in the experiment.

The emittance measurement experiment setup is shown in Figure 3. The laser pulse was focused by an F3.5 OAP onto 5-micron-thick plastic foils at 30° with respect to the target's normal direction. The originally accelerated TNSA proton beams had exponential decaying energy distribution with a cutoff energy of around 6.5 MeV and a divergence of hundreds of mrad. The protons were first focused by a quadrupole triplet electromagnet with an entrance at 14 cm behind the target, and then the energy that was dispersed by a 45° dipole magnet that was placed 1.2 m behind the triplet. Only those protons with a divergence that was smaller than ±20 mrad (corresponding to rms divergence of about 8.2 mrad) were input into the beamline in the emittance measurement experiment in order to avoid the effect of non-linearity in the applied forces of the magnets on the result. The following three methods were employed: (a) pepper-pot right after the target, (b) a quadrupole scan technique using the magnet triplet, and (c) single-shot emittance measurement with the dipole magnet.

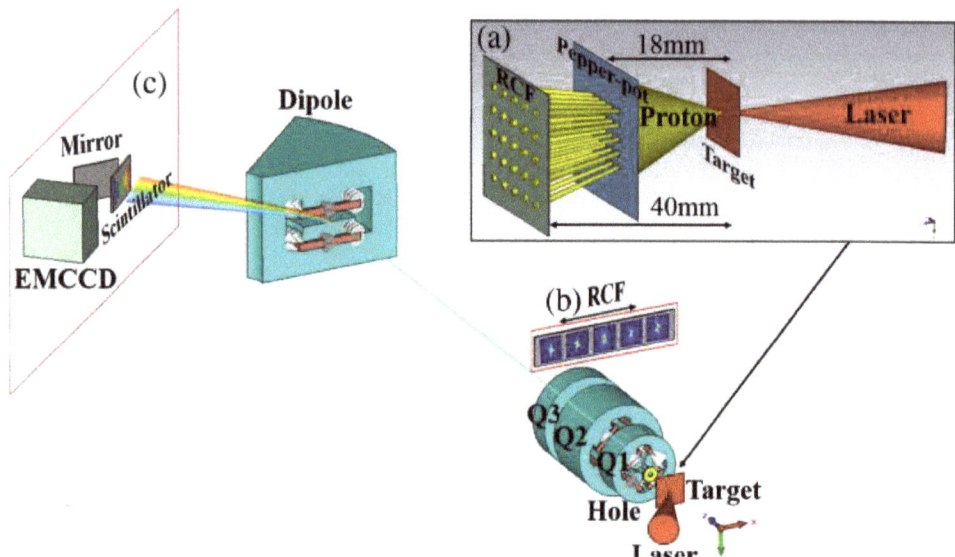

Figure 3. Setup of the emittance measurement experiment on the CLAPA beamline. Protons are accelerated along the z direction, focused by the electromagnetic quadrupole triplet lens, in which Q1 and Q3 focus in the x direction and Q2 focuses in the y direction, and are dispersed by the dipole magnet in the x direction. The following three methods were employed for the emittance measurement [33]: (**a**) pepper-pot; (**b**) quadrupole scan technique; and (**c**) single-shot emittance measurement after the dipole.

Figure 4 summarizes the emittance measurements for the 5 MeV laser-accelerated proton beam, which was measured at three different positions with the above three methods. The solid curves are the evolution of the emittance, as simulated with the program CST, in which protons with a source size of 50 μm, an energy spread of ±2%, and a divergence of ± 20 mrad were simulated, corresponding to an original emittance $\varepsilon_{n,tr,rms} \approx \varepsilon_{n,rms} = 0.02$ mm mrad. Here, $\varepsilon_{n,tr,rms}$ is the normalized root mean square (rms) emittance that was derived in the trace space $(x; x')$ and $\varepsilon_{n,rms}$ is the rms emittance that was derived in the phase space $(x; px)$ [31]. There is clear growth in $\varepsilon_{n,rms}$, both inside of the triplet and in the drift space, which matches the simulation well. The symbols with error bars are the experiment result. We have shown that the initial extremely small emittance at the source point (less than 0.004 mm mrad, as measured by Cowan [32]) increases by more than one order of magnitude after a few centimeters of propagation and remains between 0.04 mm mrad and 0.10 m mrad for the subsequent transport. This conclusion is suitable for the measured protons with ±2% energy spread and ±20 mrad angle in order to meet with the paraxial condition, which means that for the design of a monoenergetic beamline, the laser accelerator can be regarded as the same as the conventional accelerator. However, in order to fully use the laser-accelerated protons, an achromatic beamline with a large acceptance angle is recommended. In this condition, the emittance will increase significantly under the double effects of energy chromatic aberrations and the nonlinear edge field of the magnet components, bringing great challenge to the beamline design.

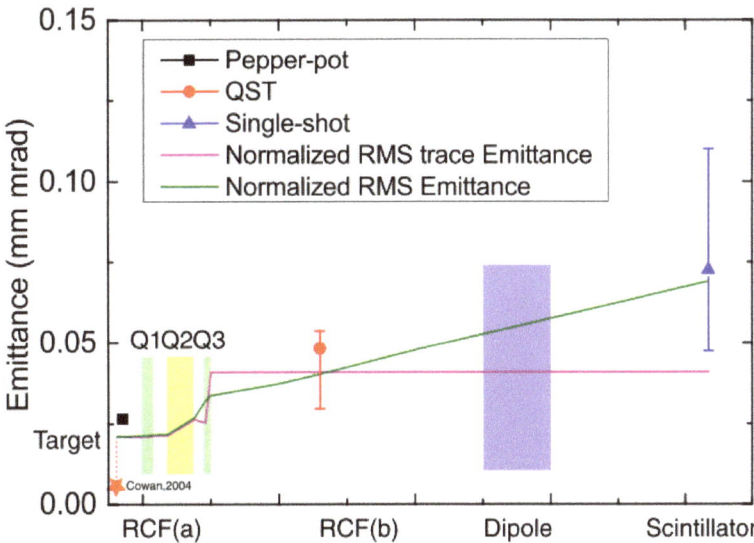

Figure 4. Emittance values from simulations and experiments. The solid lines are the emittance evolution during transport in simulations. The points with error bars are experimental results.

4. Production of the Spread-Out Bragg Peak (SOBP) by a Tailored Energy Deposition

Compact and low-cost proton radiotherapy is one important application that is expected to be implemented by the laser accelerator. In proton radiotherapy, the parameters of a continuous incident proton beam must be adjusted according to the requirements of the treatment plan, so that the irradiated dose accurately covers the whole three-dimensional volume of a tumor tissue. In other words, the narrow Bragg peak of the monoenergetic protons has to be broadened to the spread-out Bragg peak (SOBP) by combining separate shots at different energies. The SOBP is one of the key technologies of radiotherapy, and it requires high-precision beam control of energy, energy spread, energy spectrum, beam source position, beam spot size, and uniformity, which is a challenge, especially for a laser accelerator.

We have tested this ability by accumulating 203 shots of laser-driven protons with central energies of 3.45 MeV (two shots), 3.66 MeV (four shots), 3.88 MeV (six shots), 4.11 MeV (15 shots), 4.36 MeV (30 shots), 4.62 MeV (146 shots), and an energy spread of ± 3%, then, the total energy range was from 3.35 to 4.76 MeV [34]. We used the CLAPA beamline to select the proton beams from the initial exponentially decaying energy spectra (the dashed black line in Figure 5b) and accumulated them into an ascending energy spectrum (the red curve in Figure 5b), so as to obtain the tailored energy deposition that is required for the SOBP at the irradiation platform.

A stack of three layers of HD-V2 RCFs was used to record the three-dimensional dose distributions. A 30 μm thick aluminum foil was put in front of the lower half of the first RCF, so that the corresponding Bragg peak energy in each RCF-sensitive layer (the lower part) was shifted. We can see that the dose distributions at different depths of energy deposition are nearly radially symmetric, as shown in Figure 5a. Using a ± 3% energy spread increases the utilization of the proton beams and maintains a radially symmetric proton distribution. It is important to note that the carbon and oxygen ions with the same beam rigidity $q^2 \times E/A$ were inevitably transported with the same transverse envelope, with the protons in the beamline being composed of only magnetic field components. The penetration depth of the heavy ions was much smaller than that of the protons at the same energy, hence, they could be easily blocked by a thin foil. In Figure 5a, the upper half of the first RCF acts as a shield for these heavy ions, which caused excessive dosage.

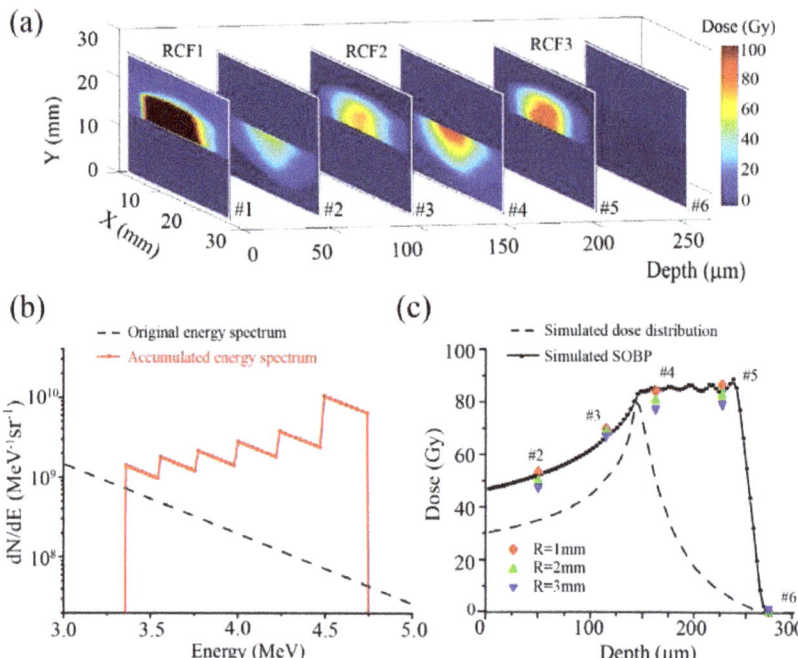

Figure 5. Production of a spread-out Bragg peak with accumulated proton shots at different energies. (**a**) Dose distributions at different depths recorded on the RCF stack. The depth shift of the Bragg peak, due to the aluminum foil, is converted to an equivalent depth for the RCF film. (**b**) The black dashed curve is the original exponentially decaying energy spectrum measured directly behind the foil target in the acceleration chamber. The red curve is the total spectrum of proton beams accumulated to form the SOBP on the irradiation platform. (**c**) Comparison of the experimental results with a simulated depth profile. The black curve is the accumulated dose distributions of all 203 shots of protons, as simulated using SRIM. The red, green, and blue dots represent the average doses within a 1, 2, and 3 mm radius of the beam center, respectively, at the different depths obtained in the experiment. The black dashed curve represents the expected dose profile if we were to use the exponentially decaying energy spectrum directly. The dose coordinate of the black dashed curve is magnified for ease of comparison, while the shape of the curve is not changed.

Figure 5c shows the calculated dose distribution (the black solid curve) at different depths and the experimental average doses within 1 mm (the red diamond), 2 mm (the green triangle), and 3 mm (the blue triangle) radius of the beam spots. The results show a good fit to the expected depth profile, demonstrating that it is possible to produce a SOBP with a laser accelerator. The black dashed curve in Figure 5c shows the expected dose curve if we were to use the original exponentially decaying spectrum directly (the dashed curve in Figure 5a), for comparison. Hence, tailoring the number of shots for different central energies changes the final dose depth profile, and enables an initially exponentially decaying spectrum in order to satisfy the requirements of the SOBP. The result also shows the potential feasibility of future irradiation based on laser-accelerated proton beams.

5. The Beamline Design for CLAPA II

5.1. Achromatic Beamline Design for CLAPA II

A new petawatt laser-driven proton therapy facility (CLAPA II) is being designed and constructed by Peking University. In the CLAPA platform that has been introduced above, the proton beams are generated mainly in the TNSA regime in a relatively low laser intensity, and the micrometer thickness targets are used to maintain stable operation. In the new therapy facility, light pressure acceleration (RPA) [27,28], the coherent acceleration of ions by laser (CAIL) [35,36] mechanisms, or in combination with a critical density plasma [37–40], will be dominant, in order to improve the acceleration efficiency. This is because under the RPA mechanism, the energy of the proton beam is directly proportional to the laser intensity [41–44], while it is proportional to the half power of the laser intensity in the TNSA mechanism [15,45]. Therefore, as the laser power increases to the PW level, the RPA will demonstrate greater advantages in obtaining higher proton energy. There is an optimal matching parameter between the target and the laser, which is expressed as $a_0 \sim \frac{n_0 d}{n_c \lambda}$, where a_0 is the normalized amplitude that is related to the laser intensity by $a_0 = 0.85 \left(\frac{I \lambda_{\mu m}^2}{10^{18} \text{ W/cm}^2} \right)^{1/2}$, $n_c = 1.1 \times 10^{21} \text{cm}^{-3} \lambda_{\mu m}^{-2}$ is the critical density, d and n_0 are the target thickness and density, respectively. It should be noted that the optimal solid target thickness for a PW laser intensity is still in the nanometer scale, which requires both a high contrast and a steep rising edge of the laser pulse. In CLAPA II, the protons will be produced by using a 2-PW laser to reach the proton energies exceeding 100 MeV. We hope that the construction of this facility will promote the real-world applications of laser accelerators.

The CLAPA II beam transmission system is designed for a 100 MeV proton beam that is produced by PW laser acceleration, and its feasibility is tested through theoretical simulations [46]. It is designed with two transport lines in order to provide both horizontal and vertical irradiation modes, as demonstrated in Figure 6. The length and the bending angle of the horizontal beamline are 12.96 m and 90°, respectively, and for the vertical beamline these values are 22.56 m and 270°, respectively. Compared to the original CLAPA beamline, the new design includes magnets with multiple functions and has several notable advantages, including an improved acceptance angle, achromatic ability, and a better spot uniformity. A locally-achromatic design method with new canted-cosine-theta (CCT) magnets [47] has been used to mitigate the negative effects of the large energy spread that is produced by laser acceleration, and to reduce the overall weight of the vertical beamline. The beamline contains a complete energy selection system, which can reduce the energy spread of the laser-accelerated beam enough to meet the application requirements. The users can select the proton beam energy within the range of 40–100 MeV, which is then transmitted through the rest of the beamline. A beam spot with a diameter of less than 15 mm and an energy spread of less than 5% can be provided at the horizontal and vertical irradiation targets. Each bending element of the beamline is locally achromatic, which allows us to significantly limit the envelope growth of the beam, due to dispersion. The use of CCT magnet technology in the vertical beamline can provide design experience for follow-up work with a superconducting gantry. CLAPA II and the beamline is expected to be operational in the Beijing Laser Accelerator Innovation Center (BLAIC) in 2024.

5.2. Designing of Active Plasma Lens for CLAPA II

Compared with the traditional beam, the laser-accelerated beam has several different properties. Therefore, in addition to catching up with the parameters and the technologies of the traditional beam, we must also explore new methods for laser-beam transmission and application. The plasma medium has high energy storage and regulation capabilities, which can support extremely high electromagnetic fields, making it a potential candidate for a suitable beam transmission element.

Capillary plasma has been used for both electron wakefield acceleration [48] and as a beam transport component [49]. In a gas-filled capillary discharges device, a current pulse is passed through a channel with an inner diameter of a few hundred microns and a scaling length of several, or even tens of, centimeters, which is prefilled with gas at a pressure of tens to hundreds of millibar. The current pulse has a peak of a few hundred amperes and a duration of the order of hundreds of nanoseconds. According to the Ampère law, an azimuthal magnetic field with a gradient of up to kT/m is generated, which provides the symmetric focusing of the particles that are comoving with the current. This current-based magnetic lens is also called the active plasma lens (APL) [50–52]. We have theoretically studied the feasibility of using a discharged-capillary-based high-gradient APL to focus the laser-accelerated pulsed proton beams, as shown in Figure 7 [53]. Several fundamental restrictions have been set in order to avoid the plasma affecting the beam quality, including the energy loss, the magnetic skin depth, the z-pinch effect, and the wakefield-induced collective effect. We have specified the equations of the motion of the proton beams in both straight and curved discharge-capillary APLs, on which the regulation law of a specific APL focusing and tuning protons can be calculated. The results show that the APL, whose parameters can be adjusted flexibly, is suitable for focusing and transporting the proton beams with an energy of 1–100 MeV.

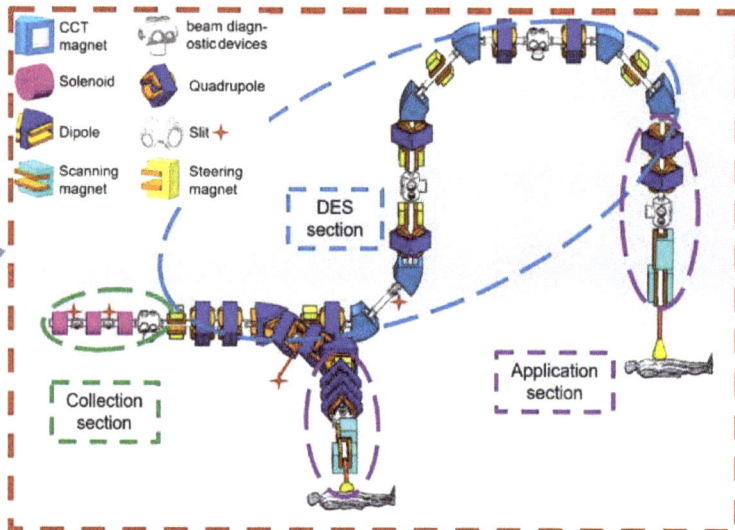

Figure 6. Layout of CLAPA II and its transport system. The overall layout of the beam transport system is in the red dotted box. The different sections of the beam transport system are circled by dashed lines of different colors.

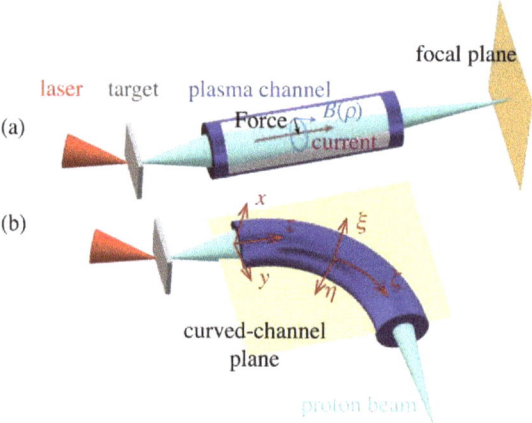

Figure 7. Schematic concept of a proton beam focusing on propagating in a straight (**a**) and a curved (**b**) APL.

This study confirms that the APL has a one order of magnitude higher magnetic field gradient, a shorter scale focal length, and a weaker energy dependence, compared with solenoids and quadrupoles. The hundred-of-ns discharge is suitable for laser-accelerated proton beams with an ultra-short pulse duration. The APL has the ability to tightly focus the protons to a micrometer transverse size spot with good tunability. It can also be used as a windowless vacuum sealing device with heat and radiation damage resistance, simplifying the structure of the irradiation platform [54]. By combining the plasma acceleration with the APL, we can not only complete the miniaturization of the laser–plasma accelerator, but also improve the efficiency of the beam transmission and utilization. Such a compact tabletop laser accelerator can have a significant impact on various areas, such as accelerator physics [55], inertial fusion science [56], astrophysics [57], and proton oncology [58].

6. Application of Laser Proton Acceleration

6.1. Laser-Accelerated Proton Radiography of Biological Samples

Compared with attenuation-based X-ray radiography, proton radiography has advantages in fine density resolution and the imaging of biological samples [59–62]. We have studied contact imaging based on MeV energy laser-accelerated protons irradiating on ant samples [63]. The sample was placed 4 cm behind the target and was sandwiched between a 70 μm-thick Al foil (which was used to shield the transmitted laser, the target debris, and the low energy ions) and an RCF stack (one HD-V2 RCF and one EBT3 RCF). The energies of the protons that were detected by the active layers were 2.9 and 5.6 MeV for the HD-V2 RCF and the EBT3 RCF, respectively. Since the sample was attached to the RCF stack, the distance between the object and the detector was ~0, and the magnification of the system was ~1. The contact imaging setup was configured to reduce the blurring caused by multiple Coulomb scattering and to increase the spatial resolution.

Figure 8 shows the images of the ant that were recorded on (a) the HD-V2 RCF and (b) the EBT3 RCF, where the dark areas are irradiated by the proton spots. The small graphs that are inserted into the lower right corner are the entirety of the radiography images. Since the ants block a part of the low-energy protons, their shapes and their internal structures are imprinted by the color changing on the background of the proton beam spots. In the magnified images of the center big ant, both the external structure and the internal organs can be distinguished with a micrometer spatial resolution. Comparing Figure 8a,b, we find that the protons of different energies can clearly distinguish the different structures of the ants. For example, the antennae of the ant (marked by the solid red line in the figure) can be better distinguished on the HD-V2 RCF with the 2.9 MeV protons, while the tibia of the ant (marked by the red dashed line) is much clearer on the EBT3 RCF with the 5.6 MeV protons. It provides a feasible method that uses the laser-accelerated proton beam with a broad energy spectrum to analyze the structure of different depths inside the irradiated object by one single shot.

6.2. Laser-Accelerated Ultra-High Dose Rate FLASH Radiation of Normal Cells and Tumor-Cells

The ultra-high dose rate FLASH-radiotherapy (FLASH-RT) has attracted wide attention in recent years [64]. It greatly protects normal tissues from damage, while effectively killing tumor tissues, which is suggested to be related to oxygen depletion. Due to ultra-short pulse duration, laser-accelerated protons have natural advantages in FLASH-RT, which has gradually become a hot research topic [58,65,66]. However, the detailed cell death profile and the pathways thereof are still unclear.

Normal mouse embryonic fibroblast cells were FLASH irradiated (~10^9 Gy/s) at a dose of ~10–40 Gy in hypoxic and normoxic conditions, with ultra-fast laser-generated particles that were generated on CLAPA [67,68]. The experiment setup is shown in Figure 9. The laser was focused onto a 100 nm plastic target using an F/2.5 OAP. The laser energy that was on target was ~1 J and the peak intensity was 5.6×10^{19} W/cm^2. The ion energy spectra were measured with a Thomson parabola spectrometer (TPS) along the direction that was normal to the back surface of the target. The cells irradiation system was plugged in after the ion energy spectra were measured (Figure 9A). The ion beams entered the cells' radiation system through a vacuum window and irradiated normally upon the cells. The vacuum window was composed of an aluminum film for light-shielding and a Kapton film for vacuum sealing. The monolayer cells that were cultured on a Mylar film were mounted on a stainless steel cell-culture cylinder, which faced toward the inner space of the cylinder, as shown in Figure 9B,C. Another Mylar film was taped onto the other side of the holder in order to seal the cylinder, avoiding the contamination and dryout of the cells during irradiation. Each cell sample was irradiated by a single shot.

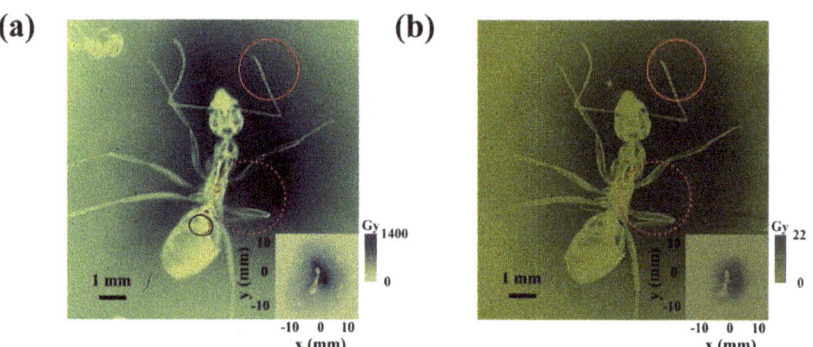

Figure 8. Proton radiography images of an ant on the (**a**) HD-V2 and (**b**) EBT3 RCF. The small images inserted in the lower right corners of (**a**,**b**) show the complete images of the proton radiography of ants with a proton energy of 2.9 and 5.6 MeV, respectively. The part marked by the solid red line is the antennae, and the part marked by the red dashed line is the tibia.

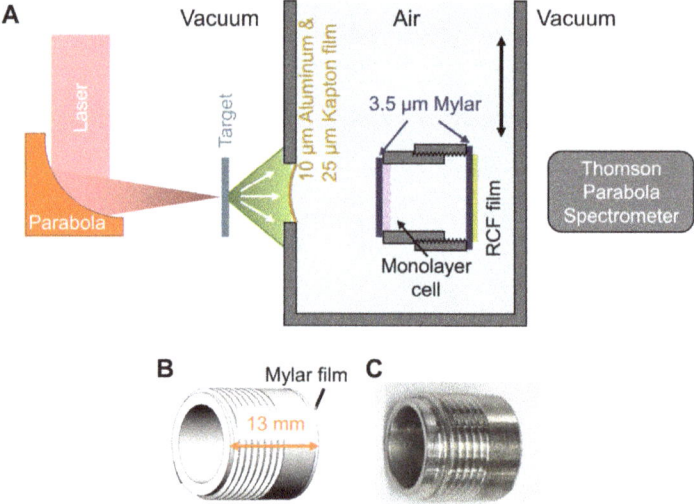

Figure 9. Experimental setup for FLASH irradiation. (**A**) Schematic drawing of the experimental setup. (**B**,**C**) Side view of the cell-culture cylinder. The cells were cultured on the 3.5 μm Mylar film adhered to inner side of the cylinder.

While the cells' irradiation system was plugged in, customized EBT3 films for dose verification were placed directly behind the sealing Mylar film. The deposited dose in the cell was calculated by the Monte-Carlo code FLUKA, with the measured energy spectra of the protons and the measured dose in the EBT3 films. The laser acceleration was completed within 1 ps. Considering the broadening of the beam duration due to the difference in the flying speed of the protons, the duration of the proton pulse that was delivered to the cell plane was ~10 ns, corresponding to the dose rate in the order of 10^9 Gy/s.

We revealed early apoptosis, late apoptosis, and necrosis induced by FLASH irradiation in both cyt c+/+ and cyt c−/− mouse embryonic fibroblast cells. The apoptosis proportion of the cyt c+/+ cell was significantly lower in hypoxia than that in normoxia, indicating the increased resistance of the normal fibroblast cell after FLASH irradiation in hypoxia. The late apoptosis and necrosis proportion of the irradiated cyt c−/− was significantly lower in both hypoxia and normoxia compared to the irradiated normal cyt c+/+ cells, indicating that mitochondrial dysfunction enhanced the radio-resistance of the mouse embryonic fibroblast cells after FLASH irradiation.

We also studied the killing effect of ultra-high dose rate FLASH-IR on MCF-7 and its cancer stem cell (CSC) [67]. The ratio of apoptosis, pyroptosis, and necrosis was determined at 6, 12, and 24 h after irradiation. At the same time, we also labeled the lysosomes and detected autophagy in the cells. The results showed that the apoptosis of the irradiated CSCs was significantly lower than that of MCF-7, and the pyroptosis and the necrosis of the irradiated CSCs were also slightly lower than that of MCF-7. In addition, the response of the CSC to irradiation was slower. These results suggested the radio-resistance of the CSCs under FLASH-IR. By detecting cells' autophagy, as well as the lysosomes, after irradiation, we found that the lysosomes and the autophagy in the CSCs were much higher (Figure 10), suggesting that CSCs may enhance their radio-resistance by increasing lysosome-mediated autophagy and decreasing apoptosis after FLASH-IR.

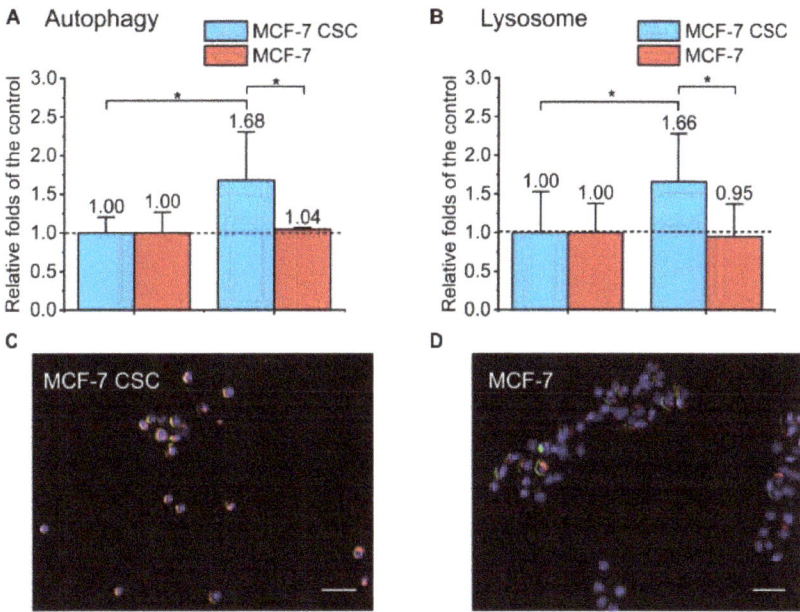

Figure 10. Detection of autophagy and lysosomes in the irradiated MCF-7 cells and MCF-7 CSCs. (**A**) Compared with the control, the increase in the autophagy proportion of the irradiated group. (**B**) Compared with the control, the increase in lysosomes of the irradiated group. All results are expressed as means ± SD, Student's t-test or one-way ANOVA are used for analyzing significance between the controls and the experimental groups, where $p < 0.05$ was marked as *. (**C,D**) Representative images of irradiated MCF-7 cells and MCF-7 CSCs stained with MDC autophagy detection kit and lysoTracker Red DND-99. The blue is the nucleus, the red is the lysosome, and the green is labeled autophagy.

6.3. Preparation of Graphene on SiC by Laser-Accelerated Pulsed Ion Beams

The proton beam that is driven by the ultra-intense laser has an ultra-short pulse duration of picoseconds to nanoseconds. When such a proton beam irradiates a sample, the rapid energy deposition will instantaneously heat the sample to a high temperature, which will lead to significant changes in the physical and chemical properties of the material. For example, if the irradiation distance is in the order of hundred microns, the sample temperature can reach up to eV and change to a warm, dense matter state [69,70]. When the irradiation distance is in the order of cm or mm, the temperature of the sample will also rise rapidly, until it reaches the melting point or the boiling point of the material. Therefore, it is possible to carry out material irradiation application research, such as testing the radiation resistance of materials under extreme conditions [71–73], or to realize the ultra-fast synthesis of some new materials [74,75].

We have carried out an application experiment using laser-accelerated ion beams to prepare graphene, utilizing the extremely high beam current [76]. Graphene that is grown on the surface of silicon carbide can be directly made into semiconductor devices, avoiding the damage that is caused by the transfer from other substrates, which leads to the decline of the electrical properties of graphene. The incident ions can break the Carbon-silicon chemical bond on the surface. In the process of high temperature annealing, silicon atoms sublimate before carbon atoms and desorb from the surface, and the enriched carbon atoms on the surface will recombine to form the graphene films. We first combined the laser-accelerated ion beam and graphene growth as demonstrated in Figure 11. After the ion irradiation, the SiC samples were annealed in a graphite enclosure at a pressure of 10^{-3} Pa, where the samples were heated to 1100 °C for 60 min. Finally, they were slowly cooled down to room temperature. Due to the closed environment of the graphite boat, the sublimation of the silicon atoms during the annealing process was reduced. The excess carbon atoms self-assembled into graphene on the SiC surface, as shown in Figure 11c.

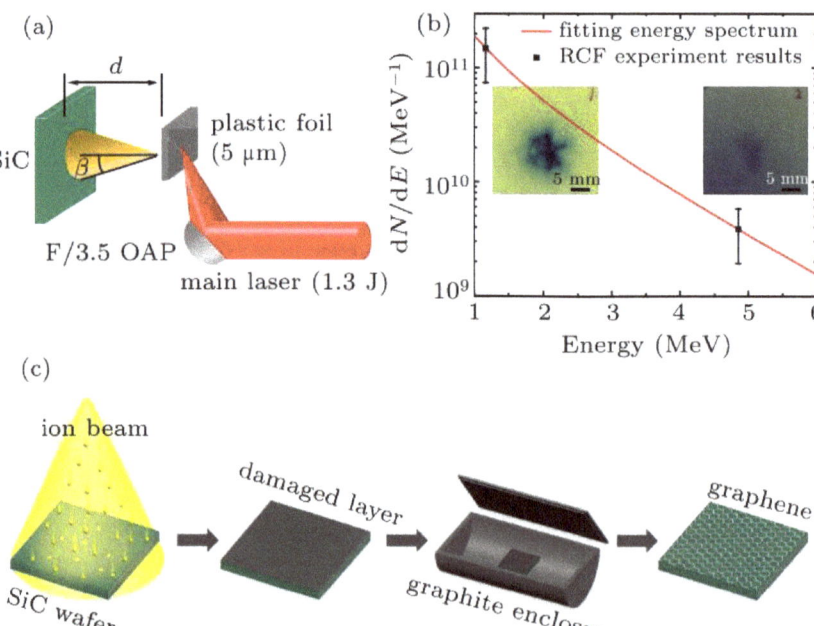

Figure 11. (a) Schematic diagram of the experiment setup. (b) The laser-accelerated proton beam energy spectrum measured with the RCF stack detector. (c) Schematic diagram of graphene preparation after laser-accelerated ion beam irradiation and annealing.

Raman spectroscopy was used to characterize the properties of the graphene, and the results are shown in Figure 12. The D peak (~1350 cm^{-1}) presents a disordered vibration. The characteristic G peak (~1580 cm^{-1}) of the sp2 hybridized carbon atom is caused by the in-plane vibration of the carbon atoms. The 2D peak (~2700 cm^{-1}) was used to characterize the stacking mode of the carbon atoms. Figure 12a shows the pristine and annealed Raman spectra of one SiC sample after it was irradiated with 10 shots at a radiation distance of 4 cm. The red and pink curves are the spectra before the irradiation and the other curves in the upper part are the spectra after irradiation. Figure 12c is the optical microscope image of the sample. As can be seen, (1) without ion irradiation, no graphene is synthesized; (2) the graphene only formed in the dark areas of Figure 12c (which corresponds to the curve of the 10-shots-D (L)); (3) in the other, brighter areas, there was no formation of graphene (which corresponds to the curve of the 10-shots-A (L)). This indicates that graphene was only synthesized after being irradiated by laser-accelerated ion beams and annealed in the subsequent process. The Raman spectra of the sample, after it was irradiated by 190 shots of the laser-accelerated ion, are shown in Figure 12b. The difference from 10-shots is that the connected D and G peaks representing the amorphous carbon peaks appeared right after the 190 shots (the blue line in Figure 12b), which indicates that there are already independent carbons on the surface of the SiC after high dose irradiation. The black and green lines correspond to the light and dark areas in Figure 12d. It can be concluded that, as the dose of irradiation increased, the area where graphene was synthesized changed from a local black spot to the entire plane.

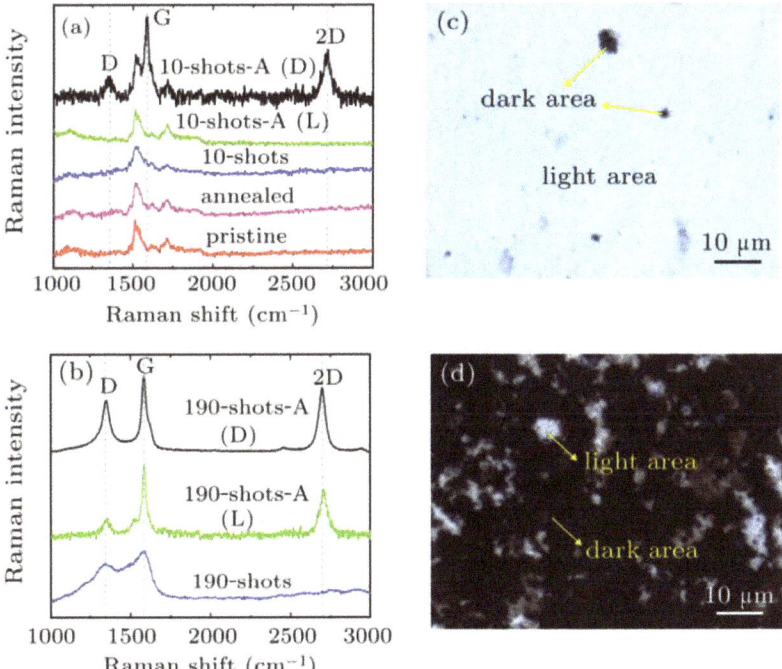

Figure 12. (**a**) Raman spectra of pristine, annealed, 10-pulse irradiated (10-shots), and 10-pulse irradiated with annealed (10-shots-A) samples. (**b**) Raman spectra of 190 pulses irradiated (190-shots) and 190 pulses irradiated with annealed (190-shots-A) SiC samples. The D and L correspond to the dark and light areas in (**c**,**d**), respectively. Optical microscope images of samples (**c**) 10-shots-A and (**d**) 190-shots-A, respectively. Raman mapping images.

We carried out a control experiment using the continuous mono-energy protons from a traditional accelerator with the same beam fluence. We found that no graphene was generated under this condition. Although the laser-accelerated ion beams maintained a small radiation dose, the thermal effect that was caused by the continuous small interval bombardment of the instantaneous pulse beam caused more serious damage to the sample surface than the traditional ion accelerator. Apart from this, in consideration of the thermal effect that was caused by the large instantaneous beam current, the self-annealing had a certain effect on the graphene under a closer irradiation distance, as demonstrated in Figure 13a. We shortened the irradiation distance to 1 cm. Figure 13b is the Raman spectrum of the sample that was measured after it was irradiated by 100-shots. Graphene of a high quality was synthesized without annealing, and the very small D peak showed the high quality of that graphene dot.

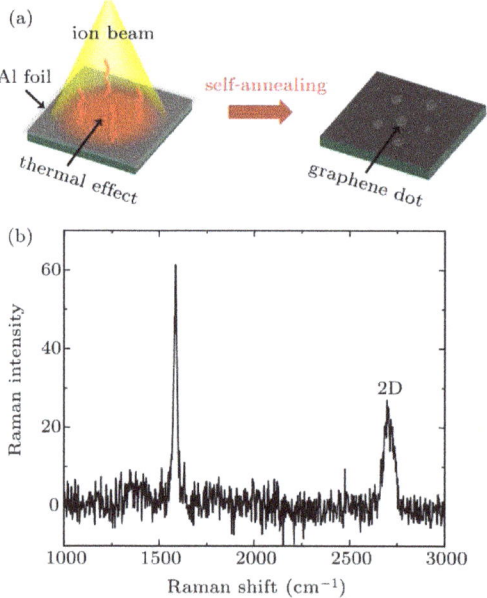

Figure 13. (a) Schematic diagram of self-annealing graphene prepared by the thermal effect of laser-accelerated ion beam irradiation at a closer irradiation distance (d $\leq$ 1 cm). (b) Raman spectrum of 1 cm-100-shot SiC sample with self-annealing (baseline drift corrected).

6.4. Laser-Accelerated Ion-Beam Trace Probe (LITP) for Measuring the Electromagnetic Fields in a Magnetic Confinement Fusion Device

When an ion enters into a magnetic confinement fusion device, for example, a tokamak, its orbit will be changed by the electromagnetic field. Based on that, a new method was proposed to diagnose the profiles of both the poloidal magnetic field ($B_{|p}$) and the radial electric field (E_r), which consists of a laser ion beam (LIB) and a detector with high temporal and spatial resolution, and was named as Laser-accelerated Ion-beam Trace Probe (LITP) [77]. The principle of the LITP is shown in Figure 14. The broad energy spread and the large divergence of the LIB makes its traces almost cover the whole core plasma area, which gives the LITP more capabilities, such as obtaining the 2D B_p profile or the 1D profile of both the poloidal and the radial magnetic fields at the same time [77,78], as well as the 2D electron density profile [79]. Furthermore, the LITP can be used in superconductive tokamaks, such as EAST, KSTAR, ITER, etc., because only a small window is needed to inject a laser pulse. By improving the nonlinear reconstruction method, the LITP could be applied not only in tokamak devices, but also in other toroidal devices, such as the spherical tokamak [80], reversal field pinch (RFP), etc.

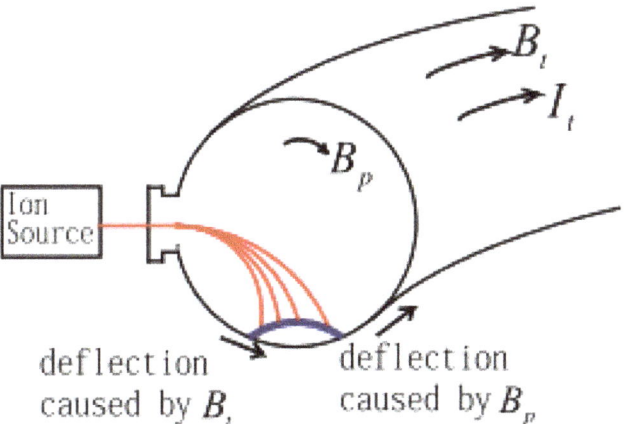

Figure 14. A diagram to show the concept of LITP. The traces of ions with different energy are shown as the red lines, and the blue line shows the ion positions on the detector.

As a new diagnostic method of the core electromagnetic field, the LITP is expected to realize the first application of the advanced laser accelerator in magnetic confinement fusion. We have designed and verified the feasibility of the LITP ion detection through systemic experiments [81]. A CsI(Tl) scintillator that was coupled with an imaging system that was composed of an optical lens and an optical fiber array for LITP was designed and tested on the HL-2A tokamak device in the Southwestern Institute of Physics. The scintillator detector was set at 100 mm to the edge of the plasma and the temperature at its location was about 110 °C–340 °C. The detector was sent into the plasma region using a long-range stepper motor translation linear stage. The signal light from the scintillator was transported by a well-shielded image system and recorded with an ultrafast CCD. The CsI scintillator was not damaged by the harsh environment after being placed in the tokamak for three days, and the real background noise that was caused by the hot plasma electrons and the radiation was measured. We found that the background noise was completely suppressed when using an ultrafast camera and a microsecond shutter. The black curve in Figure 15, which is the intensity of the background signal caused by soft X-rays in the HL-2A tokamak, decreases rapidly (from 1000 to 10) as the shutter time decreases (from 10 ms to 0.1 ms). The corresponding CCD images at the exposure times of A (10 ms), B (1 ms), and C (0.1 ms) are illustrated below. When the exposure time was shorter than 0.2 ms, the background signal was reduced to the same level as the dark noise of the CCD.

The change in the proton beam signal with the CCD shutter time was also detected on CLAPA. The 45 TW laser-accelerated protons with a central energy of 1 MeV were collected by the magnet triplet and transported onto the CsI scintillator. The signal that was detected by the ultrafast CCD with different exposure times of D (9.9 ms), E (99 μs), and F (2 μs) is shown as the blue line in Figure 15. With the shortening of the exposure time, there was no significant change in the signal intensity on the scintillator for the laser-accelerated protons. At the exposure time of 1 ms, the proton signal intensity was already more than one order of magnitude of the background intensity in HL-2a. Based on the result above, only the dark noise of the detection instrument needs to be considered in the LITP experiment. These calibrations and tests verified the feasibility of the LITP.

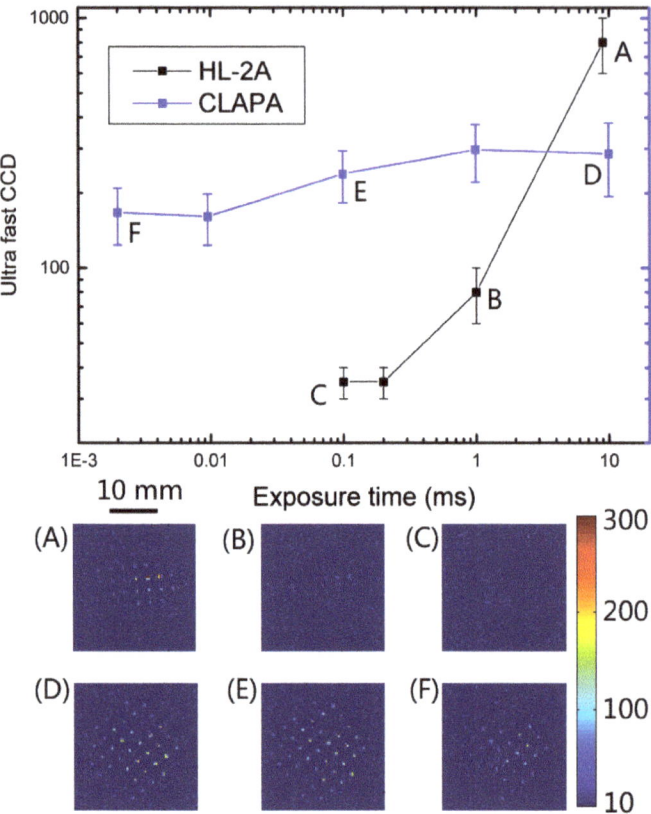

Figure 15. The black points are the intensity of the background signal in the HL-2A tokamak versus the exposure time, the corresponding CCD images at the exposure times of (**A**) 10 ms, (**B**) 1 ms, and (**C**) 0:1 ms. The background signal is mainly soft X-ray in the tokamak device that was caused by the bremsstrahlung of electrons. When the exposure time is shorter than 0.2 ms, the background signal is reduced to the same level as the dark noise of the CCD. The blue points are the result of the proton signal intensity detected by the ultrafast CCD with different exposure times of (**D**) 9 ms, (**E**) 99 μs, and (**F**) 2 μs on CLAPA. At the exposure time of 1 ms, the proton signal intensity is already more than one order of magnitude of the background intensity.

7. Summary

Due to the ultra-high acceleration gradient, laser-driven proton acceleration has attracted the attention of scientists in many fields. This paper has introduced the recent progress of laser proton acceleration and its application at Peking University, mainly in the last five years. The compact laser plasma accelerator (CLAPA) was established in 2018, and it can stably produce and transport proton beams with energies of less than 10 MeV, an energy spread of less than 1%, and several to tens of pC charge. The CLAPA beamline is an object-image point analyzing system that ensures the transmission efficiency and the energy selection accuracy for proton beams with a large initial divergence angle and energy spread. Based on CLAPA, we have developed a variety of beam regulation methods and have systematically measured the emittance of laser-accelerated proton beams for the first time. A spread-out Bragg peak (SOBP) has been produced with high-precision beam control, which is essential for cancer therapy. Some application experiments that are based on laser-accelerated proton beams have also been carried out, such as proton radiographs, ion-beam trace probes for plasma diagnosis, the preparation of graphene on SiC, ultra-high dose FLASH radiation of cancer cells, and so on. The above applications utilize the unique characteristics of laser-accelerated protons, even though some of the characteristics are considered to be shortcomings (e.g., wide energy spread). It indicates that it is important to find suitable application fields and methods for this new accelerator and beam. CLAPA II, which is a 100 MeV proton beam accelerator that is based on a 2-PW laser, as well as a prototype of tumor radiotherapy, is under construction. CLAPA II will greatly improve the performance of laser accelerators and may promote the real-world application of laser accelerators, especially in malignant tumor radiotherapy.

This work was supported by the Natural Science Foundation of China (Grants No. 11975037, 12122501, and 11921006), National Grand Instrument Project (No. 2019YFF01014400, No. 2019YFF01014404, No. 2019YFF01014403 and No. 2019YFF01014402), Beijing outstanding young scientists project, and ITER-CHINA program (grant 2015GB120001).

The simulations were supported by the High-performance Computing Platform of Peking University.

Author Contributions: Conceptualization, C.L. (Chen Lin), X.Y., W.M., K.Z., C.X. and G.Y.; Methodology, formal analysis, investigation, visualization, data curation, D.L., T.Y. and M.W. contributed to the CLAPA proton acceleration and beamline experiments; K.W. contributed to the CLAPAII beamline design; Z.M., C.L. (Chunyang Lu) and G.Y. contributed to the FLASH irradiation; M.W. contributed to the LITP application; D.L. contributed to ion irradiation experiment; Investigation, Resources, Y.Z., Y.G. and J.C. contributed to the laser system; writing—original draft preparation, D.L., T.Y., M.W., K.W. and Z.M.; writing—review and editing, C.L. (Chen Lin); Supervision, C.L. (Chen Lin), X.Y., W.M., K.Z., T.T. and J.C.; project administration, X.Y. and C.L. (Chen Lin); Funding acquisition, X.Y., C.L. (Chen Lin), W.M. and K.Z. All authors have read and agreed to the published version of the manuscript.

Funding: This work was supported by the Natural Science Foundation of China (Grants No. 11975037, 12122501, and 11921006), National Grand Instrument Project (No. 2019YFF01014400, No. 2019YFF01014404, No. 2019YFF01014403 and No. 2019YFF01014402), Beijing outstanding young scientists project, and ITER-CHINA program (grant 2015GB120001).

Institutional Review Board Statement: Not applicable.

Informed Consent Statement: Not applicable.

Data Availability Statement: The data that support the findings of this study are available from the corresponding author upon reasonable request.

Conflicts of Interest: The authors declare no conflict of interest.

References

1. Tajima, T.; Dawson, J.M. Laser electron accelerator. *Phys. Rev. Lett.* **1979**, *43*, 267. [CrossRef]
2. Danson, C.; Haefner, C.; Bromage, J.; Butcher, T.; Chanteloup, J.-C.; Chowdhury, E.; Galvanauskas, A.; Gizzi, L.; Hein, J.; Hillier, D.; et al. Petawatt and exawatt class lasers worldwide. *High Power Laser Sci. Eng.* **2019**, *7*, e54. [CrossRef]
3. Mourou, G. Nobel lecture: Extreme light physics and application. *Rev. Mod. Phys.* **2019**, *91*, 030501. [CrossRef]
4. Esarey, E.; Schroeder, C.B.; Leemans, W.P. Physics of laser-driven plasma-based electron accelerators. *Rev. Mod. Phys.* **2009**, *81*, 1229. [CrossRef]
5. Macchi, A.; Borghesi, M.; Passoni, M. Ion acceleration by superintense laser-plasma interaction. *Rev. Mod. Phys.* **2013**, *85*, 751–793. [CrossRef]
6. Gonsalves, A.J.; Nakamura, K.; Daniels, J.; Benedetti, C.; Pieronek, C.; de Raadt, T.C.H.; Steinke, S.; Bin, J.H.; Bulanov, S.S.; van Tilborg, J.; et al. Petawatt laser guiding and electron beam acceleration to 8 GeV in a laser-heated capillary discharge waveguide. *Phys. Rev. Lett.* **2019**, *122*, 084801. [CrossRef]
7. Higginson, A.; Gray, R.J.; King, M.; Dance, R.J.; Williamson, S.D.; Butler, N.M.; Wilson, R.; Capdessus, R.; Armstrong, C.; Green, J.S.; et al. Near-100 MeV protons via a laser-driven transparency-enhanced hybrid acceleration scheme. *Nat. Commun.* **2018**, *9*, 724. [CrossRef] [PubMed]
8. Daido, H.; Nishiuchi, M.; Pirozhkov, A.S. Review of laser-driven ion sources and their applications. *Rep. Prog. Phys.* **2012**, *75*, 056401. [CrossRef]
9. Raffestin, D.; Lecherbourg, L.; Lantuéjoul, I.; Vauzour, B.; Masson-Laborde, P.E.; Davoine, X.; Blanchot, N.; Dubois, J.L.; Vaisseau, X.; d'Humières, E.; et al. Enhanced ion acceleration using the high-energy petawatt PETAL laser. *Matter Radiat. Extrem.* **2021**, *6*, 056901. [CrossRef]

10. Okamura, M. Laser ion source for heavy ion inertial fusion. *Matter Radiat. Extrem.* **2018**, *3*, 61. [CrossRef]
11. Martinez, B.; Chen, S.N.; Bolaños, S.; Blanchot, N.; Boutoux, G.; Cayzac, W.; Courtois, C.; Davoine, X.; Duval, A.; Horny, V.; et al. Numerical investigation of spallation neutrons generated from petawatt-scale laser-driven proton beams. *Matter Radiat. Extrem.* **2022**, *7*, 024401. [CrossRef]
12. Romano, F.; Schillaci, F.; Cirrone, G.A.P.; Cuttone, G.; Scuderi, V.; Allegra, L.; Amato, A.; Amico, A.; Candiano, G.; De Luca, G.; et al. The ELIMED transport and dosimetry beamline for laser-driven ion beams. *Nucl. Instrum. Methods Phys. Res. Sect. A* **2016**, *829*, 153. [CrossRef]
13. Masood, U.; Bussmann, M.; Cowan, T.E.; Enghardt, W.; Karsch, L.; Kroll, F. A compact solution for ion beam therapy with laser accelerated protons. *Appl. Phys. B* **2014**, *117*, 41. [CrossRef]
14. Pommarel, L.; Vauzour, B.; Mégnin-Chanet, F.; Bayart, E.; Delmas, O.; Goudjil, F.; Nauraye, C.; Letellier, V.; Pouzoulet, F.; Schillaci, F.; et al. Spectral and spatial shaping of a laser-produced ion beam for radiation-biology experiments. *Phys. Rev. Accel. Beams* **2017**, *20*, 032801. [CrossRef]
15. Mora, P. Plasma expansion into a vacuum. *Phys. Rev. Lett.* **2003**, *90*, 185002. [CrossRef] [PubMed]
16. Pukhov, A. Three-dimensional simulations of ion acceleration from a foil irradiated by a short-pulse laser. *Phys. Rev. Lett.* **2001**, *86*, 3562. [CrossRef] [PubMed]
17. Palmer, C.A.J.; Schreiber, J.; Nagel, S.R.; Dover, N.P.; Bellei, C.; Beg, F.N.; Bott, S.; Clarke, R.J.; Dangor, A.E.; Hassan, S.M.; et al. Rayleigh–Taylor instability of an ultrathin foil accelerated by the radiation pressure of an intense laser. *Phys. Rev. Lett.* **2012**, *108*, 225002. [CrossRef]
18. Wan, Y.; Andriyash, I.A.; Lu, W.; Mori, W.B.; Malka, V. Effects of the transverse instability and wave breaking on the laser-driven thin foil acceleration. *Phys. Rev. Lett.* **2020**, *125*, 104801. [CrossRef]
19. Zhu, J.G.; Wu, M.J.; Liao, Q.; Geng, Y.X.; Zhu, K.; Li, C.C.; Xu, X.H.; Li, D.Y.; Shou, Y.R.; Yang, T.; et al. Experimental demonstration of a laser proton accelerator with accurate beam control through image-relaying transport. *Phys. Rev. Accel. Beams* **2019**, *22*, 061302. [CrossRef]
20. Geng, Y.X.; Liao, Q.; Shou, Y.R.; Zhu, J.G.; Xu, X.H.; Wu, M.J.; Wang, P.J.; Li, D.Y.; Yang, T.; Hu, R.H.; et al. Generating proton beams exceeding 10 MeV using high contrast 60 TW laser. *Chin. Phys. Lett.* **2018**, *35*, 092901. [CrossRef]
21. Geng, Y.X.; Wu, D.; Yu, W.; Sheng, Z.M.; Fritzsche, S.; Liao, Q.; Wu, M.J.; Xu, X.H.; Li, D.Y.; Ma, W.J.; et al. Proton beams from intense laser-solid interaction: Effects of the target materials. *Matter Radiat. Extrem.* **2020**, *5*, 064402. [CrossRef]
22. Zhu, J.G.; Zhu, K.; Tao, L.; Geng, Y.X.; Lin, C.; Ma, W.J.; Lu, H.Y.; Zhao, Y.Y.; Lu, Y.R.; Chen, J.E.; et al. Beam line design of compact laser plasma accelerator. *Chin. Phys. Lett.* **2017**, *34*, 054101. [CrossRef]
23. Zhu, J.G.; Zhu, K.; Tao, L.; Xu, X.H.; Lin, C.; Ma, W.J.; Lu, H.Y.; Zhao, Y.Y.; Lu, Y.R.; Chen, J.E.; et al. Distribution uniformity of laser-accelerated proton beams. *Chin. Phys. C* **2017**, *41*, 097001. [CrossRef]
24. Wilks, S.C.; Langdon, A.B.; Cowan, T.E.; Roth, M.; Singh, M.; Hatchett, S.; Key, M.H.; Pennington, D.; MacKinnon, A.; Snavely, R.A. Energetic proton generation in ultra-intense laser–solid interactions. *Phys. Plasmas* **2001**, *8*, 542–549. [CrossRef]
25. Xu, X.H.; Liao, Q.; Wu, M.J.; Geng, Y.X.; Li, D.Y.; Zhu, J.G.; Li, C.C.; Hu, R.H.; Shou, Y.R.; Chen, Y.H.; et al. Detection and analysis of laser driven proton beams by calibrated Gafchromic HD-V2 and MD-V3 radiochromic films. *Rev. Sci. Instrum.* **2019**, *90*, 033306. [CrossRef] [PubMed]
26. Wu, M.; Zhu, J.; Li, D.; Yang, T.; Liao, Q.; Geng, Y.; Xu, X.; Li, C.; Shou, Y.; Zhao, Y.; et al. Collection and focusing of laser accelerated proton beam by an electromagnetic quadrupole triplet lens. *Nucl. Instrum. Methods Phys. Res. Sect. A* **2020**, *955*, 163249. [CrossRef]
27. Yan, X.Q.; Lin, C.; Sheng, Z.M.; Guo, Z.Y.; Liu, B.C.; Lu, Y.R.; Fang, J.X.; Chen, J.E. Generating high-current monoenergetic proton beams by a circularly polarized laser pulse in the phase-stable acceleration regime. *Phys. Rev. Lett.* **2008**, *100*, 135003. [CrossRef]
28. Esirkepov, T.; Borghesi, M.; Bulanov, S.V.; Mourou, G.; Tajima, T. Highly efficient relativistic-ion generation in the laser-piston regime. *Phys. Rev. Lett.* **2004**, *92*, 175003. [CrossRef]
29. Kar, S.; Ahmed, H.; Prasad, R.; Cerchez, M.; Brauckmann, S.; Aurand, B.; Cantono, G.; Hadjisolomou, P.; Lewis, C.L.S.; Macchi, A.; et al. Guided post-acceleration of laser-driven ions by a miniature modular structure. *Nat. Commun.* **2016**, *7*, 10792. [CrossRef]
30. Bardon, M.; Moreau, J.G.; Romagnani, L.; Rousseaux, C.; Ferri, M.; Lefévre, F.; Lantuéjoul, I.; Etchessahar, B.; Bazzoli, S.; Farcage, D.; et al. Physics of chromatic focusing, post-acceleration and bunching of laser-driven proton beams in helical coil targets. *Plasma Phys. Control. Fusion* **2020**, *62*, 125019. [CrossRef]
31. Floettmann, K. Some basic features of the beam emittance. *Phys. Rev. ST Accel. Beams* **2003**, *6*, 034202. [CrossRef]
32. Cowan, T.E.; Fuchs, J.; Ruhl, H.; Kemp, A.; Audebert, P.; Roth, M.; Stephens, R.; Barton, I.; Blazevic, A.; Brambrink, E.; et al. Ultralow emittance, multi-MeV proton beams from a laser virtual-cathode plasma accelerator. *Phys. Rev. Lett.* **2004**, *92*, 204801. [CrossRef] [PubMed]
33. Wu, M.J.; Li, D.Y.; Zhu, J.G.; Yang, T.; Hu, X.Y.; Geng, Y.X.; Zhu, K.; Easton, M.J.; Zhao, Y.Y.; Zhang, A.L.; et al. Emittance measurement along transport beam line for laser driven protons. *Phys. Rev. Accel. Beams* **2020**, *23*, 031302. [CrossRef]
34. Zhu, J.G.; Wu, M.J.; Zhu, K.; Geng, Y.X.; Liao, Q.; Li, D.Y.; Yang, T.; Eatson, M.J.; Li, C.C.; Xu, X.H.; et al. Demonstration of tailored energy deposition in a laser proton accelerator. *Phys. Rev. Accel. Beams* **2020**, *23*, 121304. [CrossRef]
35. Tajima, T.; Habs, D.; Yan, X. *Laser Acceleration of Ions for Radiation Therapy*; World Scientific: Singapore, 2009; pp. 201–228.
36. Yan, X.Q.; Tajima, T.; Hegelich, M.; Yin, L.; Habs, D. Theory of laser ion acceleration from a foil target of nanometer thickness. *Appl. Phys. B* **2009**, *98*, 711–721. [CrossRef]

37. Wang, H.Y.; Yan, X.Q.; Chen, J.E.; He, X.T.; Ma, W.J.; Bin, J.H.; Schreiber, J.; Tajima, T.; Habs, D. Efficient and stable acceleration by irradiating a two-layer target with a linearly polarized laser pulse. *Phys. Plasmas* **2013**, *20*, 013101. [CrossRef]
38. Esirkepov, T.; Bulanov, S.V.; Nishihara, K.; Tajima, T.; Pegoraro, F.; Khoroshkov, V.S.; Mima, K.; Daido, H.; Kato, Y.; Kitagawa, Y.; et al. Proposed double-layer target for the generation of high-quality laser-accelerated ion beams. *Phys. Rev. Lett.* **2002**, *89*, 175003. [CrossRef]
39. Necas, A.; Tajima, T.; Mourou, G.; Osvay, K. Laser ion acceleration in a near critical density trap. *Photonics* **2022**, *9*, 453. [CrossRef]
40. Ma, W.J.; Kim, I.J.; Yu, J.Q.; Choi, I.W.; Singh, P.K.; Lee, H.W.; Sung, J.H.; Lee, S.K.; Lin, C.; Liao, Q.; et al. Laser Acceleration of highly energetic carbon ions using a double-layer target composed of slightly underdense plasma and ultrathin foil. *Phys. Rev. Lett.* **2019**, *122*, 014803. [CrossRef] [PubMed]
41. Esirkepov, T.; Yamagiwa, M.; Tajima, T. Laser ion-acceleration scaling laws seen in multiparametric particle-in-cell simulations. *Phys. Rev. Lett.* **2006**, *96*, 105001. [CrossRef]
42. Henig, A.; Steinke, S.; Schnürer, M.; Sokollik, T.; Hörlein, R.; Kiefer, D.; Jung, D.; Schreiber, J.; Hegelich, B.M.; Yan, X.Q.; et al. Radiation-pressure acceleration of ion beams driven by circularly polarized laser pulses. *Phys. Rev. Lett.* **2009**, *103*, 245003. [CrossRef]
43. Kar, S.; Kakolee, K.F.; Qiao, B.; Macchi, A.; Cerchez, M.; Doria, D.; Geissler, M.; McKenna, P.; Neely, D.; Osterholz, J.; et al. Ion acceleration in multispecies targets driven by intense laser radiation pressure. *Phys. Rev. Lett.* **2012**, *109*, 185006. [CrossRef]
44. Kim, I.J.; Pae, K.H.; Choi, I.W.; Lee, C.L.; Kim, H.T.; Singhal, H.; Sung, J.H.; Lee, S.K.; Lee, H.W.; Nickles, P.V.; et al. Radiation pressure acceleration of protons to 93 MeV with circularly polarized petawatt laser pulses. *Phys. Plasmas* **2016**, *23*, 070701. [CrossRef]
45. Fuchs, J.; Antici, P.; d'Humières, E.; Lefebvre, E.; Borghesi, M.; Brambrink, E.; Cecchetti, C.A.; Kaluza, M.; Malka, V.; Manclossi, M.; et al. Laser-driven proton scaling laws and new paths towards energy increase. *Nat. Phys.* **2008**, *2*, 28. [CrossRef]
46. Wang, K.D.; Zhu, K.; Easton, M.J.; Li, Y.J.; Lin, C.; Yan, X.Q. Achromatic beamline design for a laser-driven proton therapy accelerator. *Phys. Rev. Accel. Beams* **2020**, *23*, 111302. [CrossRef]
47. Brouwer, L.; Caspi, S.; Edwards, K.; Godeke, A.; Prestemon, S. Design and test of a curved superconducting dipole magnet for proton therapy. *Nucl. Instrum. Methods Phys. Res. Sect. A* **2020**, *957*, 163414. [CrossRef]
48. Leemans, W.P.; Nagler, B.; Gonsalves, A.J.; Toth, C.; Nakamura, K.; Geddes, C.G.R.; Esarey, E.; Schroeder, C.B.; Hooker, S.M. GeV electron beams from a centimetre-scale accelerator. *Nat. Phys.* **2006**, *2*, 696–699. [CrossRef]
49. Steinke, S.; van Tilborg, J.; Benedetti, C.; Geddes, C.G.R.; Schroeder, C.B.; Daniels, J.; Swanson, K.K.; Gonsalves, A.J.; Nakamura, K.; Matlis, N.H.; et al. Multistage coupling of independent laser-plasma accelerators. *Nature* **2016**, *530*, 190. [CrossRef]
50. Van Tilborg, J.; Steinke, S.; Geddes, C.G.R.; Matlis, N.H.; Shaw, B.H.; Gonsalves, A.J.; Huijts, J.V.; Nakamura, K.; Daniels, J.; Schroeder, C.B.; et al. Active plasma lensing for relativistic laser-plasma-accelerated electron beams. *Phys. Rev. Lett.* **2015**, *115*, 184802. [CrossRef]
51. Pompili, R.; Anania, M.P.; Bellaveglia, M.; Biagioni, A.; Bini, S.; Bisesto, F.; Brentegani, E.; Castorina, G.; Chiadroni, E.; Cianchi, A.; et al. Experimental characterization of active plasma lensing for electron beams. *Appl. Phys. Lett.* **2017**, *110*, 104101. [CrossRef]
52. Lindstrøm, C.A.; Adli, E.; Boyle, G.; Corsini, R.; Dyson, A.E.; Farabolini, W.; Hooker, S.M.; Meisel, M.; Osterhoff, J.; Röckemann, J.-H.; et al. Emittance preservation in an aberration-free active plasma lens. *Phys. Rev. Lett.* **2018**, *121*, 194801. [CrossRef] [PubMed]
53. Yang, T.; Cheng, H.; Yan, Y.; Wu, M.; Li, D.; Li, Y.; Xia, Y.; Lin, C.; Yan, X. Designing of active plasma lens for focusing laser-plasma-accelerated pulsed proton beams. *Phys. Rev. Accel. Beams* **2021**, *24*, 031301. [CrossRef]
54. Hershcovitch, A. High-pressure arcs as vacuum-atmosphere interface and plasma lens for nonvacuum electron beam welding machines, electron beam melting, and nonvacuum ion material modification. *J. Appl. Phys.* **1995**, *78*, 5283. [CrossRef]
55. Lu, L.; Ma, W.; Li, C.; He, T.; Yang, L.; Sun, L.; Xu, X.; Wang, W.; Shi, L. New developments of HIF injector. *Matter Radiat. Extrem.* **2018**, *3*, 50. [CrossRef]
56. Hofmann, I. Review of accelerator driven heavy ion nuclear fusion. *Matter Radiat. Extrem.* **2018**, *3*, 1. [CrossRef]
57. Yao, W.; Fazzini, A.; Chen, S.N.; Burdonov, K.; Antici, P.; Béard, J.; Bolaños, S.; Ciardi, A.; Diab, R.; Filippov, E.D.; et al. Detailed characterization of a laboratory magnetized supercritical collisionless shock and of the associated proton energization. *Matter Radiat. Extrem.* **2022**, *7*, 014402. [CrossRef]
58. Kroll, F.; Brack, F.; Bernert, C.; Bock, S.; Bodenstein, E.; Brüchner, K.; Cowan, T.E.; Gaus, L.; Gebhardt, R.; Helbig, U.; et al. Tumour irradiation in mice with a laser-accelerated proton beam. *Nat. Phys.* **2022**, *18*, 316. [CrossRef]
59. Scott, W.T. The theory of small-angle multiple scattering of fast charged particles. *Rev. Mod. Phys.* **1963**, *35*, 231. [CrossRef]
60. Faenov, A.Y.; Pikuz, T.A.; Fukuda, Y.; Kando, M.; Kotaki, H.; Homma, T.; Kawase, K.; Kameshima, T.; Pirozhkov, A.; Yogo, A.; et al. Submicron iconography of nanostructures using a femtosecond-laser-driven-cluster-based source. *Appl. Phys. Lett.* **2009**, *95*, 101107. [CrossRef]
61. Son, J.; Lee, C.H.; Kang, J.; Jang, D.Y.; Park, J.; Kim, Y.H.; Kim, Y.K.; Choi, C.I.; Kim, I.J.; Choi, I.W.; et al. Fine phantom image from laser-induced proton radiography with a spatial resolution of several μm. *J. Korean Phys. Soc.* **2014**, *65*, 6. [CrossRef]
62. Wang, W.; Shen, B.; Zhang, H.; Lu, X.; Wang, C.; Liu, Y.; Yu, L.; Chu, Y.; Li, Y.; Xu, T.; et al. Large-scale proton radiography with micrometer spatial resolution using femtosecond petawatt laser system. *AIP Adv.* **2015**, *5*, 107214.

63. Li, D.Y.; Xu, X.H.; Yang, T.; Wu, M.J.; Zhang, Y.F.; Cheng, H.; Hu, X.Y.; Geng, Y.X.; Zhu, J.G.; Zhao, Y.Y.; et al. Influence factors of resolution in laser accelerated proton radiography and image deblurring. *AIP Adv.* **2021**, *11*, 085316. [CrossRef]
64. Bourhis, J.; Sozzi, W.J.; Jorge, P.G.; Gaide, O.; Bailat, C.; Duclos, F.; Patin, D.; Ozsahin, M.; Bochud, F.; Germond, J.; et al. Treatment of a first patient with FLASH-radiotherapy. *Radiother. Oncol.* **2019**, *139*, 18–22. [CrossRef] [PubMed]
65. Bin, J.; Obst-Huebl, L.; Mao, J.; Nakamura, K.; Geulig, L.D.; Chang, H.; Ji, Q.; He, L.; Chant, J.D.; Kober, Z.; et al. A new platform for ultra-high dose rate radiobiological research using the BELLA PW laser proton beamline. *Sci. Rep.* **2022**, *12*, 1484. [CrossRef] [PubMed]
66. Bayart, E.; Flacco, A.; Delmas, O.; Pommarel, L.; Levy, D.; Cavallone, M.; Megnin-Chanet, F.; Deutsch, E.; Malka, V. Fast dose fractionation using ultra-short laser accelerated proton pulses can increase cancer cell mortality, which relies on functional PARP1 protein. *Sci. Rep.* **2019**, *9*, 10132. [CrossRef]
67. Yang, G.; Lu, C.; Mei, Z.; Sun, X.; Han, J.; Qian, J.; Liang, Y.; Pan, Z.; Kong, D.; Xu, S.; et al. Association of cancer stem cell radio-resistance under ultra-high dose rate FLASH irradiation with lysosome-mediated autophagy. *Front. Cell Dev. Biol.* **2021**, *9*, 1032. [CrossRef]
68. Han, J.; Mei, Z.; Lu, C.; Qian, J.; Liang, Y.; Sun, X.; Pan, Z.; Kong, D.; Xu, S.; Liu, Z.; et al. Ultra-high dose rate FLASH irradiation induced radio-resistance of normal fibroblast cells can be enhanced by hypoxia and mitochondrial dysfunction resulting from loss of cytochrome C. *Front. Cell Dev. Biol.* **2021**, *9*, 1089. [CrossRef]
69. Patel, P.K.; Mackinnon, A.J.; Key, M.H.; Cowan, T.E.; Foord, M.E.; Allen, M.; Price, D.F.; Ruhl, H.; Springer, P.T.; Stephens, R. Isochoric heating of solid-density matter with an ultrafast proton beam. *Phys. Rev. Lett.* **2003**, *91*, 125004. [CrossRef]
70. Dyer, G.M.; Bernstein, A.C.; Cho, B.I.; Osterholz, J.; Grigsby, W.; Dalton, A.; Shepherd, R.; Ping, Y.; Chen, H.; Widmann, K.; et al. Equation-of-state measurement of dense plasmas heated with fast protons. *Phys. Rev. Lett.* **2008**, *101*, 015002. [CrossRef]
71. Barberio, M.; Sciscià, M.; Vallières, S.; Cardelli, F.; Chen, S.N.; Famulari, G.; Gangolf, T.; Revet, G.; Schiavi, A.; Senzacqua, M.; et al. Laser-accelerated particle beams for stress testing of materials. *Nat. Commun.* **2018**, *9*, 372. [CrossRef]
72. Alvarez, J.; Mima, K.; Tanaka, K.A.; Fernandez, J.; Garoz, D.; Habara, H.; Kikuyama, H.; Kondo, K.; Perlado, J.M. Ultraintense lasers as a promising research tool for fusion material testing: Production of ions, X-rays and neutrons. *Plasma Fusion Res.* **2013**, *8*, 3404055. [CrossRef]
73. Barberio, M.; Vallières, S.; Sciscià, M.; Kolhatkar, G.; Ruediger, A.; Antici, P. Graphitization of diamond by laser-accelerated proton beams. *Carbon* **2018**, *139*, 531. [CrossRef]
74. Barberio, M.; Sciscià, M.; Vallières, S.; Veltri, S.; Morabito, A.; Antici, P. Laser-generated proton beams for high-precision ultra-fast crystal synthesis. *Sci. Rep.* **2017**, *7*, 12522. [CrossRef]
75. Barberio, M.; Giusepponi, S.; Vallières, S.; Sciscià, M.; Celino, M.; Antici, P. Ultra-fast high-precision metallic nanoparticle synthesis using laser-accelerated protons. *Sci. Rep.* **2020**, *10*, 9570. [CrossRef]
76. Zhou, D.; Li, D.; Chen, Y.; Wu, M.; Yang, T.; Cheng, H.; Li, Y.; Chen, Y.; Li, Y.; Geng, Y.; et al. Preparation of graphene on SiC by laser-accelerated pulsed ion beams. *Chin. Phys. B* **2021**, *30*, 116106. [CrossRef]
77. Yang, X.Y.; Chen, Y.H.; Lin, C.; Wang, L.; Xu, M.; Wang, X.G.; Xiao, C.J. A new method of measuring the poloidal magnetic and radial electric fields in a tokamak using a laser-accelerated ion-beam trace probe. *Rev. Sci. Instrum.* **2014**, *85*, 11E429. [CrossRef] [PubMed]
78. Yang, X.; Xiao, C.; Chen, Y.; Xu, T.; Lin, C.; Wang, L.; Xu, M.; Yu, Y. 2D profile of poloidal magnetic field diagnosed by a laser-driven ion-beam trace probe (LITP). *Rev. Sci. Instrum.* **2016**, *87*, 11D608. [CrossRef] [PubMed]
79. Chen, Y.H.; Yang, X.Y.; Lin, C.; Wang, L.; Xu, M.; Wang, X.G.; Xiao, C.J. 2D electron density profile measurement in tokamak by laser-accelerated ion-beam probe. *Rev. Sci. Instrum.* **2014**, *85*, 11D860. [CrossRef]
80. Yang, X.; Xiao, C.; Chen, Y.; Xu, T.; Yu, Y.; Xu, M.; Wang, L.; Wang, X.; Lin, C. Theoretical study on the laser-driven ion-beam trace probe in toroidal devices with large poloidal magnetic field. *JINST* **2018**, *13*, C03034. [CrossRef]
81. Wu, M.J.; Yang, X.Y.; Xu, T.C.; Li, D.Y.; Chen, Y.H.; Zhu, J.G.; Yang, T.; Hu, X.Y.; Ma, W.J.; Zhao, Y.Y.; et al. Calibration and test of CsI scintillator ion detection system for tokamak magnetic field diagnosis based on laser-driven ion-beam trace probe (LITP). *Nucl. Fusion* **2022**, *62*, 106028. [CrossRef]

Disclaimer/Publisher's Note: The statements, opinions and data contained in all publications are solely those of the individual author(s) and contributor(s) and not of MDPI and/or the editor(s). MDPI and/or the editor(s) disclaim responsibility for any injury to people or property resulting from any ideas, methods, instructions or products referred to in the content.

Article

Revisiting Experimental Signatures of the Ponderomotive Force

Bjorn Manuel Hegelich [1,2,†,‡], Lance Labun [1,2,*,‡] and Ou Z. Labun [1,‡]

[1] Center for High Energy Density Science, University of Texas, Austin, TX 78712, USA
[2] Tau Systems, Inc., Austin, TX 78701, USA
* Correspondence: labun@utexas.edu
† Authors alphabetical.
‡ These authors contributed equally to this work.

Abstract: The classical theory of single-electron dynamics in focused laser pulses is the foundation of both the relativistic ponderomotive force (RPF), which underlies models of laser-collective-plasma dynamics, and the discovery of novel strong-field radiation dynamics. Despite this bedrock importance, consensus eludes the community as to whether acceleration of single electrons in vacuum has been observed in experimental conditions. We analyze an early experiment on the RPF with respect to several features that were neglected in modeling and that can restore consistency between theory predictions and experimental data. The right or wrong pulse profile function, laser parameters, or initial electron distribution can each make or break the agreement between predictions and data. The laser phase at which the electron's interaction with the pulse begins has a large effect, explaining why much larger energies are achieved by electrons liberated in the focal region by photoionization from high-Z atoms and by electrons ejected from a plasma mirror. Finally, we compute the difference in a typical electron spectrum arising from fluctuating focal spot size in state-of-the-art ultra-relativistic laser facilities. Our results emphasize the importance of thoroughly characterizing laser parameters in order to achieve quantitatively accurate predictions and the precision required for discovery science.

Keywords: vacuum laser acceleration; ponderomotive force

1. Introduction

High-intensity laser experiments are entering a new stage of research [1], attempting discovery science goals [2–4], and developing more consistent outcomes in order to support medical and industrial applications [5]. Both basic research and application development require robust and quantitative predictions, but cutting edge high-intensity laser experiments often move faster than accurate predictions and simulations.

To demonstrate, we examine theory and experiment on a basic process, single-electron acceleration by lasers in vacuum. The theory is relatively simple for experiments with (peak) intensities up to $I \lesssim 10^{20}$ W/cm^2 [6–13], because single-particle dynamics are accurately described by the Lorentz force. Classical radiation reaction and high-energy photon emission remain small for fields of these magnitudes, unless the electrons are counterpropagating to the laser with $E \gtrsim 1$ GeV [14]. The physics of single-electron-laser scattering is essential to many discovery goals, from theories of strong-field ionization [7–10] to strong-field corrections to particle dynamics from quantum electrodynamics [15,16] and radiation reaction [3,4]. Additionally, the relativistic ponderomotive force (RPF) should be valid around $I \simeq 10^{20}$ W/cm^2 [17], and therefore relevant to explaining electron acceleration in vacuum. The RPF underlies models of laser acceleration in more general plasma conditions [18–25].

Despite this key role, an early experiment [6] raised questions how the experimental data could be consistent with the theory of single-electron motion in a laser field [17,26]. While these questions have been revisited in the intervening years and the original experiment may no longer be considered sound, its analysis provides a good example of what is needed in relating theory derivation to experimental reality.

Citation: Hegelich, B.M.; Labun, L.; Labun, O.Z. Revisiting Experimental Signatures of the Ponderomotive Force. *Photonics* **2023**, *10*, 226. https://doi.org/10.3390/photonics10020226

Received: 29 June 2022
Revised: 10 February 2023
Accepted: 13 February 2023
Published: 20 February 2023

Copyright: © 2023 by the authors. Licensee MDPI, Basel, Switzerland. This article is an open access article distributed under the terms and conditions of the Creative Commons Attribution (CC BY) license (https://creativecommons.org/licenses/by/4.0/).

To this end, we discuss four experimental inputs that are often not well-known and their effect on the predictions of the theory of single-particle acceleration by laser fields: temporal pulse profile, phase of injection, initial momentum, and shot-to-shot variations in the laser. These four features do not exhaust the possible differences between the experiment and the theoretical models, but they suggest additional experimental measurements that become necessary to enhance confidence in the interpretation of the experiment outcome.

This work is thus a demonstration and call for the recent and coming laser-plasma experiments, in which the ultra-high intensity and beam geometry greatly increase the difficulty in measurements at ultra-high intensity. Pulse profiles are usually measured using a subaperture beam, often before full amplification and never at full pulse energy. Focal spot sizes are measured without a target present and at reduced intensity, and laser energies are also inferred from percent-level fractions of the beam. This reduction in knowledge increases uncertainty in predictions at higher intensity. Specifically the same uncertainty that hobbles analysis of Ref. [6] translates to a much larger discrepancy in an observable as intensities rise to $I \sim 10^{23}$ W/cm^2 and beyond.

2. Theory

The theory is relatively simple for experiments with (peak) intensities up to $I \lesssim 10^{20}$ W/cm^2 [6–13], because single-particle dynamics are accurately described by the Lorentz force. Classical radiation reaction and high-energy photon emission remain small for fields of these magnitudes as long as the electrons are not counterpropagating to the laser with $E \gtrsim 1$ GeV. We are concerned with particles accelerated from low energy $E_{\text{kin}} = (\gamma - 1)m \lesssim m$, e.g., from gas targets.

2.1. When Acceleration Occurs

Before addressing the general case of 3-dimensional focused laser fields, we recall a general and elementary explanation how and under what conditions plane wave fields can accelerate charged particles [27]. For a plane wave, the field tensor and vector potential are functions of only one lightcone coordinate $x_- = ct - z$, taking the z-direction to be aligned with the propagation direction, and are subject to constraining symmetries [28]. Only the momentum conjugate x_- (namely $p_+ = E + p_z c$) is not conserved; all three other components, $\vec{p}_\perp, p_- = E - p_z c$, are conserved. In this case, the Lorentz force can be integrated directly, or the action solved [29]. The resulting 4-momentum is

$$\Pi^\mu(\phi) = p^\mu_{(0)} + q\mathcal{A}^\mu(\phi) - \bar{n}^\mu \frac{2p^{(0)} \cdot \mathcal{A}(\phi) - q^2 \mathcal{A} \cdot \mathcal{A}(\phi)}{2p_-}, \quad (1)$$

where $p^\mu_{(0)}$ is the initial 4-momentum of the particle [30]. To assure ourselves Π^μ is the physically measurable momentum, we write this in terms of gauge invariant quantities only by noting that in this case the 4-potential can be defined as the integral of the field tensor [28]

$$\mathcal{A}^\mu(x_-) \equiv \epsilon^\mu_j \int_{-\infty}^{x_-} F_j(\phi) d\phi, \quad (2)$$

where ϵ^μ_j is an orthogonal pair of polarization vectors satisfying $\bar{n} \cdot \epsilon_j = 0$ for $j = 1, 2$ and the index j is implicitly summed over. The lower bound on the integral is taken to $-\infty$ assuming that the electromagnetic field vanishes sufficiently quickly as $x_- \to -\infty$ so that the initial momentum $p^{\mu(0)}$ is well-defined before the particle interacts with the field.

The final momentum of the particle is the value of Π^μ as $x_- \to +\infty$, which, therefore, differs from the initial momentum if, and only if, $\mathcal{A}^\mu(+\infty) \neq 0$. Expressing $F^{\mu\nu}$ in frequency space reveals that $\mathcal{A}^\mu(+\infty)$ is proportional to the zero-frequency mode. In other words, the particle is accelerated if, and only if, the plane wave field contains a zero-frequency mode [27],

$$\Pi^\mu(x_-) - p^\mu_{(0)} = q\epsilon_j^\mu \tilde{F}_j(0) - \bar{n}^\mu \frac{2p^{(0)} \cdot \epsilon_j \tilde{F}_j(0) - q^2 \tilde{F}^2(0)}{2p_-}, \qquad (3)$$

where $\tilde{F}_j(k)$ is the Fourier transform of $F_j(x_-)$. The magnitude of the momentum change in a planewave field is proportional to the amplitude of its zero-frequency component. This result is modified in very strong fields as classical radiation losses imply that p_- is no longer conserved [14].

Note that many models of laser pulses use the slow-envelope approximation, which in frequency space corresponds to a relatively narrow distribution around the central frequency $\Delta\omega/\omega \ll 1$. Under this slow-envelope condition, the amplitude of the zero-frequency component is exponentially suppressed. In contrast, square (box-car) pulses and sine-squared pulses violate this condition and have zero-frequency modes that are only power-law suppressed. Square pulses, in particular, notoriously result in unphysically large accelerations and heating, though they may be useful models for some very specific cases, as discussed below.

To generalize this insight to focused laser pulses and motion in 3 spatial dimensions, we observe from the classical action that for all points the mechanical 4-momentum of the particle is given by

$$\Pi^\mu(x) = p^\mu - qA^\mu(x) \qquad (4)$$

While many field configurations, including the Gaussian beam, can be modeled with 4-potentials $A^\mu(x)$ that vanish at (null) infinity, these do not manifest the change in momentum of a massive particle. We have just seen that for a planewave, the particle acquires a non-vanishing change in the gauge potential, which is exactly the change in momentum. This is an example of the recently discussed memory effect, being a phase (for a quantized particle) that can be removed by a change in gauge but nevertheless representing a physical (measurable) difference in states. The problem reduces to determining the 4-potential at time-like infinity.

This reasoning also demonstrates the importance of the relativistic effects in the acceleration. If the change in momentum is small $\Delta p/p \ll 1$, the trajectory is unperturbed, and one can simply Fourier transform the field in the lab frame along an inertial trajectory, as an approximation to a highly relativistic particle crossing the laser field. The absence of a zero-frequency mode, or in the particular case of the Gaussian beam field its derivation from a potential [26], then proves the absence of acceleration. However, in general, particularly for electrons initially nonrelativistic, the relativistic momentum of the particle in an $a_0 \gtrsim 1$ imply that the particle does not see a time-symmetric electromagnetic field on its trajectory. To visualize this effect, in Figure 1 we compare the electric field of a laser pulse as measured by an observed fixed at the center of the focal spot to the electric field of the same laser pulse as measured on the trajectory of an electron that begins initially at rest at the center of the focal spot. We have chosen an example in which the electron sees a sudden jump from zero field to $a_0 \simeq 20$, such as ionization from a high-Z atom. In this case, the electron sees less than a half-cycle of the laser oscillation and, therefore, retains much of the energy provided to it by the transverse field. Additional intuition for this outcome is provided by introducing the ponderomotive force.

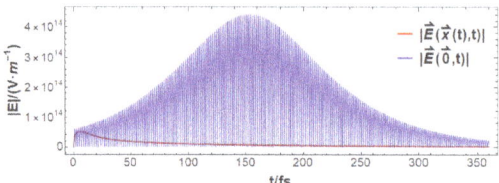

Figure 1. The magnitude of the electric field of the laser pulse measured by an observed fixed at the center of the focal spot $|\vec{E}(\vec{0},t)|$ compared to the electric field of the same laser pulse as measured on the trajectory $\vec{x}(t)$ of an electron that begins initially at rest at the center of the focal spot $|\vec{E}(\vec{x}(t),t)|$. The laser parameters are $a_0 = 64.0$, $w_0 = 1.8\ \mu\text{m}$, and $\tau = 150$ fs with hyperbolic secant temporal profile.

2.2. Relativistic Ponderomotive Force

The ponderomotive force can be derived from the single particle equation of motion by splitting the momentum into a fast, oscillating component and slow, secular component [17]. The oscillating component approximately solves the planewave equation of motion, and the resulting equation of motion is

$$\frac{d\bar{p}^i}{dt} = -\frac{1}{2m\bar{\gamma}} \nabla^i |\vec{A}|^2. \qquad (5)$$

This equation is valid to first order in ϵ, a small parameter quantifying how slowly the field strength varies from one cycle to the next. The zeroth order motion is the planewave motion which changes the energy of the particle only in proportion to the amplitude of the zero-frequency component of the field, which is typically exponentially suppressed for well-defined pulses and therefore smaller than the $\mathcal{O}(\epsilon)$ effect of the RPF Equation (3).

The ponderomotive force equation Equation (5) shows that the secular, cycle-averaged momentum evolves in response to a gradient in the intensity. This feature alone is insufficient to derive acceleration, i.e., a net gain in energy. Most models of laser pulses, and probably most real pulses near their peak intensity, are symmetric along the propagation axis. If the particle were (approximately) stationary, as for non-relativistic dynamics in lasers with $a_0 \ll 1$, then any forward force from the slowly increasing intensity before the peak is exactly balanced by a backward force from the slowly decreasing intensity after the peak. The symmetry between the forward force and backward force is broken at order ϵ by focusing of the laser, because there is a small $\mathcal{O}(\epsilon/\lambda_\ell)$ gradient pointing away from the focal plane. As a consequence of the dynamics, the particle translates even though the net transfer of momentum is (nearly) zero. When the dynamics become relativistic, for lasers $a_0 \gtrsim 1$, the symmetric shape of the laser pulse plays less of a role, because the particle is driven forward, co-propagating with the wave until the intensity drops $a_0 \ll 1$ again, typically as the laser is diverging. In this case, the particle never sees a gradient anti-parallel to the propagation direction. The particle gains forward momentum and energy. In this way, the RPF offers an intuitive explanation for the proof given in the previous subsection.

Similar reasoning applies to the transverse dynamics. For axi-symmetric models of the laser field, such as the Gaussian beam model, Equation (5) shows that the transverse momentum transfer to a particle interacting with the laser is radial from the beam axis. If the particle has zero initial transverse momentum, then its final transverse momentum is in the same direction as its displacement from the beam axis. Thus, an axisymmetric distribution of at-rest or copropagating-$\vec{p}_\perp = 0$ particles is scattered into a axisymmetric distribution with $|\vec{p}_\perp| > 0$, as found in [17]. However, if the particle has nonzero initial transverse momentum, the outcome depends on the magnitude of the momentum transfer. For small momentum transfer $\Delta \vec{p}_\perp / |\vec{p}_\perp| \ll 1$, the initial momentum (distribution) dominates, and for large momentum transfer $\Delta \vec{p}_\perp / |\vec{p}_\perp| \gtrsim 1$ the final transverse momentum distribution displays the axisymmetry of the scattering field. The more general question of whether a particle crossing the laser field with initial transverse momentum depends on the timing of the particle's crossing of the focal region, for the same reasons as the $\vec{p}_\perp = 0$ case discussed in the previous paragraph. We will demonstrate these features numerically below.

By general analysis, we have determined the conditions for a charged particle to be accelerated by a planewave or focused laser field. The general analysis also provides qualitative guidance to the outcomes of electron-laser scattering. More specific and more quantitative analysis of outcomes may be considered phenomenology of vacuum laser acceleration, i.e., the conversion of general features of the theory to more specific signals in experiment.

3. Phenomenology

The theory analysis in the previous section provides general insights into the necessary and sufficient conditions for laser acceleration in vacuum, as well as characteristics of the dynamics. Laboratory experiments differ in many ways from the thought experiment-style analysis that aids a theory investigation. We investigate four features of a realistic experimental setup: (1) the laser pulse profile, (2) the time the interaction begins, (3) the angle (relative to the beam axis) at which the electrons are traveling before the interaction begins, and (4) shot-to-shot variation in the summary parameters of the laser pulse (energy, spot size, pulse duration). Three of the four can be consistent with the application of RPF theory and, by highlighting significantly different outcomes for the same theory, point to measurements that are necessary for accurate interpretation of experimental outcomes.

3.1. Numerical Approach

We numerically integrate the Lorentz force with the electromagnetic fields modeled by the Gaussian beam. The Gaussian beam field distributions $\vec{E}(\vec{x},t)$ and $\vec{B}(\vec{x},t)$ are given explicitly in Appendix A. Next-to-leading-order corrections in the paraxial series expansion give rise to additional components of the force compared to the leading-order field. We include the first order corrections in both the weak focusing parameter $\epsilon_w = \lambda_\ell/2\pi w_0$ and the slow-envelope parameter $\epsilon_t = 1/\omega_\ell \tau_\ell$. Here, λ_ℓ and $\omega_\ell = 2\pi c/\lambda_\ell$ are the laser wavelength and angular frequency, w_0 is the focal spot radius ($\sqrt{2 \ln 2}$ times smaller than the intensity full-width half-max diameter), and τ_ℓ is the temporal intensity profile full-width half-max. For consistency of comparisons, we fix $\lambda_\ell = 1$ µm for all simulations. These expansion parameters were denoted ϵ and σ, respectively, in Ref. [17].

Individual particle trajectories are solved with standard ordinary differential equation solvers. In initial testing, multiple solvers were compared for convergence. Matlab's ode45 solver could be used in most cases, which also enabled running larger sample sizes in parallel. Truncation conditions based on time and electromagnetic field strength were checked to ensure the momentum of the particles had converged to inertial trajectories to well-within the noise level to define the final distributions. Distributions are generated by the Monte Carlo method, using several thousand samples for each parameter set: initial conditions ($\vec{x}, \vec{p}$ at $t = 0$) are randomly-generated according to the distributions described below. With these solvers, we verified quantitatively that the RPF Equation (5) gives results indistinguishable from the Lorentz force across the range of applicable parameters considered in this paper. In practice we use the Lorentz force solver in all cases and especially in Section 3.2 below where conditions of the RPF violated.

3.2. Laser Pulse Profile

The temporal profile of a laser pulse is less frequently provided in experimental descriptions. For experiments with overdense $n_e \gtrsim n_{\rm cr} = \omega_\ell^2 m_e \epsilon_0/e^2$ targets, the effect of ionizing prepulses creating preplasma up to picoseconds before the peak has been investigated to some extent [31,32]. For underdense plasma or vacuum laser acceleration, the choice of temporal profile is essential for predicting the energy gain.

For example, while Ref. [6] does not provide the temporal profile of the laser pulse in the experiment, the authors modeled their pulse with a sine-squared function. According to Ref. [26], the acceleration found using sine-squared and Gaussian profiles is unphysical, arising from the fact that these profiles do not satisfy

$$\frac{d(\ln f)}{d\varphi} \ll 1, \quad (6)$$

a condition derived together with the Gaussian beam spatial field distribution. This requires an at most exponential dependence on φ; hence Ref. [26] recommends hyperbolic secant. Consistency in the approximation scheme can be restored by including order f'/f corrections in the Gaussian beam fields [17]. In order to compare to previous simulation results and discuss the impact of these modeling choices we simulate with three profiles:

$$f_I(\varphi) = \sin^2(\varphi/\varphi_0) \quad (7)$$
$$f_{II}(\varphi) = \exp(-\varphi^2/\varphi_0^2) \quad (8)$$
$$f_{III}(\varphi) = \text{sech}(\varphi/\varphi_0), \quad (9)$$

where $\varphi = k_0(x - ct)$ is the dimensionless phase and φ_0 is linearly related to pulse duration, usually measured as the full-width half-max in intensity.

Although Gaussian profiles are formally inconsistent with Maxwell's equations, they remain useful because measured laser pulse profiles are often fit passably by Gaussians and not often fit by hyperbolic secant functions. Further, several ultra-high-intensity systems have observed multiple peaks in the temporal profile. In Figure 2, we fit a single Gaussian, a three-peak Gaussian, a hyperbolic secant function and sine-squared function to the temporal profile of the 4PW Ti:Sapphire laser system at the Center for Relativistic Laser Science (CoReLS) in Gwangju, Korea. The central peak is best fit by a Gaussian, but a model with more degrees of freedom incorporates relevant features at ∼10% peak intensity. The three-peak fit loses information, but we have found that the additional features visible in the measured profile have a small effect on the accelerated electron distribution compared to the main peaks. The early-time features at less than 1% the peak intensity effect small changes to the energy gain as long as they correspond to $a_0 < 1$. This reasoning would not hold for peak $a_0 \gg 10$, such as achieved for f/1 focusing on many petawatt-class systems. The late-time features generally have a negligible effect on the electron energies, because the electrons have been ponderomotively ejected from the focal region before these features catch up.

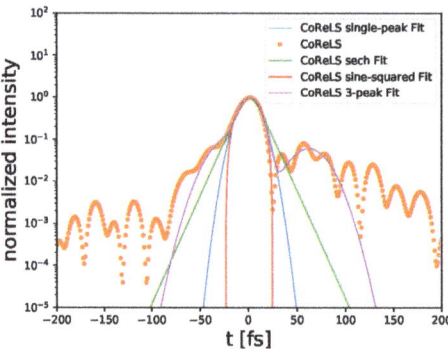

Figure 2. Temporal profile measured on CoReLS (points) compared to four possible fit functions.

Figure 3 compares the final energy distribution dN/dE of electrons accelerated by four different temporal profiles, including sine-squared and the recommended hyperbolic secant. The laser has peak intensity corresponding to $a_0 = 3$, focal spot radius $w_0 = 10\,\mu\text{m}$, and full-width half-max duration (measured on intensity) of $\Delta\tau = 350$ fs. The electrons are initially zero temperature with initial velocity parallel to the laser propagation axis, $\vec{v} = (0,0,0.2)c$, corresponding to kinetic energy $E_{kin} = m(\gamma - 1) = 10.5$ keV. The electrons are initially uniformly distributed in a cubic 3-dimensional volume around the focal spot within $3w_0$ of the beam axis. Increasing the volume covered by electron initial positions would result in more electrons receiving small or negligible acceleration and thereby increase the weight of dN/dE around the initial kinetic energy without significantly affecting the fit at higher energies.

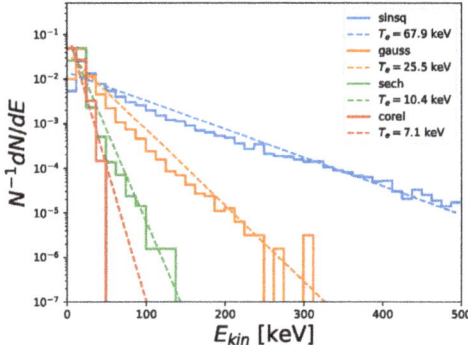

Figure 3. Normalized electron energy distributions $N^{-1}(dN/dE)$ for sine-squared, Gaussian, hyperbolic secant and three-peaked pulse measured at CoReLS. Laser parameters are $a_0 = 3.0$, $w_0 = 10$ μm and $\tau = 350$ fs. Maxwellian fits are plotted with the fit temperature shown in the key.

Recalling that the mean energy per particle in a Maxwellian distribution is $\langle E \rangle /N = T$, we see that sine-squared and Gaussian temporal profiles result in a significant gain in average energy. Compared to the sech profile, Gaussian and sine-squared profiles generally over-estimate energy gain [26]. The three-peaked Gaussian predicts even less energy gain and less heating than the hyperbolic secant. While the hyperbolic secant does not significantly change the average energy, the electron distribution is significantly heated, evolving from a zero-temperature distribution to a finite temperature distribution. Some electrons gain energy, while other electrons lose energy, showing that the reasoning of Ref. [26] is incomplete. This observation of heating without significant change in mean energy is consistent (at the provided, qualitative level) with a more recent experiment at $a_0 \simeq 5$ and much longer pulse duration ($\Delta \tau \simeq 5$ ps) [11].

3.3. Phase of Injection

Another reason Ref. [26] may not apply is that the electron–laser interaction is finite in duration, contrary to the setup of the authors' calculation. Infinite interaction time, in practice, assumes the interaction begins early enough that the switch to laser-dominated dynamics does not occur suddenly. There are two ways this assumption can be violated. First, the presence of nearby charges screens the laser field so that an individual charge is subject to a net force only after the laser field strength becomes greater than the typical electric field in the plasma $\langle \vec{E}^2 \rangle_{pl}^{1/2}$, which varies greatly depending on the creation of the plasma. This effect explains the success of plasma-mirror injection [13], since electrons are released into free space (ejected from the plasma) near the peak laser intensity and, thus, see a sudden jump from nearly zero average force in plasma to large Lorentz force in the laser field. Second, in case the electrons arise from photoionization, the ionization threshold means that electrons become free only when the laser achieves a field strength comparable to the Coulomb field of the atom. For hydrogen and helium plasmas, this effect is negligible, but for heavy inert gases such as argon or xenon, ^1S electrons may be liberated only within one or two decades of the peak intensity, which is the subject of considerable study, e.g., Refs. [9,33,34] and references therein.

A simple model of sudden turn-on is obtained by considering the net force on the particle zero until it passes a given threshold. For simulations, we modify the profile function with a step-function $f(\varphi) \rightarrow f(\varphi)\Theta(\varphi + \varphi_c)$, with $\Theta(z > 0) = 1$ the Heaviside function. With $\varphi_c > 0$ the step occurs at $\varphi = -\varphi_c$. Preceding dynamics are incorporated into the initial distribution of electron positions and momenta. If the threshold arises from screening, the electrons are free but have non-zero momentum, and we assume a maximum entropy distribution (Maxwellian).

The sharp turn-on clearly violates Equation (6), as well as the slowly-varying condition inherent in the RPF [17,35], and we expect both a greater energy gain and a significant asymmetry in the transverse momentum distribution of the final particles. As a consequence, the final particle energy and momentum distribution become sensitive to carrier–envelope phase and other non-ponderomotive effects. Only the Lorentz force solver provides accurate results in this case. The largest asymmetry arises when the electron is injected at a phase corresponding to a maximum of the electric field, and the final electron energy becomes less sensitive to the pulse profile function than the phase at which the interaction begins, in agreement with ionization studies [34].

Figure 4 shows the distribution of final transverse momentum $|\vec{p}_T| = \sqrt{p_x^2 + p_y^2}$ for $\varphi_c = 0.7$, which is chosen among many possible values of φ_c that can yield electrons with kinetic energy up to $\simeq$900 keV. Notice that the p_T distribution is not azimuthally symmetric with additional higher momenta in the $p_x > 0$ direction, corresponding to particles that first enter the laser field near the focal spot where the laser fields are maximum. As shown by the color-coding these particles also achieve the highest energy, consistent with our reasoning. This effect is particularly large for photo-ionized electrons, which begin free propagation when the peak laser field is in focal region [33]. The anisotropy arises from the maximum of the E field coinciding with the peak of the profile due to the specific value of the carrier–envelope phase in our model of the fields.

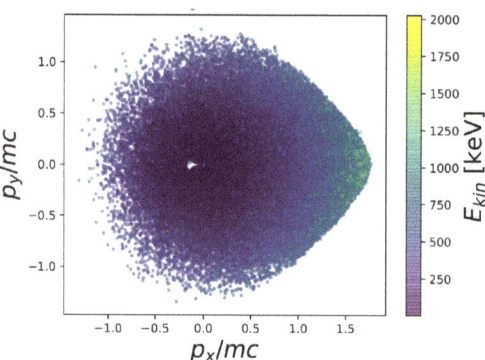

Figure 4. Scatter plot of final momenta for electrons scattered by a sech-profile pulse ($a_0 = 3$, $w_0 = 10$ μm, $\Delta \tau = 500$ fs) and initial step at $\phi_c = 0.7$.

Measuring the number of free electrons in the laser spot requires a probe with time resolution smaller than the high-intensity laser pulse, which is experimentally very difficult. For this reason, phase of injection as a parameter would probably have to be fit to the data in post-processing and analysis. Such fitting is addressed in part by ongoing efforts to observe strong-field ionization processes and validate theory calculations of the ionization rate.

3.4. Initial Transverse Momentum

In the experiment of Ref. [6], the electrons were generated by laser-ablation of a solid target situated off the axis of the acceleration laser's propagation. The schematic in Figure 1 of Ref. [6] does not give the off-axis distance, but the fact that acceleration laser was focused with an f/3 OAP suggests that the angle from which the electrons entered the focal region was greater than $\tan^{-1}(1/3) = 18.4°$. Equivalently $p_\perp = \sqrt{p_x^2 + p_y^2} \gtrsim p_z/3$.

Although the RPF is azimuthally symmetric for a Gaussian beam model of a laser field, the final distribution of electrons scattered by the laser is azimuthally symmetric if, and only if, the initial distribution is azimuthally symmetric. Ref. [17] observed a ring in the p_x–p_y plane (their Figure 9) because they initialized the electrons in an infinitely thin disk centered on the beam axis with velocity co-linear to the pulse propagation. The initial transverse momentum present in the experiment breaks the azimuthal symmetry of the scattering, and a broader three-dimensional distribution of electron initial positions shows many electrons scattering into smaller $p_\perp$ final states. Azimuthal symmetry will be visible for very large energy gain $\Delta E/E \gg 1$, because in this limit the initial state momentum is negligible compared to the final momentum.

To illustrate, we simulate electrons traveling toward the focal region at a 54° angle from the beam axis. The electrons are initially uniformly distributed off-axis between the laser pulse and focal plane and all have the same speed $|\vec{v}| = 0.3c$. The laser pulse has a Gaussian temporal profile, peak intensity $I_0 =$, focal spot size 20 µm and duration 350 fs. We verified that the same results are generated by solving either the RPF or the Lorentz force.

The distribution of final electron momentum in Figure 5 shows that most electrons remain in the injection plane, whether aligned with polarization or not. Electrons that interact with only the edges of the pulse (in space or time) are accelerated less and diverted less from their initial momentum vectors. For this reason, it remains surprising that Ref. [6] did not observe electrons upon rotating the plane of polarization; the electron source and detector remained in the same plane and only the laser's polarization changed by 90°. This suggests that more than one revision to the model of the experiment will be necessary to fit the data.

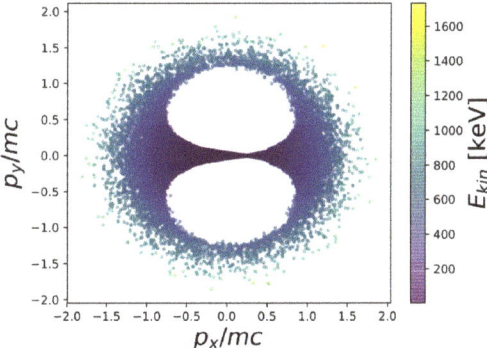

Figure 5. Scatter plot of final momenta for electrons scattered by a sine-squared profile pulse ($a_0 = 3$, $w_0 = 20$ µm, $\Delta\tau = 350$ fs). Electrons have $|\vec{v}| = 0.3c$ and enter the focal region at 54° from the laser axis.

The highest energy electrons are scattered more nearly isotropically, but only if the initial distribution of electrons accesses the full transverse distribution of the laser fields. If the electrons responsible for the detector signal arrive in the focal region before the pulse does, then they homogeneously sample the transverse intensity gradients, with different electrons seeing gradients in different radial directions. On the other hand, if the electron energy and time-of-arrival at the focal region are correlated (e.g., due to dynamics at the source), then time-of-arrival becomes another model parameter.

Figure 6 shows the final p_x (in polarization plane) as a function of the initial position for the same parameters as Figure 5. With the magnitude of the velocity fixed for all particles, initial position completely determines the time-of-arrival. Electrons arriving in the focal region ahead of the laser pulse scatter in the $+\hat{x}$ direction, because, with the highest intensity on axis and behind them, they experience a ponderomotive force in the $+\hat{x}$ direction. In contrast, electrons arriving slightly later than the laser pulse, see the ponderomotive force pointing in the $-\hat{x}$ direction. Therefore, a 100 fs variation in the source dynamics (much smaller than the ablation time scale in the experiment) enhances or suppresses the number of electrons reaching the detector, which was placed on only one side of the beam axis.

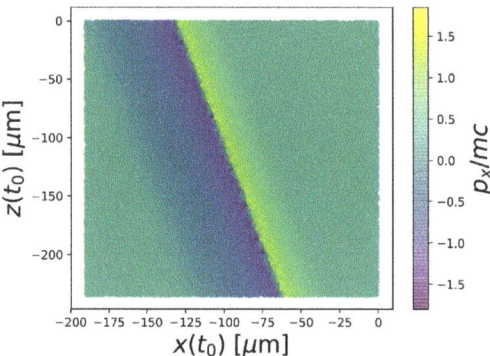

Figure 6. In-plane momentum (normalized to mass, p_x/m) as a function of initial position for the simulation that above reproduced data of [6] using initial transverse velocity.

In future experiments, the source of electrons must be thoroughly characterized before data shots with the scattering laser on. Moreover, this characterization must be accompanied by analysis of the uncertainties in order to distinguish the signal from random fluctuations of the source once the scattering laser is on.

3.5. Shot-to-Shot Variations in the Laser

Laser systems fluctuate. The energy input during amplification, the spectrum of the pulse and the pointing all vary from shot to shot. These fluctuations mean the on-target pulse profile, focal spot size, and intensity distribution in space and time [36] differ from shot to shot. Systematic changes could have a similar or greater impact: in Ref. [6] changing the polarization of the laser with an optical element could result in uncontrolled changes to the wavefront, impacting both focus quality and pulse duration.

Many changes in the laser cannot be accounted for by the gaussian beam model used here. Physically, most causes of shot-to-shot variances will result also in departures from the nominal model of the near-focus laser fields. Since approximations such as the Gaussian beam and RPF depend on the laser parameters, the accuracy of predictions also varies with the fluctuations in the laser. Even so, varying the parameters of the Gaussian beam model provides an estimate of the impact of shot-to-shot (statistical) variation in observables. Comparing spectra shows that an error or fluctuation in spot size leads to an order of magnitude difference in the number of electrons detected.

In order to quantify the typical shot-to-shot difference arising from incorrect or fluctuating laser parameters, we introduce a crude error functional,

$$\Delta\left(\frac{dN}{dE}\right) \equiv \bar{N}^{-1} \int \left|\frac{dN^{(1)}}{dE} - \frac{dN^{(2)}}{dE}\right| dE$$

$$\bar{N} = \frac{1}{2}(N^{(1)} + N^{(2)}) = \frac{1}{2}\int \left(\frac{dN^{(1)}}{dE} + \frac{dN^{(2)}}{dE}\right) dE, \quad (10)$$

which compares $dN^{(i)}/dE$ for two sets ($i = 1, 2$) of laser and plasma initial conditions and outputs a number. The error Equation (10) could be experimentally measured, provided a laser system with sufficiently precise control to run statistically distinct experiments at the parameter sets (1) and (2), in which case the average and the standard deviation of the spectrum could be obtained over $\gtrsim 30$ shots at a given parameter set. Equation (10) can be thought of as the simplest metric on the abstract space of spectra, though it is neither a standard measure of error nor a prediction interval. For the present it provides an intuitive measure of the difference between a predicted electron spectrum and a measured result in case of few ($\lesssim 10$) shots where a proper average cannot be constructed.

The particle spectrum is frequently measured with magnetic spectrometers, which require pinholes or similar mechanisms to reduce the acceptance and ensure accurate reconstruction of the particle energy. Consequently, experimental spectra are measured along narrow, predetermined sight-lines from the focal point. The small acceptance introduces additional shot-to-shot noise in the measurement, which we estimate by Monte Carlo, computing Equation (10).

Intuition from the ponderomotive force described above suggests that acceleration should strongly depend on the laser spot size, since the spot size sets the scale of transverse gradients, as well as the Rayleigh range. Spatiotemporal coupling effects in high intensity beams can produce spot size variation of order 25% [36], resulting in significant difference in the accelerated electron distribution. Figure 7 shows the error functional as the spot size deviates from the expected spot size of 10 µm. The two curves correspond to spectra measured on sight lines at 39° and 46° from the laser axis. These two sight lines are selected due to their appearance in Ref. [6]. They are representative for more recent experiments as well, because electron spectrometers typically remain off-axis while a primary diagnostic (e.g., ion spectrometer) occupies the laser axis (0°) position. The laser energy is 20 J, pulse duration 367 fs, and the temporal profile Gaussian. The laser begins 20 Rayleigh lengths from the focal plane, and the electrons are initially uniformly distributed in a box between the laser and the focal plane extending 13 microns from the beam axis. The electrons have initial momentum co-linear to the laser propagation axis and initial energy following a Maxwellian distribution with temperature 10 keV.

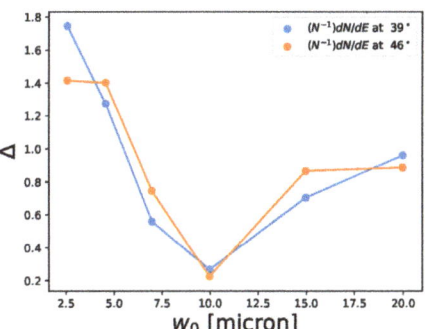

Figure 7. The error functional Equation (10) along two sight lines, 39° and 46° from the beam axis for a 20 J, 367 fs laser pulse for varying waist size w_0.

The error measure is non-zero at 10 µm because we have run two simulations with identical parameters but different random seeds which produces microscopically different electron distributions. The value at 10 µm is, thus, a measure of the shot-to-shot noise in the measurement. Smaller spot sizes significantly increase the gradients and hence the acceleration leading to broader distributions and slightly fewer electrons significantly accelerated. Both effects enhance the error functional. Larger spot sizes decrease the gradients but have a smaller effect on the number of electrons significantly accelerated since the field strengths and gradients in the larger focal region have been reduced. The quantitative size of these effects also depends on the error measure chosen. This reasoning suffices to predict a larger difference when the spot size is smaller than expected as observed in Figure 7. On the other hand, effects such as spatiotemporal coupling are more likely to cause error in the direction of larger spot size than expected.

Addressing the shot-to-shot variances of laser systems will require both new measurement techniques and data analysis techniques. High-intensity lasers are technically difficult to diagnose, often because the intensity and/or physical size of the beam is too great for well-established optical diagnostics. In many cases the experimental setup precludes measuring laser parameters on-shot. These facts require complementary development of statistical analysis of laser performance, especially issues, such as the correlation between partial-beam measurements (e.g., of energy and temporal profile) to full-beam measurements.

Some measurements, such as the complete spatio-temporal profile, are only possible in scanning mode with only a tiny fraction of the full pulse energy (10^{-4}–10^{-6}). Single shot measurements do not exist, and, therefore, the variation between two single shots at full energy is unknown. At higher peak intensities, even percent or per mille level fluctuations can have an effect. Full energy shots at the largest laser systems are essentially experiments in their own right. Since experimental campaigns on large single-shot (100–1000 J) class lasers consist of a few tens of shots at most, using a significant number of those for laser characterization would have a large impact on the actual experiment. As laser performance parameters are liable to evolve over time, one would have to repeat this characterization for every experiment. Only systematic development and constant calibration of new on-shot diagnostics can rectify this situation.

4. Fitting an Example Experiment

The interpretation of the data in Ref. [6] was criticized as being incompatible with the theory of laser acceleration in a vacuum. In the experiment, an $I \simeq 10^{19}$ W/cm^2 laser interacted with low energy ($E_{kin} = m_e(\gamma - 1) \simeq 10$ keV) electrons and accelerated electrons to 200–900 keV, observed in the polarization plane but not perpendicular to it. The angle and energy distributions were considered consistent with a simple model of the laser fields. However, others argued that in the laser's parameter regime, electrons should not be able to gain energy [26], and an equal number of electrons should be observed in the plane perpendicular to laser polarization, because the RPF scatters electrons into an azimuthally symmetric distribution about the laser axis [17].

More recent experiments have also set out to measure energy gain by free electrons interacting with a laser in vacuum, but do not provide insight into the older experiment. Both Refs. [11,12] report energy gain much smaller ($\Delta E/E \lesssim 0.05$) than reported by [6] ($\Delta E/E \simeq 90$), and, in fact, the data provided in those works are insufficient to determine whether significant energy gain was detected. In both Refs. [11,12] electrons initially have finite kinetic energy and significant dispersion in energy. One qualitatively observes increased dispersion, showing that some electrons gain energy, but does not show that the average energy of the electron increases [11]. The other omits the data necessary to distinguish increased dispersion from an increased average energy [12]. Acceleration of photoionized electrons is not comparable, because the electron becomes free to move under influence of the laser field only at a finite time, typically close the peak laser intensity. As we discuss below, this semi-infinite interaction time has an important impact on the electron dynamics and possibility of energy gain. However, in one experiment, measurements in the plane perpendicular to polarization suggest that photoionized electrons may have been accelerated into a more azimuthally symmetric distribution [37].

Theory and experiment work has suggested that improved modeling of the electrons' initial momentum distribution could help explain the discrepancy [33], but dedicated modeling of the experiment conditions is necessary to see whether or not a particular missing effect suffices to explain the data in Ref. [6]. Indeed, a significant reason for the disagreement is that theory contributions often work on generalities, simulate special cases, and, therefore, miss the impact of experiments' specific conditions.

We may now proceed to explain the data of Ref. [6]. The most difficult feature to fit is the absence of electrons perpendicular to the polarization plane. To compare electron numbers in-plane of polarization to out-of-plane of polarization, the authors kept the apparatus fixed and rotated the polarization of laser. However, this method actually changes two parameters, both the initial momentum vector and the observation line of sight being rotated into the plane perpendicular to polarization. Thus, the experiment did not measure how much electrons are scattered out of the initial plane, which is defined by the initial momentum and laser propagation vectors. As noted above (cf. Section 3.4), the RPF leads one to expect the highest energy electrons are scattered azimuthally symmetrically while lower energy electrons remain closer to the initial plane. The absence of signal even at low energy suggests that the result may be partially due to different numbers of electrons from the source on different shots.

Nevertheless, we fit the data assuming the electron source remains consistent between shots to demonstrate the importance of the missing pieces of the model we identified above. Each of the four effects can enhance or suppress the number of electrons detected along the chosen sightline by a factor 10, and each alone is insufficient to explain the $\gtrsim$100-times difference in electron number between the in-plane and out-of-plane shots. To obtain the $\sim$100-fold difference, we combine a change in laser spot size with either the sudden turn-on or the initial transverse momentum. Although, in a simplistic model, varying w_0 may be the most relevant change in the laser since wavefront differences from rotating the polarization can easily translate into less energy enclosed in the FWHM central disk.

The first fit is shown in Figure 8. In comparing to the data, we fix the laser energy, pulse duration and select an injection phase by fitting dN/dE at 39° and 46° in the plane of polarization. We set the overall normalization of the predicted dN/dE to fit the data, since it reflects the total number of electrons in the experiment (which in turn depends on efficiency of the source) and is not part of our modeling. We then vary the spot size to obtain a second prediction such that the out-of-polarization-plane dN/dE prediction fits the (absence of) signal. We plot the predictions together with the data in the same manner as Figure 2 of Ref. [6].

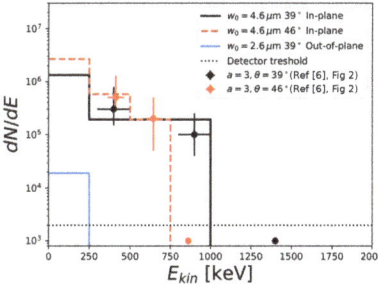

Figure 8. Measured spectra for a 20 J, 367 fs laser pulse, allowing w_0 to differ between in-plane ($w_0 = 4.6$ μm) and out-of-plane ($w_0 = 2.6$ μm) measurements.

For this first fit, we use a Gaussian temporal profile. The specific parameters that fit the data depend on the pulse profile function, but we have found fitting parameters for each profile function.

In the second fit, Figure 9, we follow the same procedure, choosing the laser parameters and initial transverse momentum to fit the in-plane measurements of dN/dE and then varying the spot size to reproduce the relative suppression of out-of-plane electron number. In this case, we use a sine-squared temporal profile, which yields higher energy electrons without any sudden turn-on (recall Figure 3). Computing $\Delta(dN/dE)$ for the in-plane and out-of-plane measurements, we obtain 1.98 and 1.87 at 39° and 46°, respectively, showing how the functional $\Delta(dN/dE)$ signifies a nearly 0 or 1 difference in signal.

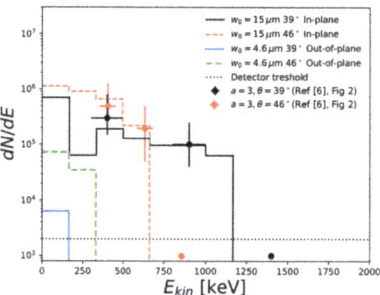

Figure 9. Measured spectra for a 16 J, 350 fs laser pulse, allowing w_0 to differ between in-plane ($w_0 = 15$ μm) and out-of-plane ($w_0 = 4.6$ μm) measurements.

Quantifying the goodness of fit is not productive in this case, because even this almost-minimal modeling has more parameters than the data have points to fit. Qualitative comments are in order though: the goodness of the fit depends also on how the simulation and experiment data are binned. We have chosen bin sizes roughly equal to the displayed uncertainty in the energy measurements presented in Ref. [6]. If we reduce the bin size, more information in the spectrum would become visible, which might provide more information about the physics of the interaction. However, even constrained to the bin size suggested by the experimental resolution, the fit can be improved or degraded by changing bin size.

5. Conclusions

We have investigated how several unmeasured and unmodeled conditions of the experiment in Ref. [6] affect widely-recognized phenomenological features of laser acceleration in vacuum. We showed that these differences between application of the theory and the experiment suffice to change qualitatively the predicted electron distributions and, thus, could have obscured the physics in the experiment. Our results suggest that any one or more of these unaccounted effects can make predictions consistent the experimental data, but too little information makes it impossible to fit the data uniquely. We cannot conclude with an overall "best fit" interpretation of the data.

Since that early publication, other experiments have added data, all of which are consistent with the theoretical understanding of laser acceleration in vacuum. Very long laser pulses interacting with low-energy free electrons result in very little average energy gain but do increase electrons' energy spread [11,12]. The sudden turn-on of the laser–electron interaction, whether due to ionization near the peak intensity [7–10,34] or ejection from a dense plasma [13], can yield much higher energy gain. Sudden turn-on makes the electron energy less sensitive to the temporal profile and more sensitive to precise magnitude of the field and initial momentum distribution of the electrons at the beginning of the interaction.

Some of the lessons of this exercise have appeared in the laser-plasma literature, but in our opinion remain under-appreciated. For instance, simulations including the dynamic development of preplasma [31] emphasize the importance of the initial plasma or electron distribution. Measuring the laser's shot-to-shot variations in performance is now recognized as important to stabilizing Wakefield accelerators [38]. Knowing the laser pulse's temporal profile is important when the electrons are likely to see the early-time features, whether a slow exponential turn-on (such as a sech profile) or an extra peak in the pre-pulse. It is less important when the electrons start to interact with the laser later in the pulse, particularly near the peak. Provided this more detailed information of the conditions, we can try to fit the more-difficult-to-measure parameters, such as the time at which the free particle–laser interaction begins. For example, ion energy correlates with focal spot size [39], pointing the way toward an in situ measurement of peak intensity. Such an approach must be validated with correct statistical analysis.

Developing these measurement and data analysis procedures is essential to discovery goals in future laser–plasma experiments. Precise single-electron dynamics are crucial to validating theories of radiation reaction and strong-field ionization, particularly as experiments continue to much higher intensity. To demonstrate the importance of accurate knowledge of laser parameters, we compute $\Delta(dN/dE)$ Equation (10) for deviations from nominal parameters at selected high-intensity laser facilities given in Table 1. We compare predictions for two different values of the laser spot size w_0, one the nominal focal spot size given in the table and second a focal spot twice as large. Only the laser spot size differs for the spectra compared in each value of $\Delta(dN/dE)$; all other laser parameters and electron initial conditions remain the same. The pulse temporal profile is Gaussian and the spectra are integrated over 4π.

Table 1. The pulse duration is measured as intensity full-width half-max. The pulse profile is always Gaussian. Malka 1 uses the laser energy and pulse duration of Ref. [6] with the nominal best focus for an f/3 mirror. Malka 2 has mostly the same laser parameters as Malka 1 but is compressed to 50 fs, as would be possible with current laser technology.

Facility	Energy [J]	Duration [fs]	w_0 [μm]	I_0 [W/cm^2]	a_0 (Peak)
Malka 1 [6]	20	300	2.6	4.25×10^{20}	17.7
Malka 2	20	50	2.6	2.55×10^{21}	43.3
BELLA PW [40]	40	30	1.8	1.77×10^{22}	91.4
TPW f/3 low-P	50	150	2.6	2.13×10^{21}	39.55
TPW f/1	150	150	1.25	2.76×10^{22}	142.5
CoReLS	50	30	1.8	2.22×10^{22}	127.7
OPAL	600	20	1.25	8.28×10^{23}	702.4

Figure 10 shows a large difference in the accelerated electron spectra. For comparison, the baseline value of Δ for two simulations with the same laser parameters but different randomized electron positions and momenta is less than 0.2 as shown in Figure 7. $\Delta(dN/dE)$ increases with intensity, suggesting that uncertainty arising from unknown or fluctuating laser parameters becomes a more serious problem on higher-intensity laser systems. The four issues addressed here do not cover all the myriad ways in which experiments depart from theorists' idealized conditions. Our concern is that without improved modeling and data-analytic efforts, experiments can misidentify as signal what is actually shot-to-shot fluctuation in laser or plasma conditions.

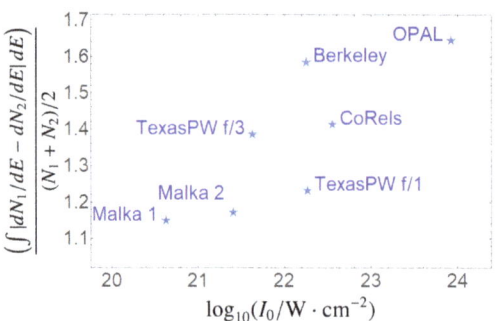

Figure 10. The error measure Δ for current and future laser facilities' nominal operating parameters in Table 1. For each point marked by a star plotted at the facility's nominal peak intensity, laser energy is constant while the waist size w_0 increased by a factor 2. Other laser and electron parameters remain the same between the simulated spectra.

Author Contributions: Conceptualization, B.M.H., L.L. and O.Z.L.; methodology, L.L. and O.Z.L.; software, O.Z.L.; validation, L.L. and O.Z.L.; formal analysis, L.L. and O.Z.L.; investigation, L.L. and O.Z.L.; data curation, L.L. and O.Z.L.; writing—original draft preparation, L.L.; writing—review and editing, B.M.H.; visualization, L.L. and O.Z.L.; supervision, B.M.H.; project administration, B.M.H.; funding acquisition, B.M.H. All authors have read and agreed to the published version of the manuscript.

Funding: This work is supported by Air Force Office of Scientific Research (FA9550-14-1-0045), the Los Alamos National Lab Office of Experimental Sciences (RFP475852), and Tau Systems, Inc.

Institutional Review Board Statement: Not applicable.

Informed Consent Statement: Not applicable.

Data Availability Statement: Experimental data are previously published in Ref. [6].

Acknowledgments: L.L. and O.Z.L. thank the Center for Relativistic Laser Science at the Gwangju Institute for Science and Technology for hospitality and Lynn Labun for continuing support.

Conflicts of Interest: The authors declare no conflict of interest.

Appendix A. Gaussian Beam Model

If we assume the intensity distribution in the focal plane is Gaussian, the solution to Maxwell's equations reproduces the Gaussian beam as an expansion in powers of [17]

$$\epsilon_w = \frac{1}{k_0 w_0}. \tag{A1}$$

In practice, $\epsilon_w \lesssim 0.13$ with the upper bound attained by the most strongly focused systems where the waist size is similar to the wavelength $w_0 \simeq \lambda_l$. Second order corrections $\epsilon_w^2 \lesssim 0.017$ are, therefore, of the same order as shot-to-shot variance in other laser parameters and smaller than corrections to wavefronts [36,41]. As coefficients of the higher order corrections appear to grow less than factorially [42], the series should be reasonably convergent. No new field components appear at higher orders at the expansion, meaning that new qualitative changes to the trajectories are excluded. Together, these facts justify truncating after $\mathcal{O}(\epsilon_w)$.

Finite pulse duration effects on the field distribution can be derived analytically [17], and the corresponding expansion parameter is defined as

$$\epsilon_t = \frac{\lambda_l}{c \Delta \tau}. \tag{A2}$$

We do not model here experimental effects due to variations in the amplification spectrum [36].

The resulting set of fields is,

$$\vec{E}(\vec{x},t) = \vec{E}^{(0)}(\vec{x},t) + \epsilon_w \vec{E}^{(1)}(\vec{x},t) + \epsilon_w^2 \vec{E}^{(2)}(\vec{x},t) + \dots \quad \text{(A3)}$$

$$\vec{B}(\vec{x},t) = \vec{B}^{(0)}(\vec{x},t) + \epsilon_w \vec{B}^{(1)}(\vec{x},t) + \epsilon_w^2 \vec{B}^{(2)}(\vec{x},t) + \dots \quad \text{(A4)}$$

for linear polarization,

$$\vec{E}^{(0)}(\vec{x},t) = \vec{e} E_0 \frac{w_0}{w(z)} e^{-r^2/w(z)^2} \sin\left(\Phi^{(0)}(t,z)\right) \quad \text{(A5)}$$

$$\vec{B}^{(0)}(\vec{x},t) = c^{-1} \hat{k} \times \vec{E}^{(0)} \quad \text{(A6)}$$

$$\vec{E}^{(1)}(\vec{x},t) = \hat{k} 2\epsilon_w E_0 (\vec{x}\cdot\vec{e}) \frac{w_0}{w(z)} e^{-r^2/w(z)^2} \cos\left(\Phi^{(1)}(t,z)\right) \quad \text{(A7)}$$

$$\vec{B}^{(1)}(\vec{x},t) = c^{-1} 2\epsilon_w E_0 (\hat{k}\times\vec{x}) \frac{w_0}{w(z)} e^{-r^2/w(z)^2} \cos\left(\Phi^{(1)}(t,z)\right) \quad \text{(A8)}$$

where $\vec{e}$ is a polarization unit vector orthogonal to the wavevector $\vec{k} = \hat{k}\omega_0/c$, w_0 is the waist radius, $r^2 = x^2 + y^2$, and E_0 is the peak electric field. The beam radius varies as a function of distance from the focal plane,

$$w(z) = w_0 \sqrt{1 + z^2/z_R^2}, \quad \text{(A9)}$$

and the phase is also a function of distance from the focal plane,

$$\Phi^{(0)}(t,z) = \omega_0(t - z/c) + \tan^{-1}(z/z_R) - \frac{zr^2}{z_R w(z)^2} - \phi_0 \quad \text{(A10)}$$

$$\Phi^{(1)}(t,z) = \Phi^{(0)}(t,z) + \tan^{-1}(z/z_R). \quad \text{(A11)}$$

The $\mathcal{O}(\epsilon_t)$ fields differ for each profile function $f(t - z/c)$ and are derived by expanding the Fourier transform with respect to t,

$$\vec{E}(\vec{x},t) \simeq \vec{e}\tilde{E}(\vec{x},\omega_0) e^{i\omega_0(t-z/c)} f(t-z/c) + \vec{e}\frac{\partial \tilde{E}}{\partial \omega}(\vec{x},\omega_0) e^{i\omega_0(t-z/c)} f'(t-z/c) + \dots \quad \text{(A12)}$$

where the second term is $\mathcal{O}(\epsilon_t)$ since the derivative on the profile function f' brings in powers of ϵ_t.

Using superscripts (a,b) to denote the order in each of the respective small parameters ϵ_w, ϵ_t, we have

$$\vec{E}(\vec{x},t) \equiv \vec{E}^{(0,0)}(\vec{x},t) + \epsilon_w \vec{E}^{(1,0)}(\vec{x},t) + \epsilon_t \vec{E}^{(0,1)}(\vec{x},t) + \dots \quad \text{(A13)}$$

to order implemented in our simulations. The same form holds for $\vec{B}(\vec{x},t)$.

References

1. Falcone, R.; Albert, F.; Beg, F.; Glenzer, S.; Ditmire, T.; Spinka, T.; Zuegel, J. Workshop Report: Brightest Light Initiative (March 27–29 2019, OSA Headquarters, Washington, DC). *arXiv* **2020**, arXiv:2002.09712.
2. Hegelich, B.M.; Labun, L.; Labun, O.Z. Finding quantum effects in strong classical potentials. *J. Plasma Phys.* **2017**, *83*, 595830301. [CrossRef]
3. Cole, J.; Behm, K.; Gerstmayr, E.; Blackburn, T.; Wood, J.; Baird, C.; Duff, M.J.; Harvey, C.; Ilderton, A.; Joglekar, A.; et al. Experimental evidence of radiation reaction in the collision of a high-intensity laser pulse with a laser-wakefield accelerated electron beam. *Phys. Rev. X* **2018**, *8*, 011020. [CrossRef]
4. Poder, K.; Tamburini, M.; Sarri, G.; Di Piazza, A.; Kuschel, S.; Baird, C.; Behm, K.; Bohlen, S.; Cole, J.; Corvan, D.; et al. Experimental signatures of the quantum nature of radiation reaction in the field of an ultraintense laser. *Phys. Rev. X* **2018**, *8*, 031004. [CrossRef]

5. Jaroszynski, D.; Bingham, R.; Brunetti, E.; Ersfeld, B.; Gallacher, J.; van Der Geer, B.; Issac, R.; Jamison, S.; Jones, D.; De Loos, M.; et al. Radiation sources based on laser–plasma interactions. *Philos. Trans. R. Soc. Lond. A Math. Phys. Eng. Sci.* **2006**, *364*, 689–710. [CrossRef]
6. Malka, G.; Lefebvre, E.; Miquel, J.L. Experimental Observation of Electrons Accelerated in Vacuum to Relativistic Energies by a High-Intensity Laser. *Phys. Rev. Lett.* **1997**, *78*, 3314. [CrossRef]
7. McNaught, S.; Knauer, J.; Meyerhofer, D. Photoelectron initial conditions for tunneling ionization in a linearly polarized laser. *Phys. Rev. A* **1998**, *58*, 1399. [CrossRef]
8. Moore, C.; Ting, A.; McNaught, S.; Qiu, J.; Burris, H.; Sprangle, P. A laser-accelerator injector based on laser ionization and ponderomotive acceleration of electrons. *Phys. Rev. Lett.* **1999**, *82*, 1688. [CrossRef]
9. DiChiara, A.; Ghebregziabher, I.; Sauer, R.; Waesche, J.; Palaniyappan, S.; Wen, B.; Walker, B. Relativistic MeV photoelectrons from the single atom response of argon to a 10^{19} W/cm^2 laser field. *Phys. Rev. Lett.* **2008**, *101*, 173002. [CrossRef]
10. Payeur, S.; Fourmaux, S.; Schmidt, B.; MacLean, J.; Tchervenkov, C.; Légaré, F.; Piché, M.; Kieffer, J. Generation of a beam of fast electrons by tightly focusing a radially polarized ultrashort laser pulse. *Appl. Phys. Lett.* **2012**, *101*, 041105. [CrossRef]
11. Cline, D.; Shao, L.; Ding, X.; Ho, Y.; Kong, Q.; Wang, P. First observation of acceleration of electrons by a laser in a vacuum. *J. Mod. Phys.* **2013**, *4*, 26491. [CrossRef]
12. Carbajo, S.; Nanni, E.A.; Wong, L.J.; Miller, R.; Kärtner, F.X. Direct laser acceleration of electrons in free-space. *arXiv* **2015**, arXiv:1501.05101.
13. Thévenet, M.; Leblanc, A.; Kahaly, S.; Vincenti, H.; Vernier, A.; Quéré, F.; Faure, J. Vacuum laser acceleration of relativistic electrons using plasma mirror injectors. *Nat. Phys.* **2016**, *12*, 355–360. [CrossRef]
14. Hadad, Y.; Labun, L.; Rafelski, J.; Elkina, N.; Klier, C.; Ruhl, H. Effects of Radiation-Reaction in Relativistic Laser Acceleration. *Phys. Rev.* **2010**, *82*, 096012. [CrossRef]
15. Bula, C.; McDonald, K.T.; Prebys, E.J.; Bamber, C.; Boege, S.; Kotseroglou, T.; Melissinos, A.C.; Meyerhofer, D.D.; Ragg, W.; Burke, D.L.; et al. Observation of nonlinear effects in Compton scattering. *Phys. Rev. Lett.* **1996**, *76*, 3116–3119. [CrossRef]
16. Bamber, C.; Boege, S.J.; Koffas, T.; Kotseroglou, T.; Melissinos, A.C.; Meyerhofer, D.D.; Reis, D.A.; Ragg, W.; Bula, C.; McDonald, K.T.; et al. Studies of nonlinear QED in collisions of 46.6-GeV electrons with intense laser pulses. *Phys. Rev.* **1999**, *60*, 092004. [CrossRef]
17. Quesnel, B.; Mora, P. Theory and simulation of the interaction of ultraintense laser pulses with electrons in vacuum. *Phys. Rev.* **1998**, *58*, 3719–3732. [CrossRef]
18. Beg, F.; Bell, A.; Dangor, A.; Danson, C.; Fews, A.; Glinsky, M.; Hammel, B.; Lee, P.; Norreys, P.; Tatarakis, M. A study of picosecond laser–solid interactions up to 1019 W cm^{-2}. *Phys. Plasmas* **1997**, *4*, 447–457. [CrossRef]
19. Key, M.; Cable, M.; Cowan, T.; Estabrook, K.; Hammel, B.; Hatchett, S.; Henry, E.; Hinkel, D.; Kilkenny, J.; Koch, J.; et al. Hot electron production and heating by hot electrons in fast ignitor research. *Phys. Plasmas* **1998**, *5*, 1966–1972. [CrossRef]
20. Wilks, S.; Langdon, A.; Cowan, T.; Roth, M.; Singh, M.; Hatchett, S.; Key, M.; Pennington, D.; MacKinnon, A.; Snavely, R. Energetic proton generation in ultra-intense laser–solid interactions. *Phys. Plasmas* **2001**, *8*, 542–549. [CrossRef]
21. Esirkepov, T.; Yamagiwa, M.; Tajima, T. Laser ion-acceleration scaling laws seen in multiparametric particle-in-cell simulations. *Phys. Rev. Lett.* **2006**, *96*, 105001. [CrossRef] [PubMed]
22. Haines, M.; Wei, M.; Beg, F.; Stephens, R. Hot-electron temperature and laser-light absorption in fast ignition. *Phys. Rev. Lett.* **2009**, *102*, 045008. [CrossRef] [PubMed]
23. Yang, J.; Craxton, R.; Haines, M. Explicit general solutions to relativistic electron dynamics in plane-wave electromagnetic fields and simulations of ponderomotive acceleration. *Plasma Phys. Control Fusion* **2011**, *53*, 125006. [CrossRef]
24. Ebisuzaki, T.; Tajima, T. Pondermotive acceleration of charged particles along the relativistic jets of an accreting blackhole. *Eur. Phys. J. Spec. Top.* **2014**, *223*, 1113–1120. [CrossRef]
25. Lau, C.; Yeh, P.C.; Luk, O.; McClenaghan, J.; Ebisuzaki, T.; Tajima, T. Ponderomotive acceleration by relativistic waves. *Phys. Rev. Spec.-Top.-Accel. Beams* **2015**, *18*, 024401. [CrossRef]
26. McDonald, K.T. Comment on Experimental observation of electrons accelerated in vacuum to relativistic energies by a high-intensity laser. *Phys. Rev. Lett.* **1998**, *80*, 1350. [CrossRef]
27. Dinu, V.; Heinzl, T.; Ilderton, A. Infra-Red Divergences in Plane Wave Backgrounds. *Phys. Rev.* **2012**, *D86*, 085037. [CrossRef]
28. Schwinger, J.S. On gauge invariance and vacuum polarization. *Phys. Rev.* **1951**, *82*, 664–679. [CrossRef]
29. Landau, L.; Lifshitz, E. *The Classical Theory of Fields, Course of Theoretical Physics*; Pergamon Press: Oxford, UK, 1971.
30. Sarachik, E.; Schappert, G. Classical theory of the scattering of intense laser radiation by free electrons. *Phys. Rev. D* **1970**, *1*, 2738. [CrossRef]
31. Sentoku, Y.; Iwata, N.; Koga, J.; Dover, N.; Nishiuchi, M. Plasma formation and target preheating by prepulse of PW laser light. In Proceedings of the APS Division of Plasma Physics Meeting Abstracts, Milwaukee, WI, USA, 23–27 October 2017; Volume 2017, p. PP11.00016.
32. Kumar, S.; Gopal, K.; Gupta, D.N. Proton acceleration from overdense plasma target interacting with shaped laser pulses in the presence of preplasmas. *Plasma Phys. Control Fusion* **2019**, *61*, 085001. [CrossRef]
33. Chowdhury, E.A.; Ghebregziabher, I.; MacDonald, J.; Walker, B.C. Electron momentum states and bremsstrahlung radiation from the ultraintense field ionization of atoms. *Opt. Express* **2004**, *12*, 3911–3920. [CrossRef] [PubMed]

34. Yandow, A.; Toncian, T.; Ditmire, T. Direct laser ion acceleration and above-threshold ionization at intensities from 10^{21} W/cm^2 to 3×10^{23} W/cm^2. *Phys. Rev. A* **2019**, *100*, 053406. [CrossRef]
35. Startsev, E.; McKinstrie, C. Multiple scale derivation of the relativistic ponderomotive force. *Phys. Rev. E* **1997**, *55*, 7527. [CrossRef]
36. Pariente, G.; Gallet, V.; Borot, A.; Gobert, O.; Quéré, F. Space–time characterization of ultra-intense femtosecond laser beams. *Nat. Photonics* **2016**, *10*, 547. [CrossRef]
37. Kalashnikov, M.; Andreev, A.; Ivanov, K.; Galkin, A.; Korobkin, V.; Romanovsky, M.; Shiryaev, O.; Schnuerer, M.; Braenzel, J.; Trofimov, V. Diagnostics of peak laser intensity based on the measurement of energy of electrons emitted from laser focal region. *Laser Part. Beams* **2015**, *33*, 361–366. [CrossRef]
38. Maier, A.R.; Delbos, N.M.; Eichner, T.; Hübner, L.; Jalas, S.; Jeppe, L.; Jolly, S.W.; Kirchen, M.; Leroux, V.; Messner, P.; et al. Decoding sources of energy variability in a laser-plasma accelerator. *Phys. Rev. X* **2020**, *10*, 031039. [CrossRef]
39. Vais, O.; Thomas, A.; Maksimchuk, A.; Krushelnick, K.; Bychenkov, V.Y. Characterizing extreme laser intensities by ponderomotive acceleration of protons from rarified gas. *New J. Phys.* **2020**, *22*, 023003. [CrossRef]
40. Nakamura, K.; Mao, H.S.; Gonsalves, A.J.; Vincenti, H.; Mittelberger, D.E.; Daniels, J.; Magana, A.; Toth, C.; Leemans, W.P. Diagnostics, control and performance parameters for the BELLA high repetition rate petawatt class laser. *IEEE J. Quantum Electron.* **2017**, *53*, 1–21. [CrossRef]
41. Tiwari, G.; Gaul, E.; Martinez, M.; Dyer, G.; Gordon, J.; Spinks, M.; Toncian, T.; Bowers, B.; Jiao, X.; Kupfer, R.; et al. Beam distortion effects upon focusing an ultrashort petawatt laser pulse to greater than 10^{22} W/cm^2. *Opt. Lett.* **2019**, *44*, 2764–2767. [CrossRef]
42. Salamin, Y.I. Fields of a Gaussian beam beyond the paraxial approximation. *Appl. Phys. B* **2007**, *86*, 319. [CrossRef]

Disclaimer/Publisher's Note: The statements, opinions and data contained in all publications are solely those of the individual author(s) and contributor(s) and not of MDPI and/or the editor(s). MDPI and/or the editor(s) disclaim responsibility for any injury to people or property resulting from any ideas, methods, instructions or products referred to in the content.

Review

High-Quality Laser-Accelerated Ion Beams from Structured Targets

Martin Matys [1,2,*], Jan Psikal [1,2], Katsunobu Nishihara [3], Ondrej Klimo [1,2], Martin Jirka [1,2], Petr Valenta [1,2] and Sergei V. Bulanov [1,4]

1. Extreme Light Infrastructure ERIC, ELI Beamlines Facility, Za Radnici 835, 252 41 Dolni Brezany, Czech Republic
2. Faculty of Nuclear Sciences and Physical Engineering, Czech Technical University in Prague, Brehova 7, 11519 Prague, Czech Republic
3. Institute of Laser Engineering, Osaka University, Suita 565-0871, Osaka, Japan
4. Kansai Photon Science Institute, National Institutes for Quantum Science and Technology, 8-1-7 Umemidai, Kizugawa-shi 619-0215, Kyoto, Japan
* Correspondence: Martin.Matys@eli-beams.eu

Abstract: In this work, we reviewed our results on the prospect of increasing the quality of ion acceleration driven by high-intensity laser pulses using low-Z structured targets. It is shown that the radiation pressure acceleration mechanism dominates over target normal sheath acceleration for assumed laser target parameters when the laser intensity is high enough. The target thickness is optimized for this regime and double-layer structure is investigated. When a corrugation is fabricated on the interface of such a target, a relativistic instability with Rayleigh–Taylor and Richtmyer–Meshkov like features can be driven by the target interaction with a high intensity laser pulse. The proper development of this instability leads to the generation of a collimated quasi-monoenergetic ion beam with lower emittance, divergence, and energy spread compared to a single and double-layer target with planar interface. A steep-front laser pulse is used in our simulations to mitigate other type of instabilities arising at the target surface from the laser–target interaction. We discuss the use of a plasma shutter to generate the required pulse profile, which also locally increases intensity. The obtained shape improves the ion acceleration, including higher maximal energy and lower beam divergence, in our simulation of a high-Z target.

Keywords: high quality; monoenergetic; ion acceleration; laser-driven; plasma; low divergence; particle-in-cell; instability; steep front; plasma shutter

1. Introduction

Laser driven ion acceleration is currently receiving particular scientific attention for its impressive applications, such as hadron therapy [1–3], nuclear fusion [4,5], use in material sciences and nuclear physics research [6], and other areas [7–9]. Cryogenic (solid) hydrogen targets provide an interesting medium for ion acceleration as they can be made relatively thin, with low density, lacking contaminants, debris-free, and can be used in high-repetition laser–target experiments [10–13].

In this work, we review our results on the prospect of increasing the quality of future ion acceleration driven by the current and forthcoming multi-(tens) PW laser systems (such as ELI Beamlines [14–16], APOLLON [17], ELI NP [18], and SEL [19]) using structured cryogenic targets. It is shown that, with the use of a 10 PW-class laser system with pulse duration over 100 fs and cryogenic targets of current thickness [11], the radiation pressure acceleration (RPA) [20] mechanism dominates over the target normal sheath acceleration (TNSA) [21,22] in both the number of accelerated protons (with energy > 10 MeV) and the maximal reached energies [23]. The laser–target conditions relevant for RPA has been thoroughly investigated in this millennia, e.g., in Refs. [24–26], and the experimental indications of the RPA regime have already been observed [27–30]. Note that the laser–target condition optimal for RPA overlaps with other mechanisms investigated at moderately relativistic intensities [31], such as phase stable acceleration (PSA) [32,33], which is also referred to as coherent acceleration of ions by laser (CAIL) [34]. Usually, two subregimes of RPA are distinguished, the hole boring [35–37] for a relatively thick target and light sail [38,39] for ultrathin targets; the transitions between them can occur by decreasing the target areal density and/or increasing the laser pulse intensity [40]. Therefore, the thickness of the cryogenic target for the use of a 100 PW class laser system was reduced in our simulations [41] to be optimized for the RPA mechanism [20]. The properties of the generated particles can be improved using structured targets made of heavy and light ion layers [1,42–44] and by properly introducing instability, transforming the target into compact ion bunches either from the planar target [45] or the target with a modulated surface [46]. We investigate the introduction of the initial corrugation on the interface between the double-layer target [41] with a high intensity laser pulse. In these conditions a relativistic instability arises, which is determined by the target geometry, having features of the Rayleigh–Taylor (RTI) [47,48] and Richtmyer–Meshkov (RMI) [49,50] instabilities. Both of them are currently being thoroughly investigated [51–59]. They can be found on different space scales ranging from the parsec-size in astrophysics (e.g., the development of the filament structure of the Crab Nebula [60]) to a μm-size in laser-plasma, e.g., affecting the creation of the hot spot in the inertial fusion [61]. The main differences between RTI and RMI are shown via the experimental results [62,63] in Figure 1. The driving force is in principle continuous for RTI, resulting in exponential growth, therefore experiencing slower growth in early time in Figure 1 (left). RTI can occur only when the acceleration is being driven from lighter to heavier media [51]. In contrast, the RMI behavior is rather impulsive and a perturbation grows linearly in time, as shown in Figure 1 (right), and it can occur for shocks directed toward either side of the interface. In the case of heavy-light direction of acceleration, RMI exhibits a characteristic phase inversion of the corrugated interface, as was predicted in theory [53,64,65] and shown via experiment [63]. The inversion (switch of corrugation maxima and minima) is visible in Figure 1 (right), e.g., compare the position of maxima and minima in sub-figures (a) and (d). In contrast, the maxima and minima stay at the same position for RTI in Figure 1 (left).

The instability can be influenced by the fabricated interface corrugation to generate a high-density proton bunch, which can be accelerated by the radiation pressure as a compact structure. Therefore, the generated proton beam has good quality and properties such as low energy spread, divergence, and emittance [41].

In our simulations, we use a steep-front laser pulse to mitigate the development of other transverse instabilities (with relatively short wavelength) arising from laser–target interaction on the target surface, usually ascribed to Rayleigh–Taylor [45,66,67] or electron-ion coupled instability [68,69], as was proposed by theory [45] to increase the target stability. Without this treatment, the target can be shattered into many small bunches, ignoring the target geometry. We discuss the use of the plasma shutter (usually a thin solid foil attached to the front surface of the target with a gap between them) [70–79] to obtain the required pulse profile. In addition to the steep-rising front, the shutter can also locally increase the peak intensity of the laser pulse [78]. The obtained shape can improve the ion acceleration from the target located behind the plasma shutter, including higher maximal energy and lower divergence [79].

The paper is organized as follows. The simulation method and parameters of the simulations used in the particular subsections of results are described in Section 2. Section 3, which contains the results, is divided into three sections. First, the dominance of the RPA mechanism for the assumed parameters is shown in Section 3.1. The target thickness is then reduced, and the influence of the corrugated interface of the double-layer target, including the bunch generation with low emittance, divergence, and energy spread, is investigated and compared to similar targets in Section 3.2. Finally, the foil stability is discussed in

Section 3.3, comparing the results using steep-front and full-front laser pulses. The use of the plasma shutter for our concept and for heavy ion acceleration from different targets is also discussed in this section. Appendix A contains the description of the virtual reality application (called VBL-Virtual BeamLine) used for visualization of our results.

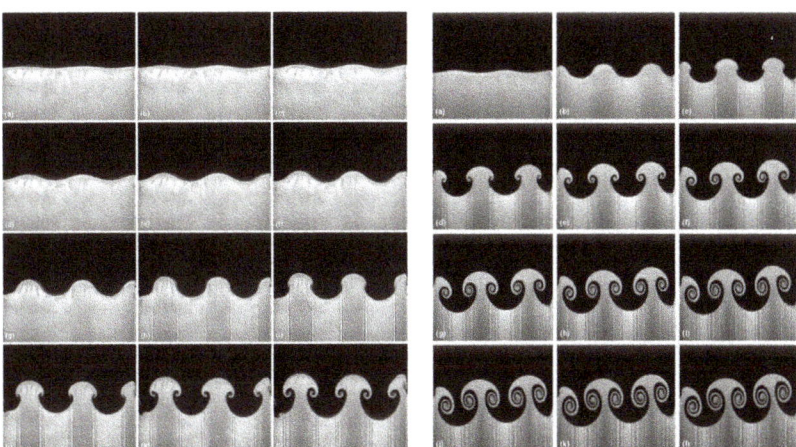

Figure 1. Difference between RTI and RMI in a sled experimental setup. (**left**) RTI, the time increment between each subsequent image is 33 ms. Reprinted from [62], with the permission of AIP Publishing. (**right**) RMI, the first image is at time before the shock is delivered, the time increment between each other subsequent image is about 83.5 ms (66 ms between the last two ones). Source [63], reproduced with permission.

2. Methods

We performed 2D and 3D particle-in-cell simulations using the code EPOCH [80]. In Sections 3.1 and 3.2, the quantum electrodynamics (QED) module [81] resolving non-linear Compton scattering is included in the simulations, assuming high intensity interaction. The EPOCH default Yee solver was used, and current smoothing option was applied. In Section 3.1, the triangular shape of particles was used, whereas the preprocessor directive for 3rd order b-spline shape function of the quasi-particles (PARTICLE_SHAPE_BSPLINE3) was used in Sections 3.2 and 3.3. The main laser–target simulation parameters are shown in Table 1, and further simulation details are described in the following paragraphs of this section.

Table 1. The main laser–target simulation parameters. In order: Intensity I, polarization, wavelength λ, width of Gaussian space profile at FWHM, temporal shape-duration for $\sin^2(t)$ and FWHM for Gaussian, target material, thickness, and electron density n_e in the corresponding critical density n_c.

Section	I [W/cm^2]	Pol.	λ [µm]	Width [µm]	t-Shape	Target	Thickness	n_e [n_c]
3.1-2D	3×10^{22}	p	1.1	5	$\sin^2(t)$ 320 fs	H	25 µm	56
3.1-3D	1.5×10^{22}	p	1.1	5	$\sin^2(t)$ 200 fs	H	15 µm	56
3.1-VR	3×10^{22}	p	1.1	5	$\sin^2(t)$ 200 fs	H	15 µm	56
3.2-2D	1.37×10^{23}	s	1.0	10	Gauss 26.7 fs	^{2}H-H	$(1+1)$ µm	48
3.3-3D	1×10^{22}	p	1.0	3	$\sin^2(t)$ 64 fs	Shutter Si$_3$N$_4$	20 nm	835
						Target Ag	20 nm	2100

In Section 3.1, the laser pulse parameters of the reference 2D case are as follows: p-polarization, peak intensity $I = 3 \times 10^{22}$ W/cm^2, wavelength $\lambda = 1.1$ µm, beam width is 5 µm, and full pulse duration is 320 fs for $\sin^2(t)$ shape in intensity. Its energy corresponds to a Gaussian temporal profile with 150 fs FWHM. The peak power is about 9 PW and energy is 1.35 kJ. Dependence on intensity ranging between $I = 0.375 \times 10^{22}$ W/cm^2 and $I = 3 \times 10^{22}$ W/cm^2 is also discussed while keeping the other parameters same (i.e., changing pulse energy and power). The intensity of $I = 1.5 \times 10^{22}$ W/cm^2 was used for 3D simulation. The target is made by 25 µm thick fully ionized hydrogen target with electron density of 56 $n_{c1.1}$, where $n_{c1.1}$ is the non-relativistic critical density for $\lambda = 1.1$ µm. For the 3D simulations and virtual reality visualization, the laser and target parameters were reduced by a factor of 5/3 to 200 fs and 15 µm. For 2D simulations, square cells with the size of 20 nm are used. Each cell occupied by plasma contains 56 electrons and 56 protons. For the 3D simulation, the cell size is 20 nm in the longitudinal direction and 30 nm in the transverse direction. The number of particles per cell was reduced to 10 electrons and 10 protons. More information about simulation parameters can be found in [23].

In Section 3.2 (and the first part of Section 3.3), the laser pulse parameters are as follows: s-polarization (electric field is perpendicular to the plane of incidence), peak intensity $I = 1.37 \times 10^{23}$ W/cm^2, wavelength $\lambda = 1$ µm, beam width is 10 µm, beam duration at FWHM is equal to 8 laser periods T. The steep front is realized by filtering out the low-intensity part at the front of the laser pulse until 2.4 T (i.e., 30% of FWHM) before the peak of the temporal Gaussian profile. The double-layer target consists of light (solid hydrogen) and heavy (deuterium) ion layers. The electron density is same in both layers $n_e = 48$ n_c, where n_c is the non-relativistic critical density for $\lambda = 1$ µm. The deuterium layer has the same electron and ion number density as the proton layer, but two times heavier ion mass. Square cells with the size of 10 nm are used. Each cell occupied by plasma contains 48 electrons and 48 protons/deuterium ions. More information about simulation parameters can be found in [41].

In the rest of Section 3.3 (results with the plasma shutter), the laser pulse parameters are as follows: p-polarization, peak intensity $I = 1 \times 10^{22}$ W/cm^2, wavelength $\lambda = 1$ µm, beam width is 3 µm, and full pulse duration is 64 fs for $\sin^2(t)$ shape in intensity. Its energy corresponds to Gaussian temporal profile with 30 fs FWHM of 1 PW laser pulse. The plasma shutter is made of silicon nitride (Si$_3$N$_4$) solid foil. Full ionization of the foil is assumed with electron density $n_e = 835$ n_c, where n_c is the non-relativistic critical density for $\lambda = 1$ µm. The thickness of the plasma shutter is set to 20 nm. The target, located behind the plasma shutter, corresponds to a silver solid foil with thickness of 20 nm. Partial ionization of the target is assumed (charge number $Z = 40$), electron density is $n_e = 2100$ n_c. The mesh has square cells of the size 3 nm in 2D simulations and cuboid cells of the size 5 nm in the laser propagation direction and 25 nm in the transverse ones in 3D. The number of electrons in 2D is 835 particles per cell inside the plasma shutter (400 in 3D) and 1050 inside the target (1000 in 3D), respectively. The numbers of ions correspond to their charge ratios. More information about simulation parameters can be found in [78,79].

3. Results

3.1. The Prominence of Different Acceleration Mechanisms Using Cryogenic Targets

In order to properly optimize the target thickness and structure, one first needs to know which acceleration mechanism to focus on. More mechanisms usually occur during the laser–target interaction, and their interplay depends on the target and laser parameters [82]. Currently, the most employed acceleration mechanism is the target normal sheath acceleration (TNSA) [21,22]. In this section, we examine the shift from the TNSA dominated regime with the increasing laser pulse intensity for low density cryogenic targets of current thicknesses [11] and 10 PW class laser systems with pulse duration over 100 fs. Understanding of this topic then helps with choosing the parameters used for the structured cryogenic target in Section 3.2.

In our simulations [23], the assumed intensity ranges between $I = 0.375 \times 10^{22}$ W/cm^2 and $I = 3 \times 10^{22}$ W/cm^2; the thickness of the fully ionized hydrogen target is 25 µm. We focuses on the difference of the well established TNSA mechanism and the emerging mechanisms that differ from it, mainly radiation pressure acceleration (RPA). These two mechanisms can be clearly distinguished from each other at the early and middle stages as they act at different positions of the target. The TNSA gets involved on the rear side of the target, whereas the RPA is acting on the front side and interior of the target. This behavior is shown in Figure 2 using the proton energy layers (i.e., protons at various energy intervals in the 2D simulation area) for the peak laser intensity $I = 3 \times 10^{22}$ W/cm^2. The conversion efficiency of the laser pulse energy to the high-energy protons (exceeding 10 MeV) in this case is about 27%.

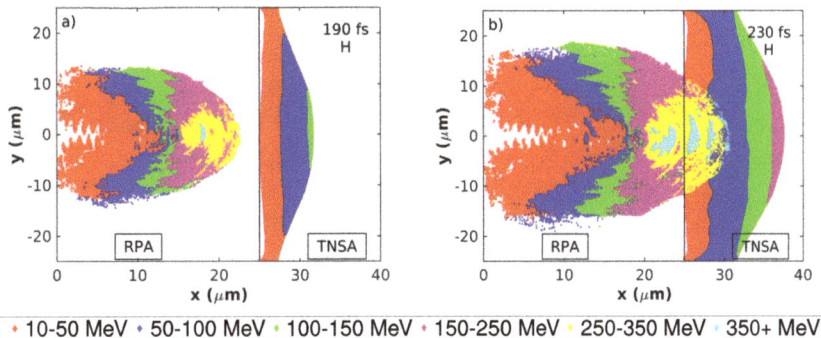

Figure 2. Proton energy layers for hydrogen target: (**a**) at 190 fs (**b**) at 230 fs from the beginning of laser–target interaction. The initial position of the target is between 0 µm and 25 µm (denoted by the black line). Republished with permission of IOP Publishing, Ltd., from [23], permission conveyed through Copyright Clearance Center, Inc.

The highest energies in the first stage (Figure 2a) are achieved by the RPA regime in the target interior. Here, the low density of the target provides good conditions for the hole boring phase of the RPA mechanism. The hole boring velocity inferred from our simulation is $u_{hb} = 0.31\ c$, which is slightly higher than the theoretical value of $u_{hb} = 0.26\ c$ calculated using the analytical model [36]. The character c denotes speed of light in vacuum. In the second stage (Figure 2b), the target is still not transparent for the laser pulse, and the most energetic protons from the inside of the target (accelerated to velocities higher than u_{hb}) enter into the TNSA field behind the initial position of the target rear side (denoted by the black line). Although the ions from both populations are now located in the same area, they can still be distinguished from one another by the combination of their energy and position. The energy of protons accelerated by the TNSA mechanism strongly depends on their distance from the target rear side, with the most energetic protons located on top of the proton cloud, as can be seen in Figure 2a. Therefore, the entering RPA protons can be distinguished by their significantly higher energy, which does not fit the energy layer of the surrounding TNSA protons. Thus, RPA results in higher proton energy than TNSA also in this stage. The separation of the two populations is more visible in the pseudo-3D visualization, with the proton energy represented also by the vertical height (Figure 3). Here, the laser pulse (incoming from left) is represented in the gray scale, the electron density by the turquoise scale, and the scale for proton energy is ranging from white (zero energy) to purple (about 400 MeV) to light blue (over 600 MeV). Note that for this visualization, the laser and target parameters were reduced in the similar way as for the 3D simulations (factor of 5/3) discussed below, and only the protons reaching the highest energy at the end of the simulation (above 300 MeV) are being tracked (see more information in [83] and in Appendix A). The interactive visualization (available online [84]) is made in the virtual reality web-based application [85], discussed in Appendix A.

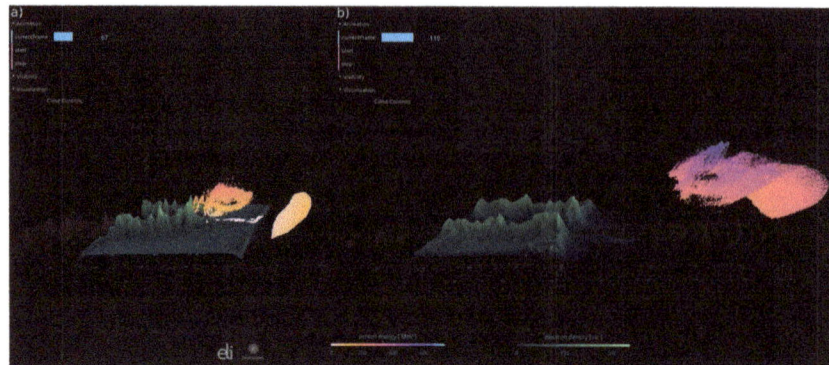

Figure 3. VBL visualization of different proton populations using the hydrogen target: (**a**) at time frame 67, (**b**) at time frame 110. The dots represent the simulated protons (only protons that exceed 300 MeV at the end of the simulations are included); the vertical height and color denote their energy using the white–red–blue scale. Laser pulse intensity is represented by the gray scale, electron density by the turquoise scale, and both values are also visualized using the vertical height. The interactive VBL application of the full time evolution is accessible online [84].

The third stage may occur if the laser pulses reach the rear side of the target and eventually punch through it, which happens around time $t = 270$ fs in the simulation with maximal intensity shown in Figure 2. The protons can be further accelerated to very high energies around the onset of the relativistic transparency by regimes such as the hybrid RPA-TNSA mechanism [86,87], break-out afterburner [88,89] and directed Coulomb explosion [90]. To see the dependence of the mechanisms interplay on intensity, other simulations were performed with the same parameters but with lower pulse intensities (and thus lower pulse power). Figure 4a shows the time evolution of the maximal reached proton energy by RPA (solid lines) and TNSA (dashed lines) in these simulations. Note that, for the times after the laser pulse burns through the target, all the ions originated from the target interior are labeled as RPA in Figure 4a for the sake of brevity.

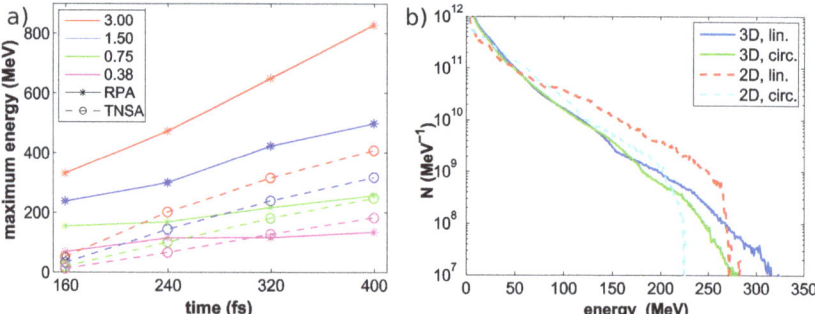

Figure 4. Maximal proton energy and ion spectra from hydrogen target. (**a**) Temporal evolution of maximum energies of protons accelerated by the RPA and TNSA mechanisms for various laser intensities. (**b**) Proton energy spectra for linearly and circularly polarized laser beams in 2D and 3D simulations at 260 fs from the beginning of the laser pulse interaction. Target thickness is reduced to 15 µm and pulse duration to 200 fs. Peak intensity $I = 1.5 \times 10^{22} \text{W/cm}^2$. Republished with permission of IOP Publishing, Ltd., from [23], permission conveyed through Copyright Clearance Center, Inc.

The RPA mechanism accelerates protons to higher energies than the TNSA in our simulations with intensities above 0.75×10^{22} W/cm^2. Note that, for these simulations, the laser pulse reached the rear side of the target, as further discussed in reference [23]. For the lowest intensity case, the target is too thick for an efficient RPA acceleration, and the TNSA plays the role of the dominating mechanism in the sense of proton energy.

Two-dimensional simulations are known to usually overestimate the maximal reached energy and heating of electrons (especially in the linear p-polarization) [89,91]. Therefore, our findings are also verified via 3D simulations. Intensity $I = 1.5 \times 10^{22}$ W/cm^2 is chosen for the demonstration. Both the laser pulse duration and target thickness are reduced by a factor of 5/3 to 200 fs and 15 µm due to computational constraints. Corresponding 2D simulations with the same reductions and simulations with the circular polarization were also performed for comparison. The proton energy spectra at the time 260 fs are shown in Figure 4b. Unexpectedly, the 3D simulations resulted in higher maximal energy than their 2D counterparts for our parameters with a relatively thick target. Further examination by separation of TNSA and RPA protons shows that only the energy of ions accelerated by RPA is higher in the 3D simulations. For example, before mixing these two populations at time 180 fs, the maximal energy of RPA protons increases from 180 MeV to 255 MeV when the third dimension is included. In this stage, the RPA mechanism represents a clear hole boring phase. This increase can be explained with the effect of the self-focusing of the laser beam propagating in the plasma. The laser pulse intensity is thus higher in 3D, as the self-focusing is not limited into just one plane as it is in 2D (see the comparison of electron density and electric field in Figure 6 in [23]). Consequently, the hole boring velocity (and thus the proton energy) is higher in 3D.

In contrast, at the same time instant, the energy of protons accelerated by pure TNSA decreases from 155 MeV to 80 MeV, which corresponds to the previous observations related to higher electron heating in 2D [91].

Circular polarization is often proposed for the laser pulse interaction with ultra-thin targets as it can improve the foil stability and reduce the electron heating and consequently results in higher ion energy [28,66,67,92]. In our simulations, these advantages diminish as the larger thickness of the target prevents it from immediately breaking. The electron heating at later stages is also similar in the linear and circular polarization due to the bending of the target surface (see the discussion in [23]). Therefore, the proton energy spectra of 3D simulations are similar until the energy is approximately 185 MeV. The linear polarization enhances the tail of the proton spectrum, resulting in higher maximal energy than the circular one in our simulations. This behavior can be ascribed to the presence of the oscillatory component of the ponderomotive force.

3.2. Improving Ion Properties Using Double-Layer Targets with Interface Corrugation

On the basis of our findings in the previous section, we choose the cryogenic target optimized for the RPA mechanism in our next study involving future 100 PW class laser systems. The optimal thickness l [20] of such a target can be expressed as:

$$\frac{l}{\lambda} = \frac{a_0}{\pi} \frac{n_c}{n_e}, \tag{1}$$

yielding the thickness of 2 µm for our laser and target parameters (see Section 2). Here, a_0 is the dimensionless amplitude of the laser electric field.

The properties of the ions accelerated from the solid target can be improved by its proper structuring. In our preliminary results in [93], we briefly compared the sinusoidal corrugation on the interface of a double-layer target with the one on the surface of single-layer-target and with the target without a corrugation (see Figure 5a–c).

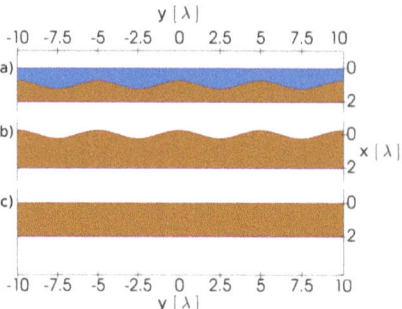
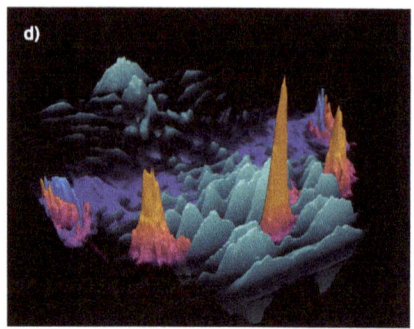

Figure 5. Structured targets and generation of proton bunch, source of the left part (**a–c**) [76]. Initial configuration of deuterium layer (blue) and proton layer (orange) in the cases: (**a**) double–layer target with the modulation on the interface, (**b**) single–layer target with the modulation on the front surface, (**c**) without the modulation. (**d**) Visualization of case (**a**) during the laser–target interaction. Coloring: electric field (gray), density of deuterium (blue) and hydrogen (orange). Colors saturated with maximum value set to the initial density. Values are also represented by the vertical height. The distinguished high density proton bunch enfolded by the laser pulse is developed. Source of (**d**): [94].

The corrugation located at the interface of a double-layer target is especially interesting as it resulted in a significant peak in ion spectra (more significant than in the reference case of surface modulation as is briefly discussed in Section 3.3). The interface corrugation was then thoroughly investigated in [41]. Figure 5d contains the visualization of the target density (deuterium: blue, proton: orange) and laser pulse electric field (gray). The values are also represented by the vertical height. The interaction of the laser pulse with the target results in the rise of the relativistic instability, with RTI and RMI features depending on the target geometry. The target is fractured into high density regions (located around the initial corrugation maxima at positions −5 μm, 0 μm, and 5 μm) and low density regions between them (around the initial minima). Moreover, as can be seen in Figure 5d, the laser pulse enfolds the central proton bunch, limiting the bunch broadening in space. Therefore, the ions are accelerated by the radiation pressure as a compact structure, having a low energy spread. The quality and properties of these protons are summarized in Figure 6a–c.

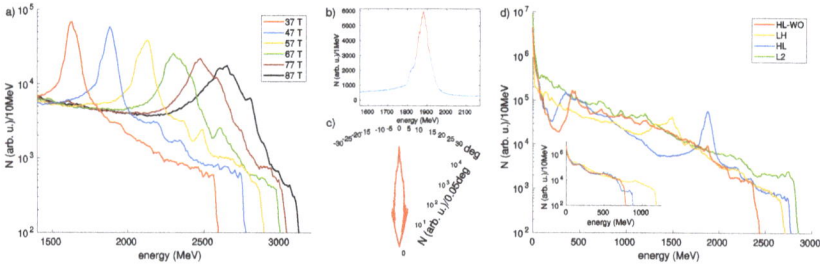

Figure 6. Properties of the ion beam. (**a**) Time evolution of the tail of the proton energy spectra in the HL case, (**b**) proton energy spectra of the HL case at time t = 47 T, with highlighted FWHM section used for (**c**) angular distribution, (**d**) proton energy spectra (corresponding deuteron energy spectra in inset) for various targets (see details in the text) at time t = 47 T. Reprinted from [41], with permission from Elsevier.

Figure 6a shows the time evolution of the tail of the proton energy spectra. Although the bunch structure is spreading in the later stages, the bunch structure is presented until the end of the simulation. Moreover, the structure is gradually shifting towards the end of the energy spectra with time. The time at 47 T (blue line) is further examined in Figure 6b,c. The average energy of the bunch is 1882 MeV, its bandwidth at FWHM is 67 MeV, and energy spread is about 3.7%. The energy conversion of the laser pulse into the protons inside the bunch is around 3.4%. The conversion into all protons propagating in the forward direction is around 28.7%. The red part of Figure 6b denotes the part of the beam above its FWHM. The angular spectrum of this red part is shown in Figure 6c using the logarithmic scale. The beam is well collimated, with the angular spread $2\theta = 0.65°$ (at FWHM), the solid angle $\Omega = 2\pi(1 - \cos(\theta)) = 0.1$ mrad, the normalized rms transverse emittance [95] $\epsilon_{rms} = \sqrt{\langle y^2 \rangle \langle p_y^2 \rangle - \langle y p_y \rangle^2}/m_p c = 0.046$ mm·mrad, where m_p and p_y are proton mass and momentum in the y-direction. This emittance is one order of magnitude lower than in the case of conventional proton accelerators [96], but still one order of magnitude higher than the emittance reported in [97] (where the energy range of protons was lower than in our case, up to 10 MeV). The transverse emittance can be also defined in real space via the beam divergence as in [98], yielding emittance $\epsilon_y = 0.218$ mm·mrad and divergence $\Theta_{div} = 0.038$ rad.

To show the effect of the corrugation, this simulation of the deuterium-proton layer (configuration shown in Figure 5a), denoted as HL (heavy-light), is compared with other simulations. Specifically, simulations of a double-layer target without corrugation (HL-WO), the double-layer target with corrugation, but with opposite order of layers (LH, light-heavy), and the single-layer hydrogen target (L2), (see the details in [41]). Both cases without the corrugation (HL-WO and L2) do not provide a significant peak in the energy spectrum (Figure 6d). The LH case provides a peak but with lower energy and higher energy spread. This behaviors correspond to the proton density shown in Figure 7. Here, the density is denoted by the vertical height, and the color represents the proton energy at that position. Both simulations with corrugations (Figure 7a,b) generate and maintain the high density bunches influenced by the target geometry as described above. In contrast, the non-corrugated cases (Figure 7c,d) generate a bubble structure typical for RPA acceleration of a planar target [45]. The RPA mechanism then can accelerate a smaller part of the particles at the bubble front to very high energies, but without the desired peak in the proton energy spectra, which is provided by the corrugation.

The influence of different laser polarization and corrugation wavelengths in the HL case is also thoroughly investigated in [41]. The instability leading to bunch generation (and peak in the ion energy spectra) also developed in the case of p-polarization. However, the central bunch was significantly smaller compared to the s-polarization case (shown in this section). This behavior was explained by artificially greater electron heating in the simulation plane in the p-polarization, as previously demonstrated in [89,91]. In contrast, the instability was mitigated in the case of circular polarization, and the ion bunch was not generated. The optimal corrugation wavelength was shown to be around the half of the size of the focal spot, which is used in the simulations in this section.

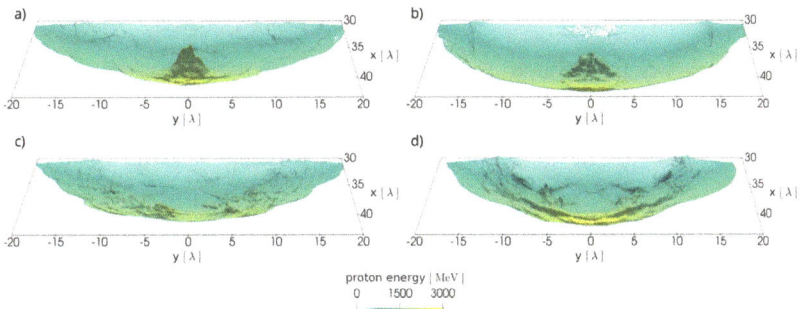

Figure 7. Spatial density distributions at time t = 47 T. The proton density is represented by the vertical height, and proton energy is represented by the blue to yellow scale. The simulated cases are: (**a**) HL, (**b**) LH, (**c**) HL–WO, (**d**) L2 (see parameters of all the targets in the text). Reprinted from [41], with permission from Elsevier.

3.3. Target Stability and Generation of the Steep-Front Laser Pulse

The foil stability is often worsened by the onset of unwanted kinds of instabilities. Especially with the treatment of a relatively short wavelength (independent on the target geometry), transverse instability arising from the laser–target interaction needs to be assumed. This instability is usually ascribed to Rayleigh–Taylor [45,66,67] or electron–ion coupled instability [68,69]. For the sake of brevity and its shorter wavelength compared to the desired instability driving the bunch generation discussed in Section 3.2, this instability will be referred to as short-wavelength instability regardless of its origin hereinafter. Its uncontrolled development results in the lower efficiency of ion acceleration in our case, as the target is shattered into many small bunches, as can be seen in Figure 8a.

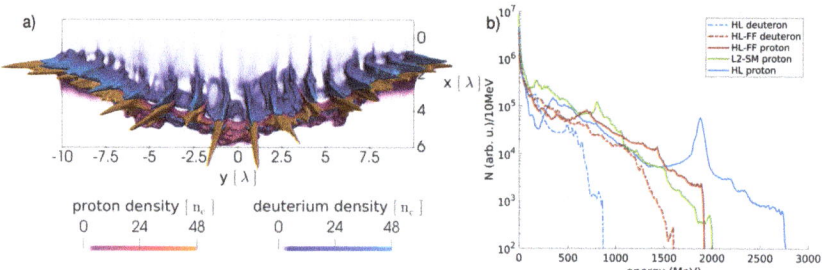

Figure 8. Short-wavelength instability. (**a**) Spatial distributions in the HL-FF (with full-front laser pulse) case at time t = 14 T. Blue and red scales represent deuterium and proton densities, with maximum value set to the initial density. Full density is indicated by the vertical height. (**b**) Proton and deuteron energy spectra for HL (steep-front, interface corrugation), HL-FF (full-front, interface corrugation), and L2-SM (steep-front, surface corrugation) cases at time t = 47 T. Reprinted from [41], with permission from Elsevier.

As noted in Section 3.1, circular polarization is often used for improving foil stability by mitigation of instabilities. However, circular polarization cannot be applied to our scheme, as it would weaken both the desired and unwanted instabilities, lowering the energy and quality of the proton beam in our simulations (see details about polarization dependence in [41]).

In our simulations, we use a steep-front laser pulse as proposed by theory [45]. Under this condition, the unwanted short-wavelength (RTI-like) instability does not have enough time to significantly develop. On the contrary, the wanted relatively long-wavelength instability induced by the target geometry (with RMI features) can immediately respond to the high radiation pressure and develop properly. This approached was used in all simulations presented in Section 3.2, where the steep-front was simulated by filtering out the beginning of the laser pulse until 2.4 T before the peak of the laser pulse. The simulation shown in Figure 8a represents the uncut full front, being 8 T longer. The effect of the laser front steepness on ion acceleration is shown in the ion energy spectra in Figure 8b. With the use of the full-front laser pulse (HL-FF), the distinctive good-quality peak in the proton spectrum is not developed. A less distinctive, relative broad peak is present, but at significantly lower energy compared to the steep-front case. The proton spectrum is somehow similar to the one of a single-layer hydrogen target with corrugation on its surface (L2-SM, configuration shown in Figure 5b), where the driving instability also originated from the surface. The foil disruption in the HL-FF case also reduces the maximal proton energy. In contrast, the energy of deuterons from the first layer is enhanced compared to the steep-front case, as they are more mixed with the protons.

The required steep-front laser pulse can be generated by several phenomena. If the laser pulse propagates through an underdense plasma [99–101] or a near critical density plasma [102–108], the desired shape can develop through the nonlinear evolution of the laser pulse. Another method is to use a thin overdense plasma foil (usually referred to as a plasma shutter [70–79]). The front of the laser pulse (with low intensity) is filtered out and the desired (high intensity) part propagates through the foil undergoing relativistic transparency, gaining the steep-front profile. In our further research, we focuses on the plasma shutter technique, first with a PW-class laser pulse utilizing a silicon nitride (Si_3N_4) plasma shutter. The plasma shutter made of this material has several advantages, such as a well defined surface, commercial availability in various thicknesses, and high quality of mechanical and optical properties [109,110]. A visualization of our 3D simulation [78] is shown in Figure 9a.

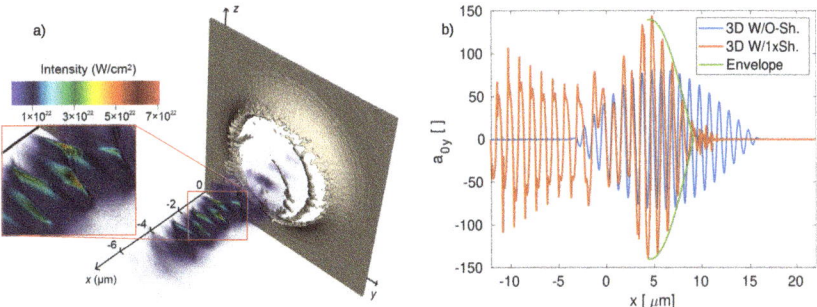

Figure 9. Plasma shutter. (**a**) The distribution of the laser intensity in the horizontal slice of the laser pulse from 3D simulation with the plasma shutter when the maximum intensity value is reached, source [78]. (**b**) The 1D profile (at $y = 0$ and $z = 0$) of dimensionless amplitude of the electric field in the y-direction (a_{0y}) after the laser pulse propagates through the plasma shutter in the 3D simulation. Comparison of the transmitted laser pulse (W/1xSh) with the original one (W/O–Sh). Steep front is generated, its envelope is approximated using the equation $y = 140 \cdot \sin(\pi \cdot x/9.2)$. Source [79]. Figures reprinted under the terms of the Creative Commons Attribution 4.0.

The laser pulse burns through the plasma shutter, shaping its profile and creating the so-called relativistic plasma aperture [111]. Consequently, the laser pulse is diffracted on such an aperture and, due to its constructive interference with generated high harmonics, the local intensity is amplified [78]. Local amplification by a factor of 7 (from the initial intensity of 1×10^{22} W/cm^2) can be seen in the highlighted area of Figure 9a, where the 2D profile of the laser pulse intensity in the polarization plane (x-y) is shown. Figure 9b shows the 1D profile (at the center of the pulse) at a later time, when the envelope stabilizes [76]. The blue line represents the original pulse in the simulation without the plasma shutter (W/O-Sh), and the red line is from the simulation with the plasma shutter (W/1xSh). The pulse front is about five periods shorter and significantly steeper compared to the original pulse. The maximal amplitude of this central (1D) profile is also enhanced, although the main intensity amplification occurs off-axis, as shown in Figure 9a. The application of the produced laser pulse for ion acceleration from a silver target was briefly investigated, with the preliminary results in [76], and then thoroughly discussed in [79], where the position of the target was also optimized. The setup of this 3D simulation is shown in our VR application in Figure 10, where the laser pulse (incoming from the left) is represented by the red color scale, electron density of the shutter is represented by the blue scale, and the density of silver ions from the target are represented by the green scale.

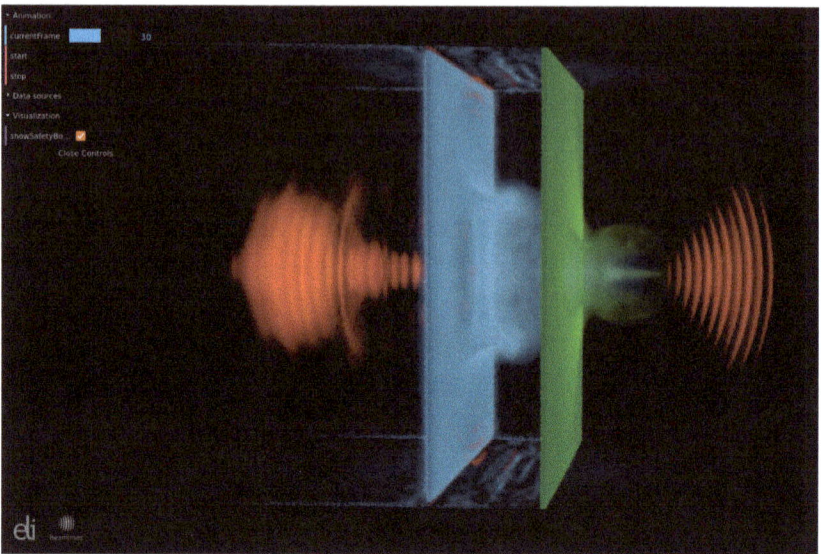

Figure 10. Application of the plasma shutter with a silver target: VBL visualization of our simulation of 1 PW laser (electric field: red color) interacting with the plasma shutter (blue: electron density) and the silver target (green: ion density). Laser pulse is shaped by the plasma shutter (resulting in the aperture) and accelerates ions from the silver target. A high energy ion beam with low divergence is generated. Data used for this visualization come from [79]. The interactive VBL application of the full time evolution is accesible online [112].

The use of the plasma shutter can result in an increase in maximal energy of heavy ions, as shown in Figure 11a, although a part of the laser pulse energy is lost during the development of the aperture [79]. For the linear polarization, the maximal energy of silver ions at the end of the simulation increases from 115 to 155 MeV per nucleon (about 35%) when the plasma shutter is included in the simulation. The same effect is also observed for the circular polarization, where the maximal energy increase is even slightly higher (about 44%). Moreover, in the case of linear polarization, the divergence of the accelerated ion beam in the x-z plane (Figure 11c) significantly decreases as the ions are focused towards the laser axis in the plane perpendicular to the laser polarization. This beam-like structure is visible in Figure 10 behind the silver target (green color) around the laser axis. The shutter also has a positive effect on the beam divergence in the x–y plane, as shown in Figure 11d; this effect was ascribed to the steep-front generation. The transverse instability in ion density (similar to the instability in Figure 8a) is also reduced when the shutter is included (and the steep-front is generated); see the full discussion in [79]. This finding corresponds to the results discussed above. In addition, two (or a series of) plasma shutters can be used to mitigate the prepulses accompanying the main pulse, thus also improving the laser contrast. The double-shutter scenario was investigated using a combination of 2D PIC and hydrodynamic simulations in [79]. The first shutter can withstand the assumed sub-ns prepulse (treatment of ns and ps prepulses by other techniques is assumed; alternatively increasing the thickness of the first shutter may filter out longer prepulses), whereas the steep front generation and the local intensity increase occurred via interaction with the second non-expanded shutter. The increase in the maximal ion energy compared to the 2D simulation without any shutter is also demonstrated in this case. A prototype of such a double shutter is presented and the design of the whole shutter-target setup is discussed in [79].

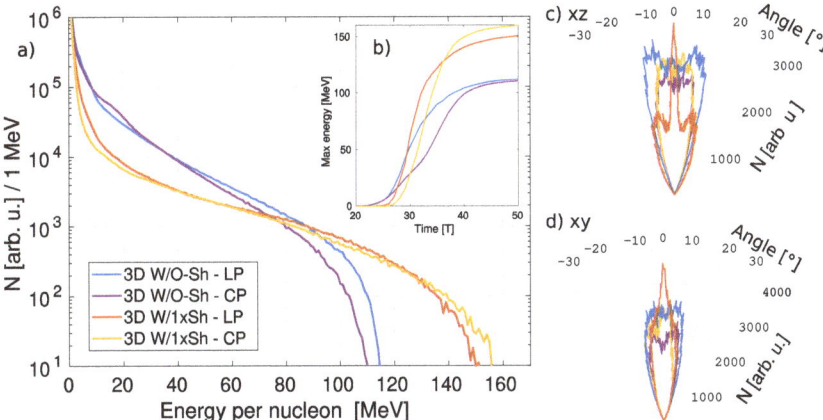

Figure 11. Properties of silver ions from the 3D simulations with the plasma shutter (W/1xSh) and without (W/O-sh) for linear (LP) and circular (CP) polarization. (**a**) Energy spectra at the end of the simulation ($t = 70\,T$), (**b**) time evolution of the maximal energy. Angular distributions of ions with energy over 55 MeV per nucleon in the x-z plane (**c**) and x-y plane (**d**). Source: [79]. Figures reprinted under the terms of the Creative Commons Attribution 4.0.

According to our findings, the plasma shutter provides a promising possible solution to the question of target stability via steep-front laser pulse generation. However, further research and optimization is required for its application for the interaction of 100 PW class lasers with double-layer targets.

4. Discussion

In this work, we review our results on the prospect of improving the quality and properties of protons accelerated by future laser systems using cryogenic targets. It is shown that, for these low density targets, the RPA mechanism can become the dominant acceleration regime. The domination is stronger with increasing laser intensity. The use of structured double-layered targets with interface corrugation in our simulations results in the occurrence of a relativistic instability influenced by the target geometry. Its development leads to the generation of a high-density and high-energy proton bunch. This bunch is accelerated by the dominant RPA mechanism as a compact structure, resulting in a proton beam of high quality. It includes low divergence, transverse emittance, and energy spread of accelerated protons. This beam is not developed in the reference cases without the corrugation on the target interface.

We further discuss the stability of this laser–target interaction. Another instability arising rather from the laser interaction with the target surface (with shorter wavelength compared to the interface corrugation assumed) needs to be reduced in order to generate the high-quality proton bunch. It is shown that the development of this short-wavelength instability is mitigated using a steep-front laser pulse. We propose the use of the plasma shutter to obtain the required laser pulse shape. Although a part of the laser pulse energy would be lost, the transmitted laser pulse will gain the steep-front time profile and locally increase the peak pulse intensity. This concept has been shown advantageous for ion acceleration using a PW-class laser pulse, improving both the maximal ion energy and beam properties [79].

The optimization of shutter parameters for use with the structured targets and laser systems with higher power assumed in this work will require additional research. The fully 3D simulation of this concept will be performed in the future.

Author Contributions: M.M. wrote the bulk of the manuscript, carried out most of the the simulations, and analyzed the results; J.P. carried out the 3D simulations in Section 3.1; K.N. contributed by determining simulation parameters and analysis of the instability in Section 3.2; M.J. analyzed and visualized the data of the plasma shutter in Figure 9a; P.V. helped to prepare the appendix about virtual reality; O.K. helped with the analysis of results regarding the plasma shutter in Section 3.3; S.V.B. provided overall supervision. All the authors have contributed to preparation and correction of this paper. All authors have read and agreed to the published version of the manuscript.

Funding: Portions of this research were carried out at ELI Beamlines, a European user facility operated by the Institute of Physics of the Academy of Sciences of the Czech Republic. Our work is supported by projects High Field Initiative (CZ.02.1.01/0.0/0.0/15_003/0000449) and Center of Advanced Applied Sciences (CZ.02.1.01/0.0/0.0/16_019/0000778) from the European Regional Development Fund. This work was supported by the Ministry of Education, Youth and Sports of the Czech Republic through the e-INFRA CZ (ID:90140). The support of Grant Agency of the Czech Technical University in Prague is appreciated, grant no. SGS22/185/OHK4/3T/14.

Data Availability Statement: The datasets generated and analyzed during the current study are available from the corresponding author on reasonable request.

Acknowledgments: We appreciate the collaboration with Virtual Beamline team of ELI Beamlines Centre, namely M. Kecova, P. Janecka, and J. Grosz with the work done towards the virtual reality visualization of our results. The discussions with G. Korn from ELI Beamlines are appreciated.

Conflicts of Interest: The authors declare no conflict of interest.

Abbreviations

The following abbreviations are used in this manuscript:

RPA	Radiation Pressure Acceleration
TNSA	Target Normal Sheath Acceleration
RTI	Rayleigh–Taylor Instability
RMI	Richtmyer–Meshkov Instability
HL	Heavy-Light
LH	Light-Heavy
HL-WO	HL without Modulation
L2	Light Single-Layer with the Same Thickness as HL
HL-FF	HL with Full-Front Laser Pulse
L2-SM	L2 with Surface Modulation
W/O-Sh	Without Plasma Shutter
W/1xSh	With Plasma Shutter
VBL	Virtual BeamLine
VR	Virtual Reality

Appendix A. Virtual Reality Visualization

Virtual reality (VR) technology is receiving more and more attention in the field of scientific visualization. It utilizes computational power and human–machine interaction concepts to emulate the effect of a 3D world. The audience uses a VR headset (i.e., a device worn on the head having small display(s), with embedded lenses and semi-transparent mirrors) and VR controllers to interact with the objects representing the scientific datasets and explore their complicated spatial and temporal structures in a way that makes them easy to understand.

At ELI Beamlines, we use a custom WebGL [113] render solution in the form of a complex web client–server application running inside a regular web browser. The application, called Virtual Beamline—VBL [114], renders the output of interactive visualization in real time (i.e., at sufficiently high frame rates) to user's regular and VR displays. The VBL application has been used not only for research itself, but also for educational purposes and science popularization. The use of the VR stations located at the atrium of ELI Beamlines is shown in the upper part of Figure A1, running the visualization discussed in Section 3.1.

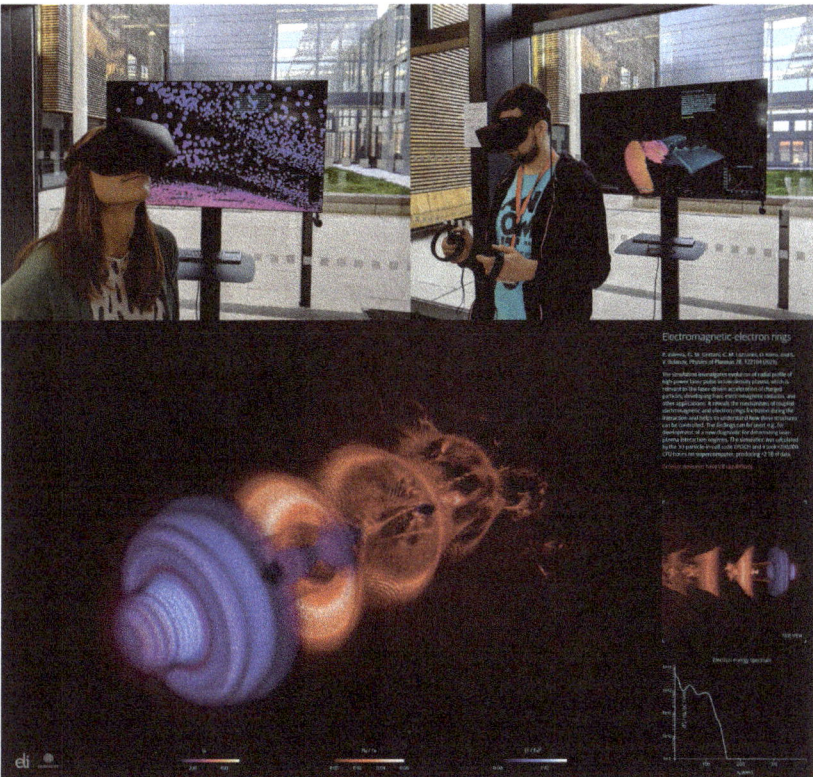

Figure A1. VBL application. (**top**) The use of the VBL application on the VR stations at ELI Beamlines (photo from [83]). (**bottom**) Example of a visualization based on the 3D PIC simulation data [116] using the VBL application.

The VBL application can visualize multi-dimensional mesh- and particle-based data that may be obtained from computer simulations or experimental measurements. The raw data must be preprocessed and converted to binary buffers that the application can read. At this point, one should also ensure that the size of the processed data complies with the capabilities of the machine used for the visualization. Finally, the resulting buffers together with a scene description in a form of a JSON [115] file are stored on a web server acting as a data input for the visualization engine of the VBL application. More details about the VBL application can be found in [85].

As can be seen in Figure A1, the application window contains multiple viewports that may show, apart from the full 3D view, the data projections along a certain plane or axis, time-dependent plots of a selected parameter, textual and numerical data, etc. On top of that, there is an additional layer containing a description of displayed dataset as well as a graphical user interface (GUI). It utilizes d3.js library for graphical elements and dat.GUI library for the interface providing animation control and layer visibility management. GUI controls together with VR controllers enable users to interact with a displayed scene by moving and scaling it in the 3D space, filtering its content, and navigating in the animation timeline.

The bottom part of Figure A1 shows an example of a visualization based on the 3D PIC simulation data. The simulation investigates evolution of the radial profile of a high-power laser pulse in a low-density plasma [116]. The VBL application helped considerably to reveal the mechanisms of coupled electromagnetic and electron rings formation during the interaction and to understand how these structures can be controlled. The simulation was calculated by the EPOCH code [80]; it took $\approx 2 \times 10^5$ core-hours, producing ≈ 2 TB of raw data. The final size of the data processed for the purpose of the visualization in the VBL application is ≈ 10 GB. The interactive visualization is available online [117] (note that the client device is required to have at least 16 GB of free memory and the VR mode has been tested for Oculus Rift in Firefox). The visualization shown in Figure 3 and the upper part of Figure A1 has lower size (as it is based on 2D simulation) and is available online [84]. Other visualizations made at ELI Beamlines can be viewed online [114], including the shutter visualization [112] from Figure 10.

References

1. Bulanov, S.V.; Esirkepov, T.; Khoroshkov, V.S.; Kuznetsov, A.V.; Pegoraro, F. Oncological hadrontherapy with laser ion accelerators. *Phys. Lett. A* **2002**, *299*, 240–247. [CrossRef]
2. Bulanov, S.V.; Wilkens, J.J.; Esirkepov, T.Z.; Korn, G.; Kraft, G.; Kraft, S.D.; Molls, M.; Khoroshkov, V.S. Laser ion acceleration for hadron therapy. *Physics-Uspekhi* **2014**, *57*, 1149–1179. [CrossRef]
3. Tajima, T. Prospect for compact medical laser accelerators. *J. Jpn. Soc. Therap. Radiol. Oncol.* **1997**, *9*, 83–85.
4. Roth, M.; Cowan, T.E.; Key, M.H.; Hatchett, S.P.; Brown, C.; Fountain, W.; Johnson, J.; Pennington, D.M.; Snavely, R.A.; Wilks, S.C.; et al. Fast ignition by intense laser-accelerated proton beams. *Phys. Rev. Lett.* **2001**, *86*, 436–439. [CrossRef] [PubMed]
5. Atzeni, S.; Temporal, M.; Honrubia, J.J. A first analysis of fast ignition of precompressed ICF fuel by laser-accelerated protons. *Nucl. Fusion* **2002**, *42*, L1. [CrossRef]
6. Nishiuchi, M.; Sakaki, H.; Esirkepov, T.Z.; Nishio, K.; Pikuz, T.A.; Faenov, A.Y.; Skobelev, I.Y.; Orlandi, R.; Sako, H.; Pirozhkov, A.S.; et al. Acceleration of highly charged GeV Fe ions from a low-Z substrate by intense femtosecond laser. *Phys. Plasmas* **2015**, *22*, 033107. [CrossRef]
7. Daido, H.; Nishiuchi, M.; Pirozhkov, A.S. Review of laser-driven ion sources and their applications. *Rep. Prog. Phys.* **2012**, *75*, 056401. [CrossRef]
8. Macchi, A.; Borghesi, M.; Passoni, M. Ion acceleration by superintense laser-plasma interaction. *Rev. Mod. Phys.* **2013**, *85*, 751–793. [CrossRef]
9. Passoni, M.; Arioli, F.M.; Cialfi, L.; Dellasega, D.; Fedeli, L.; Formenti, A.; Giovannelli, A.C.; Maffini, A.; Mirani, F.; Pazzaglia, A.; et al. Advanced laser-driven ion sources and their applications in materials and nuclear science. *Plasma Phys. Control. Fusion* **2019**, *62*, 014022. [CrossRef]
10. Garcia, S.; Chatain, D.; Perin, J.P. Continuous production of a thin ribbon of solid hydrogen. *Laser Part. Beams* **2014**, *32*, 569–575. [CrossRef]
11. Margarone, D.; Velyhan, A.; Dostal, J.; Ullschmied, J.; Perin, J.P.; Chatain, D.; Garcia, S.; Bonnay, P.; Pisarczyk, T.; Dudzak, R.; et al. Proton acceleration driven by a nanosecond laser from a cryogenic thin solid-hydrogen ribbon. *Phys. Rev. X* **2016**, *6*, 041030. [CrossRef]
12. Margarone, D.; Cirrone, G.A.P.; Cuttone, G.; Amico, A.; Andò, L.; Borghesi, M.; Bulanov, S.S.; Bulanov, S.V.; Chatain, D.; Fajstavr, A.; et al. ELIMAIA: A Laser-Driven Ion Accelerator for Multidisciplinary Applications. *Quantum Beam Sci.* **2018**, *2*, 8. [CrossRef]
13. Chagovets, T.; Stanček, S.; Giuffrida, L.; Velyhan, A.; Tryus, M.; Grepl, F.; Istokskaia, V.; Kantarelou, V.; Wiste, T.; Hernandez Martin, J.; et al. Automation of Target Delivery and Diagnostic Systems for High Repetition Rate Laser-Plasma Acceleration. *Appl. Sci.* **2021**, *11*, 1680. [CrossRef]
14. Weber, S.; Bechet, S.; Borneis, S.; Brabec, L.; Bučka, M.; Chacon-Golcher, E.; Ciappina, M.; DeMarco, M.; Fajstavr, A.; Falk, K.; et al. P3: An installation for high-energy density plasma physics and ultra-high intensity laser–matter interaction at ELI-Beamlines. *Matter Radiat. Extrem.* **2017**, *2*, 149–176. [CrossRef]
15. Condamine, F.P.; Jourdain, N.; Hernandez, J.C.; Taylor, M.; Bohlin, H.; Fajstavr, A.; Jeong, T.M.; Kumar, D.; Laštovička, T.; Renner, O.; et al. High-repetition rate solid target delivery system for PW-class laser–matter interaction at ELI Beamlines. *Rev. Sci. Instrum.* **2021**, *92*, 063504. [CrossRef]
16. Jourdain, N.; Chaulagain, U.; Havlík, M.; Kramer, D.; Kumar, D.; Majerová, I.; Tikhonchuk, V.T.; Korn, G.; Weber, S. The L4n laser beamline of the P3-installation: Towards high-repetition rate high-energy density physics at ELI-Beamlines. *Matter Radiat. Extrem.* **2021**, *6*, 015401. [CrossRef]
17. Papadopoulos, D.; Zou, J.; Le Blanc, C.; Cheriaux, G.; Georges, P.; Druon, F.; Mennerat, G.; Martin, L.; Fréneaux, A.; Beluze, A.; et al. The Apollon 10 PW laser: Experimental and theoretical investigation of the temporal characteristics. *High Power Laser Sci. Eng.* **2016**, *4*, E34. [CrossRef]
18. Zamfir, N.V. Nuclear Physics with 10 PW laser beams at Extreme Light Infrastructure-Nuclear Physics (ELI-NP). *Eur. Phys. J. Spec. Top.* **2014**, *223*, 1221–1227. [CrossRef]
19. Shao, B.; Li, Y.; Peng, Y.; Wang, P.; Qian, J.; Leng, Y.; Li, R. Broad-bandwidth high-temporal-contrast carrier-envelope-phase-stabilized laser seed for 100 PW lasers. *Opt. Lett.* **2020**, *45*, 2215–2218. [CrossRef]
20. Esirkepov, T.; Borghesi, M.; Bulanov, S.V.; Mourou, G.; Tajima, T. Highly efficient relativistic-ion generation in the laser-piston regime. *Phys. Rev. Lett.* **2004**, *92*, 175003. [CrossRef]

21. Wilks, S.C.; Langdon, A.B.; Cowan, T.E.; Roth, M.; Singh, M.; Hatchett, S.; Key, M.H.; Pennington, D.; MacKinnon, A.; Snavely, R.A. Energetic proton generation in ultra-intense laser–solid interactions. *Phys. Plasmas* **2001**, *8*, 542–549. [CrossRef]
22. Snavely, R.A.; Key, M.H.; Hatchett, S.P.; Cowan, T.E.; Roth, M.; Phillips, T.W.; Stoyer, M.A.; Henry, E.A.; Sangster, T.C.; Singh, M.S.; et al. Intense High-Energy Proton Beams from Petawatt-Laser Irradiation of Solids. *Phys. Rev. Lett.* **2000**, *85*, 2945–2948. [CrossRef] [PubMed]
23. Psikal, J.; Matys, M. Dominance of hole-boring radiation pressure acceleration regime with thin ribbon of ionized solid hydrogen. *Plasma Phys. Control. Fusion* **2018**, *60*, 044003. [CrossRef]
24. Macchi, A.; Cattani, F.; Liseykina, T.V.; Cornolti, F. Laser Acceleration of Ion Bunches at the Front Surface of Overdense Plasmas. *Phys. Rev. Lett.* **2005**, *94*, 165003. [CrossRef]
25. Schwoerer, H.; Pfotenhauer, S.; Jäckel, O.; Amthor, K.U.; Liesfeld, B.; Ziegler, W.; Sauerbrey, R.; Ledingham, K.W.D.; Esirkepov, T. Laser-plasma acceleration of quasi-monoenergetic protons from microstructured targets. *Nature* **2006**, *439*, 445–448. [CrossRef] [PubMed]
26. Hegelich, B.M.; Albright, B.J.; Cobble, J.; Flippo, K.; Letzring, S.; Paffett, M.; Ruhl, H.; Schreiber, J.; Schulze, R.K.; Fernández, J.C. Laser acceleration of quasi-monoenergetic MeV ion beams. *Nature* **2006**, *439*, 441–444. [CrossRef]
27. Kar, S.; Borghesi, M.; Bulanov, S.V.; Key, M.H.; Liseykina, T.V.; Macchi, A.; Mackinnon, A.J.; Patel, P.K.; Romagnani, L.; Schiavi, A.; et al. Plasma Jets Driven by Ultraintense-Laser Interaction with Thin Foils. *Phys. Rev. Lett.* **2008**, *100*, 225004. [CrossRef]
28. Henig, A.; Steinke, S.; Schnürer, M.; Sokollik, T.; Hörlein, R.; Kiefer, D.; Jung, D.; Schreiber, J.; Hegelich, B.M.; Yan, X.Q.; et al. Radiation-Pressure Acceleration of Ion Beams Driven by Circularly Polarized Laser Pulses. *Phys. Rev. Lett.* **2009**, *103*, 245003. [CrossRef]
29. Kar, S.; Kakolee, K.F.; Qiao, B.; Macchi, A.; Cerchez, M.; Doria, D.; Geissler, M.; McKenna, P.; Neely, D.; Osterholz, J.; et al. Ion Acceleration in Multispecies Targets Driven by Intense Laser Radiation Pressure. *Phys. Rev. Lett.* **2012**, *109*, 185006. [CrossRef]
30. Kim, I.J.; Pae, K.H.; Choi, I.W.; Lee, C.L.; Kim, H.T.; Singhal, H.; Sung, J.H.; Lee, S.K.; Lee, H.W.; Nickles, P.V.; et al. Radiation pressure acceleration of protons to 93 MeV with circularly polarized petawatt laser pulses. *Phys. Plasmas* **2016**, *23*, 070701. [CrossRef]
31. Henig, A.; Kiefer, D.; Markey, K.; Gautier, D.C.; Flippo, K.A.; Letzring, S.; Johnson, R.P.; Shimada, T.; Yin, L.; Albright, B.J.; et al. Enhanced Laser-Driven Ion Acceleration in the Relativistic Transparency Regime. *Phys. Rev. Lett.* **2009**, *103*, 045002. [CrossRef] [PubMed]
32. Yan, X.Q.; Lin, C.; Sheng, Z.M.; Guo, Z.Y.; Liu, B.C.; Lu, Y.R.; Fang, J.X.; Chen, J.E. Generating High-Current Monoenergetic Proton Beams by a CircularlyPolarized Laser Pulse in the Phase-StableAcceleration Regime. *Phys. Rev. Lett.* **2008**, *100*, 135003. [CrossRef] [PubMed]
33. Yan, X.Q.; Tajima, T.; Hegelich, M.; Yin, L.; Habs, D. Theory of laser ion acceleration from a foil target of nanometer thickness. *Appl. Phys. B* **2009**, *98*, 711–721. [CrossRef]
34. Tajima, T.; Habs, D.; Yan, X. *Laser Acceleration of Ions for Radiation Therapy*; World Scientific: Singapore, 2009; pp. 201–228. [CrossRef]
35. Naumova, N.; Schlegel, T.; Tikhonchuk, V.T.; Labaune, C.; Sokolov, I.V.; Mourou, G. Hole Boring in a DT Pellet and Fast-Ion Ignition with Ultraintense Laser Pulses. *Phys. Rev. Lett.* **2009**, *102*, 025002. [CrossRef] [PubMed]
36. Robinson, A.P.L.; Gibbon, P.; Zepf, M.; Kar, S.; Evans, R.G.; Bellei, C. Relativistically correct hole-boring and ion acceleration by circularly polarized laser pulses. *Plasma Phys. Control. Fusion* **2009**, *51*, 024004. [CrossRef]
37. Bulanov, S.V.; Esirkepov, T.Z.; Kando, M.; Pegoraro, F.; Bulanov, S.S.; Geddes, C.G.R.; Schroeder, C.B.; Esarey, E.; Leemans, W.P. Ion acceleration from thin foil and extended plasma targets by slow electromagnetic wave and related ion-ion beam instability. *Phys. Plasmas* **2012**, *19*, 103105. [CrossRef]
38. Macchi, A.; Veghini, S.; Pegoraro, F. "Light Sail" Acceleration Reexamined. *Phys. Rev. Lett.* **2009**, *103*, 085003. [CrossRef]
39. Mackenroth, F.; Bulanov, S.S. Tailored laser pulse chirp to maintain optimum radiation pressure acceleration of ions. *Phys. Plasmas* **2019**, *26*, 023103. [CrossRef]
40. Kar, S.; Kakolee, K.F.; Cerchez, M.; Doria, D.; Macchi, A.; McKenna, P.; Neely, D.; Osterholz, J.; Quinn, K.; Ramakrishna, B.; et al. Experimental investigation of hole boring and light sail regimes of RPA by varying laser and target parameters. *Plasma Phys. Control. Fusion* **2013**, *55*, 124030. [CrossRef]
41. Matys, M.; Nishihara, K.; Kecova, M.; Psikal, J.; Korn, G.; Bulanov, S.V. Laser-driven generation of collimated quasi-monoenergetic proton beam using double-layer target with modulated interface. *High Energy Density Phys.* **2020**, *36*, 100844. [CrossRef]
42. Bulanov, S.V.; Khoroshkov, V.S. Feasibility of using laser ion accelerators in proton therapy. *Plasma Phys. Rep.* **2002**, *28*, 453–456. [CrossRef]
43. Bulanov, S.V.; Esirkepov, T.Z.; Kamenets, F.F.; Kato, Y.; Kuznetsov, A.V.; Nishihara, K.; Pegoraro, F.; Tajima, T.; Khoroshkov, V.S. Generation of high-quality charged particle beams during the acceleration of ions by high-power laser radiation. *Plasma Phys. Rep.* **2002**, *28*, 975–991. [CrossRef]
44. Esirkepov, T.; Bulanov, S.V.; Nishihara, K.; Tajima, T.; Pegoraro, F.; Khoroshkov, V.S.; Mima, K.; Daido, H.; Kato, Y.; Kitagawa, Y.; et al. Proposed double-layer target for the generation of high-quality laser-accelerated ion beams. *Phys. Rev. Lett.* **2002**, *89*, 175003. [CrossRef] [PubMed]
45. Pegoraro, F.; Bulanov, S.V. Photon bubbles and ion acceleration in a plasma dominated by the radiation pressure of an electromagnetic pulse. *Phys. Rev. Lett.* **2007**, *99*, 065002. [CrossRef]

46. Echkina, E.Y.; Inovenkov, I.N.; Esirkepov, T.Z.; Pegoraro, F.; Borghesi, M.; Bulanov, S.V. Dependence of the ion energy on the parameters of the laser pulse and target in the radiation-pressure-dominated regime of acceleration. *Plasma Phys. Rep.* **2010**, *36*, 15–29. [CrossRef]
47. Lord Rayleigh. Investigation of the character of the equilibrium of an incompressible heavy fluid of variable density. *Proc. Lond. Math. Soc.* **1882**, *14*, 170–177. [CrossRef]
48. Taylor, G. The instability of liquid surfaces when accelerated in a direction perpendicular to their planes. I. *Proc. R. Soc. Lond. Ser. A Math. Phys. Sci.* **1950**, *201*, 192–196. [CrossRef]
49. Richtmyer, R.D. Taylor instability in shock acceleration of compressible fluids. *Commun. Pure Appl. Math.* **1960**, *13*, 297–319. [CrossRef]
50. Meshkov, E.E. Instability of the interface of two gases accelerated by a shock wave. *Fluid Dyn.* **1969**, *4*, 101–104. [CrossRef]
51. Zhou, Y. Rayleigh–Taylor and Richtmyer–Meshkov instability induced flow, turbulence, and mixing. I. *Phys. Rep.* **2017**, *720-722*, 1–136. [CrossRef]
52. Palmer, C.A.; Schreiber, J.; Nagel, S.R.; Dover, N.P.; Bellei, C.; Beg, F.N.; Bott, S.; Clarke, R.J.; Dangor, A.E.; Hassan, S.M.; et al. Rayleigh-Taylor instability of an ultrathin foil accelerated by the radiation pressure of an intense laser. *Phys. Rev. Lett.* **2012**, *108*, 225002. [CrossRef] [PubMed]
53. Yang, Y.; Zhang, Q.; Sharp, D.H. Small amplitude theory of Richtmyer-Meshkov instability. *Phys. Fluids* **1994**, *6*, 1856–1873. [CrossRef]
54. Wouchuk, J.G.; Nishihara, K. Asymptotic growth in the linear Richtmyer-Meshkov instability. *Phys. Plasmas* **1997**, *4*, 1028–1038. [CrossRef]
55. Nishihara, K.; Wouchuk, J.G.; Matsuoka, C.; Ishizaki, R.; Zhakhovsky, V.V. Richtmyer-Meshkov instability: Theory of linear and nonlinear evolution. *Philos. Trans. R. Soc. A Math. Phys. Eng. Sci.* **2010**, *368*, 1769–1807. [CrossRef] [PubMed]
56. Mohseni, F.; Mendoza, M.; Succi, S.; Herrmann, H.J. Relativistic effects on the Richtmyer-Meshkov instability. *Phys. Rev. D Part. Fields Gravit. Cosmol.* **2014**, *90*, 125028. [CrossRef]
57. Matsuoka, C.; Nishihara, K.; Sano, T. Nonlinear Dynamics of Non-uniform Current-Vortex Sheets in Magnetohydrodynamic Flows. *J. Nonlinear Sci.* **2017**, *27*, 531–572. [CrossRef]
58. Zhou, Y.; Clark, T.T.; Clark, D.S.; Gail Glendinning, S.; Aaron Skinner, M.; Huntington, C.M.; Hurricane, O.A.; Dimits, A.M.; Remington, B.A. Turbulent mixing and transition criteria of flows induced by hydrodynamic instabilities. *Phys. Plasmas* **2019**, *26*, 080901. [CrossRef]
59. Zhou, Y.; Williams, R.J.; Ramaprabhu, P.; Groom, M.; Thornber, B.; Hillier, A.; Mostert, W.; Rollin, B.; Balachandar, S.; Powell, P.D.; et al. Rayleigh–Taylor and Richtmyer–Meshkov instabilities: A journey through scales. *Phys. D Nonlinear Phenom.* **2021**, *423*, 132838. [CrossRef]
60. Hester, J.J. The Crab Nebula: An Astrophysical Chimera. *Annu. Rev. Astron. Astrophys.* **2008**, *46*, 127–155. [CrossRef]
61. Lindl, J.D.; Mccrory, R.L.; Campbell, E.M. Progress toward Ignition and Burn Propagation in Inertial Confinement Fusion. *Phys. Today* **1992**, *45*, 32–40. [CrossRef]
62. Waddell, J.T.; Niederhaus, C.E.; Jacobs, J.W. Experimental study of Rayleigh–Taylor instability: Low Atwood number liquid systems with single-mode initial perturbations. *Phys. Fluids* **2001**, *13*, 1263–1273. [CrossRef]
63. Niederhaus, C.E.; Jacobs, J.W. Experimental study of the Richtmyer-Meshkov instability of incompressible fluids. *J. Fluid Mech.* **2003**, *485*, 243–277. [CrossRef]
64. Velikovich, A.L. Analytic theory of Richtmyer-Meshkov instability for the case of reflected rarefaction wave. *Phys. Fluids* **1996**, *8*, 1666–1679. [CrossRef]
65. Wouchuk, J.G.; Nishihara, K. Linear perturbation growth at a shocked interface. *Phys. Plasmas* **1996**, *3*, 3761–3776. [CrossRef]
66. Klimo, O.; Psikal, J.; Limpouch, J.; Tikhonchuk, V.T. Monoenergetic ion beams from ultrathin foils irradiated by ultrahigh-contrast circularly polarized laser pulses. *Phys. Rev. Spec. Top. Accel. Beams* **2008**, *11*, 031301. [CrossRef]
67. Robinson, A.P.; Zepf, M.; Kar, S.; Evans, R.G.; Bellei, C. Radiation pressure acceleration of thin foils with circularly polarized laser pulses. *New J. Phys.* **2008**, *10*, 013021. [CrossRef]
68. Wan, Y.; Pai, C.H.; Zhang, C.J.; Li, F.; Wu, Y.P.; Hua, J.F.; Lu, W.; Gu, Y.Q.; Silva, L.O.; Joshi, C.; et al. Physical Mechanism of the Transverse Instability in Radiation Pressure Ion Acceleration. *Phys. Rev. Lett.* **2016**, *117*, 234801. [CrossRef]
69. Wan, Y.; Pai, C.H.; Zhang, C.J.; Li, F.; Wu, Y.P.; Hua, J.F.; Lu, W.; Joshi, C.; Mori, W.B.; Malka, V. Physical mechanism of the electron-ion coupled transverse instability in laser pressure ion acceleration for different regimes. *Phys. Rev. E* **2018**, *98*, 013202. [CrossRef]
70. Vshivkov, V.A.; Naumova, N.M.; Pegoraro, F.; Bulanov, S.V. Nonlinear electrodynamics of the interaction of ultra-intense laser pulses with a thin foil. *Phys. Plasmas* **1998**, *5*, 2727–2741. [CrossRef]
71. Reed, S.A.; Matsuoka, T.; Bulanov, S.; Tampo, M.; Chvykov, V.; Kalintchenko, G.; Rousseau, P.; Yanovsky, V.; Kodama, R.; Litzenberg, D.W.; et al. Relativistic plasma shutter for ultraintense laser pulses. *Appl. Phys. Lett.* **2009**, *94*, 201117. [CrossRef]
72. Palaniyappan, S.; Hegelich, B.M.; Wu, H.C.; Jung, D.; Gautier, D.C.; Yin, L.; Albright, B.J.; Johnson, R.P.; Shimada, T.; Letzring, S.; et al. Dynamics of relativistic transparency and optical shuttering in expanding overdense plasmas. *Nat. Phys.* **2012**, *8*, 763–769. [CrossRef]

73. Wei, W.Q.; Yuan, X.H.; Fang, Y.; Ge, Z.Y.; Ge, X.L.; Yang, S.; Li, Y.F.; Liao, G.Q.; Zhang, Z.; Liu, F.; et al. Plasma optical shutter in ultraintense laser-foil interaction. *Phys. Plasmas* **2017**, *24*, 113111. [CrossRef]
74. Matys, M.; Klimo, O.; Psikal, J.; Bulanov, S.V. Simulation studies on transmissivity of silicon nitride plasma shutter for laser pulse contrast enhancement. In Proceedings of the 45th EPS Conference on Plasma Physics, EPS, Prague, Czech Republic, 2–6 July 2018; Coda, S., Berndt, J., Lapenta, G., Mantsinen, M., Michaut, C., Weber, S., Eds.; 2018; pp. 1332–1335.
75. Jirka, M.; Klimo, O.; Gu, Y.J.; Weber, S. Enhanced photon emission from a double-layer target at moderate laser intensities. *Sci. Rep.* **2020**, *10*, 8887. [CrossRef] [PubMed]
76. Matys, M.; Bulanov, S.; Kecova, M.; Kucharik, M.; Jirka, M.; Janecka, P.; Psikal, J.; Nikl, J.; Grosz, J.; Korn, G.; et al. Ion acceleration enhancement by laser-pulse shaping via plasma shutter. In Proceedings of the Laser Acceleration of Electrons, Protons, and Ions VI, Online, 19–23 April 2021; Bulanov, S.S., Schreiber, J., Schroeder, C.B., Eds.; SPIE: Bellingham, WA, USA, 2021; Volume 11779. [CrossRef]
77. Nikl, J.; Jirka, M.; Matys, M.; Kuchařík, M.; Klimo, O. Contrast enhancement of ultra-intense laser pulses by relativistic plasma shutter. In Proceedings of the High Power Lasers and Applications, Online, 19–29 April 2021; Hein, J., Butcher, T.J., Bakule, P., Haefner, C.L., Korn, G., Silva, L.O., Eds.; SPIE: Bellingham, WA, USA, 2021; Volume 11777, p. 117770X. [CrossRef]
78. Jirka, M.; Klimo, O.; Matys, M. Relativistic plasma aperture for laser intensity enhancement. *Phys. Rev. Res.* **2021**, *3*, 033175. [CrossRef]
79. Matys, M.; Bulanov, S.V.; Kucharik, M.; Jirka, M.; Nikl, J.; Kecova, M.; Proska, J.; Psikal, J.; Korn, G.; Klimo, O. Design of plasma shutters for improved heavy ion acceleration by ultra-intense laser pulses. *New J. Phys.* **2022**, *24*, 113046. [CrossRef]
80. Arber, T.D.; Bennett, K.; Brady, C.S.; Lawrence-Douglas, A.; Ramsay, M.G.; Sircombe, N.J.; Gillies, P.; Evans, R.G.; Schmitz, H.; Bell, A.R.; et al. Contemporary particle-in-cell approach to laser-plasma modelling. *Plasma Phys. Control. Fusion* **2015**, *57*, 113001. [CrossRef]
81. Ridgers, C.P.; Kirk, J.G.; Duclous, R.; Blackburn, T.G.; Brady, C.S.; Bennett, K.; Arber, T.D.; Bell, A.R. Modelling gamma-ray photon emission and pair production in high-intensity laser-matter interactions. *J. Comput. Phys.* **2014**, *260*, 273–285. [CrossRef]
82. Bulanov, S.S.; Esarey, E.; Schroeder, C.B.; Bulanov, S.V.; Esirkepov, T.Z.; Kando, M.; Pegoraro, F.; Leemans, W.P. Radiation pressure acceleration: The factors limiting maximum attainable ion energy. *Phys. Plasmas* **2016**, *23*, 056703. [CrossRef]
83. Matys, M.; Psikal, J.; Danielova, M.; Valenta, P.; Bulanov, S.V. Laser-driven Ion Acceleration Using Cryogenic Hydrogen Targets. In Proceedings of the Supercomputing in Science and Engineering 2017–2018, Ostrava, Czechia, 21–25 January 2019; Pešatová, K., Poláková, B., Cawley, J., Červenková, Z., Eds.; VSB–Technical University of Ostrava: Ostrava, Czechia, 2019; pp. 149–151. ISBN 978-80-248-4289-9.
84. Laser-Driven Proton Acceleration from Cryogenic Hydrogen Target. Available online: https://vbl.eli-beams.eu/mm-track/ (accessed on 2 June 2022).
85. Danielova, M.; Janecka, P.; Grosz, J.; Holy, A. Interactive 3D Visualizations of Laser Plasma Experiments on the Web and in VR. In Proceedings of the EuroVis 2019-Posters, Porto, Portugal, 3–7 June 2019; Madeiras Pereira, J., Raidou, R.G., Eds.; The Eurographics Association: Porto, Portugal, 2019. [CrossRef]
86. Higginson, A.; Gray, R.J.; King, M.; Dance, R.J.; Williamson, S.D.; Butler, N.M.; Wilson, R.; Capdessus, R.; Armstrong, C.; Green, J.S.; et al. Near-100 MeV protons via a laser-driven transparency-enhanced hybrid acceleration scheme. *Nat. Commun.* **2018**, *9*, 724. [CrossRef]
87. Qiao, B.; Kar, S.; Geissler, M.; Gibbon, P.; Zepf, M.; Borghesi, M. Dominance of Radiation Pressure in Ion Acceleration with Linearly Polarized Pulses at Intensities of 10(21) W cm(-2). *Phys. Rev. Lett.* **2012**, *108*, 115002. [CrossRef]
88. Yin, L.; Albright, B.J.; Bowers, K.J.; Jung, D.; Fernández, J.C.; Hegelich, B.M. Three-Dimensional Dynamics of Breakout Afterburner Ion Acceleration Using High-Contrast Short-Pulse Laser and Nanoscale Targets. *Phys. Rev. Lett.* **2011**, *107*, 045003. [CrossRef] [PubMed]
89. Liu, J.L.; Chen, M.; Zheng, J.; Sheng, Z.M.; Liu, C.S. Three dimensional effects on proton acceleration by intense laser solid target interaction. *Phys. Plasmas* **2013**, *20*, 063107. [CrossRef]
90. Bulanov, S.S.; Brantov, A.; Bychenkov, V.Y.; Chvykov, V.; Kalinchenko, G.; Matsuoka, T.; Rousseau, P.; Reed, S.; Yanovsky, V.; Litzenberg, D.W.; et al. Accelerating monoenergetic protons from ultrathin foils by flat-top laser pulses in the directed-Coulomb-explosion regime. *Phys. Rev. E* **2008**, *78*, 026412. [CrossRef] [PubMed]
91. Stark, D.J.; Yin, L.; Albright, B.J.; Guo, F. Effects of dimensionality on kinetic simulations of laser-ion acceleration in the transparency regime. *Phys. Plasmas* **2017**, *24*, 053103. [CrossRef]
92. Chen, M.; Pukhov, A.; Yu, T.P.; Sheng, Z.M. Enhanced collimated GeV monoenergetic ion acceleration from a shaped foil target irradiated by a circularly polarized laser pulse. *Phys. Rev. Lett.* **2009**, *103*, 024801. [CrossRef]
93. Matys, M.; Nishihara, K.; Danielova, M.; Psikal, J.; Korn, G.; Bulanov, V.S. Generation of collimated quasi-mono-energetic ion beams using a double layer target with interface modulations. In Proceedings of the Laser Acceleration of Electrons, Protons, and Ions V, Prague, Czech Republic, 1–3 April 2019; Esarey, E., Schroeder, C., Schreiber, J., Eds.; SPIE: Bellingham, WA, USA, 2019; Volume 11037, p. 110370Z. [CrossRef]
94. Matys, M.; Valenta, P.; Kecova, M.; Nishihara, K.; Psikal, J.; Esirkepov, T.Z.; Koga, J.K.; Necas, A.; Grittani, G.M.; Lazzarini, C.M.; et al. Laser-Driven Acceleration of Charged Particles. In *Supercomputing in Science and Engineering 2019–2020*; Vondrak, V., Tomas Kozubek, B.J., Eds.; VSB–Technical University of Ostrava: Ostrava, Czechia, 2021; pp. 86–88. ISBN 978-80-248-4567-8.
95. Floettmann, K. Some basic features of the beam emittance. *Phys. Rev. Spec. Top. Accel. Beams* **2003**, *6*, 80–86. [CrossRef]

96. Zhang, T.; Peng, S.X.; Wu, W.B.; Ren, H.T.; Zhang, J.F.; Wen, J.M.; Ma, T.H.; Jiang, Y.X.; Sun, J.; Guo, Z.Y.; et al. Practical 2.45-GHz microwave-driven Cs-free H- ion source developed at Peking University. *Chin. Phys. B* **2018**, *27*, 105208. [CrossRef]
97. Cowan, T.E.; Fuchs, J.; Ruhl, H.; Kemp, A.; Audebert, P.; Roth, M.; Stephens, R.; Barton, I.; Blazevic, A.; Brambrink, E.; et al. Ultralow emittance, multi-MeV proton beams from a laser virtual-cathode plasma accelerator. *Phys. Rev. Lett.* **2004**, *92*, 204801. [CrossRef]
98. Gu, Y.J.; Zhu, Z.; Li, X.F.; Yu, Q.; Huang, S.; Zhang, F.; Kong, Q.; Kawata, S. Stable long range proton acceleration driven by intense laser pulse with underdense plasmas. *Phys. Plasmas* **2014**, *21*, 063104. [CrossRef]
99. Bulanov, S.V.; Inovenkov, I.N.; Kirsanov, V.I.; Naumova, N.M.; Sakharov, A.S. Nonlinear depletion of ultrashort and relativistically strong laser pulses in an underdense plasma. *Phys. Fluids B* **1992**, *4*, 1935–1942. [CrossRef]
100. Bulanov, S.V.; Kirsanov, V.I.; Naumova, N.M.; Sakharov, A.S.; Shah, H.A.; Inovenkov, I.N. Stationary shock-front of a relativisticaliy strong electromagnetic radiation in an underdense plasma. *Phys. Scr.* **1993**, *47*, 209–213. [CrossRef]
101. Decker, C.D.; Mori, W.B.; Tzeng, K.C.; Katsouleas, T. The evolution of ultra-intense, short-pulse lasers in underdense plasmas. *Phys. Plasmas* **1996**, *3*, 2047–2056. [CrossRef]
102. Wang, H.; Lin, C.; Sheng, Z.; Liu, B.; Zhao, S.; Guo, Z.; Lu, Y.; He, X.; Chen, J.; Yan, X. Laser Shaping of a Relativistic Intense, Short Gaussian Pulse by a Plasma Lens. *Phys. Rev. Lett.* **1996**, *107*, 265002. [CrossRef] [PubMed]
103. Bin, J.; Ma, W.; Wang, H.; Streeter, M.; Kreuzer, C.; Kiefer, D.; Yeung, M.; Cousens, S.; Foster, P.; Dromey, B.; et al. Ion Acceleration Using Relativistic Pulse Shaping in Near-Critical-Density Plasmas. *Phys. Rev. Lett.* **2015**, *115*, 064801. [CrossRef] [PubMed]
104. Fedeli, L.; Formenti, A.; Cialfi, L.; Pazzaglia, A.; Passoni, M. Ultra-intense laser interaction with nanostructured near-critical plasmas. *Sci. Rep.* **2018**, *8*, 3834. [CrossRef]
105. Horný, V.; Chen, S.; Davoine, X.; Lelasseux, V.; Gremillet, L.; Fuchs, J. High-flux neutron generation by laser-accelerated ions from single- and double-layer targets. *Sci. Rep.* **2022**, *12*, 19767. [CrossRef]
106. Park, J.; Bulanov, S.; Bin, J.; Ji, Q.; Steinke, S.; Vay, J.; Geddes, C.; Schroeder, C.; Leemans, W.; Schenkel, T.; et al. Ion acceleration in laser generated megatesla magnetic vortex. *Phys. Plasmas* **2019**, *26*, 103108. [CrossRef]
107. Hakimi, S.; Obst-Huebl, L.; Huebl, A.; Nakamura, K.; Bulanov, S.; Steinke, S.; Leemans, W.; Kober, Z.; Ostermayr, T.; Schenkel, T.; et al. Laser–solid interaction studies enabled by the new capabilities of the iP2 BELLA PW beamline. *Phys. Plasmas* **2022**, *29*, 083102. [CrossRef]
108. Yogo, A.; Daido, H.; Bulanov, S.; Nemoto, K.; Oishi, Y.; Nayuki, T.; Fujii, T.; Ogura, K.; Orimo, S.; Sagisaka, A.; et al. Laser ion acceleration via control of the near-critical density target. *Phys. Rev. E* **2008**, *77*, 016401. [CrossRef]
109. Zwickl, B.M.; Shanks, W.E.; Jayich, A.M.; Yang, C.; Bleszynski Jayich, A.C.; Thompson, J.D.; Harris, J.G.E. High quality mechanical and optical properties of commercial silicon nitride membranes. *Appl. Phys. Lett.* **2008**, *92*, 103125. [CrossRef]
110. Kaloyeros, A.E.; Jové, F.A.; Goff, J.; Arkles, B. Review—Silicon Nitride and Silicon Nitride-Rich Thin Film Technologies: Trends in Deposition Techniques and Related Applications. *ECS J. Solid State Sci. Technol.* **2017**, *6*, P691–P714. [CrossRef]
111. Gonzalez-Izquierdo, B.; Gray, R.; King, M.; Dance, R.; Wilson, R.; McCreadie, J.; Butler, N.; Capdessus, R.; Hawkes, S.; Green, J.; et al. Optically controlled dense current structures driven by relativistic plasma aperture-induced diffraction. *Nat. Phys.* **2016**, *12*, 505–512. [CrossRef]
112. Plasma Shutter for Heavy ION Acceleration Enhancement. Available online: https://vbl.eli-beams.eu/mm-shutter/ (accessed on 7 December 2022).
113. Parisi, T. *WebGL: Up and Running*, 1st ed.; O'Reilly Media, Inc.: Sebastopol, CA, USA, 2012; ISBN 144932357X.
114. Virtual BeamLine. Available online: https://vbl.eli-beams.eu/ (accessed on 2 June 2022).
115. Pezoa, F.; Reutter, J.L.; Suarez, F.; Ugarte, M.; Vrgoč, D. Foundations of JSON schema. In Proceedings of the 25th International Conference on World Wide Web. International World Wide Web Conferences Steering Committee, Montreal, QC, Canada, 11–15 May 2016; pp. 263–273. [CrossRef]
116. Valenta, P.; Grittani, G.M.; Lazzarini, C.M.; Klimo, O.; Bulanov, S.V. On the electromagnetic-electron rings originating from the interaction of high-power short-pulse laser and underdense plasma. *Phys. Plasmas* **2021**, *28*, 122104. [CrossRef]
117. Electromagnetic-Electron Rings. Available online: https://valenpe7.github.io/on_the_electromagnetic_electron_rings/ (accessed on 2 June 2022).

Disclaimer/Publisher's Note: The statements, opinions and data contained in all publications are solely those of the individual author(s) and contributor(s) and not of MDPI and/or the editor(s). MDPI and/or the editor(s) disclaim responsibility for any injury to people or property resulting from any ideas, methods, instructions or products referred to in the content.

Review

Progress in Hybrid Plasma Wakefield Acceleration

Bernhard Hidding [1,2,*], Ralph Assmann [3,4], Michael Bussmann [5,6], David Campbell [1,2], Yen-Yu Chang [5], Sébastien Corde [7], Jurjen Couperus Cabadağ [5], Alexander Debus [5], Andreas Döpp [8], Max Gilljohann [7], J. Götzfried [8], F. Moritz Foerster [8], Florian Haberstroh [8], Fahim Habib [1,2], Thomas Heinemann [1,2], Dominik Hollatz [9,10], Arie Irman [5], Malte Kaluza [9,10], Stefan Karsch [8,11], Olena Kononenko [7], Alexander Knetsch [7], Thomas Kurz [5], Stephan Kuschel [12], Alexander Köhler [5], Alberto Martinez de la Ossa [3], Alastair Nutter [1,2,5], Richard Pausch [5], Gaurav Raj [7], Ulrich Schramm [5], Susanne Schöbel [5], Andreas Seidel [9,10], Klaus Steiniger [5], Patrick Ufer [5], Mark Yeung [9,10], Omid Zarini [5] and Matt Zepf [9,10]

1 Scottish Universities Physics Alliance SUPA, University of Strathclyde, 107 Rottenrow, Glasgow G4 0NG, UK
2 The Cockcroft Institute, Keckwick Ln, Daresbury, Warrington WA4 4AD, UK
3 Deutsches Elektronen-Synchrotron DESY, 22607 Hamburg, Germany
4 Laboratori Nazionali di Frascati, 00044 Frascati, Italy
5 Helmholtz-Zentrum Dresden-Rossendorf, Bautzner Landstraße 400, 01328 Dresden, Germany
6 Center for Advanced Systems Understanding CASUS, 02826 Görlitz, Germany
7 LOA, ENSTA Paris, CNRS, Ecole Polytechnique, Institut Polytechnique de Paris, 91762 Palaiseau, France
8 Faculty of Physics, Ludwig-Maximilians-Universität München, Am Coulombwall 1, 85748 Garching, Germany
9 Institute of Optics and Quantum Electronics, Friedrich-Schiller-University of Jena, Max-Wien-Platz 1, 07743 Jena, Germany
10 Helmholtz Institute Jena, Fröbelstieg 3, 07743 Jena, Germany
11 Max Planck Institut für Quantenoptik, Hans-Kopfermann-Straße 1, 85748 Garching, Germany
12 Center for Free Electron Science, CFEL, Luruper Chaussee 149, 22761 Hamburg, Germany
* Correspondence: bernhard.hidding@strath.ac.uk

Abstract: Plasma wakefield accelerators can be driven either by intense laser pulses (LWFA) or by intense particle beams (PWFA). A third approach that combines the complementary advantages of both types of plasma wakefield accelerator has been established with increasing success over the last decade and is called hybrid LWFA→PWFA. Essentially, a compact LWFA is exploited to produce an energetic, high-current electron beam as a driver for a subsequent PWFA stage, which, in turn, is exploited for phase-constant, inherently laser-synchronized, quasi-static acceleration over extended acceleration lengths. The sum is greater than its parts: the approach not only provides a compact, cost-effective alternative to linac-driven PWFA for exploitation of PWFA and its advantages for acceleration and high-brightness beam generation, but extends the parameter range accessible for PWFA and, through the added benefit of co-location of inherently synchronized laser pulses, enables high-precision pump/probing, injection, seeding and unique experimental constellations, e.g., for beam coordination and collision experiments. We report on the accelerating progress of the approach achieved in a series of collaborative experiments and discuss future prospects and potential impact.

Keywords: plasma wakefield acceleration; LWFA; PWFA; compact particle acceleration; radiation sources

1. Introduction: LWFA and PWFA

The need for collective acceleration mechanisms as a pathway to overcome the limitations of conventional accelerators, such as the occurrence of voltage or structural breakdown, and to realize energy gains orders of magnitude larger than otherwise possible, has been discussed since the 1950s [1]. The electric fields in collective plasma electron oscillations increase with plasma density and were recognized to be suitable for achieving orders of magnitude larger energy gains. Using "lasers to accelerate electrons to high energies in a short distance" was proposed by Tajima and Dawson [2] in 1979 and is today known as laser-driven plasma wakefield acceleration (LWFA). Using a "bunched relativistic electron beam in a cold plasma" was proposed by Chen et al. [3] in 1985 and is today known as particle beam-driven plasma wakefield acceleration (PWFA). Both schemes were visionary and required technological advances that were achieved over recent decades. For LWFA, a technological breakthrough came from the chirped pulse amplification (CPA) technique proposed by Strickland and Mourou [4] (interestingly, published in the same year as the seminal PWFA paper). CPA eventually made high-power, high intensity, ultra-short laser pulses commercially available, which, in turn, enabled the realization and exploitation of LWFA and the injection of electrons from background plasma wave-breaking and quasi-monoenergetic electron beam production [5] even in university-scale laboratories. For PWFA, the development was, perhaps, a little more gradual, with the first driver/witness-type double-bunch acceleration experiment performed in 1988 [6]. This was similar to the approach described in [3] as a driving/driven beam system, with two-bunch acceleration remaining a key strategy [7] as a result of the ability of linacs to provide such driver/witness beam systems.

2. Hybrid LWFA→PWFA

The LWFA and PWFA techniques have complementary advantages. Resulting from a strength and weakness analysis of both approaches, the concept of "hybrid laser-plasma accelerators" was established in 2010 [8]. The similarities, differences, and complementarities of LWFA and PWFA, and the resulting opportunities, are discussed in detail elsewhere, for example in [9–15]. As a top-level summary, the key complementary features are that laser pulses are ideal for tailored plasma production and use of LWFA for compact generation of intense, high-current electron beams, but suffer from dephasing, diffraction, and oscillatory electromagnetic field structures, whereas PWFA is ideal for dephasing-free, i.e., phase-constant and quasi-static acceleration over naturally long distances, operation in tailored pre-ionized plasma channels and ultracold electron beam production. Jointly, they provide inherent laser synchronization of systems to PWFA, for example, for probing, diagnostics and injection of high-brightness beams.

Figure 1 below illustrates the concept. In the LWFA stage, a laser pulse, with power of the order of 100 TW, propagates with a group velocity $v_g < c$ through plasma and drives a plasma wave with an elliptical "bubble" structure [16]. An electron beam is then injected by capturing plasma electrons in the accelerating longitudinal electric field, indicated by the blue profile. The electron beam is indicated in green and the transverse Lorentz-contracted fields are shown in red and blue, respectively. In the PWFA stage, this electron beam is used to drive the plasma wave in the "blowout" regime [17], with a velocity c without dephasing issues over long distances. A synchronized laser pulse(s) can then be used in arbitrary geometry for PWFA wakefield imaging or for advanced injection mechanisms and interaction experiments.

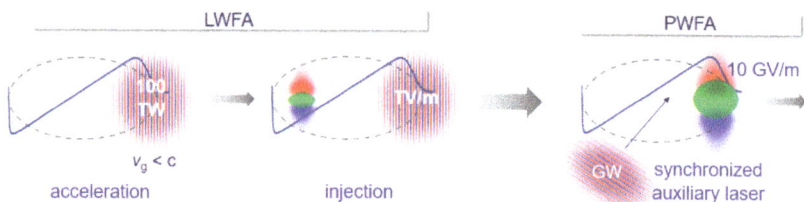

Figure 1. Schematic visualization of hybrid plasma wakefield acceleration. A 100 TW-scale laser pulse drives a wakefield (the blue line shows the profile of the longitudinal electric field on-axis); an electron beam is produced in the LWFA stage and then used as a driver for the attached PWFA stage. Here, the inherent advantages of PWFA for acceleration and injection and the inherent synchronization can be exploited.

Due to dephasing and laser depletion, a transition from laser-driven to electron-beam-driven regimes may occur quite naturally [18–24]. Figure 2a–c (adapted from [20]) shows how such a transition looks in PIC-simulations (also see Figure 8). Figure 2a depicts the plasma electron density distribution normalized by the critical density, which shows several electron bunches that have a pronounced effect on the wakefield structure. Figure 2b shows the corresponding transverse force normalized by $m_e c \omega$, and Figure 2c shows, in contrast to this, the transverse force that would be produced by the laser pulse only, without the electron bunch(es) present. Experimentally, this scenario manifests in enhanced betatron emission (length), in particular, for higher electron densities n_e, where dephasing and depletion are stronger (see Figure 2d).

While, in PWFA, laser pulses are not required, electron beams are always present in LWFA scenarios. Generally, the impact of injected electron beams is, therefore, inseparable from the LWFA process. For example, beam-loading [25] has been observed in seminal simulations that predicted mono-energetic electron bunch generation in LWFA [16], the increasing influence of the injected beam on the LWFA process was observed in simulations described in [18], beam-loading in LWFA experiments was observed in [26], and mode-transition from LWFA to PWFA [19] was encountered experimentally [21]. Such a gradual mode transition (also see Figure 8 and [15]) was suggested more recently to be responsible for energy spread improvement [24], while, conversely, it was interpreted, by the same group, for very similar beams from LWFA, that beam-driven acceleration was excluded [27] in experiments that provided highest-quality electron beams from LWFA that were used for the first demonstration of VUV-range free-electron lasing [28]. These examples underline the relevance of PWFA-like regimes for LWFA and show that both regimes may be more intertwined than is often appreciated. On the other hand, this also underlines the need for clear disentanglement between LWFA and PWFA stages and the need for 'safety margins' for purposeful, controlled injection processes, instead of sensitive at-threshold injection mechanisms and dark current production.

Reminiscent of the first driver/witness bunch pair experiments in linac-driven PWFAs, various mechanisms for the production of electron bunch trains from LWFA exist. The purposeful generation of electron bunch pairs from LWFA, for example, for driver/witness-type PWFA [7,8] was explored in [22] and measured via coherent transition radiation (CTR) of generated bunches. Figure 3 shows reconstructed electron bunch temporal profiles based on CTR signals for the cases of a short and long plasma cell, respectively. The longer plasma cell is longer than the dephasing distance, which implies a regime change from LWFA to PWFA, provided that the electron beam is strong enough when compared to the remaining laser pulse, and the injection of an additional electron bunch.

Informed by general studies of PWFA physics and enhanced energy gains, the staged combination of LWFA and PWFA become increasingly attractive as a result of the invention of the plasma photocathode, an injection scheme for generation of beams with orders of magnitude better emittance and brightness than state-of-the-art approaches. The plasma photocathode can act as a beam brightness transformer [29], in which the generated electron witness beam has much higher brightness than the incoming electron driver beam. While, for the first time, a plasma photocathode was developed with linac-driven PWFA [30], the inherent synchronization of plasma photocathode injection lasers with electron beams from LWFA, using a split-off laser pulse [31], makes this injection scheme ideally suited for hybrid LWFA→PWFA.

Plasma-lensing, a concept introduced in the context of high-energy physics [32], whereby plasma ions provide a focusing force [33], represents one of the initial stages in the quest to develop hybrid LWFA→PWFA. Figure 4 shows a setup used as a first step towards the development of staged hybrid plasma wakefield accelerators involving the use of two separated gas targets [34]. Here, the second gas target is pre-ionized by the diffracting LWFA remnant laser pulse and produces a plasma just ahead of the electron beam. The electron beam then undergoes plasma-lensing, which has a variety of applications, including capture of diverging electron beams from LWFA or transverse-matching. While, in this setup, the laser pulse diffracted sufficiently and did not drive a plasma wave in the second gas jet, in a complementary setup produced earlier the laser pulse still drove a wakefield in the second jet and generated a focusing laser-driven plasma lens effect [35].

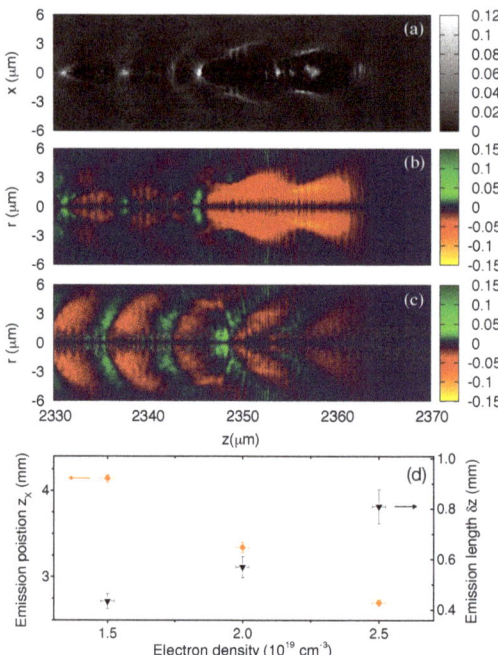

Figure 2. Mode transition: (**a**–**c**) show a PIC simulation at plasma density of 2.5×10^{19} cm^{-3}, in (**a**) plasma density n_e with the injected electron beam, in (**b**) the corresponding normalized transverse force in the wakefield and in (**c**) the transverse wakefield force as generated from the laser pulse only. This shows that, at this point, the wakefield is maintained primarily by the electron beam. In (**d**), experimental results showing that the betatron emission length and, thus, the plasma interaction length is increased with n_e at high values of n_e, contrary to LWFA scalings and in agreement with an LWFA-PWFA transition that allows for increased emission length at high plasma density (figure adapted from [20]).

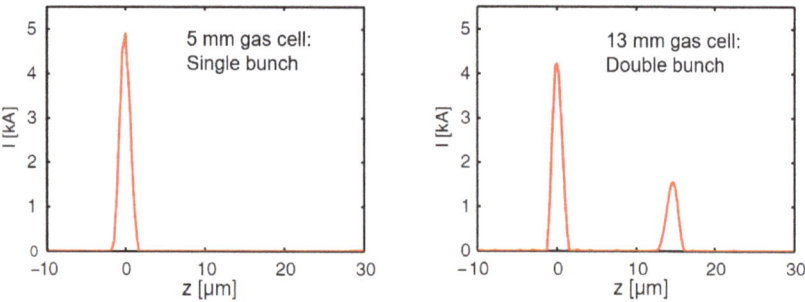

Figure 3. Single and double electron bunches produced from LWFA due to dephasing and a regime change from LWFA to PWFA, measured via coherent transition radiation (figure adapted from [22]).

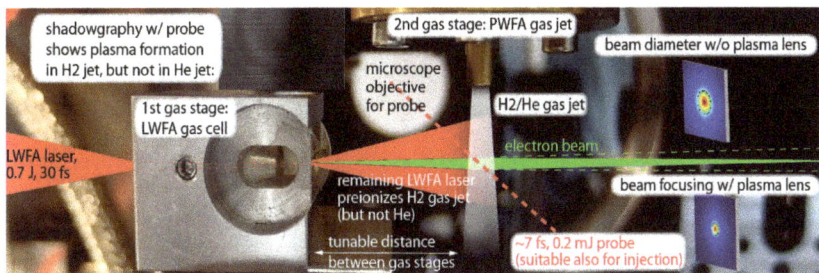

Figure 4. Hybrid setup with two separate gas targets used to show plasma-lensing of an electron beam in a second gas jet (figure adapted from [34]).

The next level of interaction intensity is reached when the electron beam from the LWFA stage has sufficient charge density and current that it begins to drive a plasma wave in the PWFA stage and, thereby, decelerates. Figure 5 shows the degree of deceleration observed when the second stage is placed at variable distances from the LWFA stage. Larger deceleration and, perhaps, some re-acceleration of decelerated electrons is obtained when the distance between both stages is shorter, consistent with the higher electron beam density and, hence, stronger wake driven by the diverging electron beam when the distance between the stages is reduced. Additionally, a steel tape was introduced in between the stages to rule out the potential for the LWFA laser remnant to interact with the PWFA stage. In this variation, the PWFA stage was self-ionized by the electric field of the electron beam—an important milestone in its own right and an indication of the high charge densities of electron beams obtainable from LWFA—and collective deceleration was observed [36].

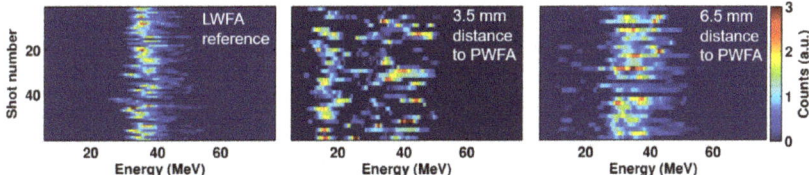

Figure 5. Collective deceleration shown using two separate targets, with varied distance of the PWFA to the LWFA jet (figure adapted from [36]).

The prospects of hybrid plasma wakefield accelerators, for example, as energy and brightness transformers, as PWFA physics test-beds, and to boost the capacities and capabilities of plasma wakefield accelerators, has increasingly fostered collaborative R&D in the US [29] and, in particular, in Europe [37], where, from 2017, a dedicated experimental collaboration, involving teams from Germany, France and the UK, was set up to systematically progress their development.

A first milestone of this collaboration was a demonstration that the capabilities of hybrid LWFA→PWFA can complement, and even exceed, those of linac-driven PWFA. In [11], a two-stage setup with a tape drive separation option was amended by a pre-ionizer laser pulse. The ultra-high electron beam density, which is obtained quite naturally from the LWFA stages, allowed driving of a plasma wave at densities of about 10^{19} cm^{-3}, about two orders of magnitude higher than those achieved in experiments conducted in the blowout regime at linac-driven PWFA facilities to date [7].

The inherent synchronization between electron beams and lasers was exploited for high-precision imaging of the dynamics at the PWFA stage via few-cycle shadowgraphy as used in LWFA [38]. Figure 6 shows that the strong, uni-polar electric field of the electron beam generates significant ion motion and an emerging cone structure. Time-resolved few-cycle shadowgrams of these dynamics are a powerful tool for PWFA research and optimization in general. For example, it was concluded in [11] that this type of directed ion motion may have immediate implications for low-density PWFA as used at linac-based facilities. Specifically, it was highlighted that bunch trains, where the plasma might not be able to recover from the perturbation between two shots, should be investigated, a scenario that was later confirmed in [39]. These results show that time-resolved shadowgraphy, a technique that is standard in LWFA and was here introduced to (hybrid) PWFA, can provide fundamental insights, for example, into the dissipation of plasma waves [40] and energy transfer mechanisms [41] in PWFA.

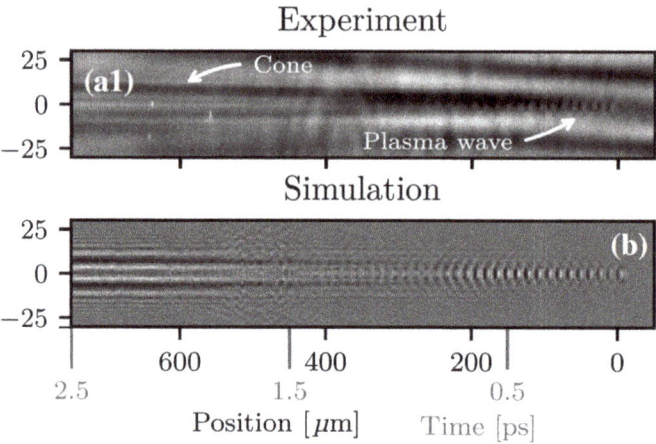

Figure 6. Experimentally imaged plasma wave obtained by shadowgraphy (**a1**) and corresponding simulation (**b**), illuminating the induced cone-shaped ion motion evolution as a result of the unipolar field kick of the PWFA (figure adapted from [11]).

The interaction of electron beams from LWFA with thin foils can involve filamentation in addition to emittance-spoiling scattering and is relevant for tape drive laser blockers between LWFA and PWFA stages, but also for staged LWFA schemes, where tape drives are used as plasma mirrors [42]. Figure 7 illustrates the effect of the laser-driven plasma instability in the foil on the LWFA electron beam, which was investigated in [43]. This research also demonstrated that the inherent synchronization between wakefield-accelerated electrons and laser pulses is very valuable for the probing and investigation of laser-plasma driven instabilities.

In [23], it was pointed out that electron beam quality optimization in LWFA is generally connected with operation at low charges (the same can be said about linacs, albeit for different reasons), while high charge beams are also required for many other applications than hybrid LWFA→PWFA. Ionization injection in LWFA [44] is naturally associated with high injection rates and, therefore, is a promising candidate for the production of heavily charged electron beams and exploitation of associated beam-loading [23]. Self-truncated ionization injection [45] has been realized as a localized, beam-loaded injection scheme with beam charges of hundreds of pC and currents of tens of kA [46], which are excellent prerequisites for laboratory-sized beam-driven plasma wakefield acceleration. Other schemes with high injection rates, such as density downramp injection, are also excellent approaches for the generation of high-current electron beams for PWFA.

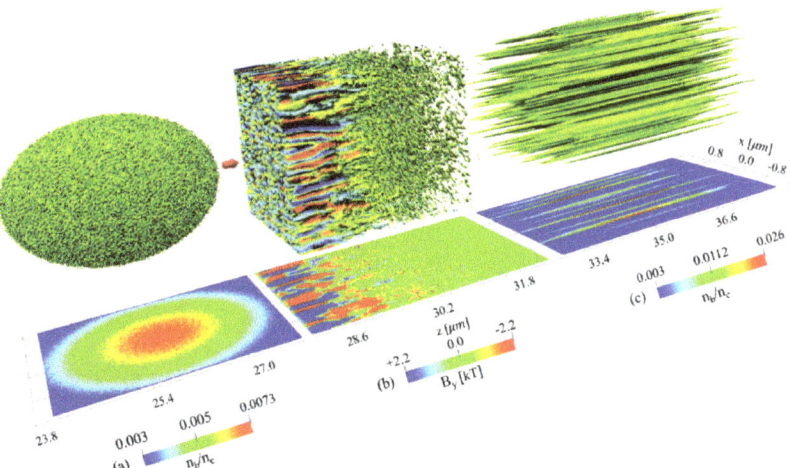

Figure 7. Laser-driven plasma instability probed by an electron beam from LWFA as a result of interaction between the laser pulse and the foil used as a laser blocker for separation of targets in LWFA→PWFA setups (figure adapted from [43]).

The physics of the transition from LWFA to PWFA, and the role of increasingly high charge, was further investigated in [15]. Figure 8 shows the different regimes and the transition from LWFA to PWFA when the laser pulse intensity and the electron beam charge, respectively, change. A pure unloaded LWFA regime is realized only when there is no injected electron beam, whereas, in contrast, a pure PWFA regime is realized only when the laser pulse vanishes. Different laser systems with different pulse durations and power levels, and two injection schemes for the LWFA stage, namely shock-front induced density downramp injection and colliding pulse injection, were used. By scanning across energies and plasma densities in the different regimes and setups, a wide range of scenarios, such as beam-loaded LWFA and beam-dominated wakefield scenarios, were experimentally realized. This included controlled production of two electron beams, which, in the context of hybrid LWFA→PWFA, are important for driver-witness-type acceleration [8] and the escort-beam loading approach for extremely high 6D-brightness beams [47].

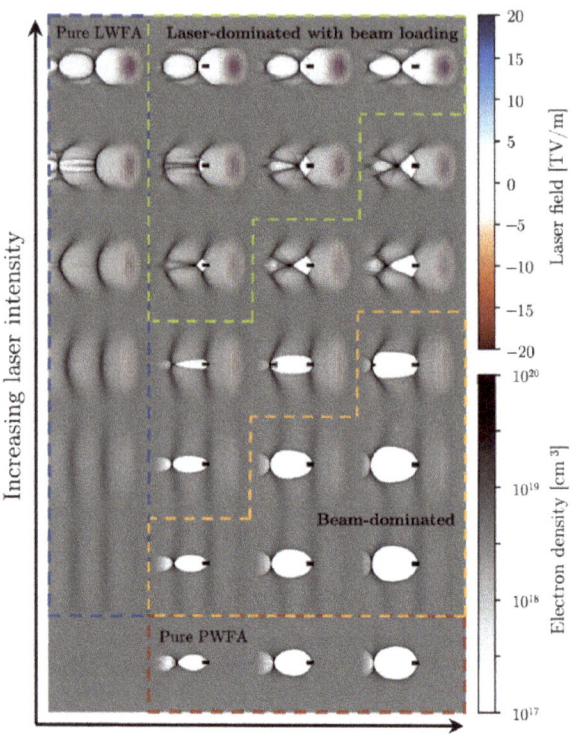

Figure 8. Overview showing a classification of laser pulse vs. electron-beam-dominated wakefield regimes (figure adapted from [15]). The electron beam charge density (x-axis) and the laser pulse intensity (y-axis) are responsible for the wake excitation and are, hence, decisive for the type of plasma wakefield that is generated.

3. Full Demonstration of Hybrid LWFA→PWFA

A breakthrough milestone was then passed that firmly established the LWFA→PWFA approach as an experimentally viable approach and platform. In [48], it was shown, for the first time, that driver/witness-type PWFA can be realized from an all-optical, laser-powered plasma wakefield accelerator. In Figure 9, the interaction setup is illustrated, along with plasma wave images of the LWFA stage, as well as the PWFA stage, in self-ionized and pre-ionized modes, respectively. The driver/witness pairs were generated via various mechanisms in the LWFA stage, separation between the two stages was realized with or without a tape drive laser blocker, and the platform was realized at two different laboratories. These results, with the feasibility as well as the variability demonstrated, and the similarity of the setups to the way they were envisioned a decade earlier [8], is a testament to the robustness and success of the approach, but also to its unique capabilities.

The inherently short duration and high charge density of electron beams from LWFA enable operation of the PWFA stage at naturally high plasma densities. The demonstrated energy gain gradient [48] of witness beams obtained in this first full-scale realization of LWFA→PWFA amounted to over 100 GeV/m, a rate similar to the highest ever achieved in linac-driven PWFA [49]. With regard to diagnostics, it is appropriate to emphasize again that the naturally synchronized interplay of up to three laser arms in these experiments [11,48], including a few-cycle optical probe beam, allows time-resolved shadowgraphy and, hence, illumination of the interaction with femtosecond resolution.

This capability is crucial for precision studies of plasma waves and dynamics and is also enormously useful for injection studies.

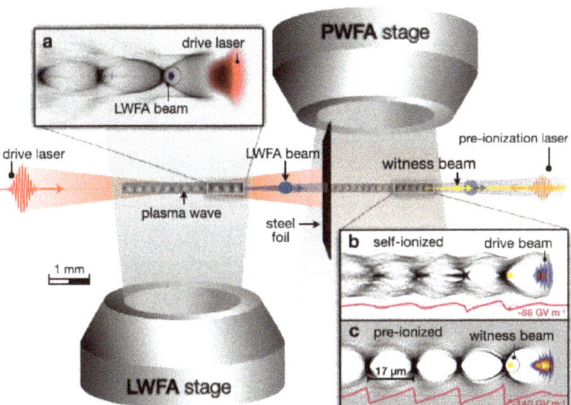

Figure 9. Hybrid LWFA→PWFA platform and driver/witness-type PWFA, using two separate gas jets and three laser arms to drive the LWFA stage and pre-ionize the PWFA stage for shadowgraphy imaging (figure adapted from [48]). The insets show simulation representations of LWFA and self-ionized and pre-ionized PWFA, respectively.

Gas-dynamic density downramp injection also represents a promising scheme for the production of high-quality electron beams. While a standard method in LWFA for more than a decade, its realization remained a long-harboured aspiration of the PWFA community until recently. Based on the now-established hybrid LWFA→PWFA platform [48], this milestone was reached in a straightforward manner. In [50], a thin wire was used to generate a (double) shock in the PWFA gas jet, with an associated downramp that captured plasma electrons and accelerated them at gradients beyond 120 GeV/m. Figure 10 shows the wire-equipped hybrid platform and the resulting hydrodynamic shock and gas density spike. The shadowgraphy was exploited to provide images of the shock(s) as well as the PWFA. Control of the injection parameters and the resulting electron beams was also demonstrated by changing the injection position as well as the plateau PWFA gas density. These results underline the rapid advance of the approach and the contributions it can make, for example, towards high-brightness electron beam generation.

The LWFA optimization priorities for electron beam generation for PWFA, such as charge and current, are different from those for traditional LWFA, where energy spread minimization is a key goal. While LWFA does not yet produce electron beams that can compete with state-of-the-art linacs in terms of stability, the variability can be exploited for passive parameter scans. In [51], an approximately inverse correlation between electron beam charge and energy [15] obtained in the LWFA due to beam loading was investigated through its impact on the PWFA stage. Jointly with PWFA shadowgraphy and other diagnostics, this allowed precision studies of the PWFA wakes to be carried through in the self-ionized and pre-ionized regimes, respectively. Relativistic plasma wave elongation, as a result of increased driver beam charge and density, was observed and, by probing the wake at different positions within the PWFA stage, the evolution of the decelerating driver beam and its corresponding plasma wake were observed. This setup will enable further in-depth studies of PWFA dynamics in the future.

In a recent study [52], for the first time, an all-optical injection scheme in hybrid LWFA→PWFA was realized. Here, an optically triggered shock provided the downramp; the approach thus complemented a first realization of the plasma photocathode [30] and plasma torch [53,54] methods, which had been first realized in linac-driven PWFAs. Moreover, Ref. [52] provided the first evidence that various aspects of stability, quality and energy transfer of the generated electron beam obtained from injection in the PWFA stage can be improved. This represents a first step towards a beam brightness transformer based on the hybrid LWFA→PWFA platform.

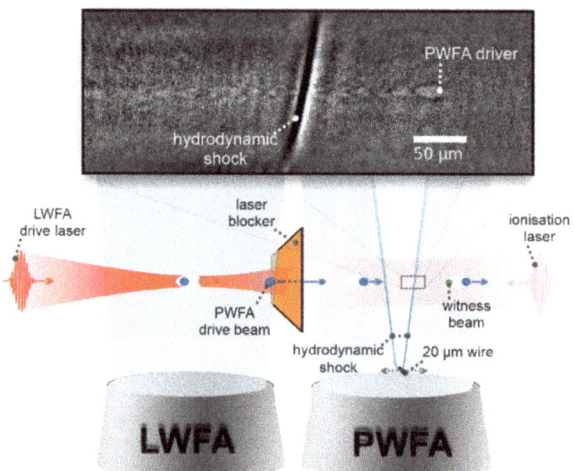

Figure 10. Gas-dynamic density downramp injection, realized by wire-induced shocks in the PWFA gas jet. Shadowgraphy reveals both the PWFA-driven plasma wave and the hydrodynamic shock profile (figure from [50]).

4. Conclusions

Both LWFA and PWFA, invented in their modern forms approximately four decades ago, have matured to become experimentally highly successful approaches. Each has particular advantages. Hybrid plasma wakefield acceleration, or LWFA→PWFA, seeks to exploit the best of both worlds and has been driven forward from innovation to realization with an increasing success rate over the last decade. This is not only because of the viability of the approach, but is also because of its capacities—there are only a small number of linac-driven PWFA facilities in the world, with corresponding limitations of access and accessible parameter ranges, constituting an R&D-capacity bottleneck. LWFA-driven PWFA systems, in contrast, can be realized in university-scale laboratories and, hence, offer a means of overcoming the capacity bottleneck that currently exists in PWFA. Moreover, LWFA→PWFA has already demonstrated capabilities beyond those of existing linac-driven PWFAs that can be exploited.

Figure 11 shows a timeline with experimental milestones passed over the last years as summarized in this paper.

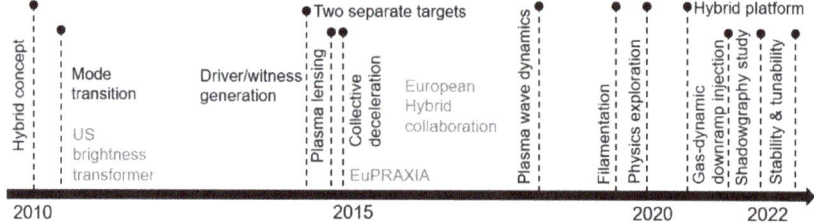

Figure 11. Timeline of hybrid LWFA→PWFA research, with selected experimental highlights. Milestones for the approach are being reached at an increasing rate based on the full experimental establishment of the hybrid plasma accelerator platform at the beginning of the 2020s.

What is next for LWFA→PWFA? One key prospect and goal is improvement in the quality of beams generated from these systems. In particular, plasma photocathodes provide promising quality boosts of several orders of magnitude, beyond even the highest-quality linac-generated electron beams and, at the same time, benefit from the inherent synchronization between electron beams and laser pulses in LWFA→PWFA. If such beam brightness transformers for laser-plasma accelerators can be realized, then this will have a transformative impact for various applications. These may include, light sources profitting from enhanced electron beam (phase space) density and brightness, creating prospects for X-ray free-electron-lasers [31,55,56], betatron radiation-based sources in X-ray and γ-ray [57] or ion channel laser regimes [55], or inverse-Compton-scattering-based γ-ray sources [9,55] driven by hybrid LWFA→PWFA. First experimental indications of free-electron-lasing in the VUV obtained from electron beams by LWFA [28] and in the IR from PWFA [58] via SASE, and as a seeded free-electron laser in the UV [59] from LWFA, have now been obtained. Start-to-end simulations show that, with high-brightness beams from plasma photocathodes, even attosecond-Angstrom-class hard X-FEL may become possible based on hybrid LWFA→PWFA systems [60]. Ultra-low emittance/ultra-high brightness beams are also of significant interest for high-energy physics research, for example, as test beams for staging and emittance preservation, and, in combination with co-located photon beams, also for, for example, nuclear- and quantum-electrodynamics research. We anticipate that, especially if the efforts that have been initiated for ultrabright electron beam production are successful with linac-driven PWFA and/or hybrid LWFA→PWFA, there will be a surge in laboratories engaging in hybrid LWFA→PWFA research as a gateway, not only to PWFA physics exploration, but also to ultrabright beam production and the myriad of resulting applications for next-generation experiments and science.

Author Contributions: All authors contributed to the experimental results obtained during the various stages and the development of the field. All authors have read and agreed to the published version of the manuscript.

Funding: Work at HZDR was fully supported by the Helmholtz association under the Matter and Technology program, Accelerator Research and Development topic. Computational resources were used at the Center for Information Services and HPC (ZIH) at TU Dresden on the HRSK-II. The work was partially funded by the Center of Advanced Systems Understanding (CASUS), which is financed by Germany's Federal Ministry of Education and Research (BMBF) and by the Saxon Ministry for Science, Culture and Tourism (SMWK) with tax funds on the basis of the budget approved by the Saxon State Parliament. Work at LOA was supported by the European Research Council (ERC) under the European Union's Horizon 2020 research and innovation programme (Miniature-beam-driven Plasma Accelerators Project, ERC Grant Agreement No. 715807). Work at the LMU by DFG was supported through the Cluster of Excellence Munich–Centre for Advanced Photonics (MAP EXC 158), the Euratom research and training program under Grant Agreement Number 633053 within the framework of the EUROfusion consortium and by the Max Planck Society. The Gauss Centre for Supercomputing e.V. provided computing time on the GCS Supercomputer SuperMUC at the Leibniz Supercomputing Centre. Work at the University of Strathclyde was supported by the European Research Council (ERC) under the European Union's Horizon 2020 research and innovation programme (NeXource: Next-generation Plasma-based Electron Beam Sources for High-brightness Photon Science, ERC Grant Agreement No. 865877) and by STFC ST/S006214/1 PWFA-FEL and used computational resources of the National Energy Research Scientific Computing Center, which is supported by DOE DE-AC02-05CH11231, and Shaheen (project k1191). The European Union's Horizon 2020 research and innovation program under Grant Agreement Number 653782 (EuPRAXIA) supported various aspects of the R&D. Work at FSU Jena was supported by the Bundesministerium für Bildung und Forschung (BMBF) Grants No. 05K19SJC, No. 05K19SJB, No. 05K22SJA, and No. 05K22SJB.

Institutional Review Board Statement: Not applicable.

Informed Consent Statement: Not applicable.

Data Availability Statement: Not applicable.

Conflicts of Interest: The authors declare no conflict of interest.

References

1. Lawson, J. Collective and coherent methods of particle acceleration. *Part. Accel.* **1972**, *3*, 21–33.
2. Tajima, T.; Dawson, J.M. Laser Electron-Accelerator. *Phys. Rev. Lett.* **1979**, *43*, 267–270. [CrossRef]
3. Chen, P.; Dawson, J.M.; Huff, R.W.; Katsouleas, T. Acceleration of Electrons by the Interaction of a Bunched Electron Beam with a Plasma. *Phys. Rev. Lett.* **1985**, *54*, 693–696. [CrossRef]
4. Strickland, D.; Mourou, G. Compression of amplified chirped optical pulses. *Opt. Commun.* **1985**, *56*, 219–221. [CrossRef]
5. Malka, V.; Faure, J.; Gauduel, Y.A.; Lefebvre, E.; Rousse, A.; Phuoc, K.T. Principles and applications of compact laser-plasma accelerators. *Nat. Phys.* **2008**, *4*, 447–453. [CrossRef]
6. Rosenzweig, J.B. Nonlinear plasma dynamics in the plasma wake-field accelerator. *Phys. Rev. Lett.* **1987**, *58*, 555–558. [CrossRef] [PubMed]
7. Litos, M.; Adli, E.; An, W.; Clarke, C.I.; Clayton, C.E.; Corde, S.; Delahaye, J.P.; England, R.J.; Fisher, A.S.; Frederico, J.; et al. High-efficiency acceleration of an electron beam in a plasma wakefield accelerator. *Nature* **2014**, *515*, 92–95. [CrossRef] [PubMed]
8. Hidding, B.; Koenigstein, T.; Osterholz, J.; Karsch, S.; Willi, O.; Pretzler, G. Monoenergetic Energy Doubling in a Hybrid Laser-Plasma Wakefield Accelerator. *Phys. Rev. Lett.* **2010**, *104*, 195002. [CrossRef]
9. Hidding, B.; Manahan, G.G.; Karger, O.; Knetsch, A.; Wittig, G.; Jaroszynski, D.A.; Sheng, Z.M.; Xi, Y.; Deng, A.; Rosenzweig, J.B.; et al. Ultrahigh brightness bunches from hybrid plasma accelerators as drivers of 5th generation light sources. *J. Phys. B At. Mol. Opt. Phys.* **2014**, *47*, 234010. [CrossRef]
10. Hidding, B.; Beaton, A.; Boulton, L.; Corde, S.; Doepp, A.; Habib, F.A.; Heinemann, T.; Irman, A.; Karsch, S.; Kirwan, G.; et al. Fundamentals and Applications of Hybrid LWFA-PWFA. *Appl. Sci.* **2019**, *9*, 2626. [CrossRef]
11. Gilljohann, M.F.; Ding, H.; Döpp, A.; Götzfried, J.; Schindler, S.; Schilling, G.; Corde, S.; Debus, A.; Heinemann, T.; Hidding, B.; et al. Direct Observation of Plasma Waves and Dynamics Induced by Laser-Accelerated Electron Beams. *Phys. Rev. X* **2019**, *9*, 011046. [CrossRef]
12. Hidding, B.; Foster, B.; Hogan, M.J.; Muggli, P.; Rosenzweig, J.B. Directions in plasma wakefield acceleration. *Philos. Trans. R. Soc. A Math. Phys. Eng. Sci.* **2019**, *377*, 20190215.
13. Martinez de la Ossa, A.; Assmann, R.W.; Bussmann, M.; Corde, S.; Cabadağ, J.P.C.; Debus, A.; Döpp, A.; Pousa, A.F.; Gilljohann, M.F.; Heinemann, T.; et al. Hybrid LWFA-PWFA staging as a beam energy and brightness transformer: conceptual design and simulations. *Philos. Trans. R. Soc. A Math. Phys. Eng. Sci.* **2019**, *377*, 20180175.
14. Manahan, G.G.; Habib, A.F.; Scherkl, P.; Ullmann, D.; Beaton, A.; Sutherland, A.; Kirwan, G.; Delinikolas, P.; Heinemann, T.; Altuijri, R.; et al. Advanced schemes for underdense plasma photocathode wakefield accelerators: Pathways towards ultrahigh brightness electron beams. *Philos. Trans. R. Soc. A Math. Phys. Eng. Sci.* **2019**, *377*, 20180182.
15. Götzfried, J.; Döpp, A.; Gilljohann, M.F.; Foerster, F.M.; Ding, H.; Schindler, S.; Schilling, G.; Buck, A.; Veisz, L.; Karsch, S. Physics of High-Charge Electron Beams in Laser-Plasma Wakefields. *Phys. Rev. X* **2020**, *10*, 041015. [CrossRef]
16. Pukhov, A.; Meyer-ter Vehn, J. Laser wake field acceleration: The highly non-linear broken-wave regime. *Appl. Phys. B-Lasers Opt.* **2002**, *74*, 355–361. [CrossRef]
17. Rosenzweig, J.B.; Breizman, B.; Katsouleas, T.; Su, J.J. Acceleration and focusing of electrons in two-dimensional nonlinear plasma wake fields. *Phys. Rev. A* **1991**, *44*, R6189–R6192. [CrossRef]
18. Tsung, F.S.; Narang, R.; Mori, W.B.; Joshi, C.; Fonseca, R.A.; Silva, L.O. Near-GeV-Energy Laser-Wakefield Acceleration of Self-Injected Electrons in a Centimeter-Scale Plasma Channel. *Phys. Rev. Lett.* **2004**, *93*, 185002. [CrossRef] [PubMed]
19. Pae, K.H.; Choi, I.W.; Lee, J. Self-mode-transition from laser wakefield accelerator to plasma wakefield accelerator of laser-driven plasma-based electron acceleration. *Phys. Plasmas* **2010**, *17*, 123104. [CrossRef]
20. Corde, S.; Thaury, C.; Phuoc, K.T.; Lifschitz, A.; Lambert, G.; Faure, J.; Lundh, O.; Benveniste, E.; Ben-Ismail, A.; Arantchuk, L.; et al. Mapping the X-ray Emission Region in a Laser-Plasma Accelerator. *Phys. Rev. Lett.* **2011**, *107*, 215004. [CrossRef] [PubMed]
21. Masson-Laborde, P.E.; Mo, M.Z.; Ali, A.; Fourmaux, S.; Lassonde, P.; Kieffer, J.C.; Rozmus, W.; Teychenné, D.; Fedosejevs, R. Giga-electronvolt electrons due to a transition from laser wakefield acceleration to plasma wakefield acceleration. *Phys. Plasmas* **2014**, *21*, 123113. [CrossRef]
22. Heigoldt, M.; Popp, A.; Khrennikov, K.; Wenz, J.; Chou, S.W.; Karsch, S.; Bajlekov, S.I.; Hooker, S.M.; Schmidt, B. Temporal evolution of longitudinal bunch profile in a laser wakefield accelerator. *Phys. Rev. ST Accel. Beams* **2015**, *18*, 121302. [CrossRef]
23. Guillaume, E.; Döpp, A.; Thaury, C.; Lifschitz, A.; Goddet, J.P.; Tafzi, A.; Sylla, F.; Iaquanello, G.; Lefrou, T.; Rousseau, P.; et al. Physics of fully-loaded laser-plasma accelerators. *Phys. Rev. ST Accel. Beams* **2015**, *18*, 061301. [CrossRef]
24. Wu, Y.; Yu, C.; Qin, Z.; Wang, W.; Zhang, Z.; Qi, R.; Feng, K.; Ke, L.; Chen, Y.; Wang, C.; et al. Energy Enhancement and Energy Spread Compression of Electron Beams in a Hybrid Laser-Plasma Wakefield Accelerator. *Appl. Sci.* **2019**, *9*, 2561. [CrossRef]
25. Katsouleas, T.; Wilks, S.; Chen, P.; Dawson, J.; Su, J. Beam loading in Plasma Accelerators. *Part. Accel.* **1987**, *22*, 81–99.
26. Rechatin, C.; Davoine, X.; Lifschitz, A.; Ismail, A.B.; Lim, J.; Lefebvre, E.; Faure, J.; Malka, V. Observation of Beam Loading in a Laser-Plasma Accelerator. *Phys. Rev. Lett.* **2009**, *103*, 194804. [CrossRef] [PubMed]

27. Ke, L.T.; Feng, K.; Wang, W.T.; Qin, Z.Y.; Yu, C.H.; Wu, Y.; Chen, Y.; Qi, R.; Zhang, Z.J.; Xu, Y.; et al. Near-GeV Electron Beams at a Few Per-Mille Level from a Laser Wakefield Accelerator via Density-Tailored Plasma. *Phys. Rev. Lett.* **2021**, *126*, 214801. [CrossRef]
28. Wang, W.; Feng, K.; Ke, L.; Yu, C.; Xu, Y.; Qi, R.; Chen, Y.; Qin, Z.; Zhang, Z.; Fang, M.; et al. Free-electron lasing at 27 nanometres based on a laser wakefield accelerator. *Nature* **2021**, *595*, 516–520. [CrossRef]
29. RadiaBeam: Plasma Photocathode Beam Brightness Transformer for Laser-Plasma-Wakefield Accelerators, DOE DESC0009533, 2013–2016. Available online: https://radiabeam.com/ (accessed on 17 December 2022).
30. Deng, A.; Karger, O.; Heinemann, T.; Knetsch, A.; Scherkl, P.; Manahan, G.; Beaton, A.; Ullmann, D.; Wittig, G.; Habib, A.; et al. Generation and acceleration of electron bunches from a plasma photocathode. *Nat. Phys.* **2019**, *15*, 1156–1160. [CrossRef]
31. Hidding, B.; Pretzler, G.; Rosenzweig, J.B.; Königstein, T.; Schiller, D.; Bruhwiler, D.L. Ultracold Electron Bunch Generation via Plasma Photocathode Emission and Acceleration in a Beam-Driven Plasma Blowout. *Phys. Rev. Lett.* **2012**, *108*, 035001. [CrossRef]
32. Chen, P. A possible final focusing mechanism for linear colliders. *Part. Accel.* **1987**, *20*, 171–182.
33. Bennett, W.H. Magnetically Self-Focussing Streams. *Phys. Rev.* **1934**, *45*, 890–897. [CrossRef]
34. Kuschel, S.; Hollatz, D.; Heinemann, T.; Karger, O.; Schwab, M.B.; Ullmann, D.; Knetsch, A.; Seidel, A.; Rödel, C.; Yeung, M.; et al. Demonstration of passive plasma lensing of a laser wakefield accelerated electron bunch. *Phys. Rev. Accel. Beams* **2016**, *19*, 071301. [CrossRef]
35. Thaury, C.; Guillaume, E.; Döpp, A.; Lehe, R.; Lifschitz, A.; Ta Phuoc, K.; Gautier, J.; Goddet, J.P.; Tafzi, A.; Flacco, A.; et al. Demonstration of relativistic electron beam focusing by a laser-plasma lens. *Nat. Commun.* **2015**, *6*, 6860. [CrossRef]
36. Chou, S.; Xu, J.; Khrennikov, K.; Cardenas, D.E.; Wenz, J.; Heigoldt, M.; Hofmann, L.; Veisz, L.; Karsch, S. Collective Deceleration of Laser-Driven Electron Bunches. *Phys. Rev. Lett.* **2016**, *117*, 144801. [CrossRef] [PubMed]
37. Eupraxia: European Plasma Research Accelerator with Excellence in Applications. 2015. Available online: https://roadmap2021.esfri.eu/projects-and-landmarks/browse-the-catalogue/eupraxia/ (accessed on 17 December 2022).
38. Sävert, A.; Mangles, S.P.D.; Schnell, M.; Siminos, E.; Cole, J.M.; Leier, M.; Reuter, M.; Schwab, M.B.; Möller, M.; Poder, K.; et al. Direct Observation of the Injection Dynamics of a Laser Wakefield Accelerator Using Few-Femtosecond Shadowgraphy. *Phys. Rev. Lett.* **2015**, *115*, 055002. [CrossRef]
39. D'Arcy, R.; Chappell, J.; Beinortaite, J.; Diederichs, S.; Boyle, G.; Foster, B.; Garland, M.J.; Caminal, P.G.; Lindstrøm, C.A.; Loisch, G.; et al. Recovery time of a plasma-wakefield accelerator. *Nature* **2022**, *603*, 58–62. [CrossRef]
40. Zgadzaj, R.; Li, Z.; Downer, M.; Sosedkin, A.; Khudyakov, V.; Lotov, K.; Silva, T.; Vieira, J.; Allen, J.; Gessner, S.; et al. Dissipation of electron-beam-driven plasma wakes. *arXiv* **2020**, arXiv:2001.09401.
41. Scherkl, P.; Knetsch, A.; Heinemann, T.; Sutherland, A.; Habib, A.F.; Karger, O.S.; Ullmann, D.; Beaton, A.; Manahan, G.G.; Xi, Y.; et al. Plasma photonic spatiotemporal synchronization of relativistic electron and laser beams. *Phys. Rev. Accel. Beams* **2022**, *25*, 052803. [CrossRef]
42. Steinke, S.; van Tilborg, J.; Benedetti, C.; Geddes, C.G.R.; Schroeder, C.B.; Daniels, J.; Swanson, K.K.; Gonsalves, A.J.; Nakamura, K.; Matlis, N.H.; et al. Multistage coupling of independent laser-plasma accelerators. *Nature* **2016**, *530*, 190–193. [CrossRef]
43. Raj, G.; Kononenko, O.; Gilljohann, M.F.; Doche, A.; Davoine, X.; Caizergues, C.; Chang, Y.Y.; Couperus Cabadağ, J.P.; Debus, A.; Ding, H.; et al. Probing ultrafast magnetic-field generation by current filamentation instability in femtosecond relativistic laser-matter interactions. *Phys. Rev. Res.* **2020**, *2*, 023123. [CrossRef]
44. Chen, M.; Sheng, Z.M.; Ma, Y.Y.; Zhang, J. Electron injection and trapping in a laser wakefield by field ionization to high-charge states of gases. *J. Appl. Phys.* **2006**, *99*, 056109. [CrossRef]
45. Zeng, M.; Chen, M.; Sheng, Z.M.; Mori, W.B.; Zhang, J. Self-truncated ionization injection and consequent monoenergetic electron bunches in laser wakefield acceleration. *Phys. Plasmas* **2014**, *21*, 030701.
46. Couperus, J.; Pausch, R.; Köhler, A.; Zarini, O.; Krämer, J.; Garten, M.; Huebl, A.; Gebhardt, R.; Helbig, U.; Bock, S.; et al. Demonstration of a beam loaded nanocoulomb-class laser wakefield accelerator. *Nat. Commun.* **2017**, *8*, 487. [CrossRef]
47. Manahan, G.; Habib, A.; Scherkl, P.; Delinikolas, P.; Beaton, A.; Knetsch, A.; Karger, O.; Wittig, G.; Heinemann, T.; Sheng, Z.; et al. Single-stage plasma-based correlated energy spread compensation for ultrahigh 6D brightness electron beams. *Nat. Commun.* **2017**, *8*, 15705. [CrossRef]
48. Kurz, T.; Heinemann, T.; Gilljohann, M.F.; Chang, Y.Y.; Couperus Cabadağ, J.P.; Debus, A.; Kononenko, O.; Pausch, R.; Schöbel, S.; Assmann, R.W.; et al. Demonstration of a compact plasma accelerator powered by laser-accelerated electron beams. *Nat. Commun.* **2021**, *12*, 2895. [CrossRef]
49. Corde, S.; Adli, E.; Allen, J.M.; An, W.; Clarke, C.I.; Clausse, B.; Clayton, C.E.; Delahaye, J.P.; Frederico, J.; Gessner, S.; et al. High-field plasma acceleration in a high-ionization-potential gas. *Nat. Commun.* **2016**, *7*, 11898. [CrossRef]
50. Couperus Cabadağ, J.P.; Pausch, R.; Schöbel, S.; Bussmann, M.; Chang, Y.Y.; Corde, S.; Debus, A.; Ding, H.; Döpp, A.; Foerster, F.M.; et al. Gas-dynamic density downramp injection in a beam-driven plasma wakefield accelerator. *Phys. Rev. Res.* **2021**, *3*, L042005. [CrossRef]
51. Schöbel, S.; Pausch, R.; Chang, Y.Y.; Corde, S.; Cabadağ, J.C.; Debus, A.; Ding, H.; Döpp, A.; Foerster, F.M.; Gilljohann, M.; et al. Effect of driver charge on wakefield characteristics in a plasma accelerator probed by femtosecond shadowgraphy. *New J. Phys.* **2022**, *24*, 083034. [CrossRef]

52. Foerster, F.M.; Döpp, A.; Haberstroh, F.; Grafenstein, K.v.; Campbell, D.; Chang, Y.Y.; Corde, S.; Couperus Cabadağ, J.P.; Debus, A.; Gilljohann, M.F.; et al. Stable and High-Quality Electron Beams from Staged Laser and Plasma Wakefield Accelerators. *Phys. Rev. X* **2022**, *12*, 041016. [CrossRef]
53. Ullmann, D.; Scherkl, P.; Knetsch, A.; Heinemann, T.; Sutherland, A.; Habib, A.F.; Karger, O.S.; Beaton, A.; Manahan, G.G.; Deng, A.; et al. All-optical density downramp injection in electron-driven plasma wakefield accelerators. *arXiv* **2020**, arXiv:2007.12634.
54. Knetsch, A.; Sheeran, B.; Boulton, L.; Niknejadi, P.; Põder, K.; Schaper, L.; Zeng, M.; Bohlen, S.; Boyle, G.; Brümmer, T.; et al. Stable witness-beam formation in a beam-driven plasma cathode. *Phys. Rev. Accel. Beams* **2021**, *24*, 101302. [CrossRef]
55. Habib, A.F.; Scherkl, P.; Manahan, G.G.; Heinemann, T.; Ullmann, D.; Sutherland, A.; Knetsch, A.; Litos, M.; Hogan, M.; Rosenzweig, J.; et al. Plasma accelerator-based ultrabright X-ray beams from ultrabright electron beams. In *Proceedings of the Advances in Laboratory-Based X-ray Sources, Optics, and Applications VII, San Diego, CA, USA, 13 August 2019*; International Society for Optics and Photonics: Bellingham, WA, USA, 2019; Volume 11110, p. 111100A.
56. Emma, C.; Van Tilborg, J.; Assmann, R.; Barber, S.; Cianchi, A.; Corde, S.; Couprie, M.E.; D'Arcy, R.; Ferrario, M.; Habib, A.F.; et al. Free electron lasers driven by plasma accelerators: Status and near-term prospects. *High Power Laser Sci. Eng.* **2021**, *9*, e57. [CrossRef]
57. Ferri, J.; Corde, S.; Döpp, A.; Lifschitz, A.; Doche, A.; Thaury, C.; Ta Phuoc, K.; Mahieu, B.; Andriyash, I.A.; Malka, V.; et al. High-Brilliance Betatron γ-Ray Source Powered by Laser-Accelerated Electrons. *Phys. Rev. Lett.* **2018**, *120*, 254802. [CrossRef]
58. Pompili, R.; Alesini, D.; Anania, M.P.; Arjmand, S.; Behtouei, M.; Bellaveglia, M.; Biagioni, A.; Buonomo, B.; Cardelli, F.; Carpanese, M.; et al. Free-electron lasing with compact beam-driven plasma wakefield accelerator. *Nature* **2022**, *605*, 659–662. [CrossRef]
59. Labat, M.; Cabadağ, J.C.; Ghaith, A.; Irman, A.; Berlioux, A.; Berteaud, P.; Blache, F.; Bock, S.; Bouvet, F.; Briquez, F.; et al. Seeded free-electron laser driven by a compact laser plasma accelerator. *Nat. Photonics* **2022**, 1–7. [CrossRef]
60. Habib, A.F.; Manahan, G.; Scherkl, P.; Heinemann, T.; Sutherland, A.; Altuiri, R.; Alotaibi, B.M.; Litos, M.; Cary, J.; Raubenheimer, T.; et al. Attosecond-Angstrom free-electron-laser towards the cold beam limit. *arXiv* **2022**, arXiv:2212.04398.

Disclaimer/Publisher's Note: The statements, opinions and data contained in all publications are solely those of the individual author(s) and contributor(s) and not of MDPI and/or the editor(s). MDPI and/or the editor(s) disclaim responsibility for any injury to people or property resulting from any ideas, methods, instructions or products referred to in the content.

Review

Review of Quality Optimization of Electron Beam Based on Laser Wakefield Acceleration

Kangnan Jiang [1,2], Wentao Wang [1,*], Ke Feng [1] and Ruxin Li [1,2]

1. State Key Laboratory of High Field Laser Physics and CAS Center for Excellence in Ultra-Intense Laser Science, Shanghai Institute of Optics and Fine Mechanics (SIOM), Chinese Academy of Sciences (CAS), Shanghai 201800, China; jiangkn@siom.ac.cn (K.J.); fengke@siom.ac.cn (K.F.); ruxinli@siom.ac.cn (R.L.)
2. School of Physical Science and Technology, Shanghai Tech University, Shanghai 200031, China
* Correspondence: wwt1980@siom.ac.cn

Abstract: Compared with state-of-the-art radio frequency accelerators, the gradient of laser wakefield accelerators is 3–4 orders of magnitude higher. This is of great significance in the development of miniaturized particle accelerators and radiation sources. Higher requirements have been proposed for the quality of electron beams, owing to the increasing application requirements of tabletop radiation sources, specifically with the rapid development of free-electron laser devices. This review briefly examines the electron beam quality optimization scheme based on laser wakefield acceleration and presents some representative studies. In addition, manipulation of the electron beam phase space by means of injection, plasma profile distribution, and laser evolution is described. This review of studies is beneficial for further promoting the application of laser wakefield accelerators.

Keywords: laser wakefield accelerator; six-dimensional phase-space brightness; beam quality optimization

1. Introduction

In 1979, Tajima and Dawson [1] proposed the concept of laser wakefield acceleration (LWFA) [2]. When a strong laser is incident on the plasma, the ponderomotive force dislodges the electrons in the background plasma and then excites a wakefield to accelerate the particles. Without the breakdown voltage limitation in the plasma, the acceleration gradient of the LWFA can reach 100 GV/m, which is three orders of magnitude higher than that of the conventional radio frequency accelerator. Therefore, it is of great significance for the development of miniaturized particle accelerators. The nonlinear wakefield, called the bubble, has a microstructure, and the accelerated electrons usually have only an fs-level pulse length and a µm-level transverse size. In addition to being affected by the longitudinal acceleration field, the electron beam also oscillates transversely in the wakefield, which generates betatron radiation covering the ultraviolet to X-ray wave bands, whose frequencies are related to the plasma frequency and electron energy. Gamma rays can also be generated by inverse Compton scattering, caused by the interaction of the electron beam with the laser beam. When the electron beam quality meets the high-gain free-electron laser (FEL) conditions, it can be applied to the FEL [3–5]. These features make LWFA a potential tabletop accelerator and radiation source.

LWFA has high requirements for laser intensity (~25 fs pulse length, 10^{18} W/cm^2 power density). It was impossible to experimentally obtain a monoenergetic electron beam for a long time, owing to the lack of a strong driving laser. In 1985, the introduction of chirped pulse amplification (CPA) [6] led to the rapid development of ultra-intense and ultra-short laser devices, providing a driving light source with relativistic intensity for the excitation of the laser wakefield. In 2004, Faure et al., Geddes et al. and Mangles et al. experimentally obtained 100 MeV level quasi-mono-energetic electron beams for the first time experimentally, which were reported on the cover of *Nature* with the title

"Dream Beam" [7–9]. LWFA ushered in a milestone breakthrough, marking the beginning of miniaturized particle accelerators. An increasing number of groups have devoted themselves to electron acceleration research based on LWFA. This research has entered a period of rapid development concentrated on energy gain improvements [10], acceleration stability [11], and electron beam quality optimization [12].

As a typical example, the group led by Leemans has carried out a lot of important work in the promotion of electron beam energy and also enhanced the electron beam energy multiple times [13–15]. The acceleration distance can be extended, and the maximum acceleration energy can be increased by optimizing laser guidance [16]. In 2019, they used a 20-cm-long capillary [17] to guide the laser to maintain good focus and electron beams with energy peaks up to 7.8 GeV [15]. These are the highest LWFA-based energy electrons that have been reported internationally. In terms of electron beam stability, Osterhoff et al. [18] used a cylindrical gas box 15 mm long and 250 μm in diameter as a gas pool structure to create a stable plasma profile distribution in 2008. An electron beam with a divergence angle of ~2.1 mrad was obtained by continuous collection. The RMS (root mean square) energy jitter from shot to shot was less than 2.5%, and the pointing jitter was less than 1.4 mrad, which was the best result for stability reported at the time. In 2020, Maier et al. conducted further experiments on the stability of LWFA [11]. They accurately measured the electron beam energy drift and jitter with a combination of diagnostic methods, which provided a basis for obtaining electron beam acceleration feedback and active control. According to the correlation between the laser and electron parameters, the electron beam quality is parameterized to enable loop feedback and fine-tuning of the accelerator, resulting in a reproducible electron beam [19,20]. The continuous acquisition of 100,000 high-stability electron beams within 24 h has realized the long-term stable operation of LWFA.

Methods for electron injection and electron phase-space manipulation have been continuously proposed and improved, with the intent of boosting the quality of electron beams based on LWFA. In 2006, Faure et al. first experimentally verified the colliding laser pulse injection proposed in the early theory [21]. They also realized a flexible adjustment of the electron beam peak energy by changing the collision position of the two pulses. Thus, the electron beam was further optimized. The phase-space volume of the injected particles can be controlled by adjusting the optical injection parameters, thereby controlling the electron beam charge and energy spread. An electron beam with 200 MeV, 10 pC, and 1% relative energy spread was experimentally obtained [22]. Along with the theory of ionization injection, in 2007, Oz et al. [23] took the lead in performing LWFA based on ionization injection in experiments. In 2014, Xu et al. and Yu et al. [24,25] conducted research on obtaining low-emittance electron beams based on two-color laser ionization injection. Zeng et al. proposed an ionization implantation scheme, in which a triple-frequency injection laser propagates co-linearly with the driving laser to obtain a low-energy spread electron beam [26].

As mentioned above, it is difficult to describe the overall quality of an electron beam using a single parameter. Drawing on conventional accelerators, we introduce the six-dimensional phase-space brightness in units of A/m^2/0.1% [12,27,28] to characterize the comprehensive quality of the electron beam, which can be defined as the total bunch charge divided by the product of the rms horizontal, vertical and longitudinal normalized emittances be expressed as

$$B_{6D} = \frac{I_P}{\varepsilon_{nx}\varepsilon_{ny}\sigma_\gamma \cdot 0.1\%}, \tag{1}$$

where I_P represents the peak current; ε_{nx} and ε_{ny} represent the horizontal and vertical transverse emittance, respectively; and σ_γ represents the RMS relative energy spread. High brightness in the 6D phase space requires the electron beam to have a low energy spread, low emittance, and high current, which results in high quality and provides guidance for optimizing the electron beam.

In this review, we briefly examine an electron beam quality optimization scheme based on LWFA. The analysis of the influencing factors indicates the direction of electron beam parameter optimization. The effects of the injection method, phase-space manipulation, and improvements of electron beam parameters at different stages are discussed. In addition, this review briefly discusses a portion of the outstanding work of related research teams on LWFA and provides guidance for future electron beam quality optimization.

2. Emittance

Emittance, which is the area of transverse phase space occupied by a beam of particles, as shown in Figure 1a, characterizes the transverse quality of the beam. It is necessary to control the electron beam injection and acceleration in the wakefield by controlling the profile of the plasma density and evolution of the laser pulse to obtain an electron beam with low emittance. An increase in the electron beam emittance was suppressed, and high-quality electron beams with low emittance were finally obtained by controlling the evolution of the phase space to match the parameters of the wakefield.

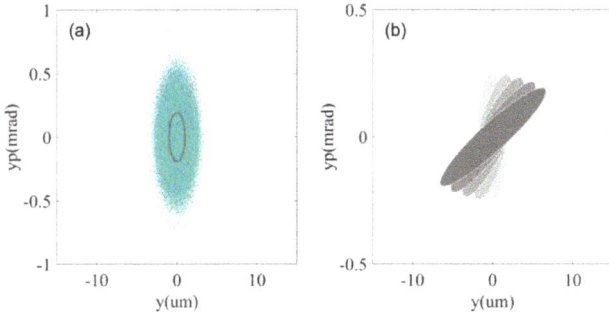

Figure 1. Transverse phase space distribution of electron beam: (**a**) definition of emittance, area (red line) = emittance $\times \pi$; (**b**) phase space distribution of electron beam with different phase.

Beam density remains constant in the phase space according to the Liouville theorem. Therefore, when particle beam density remains unchanged, the volume occupied by the particle beam in the phase space remains unchanged during motion. The injected emittance determines the lower limit of the final emittance for a mono-energetic electron beam, while neglecting collective effects, such as space charge. The transverse wave breaking threshold will be lower than the traditional one-dimensional wave breaking threshold in two-dimensional or three-dimensional structures [29], which promotes the transverse injection of the electron beam. The off-axis injected electrons maintain betatron oscillation inside the bubble, under the influence of the transverse field. Collision ionization injection reduces the influence of the transverse force. Two oppositely propagating ultrashort laser beams with the same parameters were injected transversely, and the lasers were controlled to collide precisely on the axis. The two trigger lasers were linearly polarized along the z-axis, which reduced the transverse modulation of the electrons injected from the trigger laser. The electron beam injection phase is controlled so that it enters the accelerated focusing field quickly after injection to reduce the transverse divergence, and finally, electrons with an emittance of nm rad level are obtained.

During acceleration in the wakefield, the injected electron beam is not only affected by the longitudinal acceleration field, but also by the transverse focusing and defocusing field. Matching the particle beam to the focusing and defocusing field of the plasma accelerator is critical for maintaining beam quality. While accelerated in the longitudinal direction, the electron beam also oscillates continuously in the transverse direction, and its oscillation frequency is related to the energy and longitudinal phase of the electron beam. Therefore, a strong coupling exists between the longitudinal and transverse directions of the electron beam during wakefield acceleration. This strong coupling causes the oscillation phase of the electron to change with the longitudinal position, eventually leading to complete decoherence. Phase decoherence is an important factor leading to an increase in electron beam emittance during the acceleration process. Generally, these effects are caused by a non-zero energy spread or non-zero pulse length. It is necessary to construct a specific plasma profile distribution and control the evolution of the laser pulse to control the electron beam motion in the wakefield, such that the electron beam phase space matches the wakefield and suppresses the electron beam emittance growth [30].

According to the Mathieu–Hill equation and the relationship between the Courant–Snyder parameter states, the evolution of the beta function in a line-focusing system follows a function. For a narrow electron beam ($k_p \sigma_r \ll 1$) in LWFA, the electrons can be approximately subjected to a linear transverse force [31–33], as follows:

$$K(r,z) = -\frac{e}{\gamma m c^2} \partial_r E(r,z) \bigg|_{r=0}, \tag{2}$$

where e and m represent the charge and mass of the electron, respectively. γ represents the Lorentz factor, c represents the speed of light in a vacuum, and E_r represents the transverse electric field. For a given K, the evolution of the beta function can be expressed as [30]

$$\beta(z) = \beta_0 \cos^2\left(\sqrt{K}z\right) + \frac{1}{\beta_0 K}\sin^2\left(\sqrt{K}z\right), \tag{3}$$

where β_0 denotes the initial beta function. The formula shows that the beta function of the electron beam in the normally focused channel oscillates between β_0 and $1/(\beta_0 K)$. When the initial beta function value is $K^{-1/2}$, the electron beam maintains the transverse size, which can be called a matched electron beam. Similarly, for a given electron beam envelope parameter, K can be tuned to match the electron beam by constructing a specific plasma density profile. Matching the electron beam to the mean parameter K slows the betatron oscillations, which also provides guidance for controlling emittance growth. When the single stage is extended to multiple stages, the electron beam parameters can be adjusted to match the channel and effectively avoid the increase in emittance caused by the nonlinear coupling of lateral and longitudinal motions. In both theory and simulation [30,34–37], the matched parameters can control the increase in electron beam emittance at the level of several percent.

Similar to bubbles, the energy spread also results in an increase in the electron beam emittance in the free space. When an electron beam passes through a magnet and is subjected to a magnetic field with the same gradient, electrons with different energies are focused and defocused. The energy spread causes a phase difference in the electron beam transverse phase space, as shown in Figure 1b, which is also the main reason that the projected emittance is greater than the slice emittance. Increasing the transport distance or electron beam energy spread exacerbates the increase in emittance until saturation. Therefore, it is necessary to design a compact beam transport line and strictly compress the electron beam energy spread [38–40]. The scheme of controlling electrons to achieve a low energy spread is described below.

3. Energy Spread

The final energy spread of the electron beam is affected by the initial energy spread and inhomogeneous acceleration, which originate from the inhomogeneity of the longitudinal acceleration field, beam loading, and phase slippage caused by the betatron oscillations. The electrons injected at different times are affected by the acceleration field for different durations, which means that the electrons in the head (those injected first) have higher energy. Therefore, the electron beam initially appears as a negative chirp. Continuous electron beam injection results in increased initial energy spread. Figure 2 shows a snapshot of a bubble and the on-axis longitudinal field (white line) in the PIC simulation. During the acceleration process, owing to the nonuniform longitudinal acceleration field, the energy gain of the electrons in the tail of the beam gradually becomes higher than that at the head, and the negative chirp evolves into a positive chirp. Therefore, energy spread compression is achieved by reducing the injection duration, as well as weakening the inhomogeneity of the acceleration field and chirp compensation in the injection and acceleration stages, respectively. The injection process plays an important role in the electron beam quality. Several methods, including ionization [41,42], density gradient, and collision, are used to trigger injection. There are also some improved injection methods, such as utilizing Tesla-scale magnetic fields to control self-injection and an evolved electron beam to drive plasma waves to achieve injection control. The following discussion will take an example and examine its influence on the electron beam energy spread during the injection process.

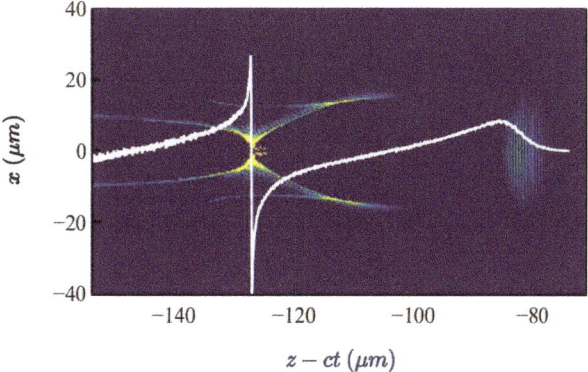

Figure 2. Snapshot of a bubble and the on-axis longitudinal field lineouts (white line) in the PIC simulation.

Density gradient injection is a controllable injection scheme that was first proposed by Bulanov [43]. He studied the wave breaking phenomenon generated in the region of a slow-varying plasma density down ramp and then explored the conditions of the injection. Subsequently, Suk et al. [44] conducted a theoretical study of the case of discontinuously varying densities. The phase velocity of the wakefield decreased as the wavelength of the plasma wave in this area increased. The magnitude of the reduction was proportional to the distance of the wakefield from the driving laser and the gradient of the density-down ramp. Electrons are injected when the wakefield phase velocity is smaller than the electron velocity.

In 2008, Geddes et al. [45] obtained low-energy electron beams with only 0.17 MeV energy spread based on density gradient injection. In 2010, Faure et al. also conducted experiments on density-gradient injection [46]. They used an inclined auxiliary laser beam to generate a plasma channel at an angle of 135° corresponding to the axis. The inclined channel generates a relatively large density gradient, and the wakefield continues to accelerate the injected electrons after the wave breaks. In 2013, Wang et al. adopted a cascade acceleration scheme based on gradient injection [47]. Active control of the density gradient is achieved by changing the distance between the two gas cells or the back-pressure difference of the gas. The absolute energy spread introduced by the injection stage can be effectively controlled in the experiment by changing the plasma density of the second stage to lower than the conditions required for electron injection. As the plasma density of the accelerating stage is further reduced, the size of the bubble becomes significantly larger, causing the electrons initially injected in the second bubble to slip into the first bubble. Through density control, the electron beam can be slipped to a better matched phase in the first bubble and finally accelerated to 0.5 GeV, resulting in a significantly reduced energy spread of approximately 3%.

The previously discussed methods are used to construct density gradients artificially, by means of auxiliary lasers or the injection of gases with different back pressures. However, these approaches make it difficult to construct plasma distributions with high-density gradients. During the interaction between the laser and gas, the evolution of the normalized intensity of the laser also affects the size of the bubble and phase velocity of the wakefield, owing to the effects of self-focusing and defocusing. When the plasma profile density gradient was small, the wavelength change in the plasma wave was less affected by the density. Compared to the influence of the evolution of the laser, the influence of the density gradient on the wakefield phase velocity is not dominant. Therefore, it is difficult to achieve low energy spread and high stability injection by relying only on the density gradient constructed in this manner.

To improve the controllability of the electron quality, several research groups have successively improved the method to construct specific plasma distributions. When supersonic gas was sprayed on a target, a shock wave with a density gradient was formed in the local area. Based on this principle, different structural targets, such as blades, capillaries, and steel wires [48–51], were used as nozzles to construct matching density distributions. Similarly, the dual-nozzle structure [52] can also be used to construct a plasma density falling edge. The upper and lower nozzles were used for gas injection. A high-density area with an adjustable width can be generated by adjusting the relative horizontal positions of the two nozzles. The second self-injection of the electron beam was suppressed by the density peak, and the injection cut-off was effectively realized. In addition, the electron beam passes through a wakefield with a negative energy chirp slope at the density down ramp, that is, the low-energy electrons at the tail of the beam obtain a higher energy gain, and the high-energy electrons at the head obtain a lower energy gain. This is beneficial for the energy-spread compression of the electron beam in the bubble. In 2016, Wang et al. used a double-nozzle structure to obtain a 530–580 MeV electron beam with an energy spread of less than 1% [12]. It can be found that the energy spread of the electron beam obtained by LWFA based on gradient injection is mostly at the level of several percent, which cannot meet the relative energy spread at the level of several thousandths required by the tabletop FEL. In the final analysis, the density gradient injection was still a wave break injection [29,53,54], but the injection threshold reduction was controlled. Therefore, the density gradient injection still has the disadvantage of wave-breaking injection, which depends on the nonlinear effect of the wakefield.

As mentioned previously, an electron beam with an energy spread of ~1% can be experimentally obtained using the cascade acceleration scheme. Furthermore, the construction of a multistage plasma distribution system to achieve further compression of the energy spread through electron beam length compression has also been proposed. However, cascade acceleration is usually complex to operate and requires high stability of each part; thus, it is challenging to stably generate electron beams with ultra-low energy spread. The increase in the energy spread in the acceleration stage was mainly affected by the inhomogeneity of the longitudinal acceleration field (usually a positive chirp). We can construct an appropriate non-uniform acceleration field (usually a negative chirp) to compress the electron energy spread and solve this problem. In recent years, researchers of conventional accelerators have designed special dechirp devices to remove energy chirps [55,56]. Such devices can make the electron beam energy spread to a level of a few thousandths. However, the dechirp devices used in conventional accelerators have a low intensity, which is not suitable for high-energy chirped electron beams generated in LWFA.

Drawing on the chirp compensation mechanism of conventional accelerators, the concept of plasma dechirp device was first proposed in 2017. The basic principle is to use the wakefield generated by an electron beam in the plasma (particle wakefield acceleration, PWFA) to remove the energy chirp [57,58]. The longitudinal field excited in the plasma by a positive-energy chirp electron beam causes the tail to decelerate more than the head. After a suitable distance, the energy chirp of the electron beam is removed. In 2019, D'Arcy et al., Shpakov et al. and Wu et al. each experimentally verified the concept of a plasma dechirper [59–61].

In addition to the external plasma dechirp device in the beamline, the wakefield acceleration process uses a similar technology called energy chirp compensation [20]. The difference between them lies in the generation of the dechirp field and interaction process. Relativistic self-focusing plays an important role in the interaction between the laser and plasma. When the laser power is sufficiently high, there will be enough critical energy for the laser to self-focus. Usually, the laser self-focusing process can be used to extend the laser transport distance and control the electron beam injection; however, the laser defocusing process is rarely considered. Experiments and simulations have shown that the laser defocusing process can degenerate the wakefield from a strong nonlinear state to a weak nonlinear state under the matched parameters. In this process, the acceleration field at the position where the injected electrons are located changes from a positive slope to a negative slope, which effectively removes the positive chirp of the electron beam. By introducing a density spike at a suitable position, Dopp et al. [62] achieved electron beam energy spread compression from tens of percent to less than ten percent. In 2021, Ke et al. used shock injection to generate 780–840 MeV, 2.4‰–4.1‰ energy spread high-quality electron beams in the experiment [63], as shown in Table 1. A suitable plasma profile distribution was constructed by adjusting the relative positions of the nozzles, such that the electron beam could inject the bubble at an appropriate position before laser defocusing. When the laser is defocused, the electron beam can interact with the formed dechirping field and carry out an effective dechirping process. The effect of plasma density on laser self-focusing and defocusing was used to control the acceleration field, and a high-energy electron beam with ultralow energy spread was obtained.

Table 1. Summary of parameters from different laboratories, as discussed in the text.

Laboratory	Energy [1] (GeV)	Energy Spread [1] (%)	Charge [1] (pC)	Emittance [1] (mm mrad)
SIOM	0.8	0.2–1.2	10–50	0.4
DESY	0.3	0.4	500	1.5/0.3
LBNL	7.8	0.2–1	25	0.3–1
LOA	1.1	3.1	120	NA

[1] The best parameters are listed when a laboratory has multiple experimental results, as discussed.

4. Current

Current, the ratio of electron beam charge to pulse length, is usually at the level of KA in LWFA (it deals with the peak current). From the definition, the electron beam current can be increased by increasing the electron beam charge or compressing the pulse length [64]. The number of injected electrons in the bubble is positively correlated with the laser intensity, according to the model established by Gordienko et al. [65,66]. However, realizing a large amount of charge does not only guarantee an electron beam with high current. More importantly, it increases the amount of charge injected per unit time. For the qualitative analysis of the injection process, the phase velocity of the plasma wave in the bubble can be expressed as [67]

$$v_{ph} = -\frac{\frac{\partial \varphi}{\partial t}}{\frac{\partial \varphi}{\partial z}} \approx \frac{v_g}{1 + \frac{z-ct}{k_p} \cdot \frac{dk_p}{dz}} = \frac{v_g}{1 + \frac{z-ct}{2n_z} \cdot \frac{dn_z}{dz}}, \quad (4)$$

where v_g is the laser group velocity, $z - ct$ is the longitudinal position in the co-moving coordinate system, and n_z is the plasma density longitudinal distribution. The formula shows that when n_z has a down ramp in the longitudinal direction, the relativistic factor of the plasma wave can be effectively reduced. The wave break threshold decreases as the plasma wave phase velocity decreases, making it easier for electrons to inject. With the further increase in the density gradient, the wave break threshold decreases more, which is beneficial to realize the high current of the electron beam. However, a decrease in plasma density means a decrease in the number of cardinality that can be injected with electrons, which suppresses the electron beam current. Therefore, it is necessary to quantitatively analyze [68,69] and optimize the density gradient to improve the electron beam current by particle-in-cell simulation.

In the experiments, the current is difficult to increase, since the charge scales with the pulse length under the same conditions. Continued injection results in a high-charge electron beam accompanied by an increase in the pulse length. This will result in a more significant difference in energy gain between the head and tail of the electron beam, which increases the beam energy spread. Focused adjustment of the electron beam quality is necessary for different radiation source requirements. As required for high-gain FELs, its Pierce parameter should be greater than the relative energy spread of the electron beam. Figure 3 shows the Pierce parameters for different currents and transverse sizes based on specific electron beam and undulator parameters. Taking the transverse size as 40 µm, when the current increases from 5 kA to 15 kA, the Pierce parameter (upper limit of relative energy spread) only increases from 0.4% to less than 0.6%, whose increase is significantly smaller than that of the current. Wang et al. presented an experimental demonstration of undulator radiation amplification in the exponential-gain regime [70]. The accelerated electron beam typically has a peak energy of ~490 MeV, with the energy spread of approximately 0.5%, an average integrated charge of around 30 pC, and r.m.s. divergence of approximately 0.2 mrad. Simulations show that the electron beam current is approximately 5 kA. Although no emphasis has been placed on optimizing the current, experimentally, the per-mille-level relative energy spread enables electrons to achieve 100-fold gain in the third undulator. Therefore, compared with high current, low energy spread plays a dominant role. For those with less demanding electron beam energy spread, such as betatron radiation, an increase in current intensity or charge is beneficial to obtain a higher photon number [71,72].

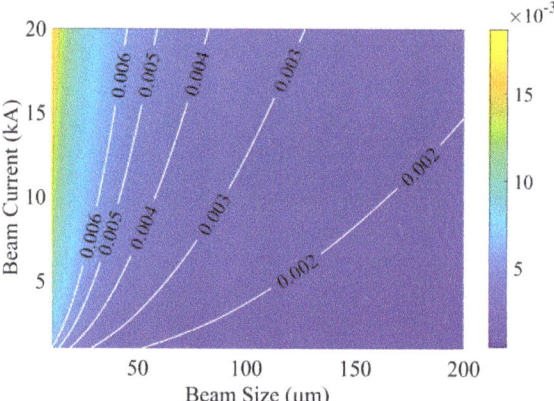

Figure 3. The Pierce parameters for different currents and transverse sizes.

5. Conclusions

With the continuous efforts of various research teams, LWFA has developed rapidly in the past ten years, and the electron beam quality has gradually improved. The brightness of the electron beam and radiation source based on LWFA have also been improved [63,73–76]. The tabletop FEL [70,77,78] based on LWFA was verified experimentally. Such proof-of-principle experiments will expedite the development of future compact facilities with broad applications. However, owing to limited high-field laser technology developments, instability in laser and plasma interactions, and acceleration field inhomogeneities, the current electron beams cannot meet the application requirements in terms of performance and repetition frequency. More theoretical and experimental research is necessary, including the exploration of new injection methods, high-resolution diagnostic schemes, ultralong low-density plasma channel development, and machine learning to promote electron beam performance optimization. It is necessary to continuously optimize the electron beam quality to meet its application requirements for various tabletop radiation sources [74,79–81], so that the LWFA can be stably available and realize miniaturization acceleration. This review briefly examines recent LWFA-based electron beam quality optimization schemes, aiming to provide a complete and clear understanding of LWFA research, while promoting cooperation and exchanges in interdisciplinary fields.

Author Contributions: Conceptualization, K.J. and K.F.; Methodology, K.J., W.W. and K.F.; Validation, W.W.; Investigation, K.J.; Software, K.J. and K.F.; Funding acquisition, W.W. and R.L.; Writing—original draft preparation, K.J.; Writing—review and editing, W.W. and K.F. All authors have read and agreed to the published version of the manuscript.

Funding: This work was supported by the National Natural Science Foundation of China (grant nos. 11991072 and 11875065), the State Key Laboratory Program of the Chinese Ministry of Science and Technology and CAS Youth Innovation Promotion Association (Y201952) and the National Natural Science Foundation of China (grant nos. 12105353).

Institutional Review Board Statement: Not applicable.

Informed Consent Statement: Not applicable.

Data Availability Statement: Not applicable.

Conflicts of Interest: The authors declare no conflict of interest.

References

1. Tajima, T.; Dawson, J.M. Laser Electron Accelerator. *Phys. Rev. Lett.* **1979**, *43*, 267. [CrossRef]
2. Tajima, T.; Nakajima, K.; Mourou, G. Laser acceleration. *Riv. Nuovo Cim.* **2017**, *40*, 33–133. [CrossRef]
3. Emma, C.; Van Tilborg, J.; Assmann, R.; Barber, S.; Cianchi, A.; Corde, S.; Couprie, M.E.; D'Arcy, R.; Ferrario, M.; Habib, A.F.; et al. Free electron lasers driven by plasma accelerators: Status and near-term prospects. *High Power Laser Sci. Eng.* **2021**, *9*, e57. [CrossRef]
4. Huang, Z.R.; Ding, Y.T.; Schroeder, C.B. Compact X-ray Free-Electron Laser from a Laser-Plasma Accelerator Using a Transverse-Gradient Undulator. *Phys. Rev. Lett.* **2012**, *109*, 204801. [CrossRef] [PubMed]
5. Pellegrini, C.; Marinelli, A.; Reiche, S. The physics of X-ray free-electron lasers. *Rev. Mod. Phys.* **2016**, *88*, 55. [CrossRef]
6. Strickland, D.; Mourou, G. Compression of amplified chirped optical pulses. *Opt. Commun.* **1985**, *56*, 219–221. [CrossRef]
7. Faure, J.; Glinec, Y.; Pukhov, A.; Kiselev, S.; Gordienko, S.; Lefebvre, E.; Rousseau, J.P.; Burgy, F.; Malka, V. A laser-plasma accelerator producing monoenergetic electron beams. *Nature* **2004**, *431*, 541–544. [CrossRef]
8. Geddes, C.G.R.; Toth, C.; van Tilborg, J.; Esarey, E.; Schroeder, C.B.; Bruhwiler, D.; Nieter, C.; Cary, J.; Leemans, W.P. High-quality electron beams from a laser wakefield accelerator using plasma-channel guiding. *Nature* **2004**, *431*, 538–541. [CrossRef]
9. Mangles, S.P.D.; Murphy, C.D.; Najmudin, Z.; Thomas, A.G.R.; Collier, J.L.; Dangor, A.E.; Divall, E.J.; Foster, P.S.; Gallacher, J.G.; Hooker, C.J.; et al. Monoenergetic beams of relativistic electrons from intense laser-plasma interactions. *Nature* **2004**, *431*, 535–538. [CrossRef]
10. Nakajima, K.; Kim, H.T.; Jeong, T.M.; Nam, C.H. Scaling and design of high-energy laser plasma electron acceleration. *High Power Laser Sci. Eng.* **2015**, *3*, e10. [CrossRef]
11. Maier, A.R.; Delbos, N.M.; Eichner, T.; Hubner, L.; Jalas, S.; Jeppe, L.; Jolly, S.W.; Kirchen, M.; Leroux, V.; Messner, P.; et al. Decoding Sources of Energy Variability in a Laser-Plasma Accelerator. *Phys. Rev. X* **2020**, *10*, 031039. [CrossRef]
12. Wang, W.T.; Li, W.T.; Liu, J.S.; Zhang, Z.J.; Qi, R.; Yu, C.H.; Liu, J.Q.; Fang, M.; Qin, Z.Y.; Wang, C.; et al. High-Brightness High-Energy Electron Beams from a Laser Wakefield Accelerator via Energy Chirp Control. *Phys. Rev. Lett.* **2016**, *117*, 124801. [CrossRef] [PubMed]
13. Leemans, W.P.; Nagler, B.; Gonsalves, A.J.; Toth, C.; Nakamura, K.; Geddes, C.G.R.; Esarey, E.; Schroeder, C.B.; Hooker, S.M. GeV electron beams from a centimetre-scale accelerator. *Nat. Phys.* **2006**, *2*, 696–699. [CrossRef]
14. Leemans, W.P.; Gonsalves, A.J.; Mao, H.S.; Nakamura, K.; Benedetti, C.; Schroeder, C.B.; Toth, C.; Daniels, J.; Mittelberger, D.E.; Bulanov, S.S.; et al. Multi-GeV Electron Beams from Capillary-Discharge-Guided Subpetawatt Laser Pulses in the Self-Trapping Regime. *Phys. Rev. Lett.* **2014**, *113*, 245002. [CrossRef]
15. Gonsalves, A.J.; Nakamura, K.; Daniels, J.; Benedetti, C.; Pieronek, C.; de Raadt, T.C.H.; Steinke, S.; Bin, J.H.; Bulanov, S.S.; van Tilborg, J.; et al. Petawatt Laser Guiding and Electron Beam Acceleration to 8 GeV in a Laser-Heated Capillary Discharge Waveguide. *Phys. Rev. Lett.* **2019**, *122*, 084801. [CrossRef] [PubMed]
16. Oubrerie, K.; Leblanc, A.; Kononenko, O.; Lahaye, R.; Andriyash, I.A.; Gautier, J.; Goddet, J.P.; Martelli, L.; Tafzi, A.; Phuoc, K.T.; et al. Controlled acceleration of GeV electron beams in an all-optical plasma waveguide. *Light-Sci. Appl.* **2022**, *11*, 180. [CrossRef]

17. Turner, M.; Gonsalves, A.J.; Bulanov, S.S.; Benedetti, C.; Bobrova, N.A.; Gasilov, V.A.; Sasorov, P.V.; Korn, G.; Nakamura, K.; van Tilborg, J.; et al. Radial density profile and stability of capillary discharge plasma waveguides of lengths up to 40 cm. *High Power Laser Sci. Eng.* **2021**, *9*, e17. [CrossRef]
18. Osterhoff, J.; Popp, A.; Major, Z.; Marx, B.; Rowlands-Rees, T.P.; Fuchs, M.; Geissler, M.; Hoerlein, R.; Hidding, B.; Becker, S.; et al. Generation of stable, low-divergence electron beams by laser-wakefield acceleration in a steady-state-flow gas cell. *Phys. Rev. Lett.* **2008**, *101*, 085002. [CrossRef]
19. Jalas, S.; Kirchen, M.; Messner, P.; Winkler, P.; Hubner, L.; Dirkwinkel, J.; Schnepp, M.; Lehe, R.; Maier, A.R. Bayesian Optimization of a Laser-Plasma Accelerator. *Phys. Rev. Lett.* **2021**, *126*, 104801. [CrossRef]
20. Kirchen, M.; Jalas, S.; Messner, P.; Winkler, P.; Eichner, T.; Hubner, L.; Hulsenbusch, T.; Jeppe, L.; Parikh, T.; Schnepp, M.; et al. Optimal Beam Loading in a Laser-Plasma Accelerator. *Phys. Rev. Lett.* **2021**, *126*, 174801. [CrossRef]
21. Faure, J.; Rechatin, C.; Norlin, A.; Lifschitz, A.; Glinec, Y.; Malka, V. Controlled injection and acceleration of electrons in plasma wakefields by colliding laser pulses. *Nature* **2006**, *444*, 737–739. [CrossRef]
22. Rechatin, C.; Faure, J.; Ben-Ismail, A.; Lim, J.; Fitour, R.; Specka, A.; Videau, H.; Tafzi, A.; Burgy, F.; Malka, V. Controlling the Phase-Space Volume of Injected Electrons in a Laser-Plasma Accelerator. *Phys. Rev. Lett.* **2009**, *102*, 164801. [CrossRef]
23. Oz, E.; Deng, S.; Katsouleas, T.; Muggli, P.; Barnes, C.D.; Blumenfeld, I.; Decker, F.J.; Emma, P.; Hogan, M.J.; Ischebeck, R.; et al. Ionization-induced electron trapping in ultrarelativistic plasma wakes. *Phys. Rev. Lett.* **2007**, *98*, 084801. [CrossRef] [PubMed]
24. Xu, X.L.; Wu, Y.P.; Zhang, C.J.; Li, F.; Wan, Y.; Hua, J.F.; Pai, C.H.; Lu, W.; Yu, P.; Joshi, C.; et al. Low emittance electron beam generation from a laser wakefield accelerator using two laser pulses with different wavelengths. *Phys. Rev. Spec. Top.-Accel. Beams* **2014**, *17*, 061301. [CrossRef]
25. Yu, L.L.; Esarey, E.; Schroeder, C.B.; Vay, J.L.; Benedetti, C.; Geddes, C.G.R.; Chen, M.; Leemans, W.P. Two-Color Laser-Ionization Injection. *Phys. Rev. Lett.* **2014**, *112*, 125001. [CrossRef] [PubMed]
26. Zeng, M.; Chen, M.; Yu, L.L.; Mori, W.B.; Sheng, Z.M.; Hidding, B.; Jaroszynski, D.A.; Zhang, J. Multichromatic Narrow-Energy-Spread Electron Bunches from Laser-Wakefield Acceleration with Dual-Color Lasers. *Phys. Rev. Lett.* **2015**, *114*, 084801. [CrossRef]
27. Di Mitri, S.; Cornacchia, M. Electron beam brightness in linac drivers for free-electron-lasers. *Phys. Rep.-Rev. Sec. Phys. Lett.* **2014**, *539*, 1–48. [CrossRef]
28. Manahan, G.G.; Habib, A.F.; Scherkl, P.; Delinikolas, P.; Beaton, A.; Knetsch, A.; Karger, O.; Wittig, G.; Heinemann, T.; Sheng, Z.M.; et al. Single-stage plasma-based correlated energy spread compensation for ultrahigh 6D brightness electron beams. *Nat. Commun.* **2017**, *8*, 15705. [CrossRef]
29. Bulanov, S.V.; Pegoraro, F.; Pukhov, A.M.; Sakharov, A.S. Transverse-wake wave breaking. *Phys. Rev. Lett.* **1997**, *78*, 4205–4208. [CrossRef]
30. Mehrling, T.; Grebenyuk, J.; Tsung, F.S.; Floettmann, K.; Osterhoff, J. Transverse emittance growth in staged laser-wakefield acceleration. *Phys. Rev. Spec. Top.-Accel. Beams* **2012**, *15*, 111303. [CrossRef]
31. Esarey, E.; Schroeder, C.B.; Leemans, W.P. Physics of laser-driven plasma-based electron accelerators. *Rev. Mod. Phys.* **2009**, *81*, 1229–1285. [CrossRef]
32. Lu, W.; Huang, C.; Zhou, M.; Tzoufras, M.; Tsung, F.S.; Mori, W.B.; Katsouleas, T. A nonlinear theory for multidimensional relativistic plasma wave wakefields. *Phys. Plasmas* **2006**, *13*, 056709. [CrossRef]
33. Rosenzweig, J.B.; Breizman, B.; Katsouleas, T.; Su, J.J. Acceleration and focusing of electrons in 2-dimensional nonlinear plasma wake fields. *Phys. Rev. A* **1991**, *44*, R6189–R6192. [CrossRef] [PubMed]
34. Migliorati, M.; Bacci, A.; Benedetti, C.; Chiadroni, E.; Ferrario, M.; Mostacci, A.; Palumbo, L.; Rossi, A.R.; Serafini, L.; Antici, P. Intrinsic normalized emittance growth in laser-driven electron accelerators. *Phys. Rev. Spec. Top.-Accel. Beams* **2013**, *16*, 011302. [CrossRef]
35. Li, X.K.; Chance, A.; Nghiem, P.A.P. Preserving emittance by matching out and matching in plasma wakefield acceleration stage. *Phys. Rev. Accel. Beams* **2019**, *22*, 021304. [CrossRef]
36. Floettmann, K. Adiabatic matching section for plasma accelerated beams. *Phys. Rev. Spec. Top.-Accel. Beams* **2014**, *17*, 054402. [CrossRef]
37. Dornmair, I.; Floettmann, K.; Maier, A.R. Emittance conservation by tailored focusing profiles in a plasma accelerator. *Phys. Rev. Spec. Top.-Accel. Beams* **2015**, *18*, 041302. [CrossRef]
38. Loulergue, A.; Labat, M.; Evain, C.; Benabderrahmane, C.; Malka, V.; Couprie, M.E. Beam manipulation for compact laser wakefield accelerator based free-electron lasers. *New J. Phys.* **2015**, *17*, 023028. [CrossRef]
39. Pousa, A.F.; de la Ossa, A.M.; Brinkmann, R.; Assmann, R.W. Compact Multistage Plasma-Based Accelerator Design for Correlated Energy Spread Compensation. *Phys. Rev. Lett.* **2019**, *123*, 054801. [CrossRef]
40. Van Tilborg, J.; Steinke, S.; Geddes, C.G.R.; Matlis, N.H.; Shaw, B.H.; Gonsalves, A.J.; Huijts, J.V.; Nakamura, K.; Daniels, J.; Schroeder, C.B.; et al. Active Plasma Lensing for Relativistic Laser-Plasma-Accelerated Electron Beams. *Phys. Rev. Lett.* **2015**, *115*, 184802. [CrossRef]
41. Hafz, N.A.M.; Li, S.; Li, G.Y.; Mirzaie, M.; Zeng, M.; Zhang, J. Generation of high-quality electron beams by ionization injection in a single acceleration stage. *High Power Laser Sci. Eng.* **2016**, *4*, e24. [CrossRef]
42. Feng, J.; Li, Y.F.; Wang, J.G.; Li, D.Z.; Zhu, C.Q.; Tan, J.H.; Geng, X.T.; Liu, F.; Chen, L.M. Optical control of transverse motion of ionization injected electrons in a laser plasma accelerator. *High Power Laser Sci. Eng.* **2021**, *9*, e5. [CrossRef]

43. Bulanov, S.; Naumova, N.; Pegoraro, F.; Sakai, J. Particle injection into the wave acceleration phase due to nonlinear wake wave breaking. *Phys. Rev. E* **1998**, *58*, R5257–R5260. [CrossRef]
44. Suk, H.; Barov, N.; Rosenzweig, J.B.; Esarey, E. Plasma electron trapping and acceleration in a plasma wake field using a density transition. *Phys. Rev. Lett.* **2001**, *86*, 1011–1014. [CrossRef] [PubMed]
45. Geddes, C.G.R.; Nakamura, K.; Plateau, G.R.; Toth, C.; Cormier-Michel, E.; Esarey, E.; Schroeder, C.B.; Cary, J.R.; Leemans, W.P. Plasma-density-gradient injection of low absolute-momentum-spread electron bunches. *Phys. Rev. Lett.* **2008**, *100*, 215004. [CrossRef] [PubMed]
46. Faure, J.; Rechatin, C.; Lundh, O.; Ammoura, L.; Malka, V. Injection and acceleration of quasimonoenergetic relativistic electron beams using density gradients at the edges of a plasma channel. *Phys. Plasmas* **2010**, *17*, 083107. [CrossRef]
47. Wang, W.T.; Li, W.T.; Liu, J.S.; Wang, C.; Chen, Q.; Zhang, Z.J.; Qi, R.; Leng, Y.X.; Liang, X.Y.; Liu, Y.Q.; et al. Control of seeding phase for a cascaded laser wakefield accelerator with gradient injection. *Appl. Phys. Lett.* **2013**, *103*, 243501. [CrossRef]
48. Schmid, K.; Buck, A.; Sears, C.M.S.; Mikhailova, J.M.; Tautz, R.; Herrmann, D.; Geissler, M.; Krausz, F.; Veisz, L. Density-transition based electron injector for laser driven wakefield accelerators. *Phys. Rev. Spec. Top.-Accel. Beams* **2010**, *13*, 091301. [CrossRef]
49. Gonsalves, A.J.; Nakamura, K.; Lin, C.; Panasenko, D.; Shiraishi, S.; Sokollik, T.; Benedetti, C.; Schroeder, C.B.; Geddes, C.G.R.; van Tilborg, J.; et al. Tunable laser plasma accelerator based on longitudinal density tailoring. *Nat. Phys.* **2011**, *7*, 862–866. [CrossRef]
50. Buck, A.; Wenz, J.; Xu, J.; Khrennikov, K.; Schmid, K.; Heigoldt, M.; Mikhailova, J.M.; Geissler, M.; Shen, B.; Krausz, F.; et al. Shock-Front Injector for High-Quality Laser-Plasma Acceleration. *Phys. Rev. Lett.* **2013**, *110*, 185006. [CrossRef]
51. Burza, M.; Gonoskov, A.; Svensson, K.; Wojda, F.; Persson, A.; Hansson, M.; Genoud, G.; Marklund, M.; Wahlstrom, C.G.; Lundh, O. Laser wakefield acceleration using wire produced double density ramps. *Phys. Rev. Spec. Top.-Accel. Beams* **2013**, *16*, 011301. [CrossRef]
52. Hansson, M.; Aurand, B.; Davoine, X.; Ekerfelt, H.; Svensson, K.; Persson, A.; Wahlstrom, C.G.; Lundh, O. Down-ramp injection and independently controlled acceleration of electrons in a tailored laser wakefield accelerator. *Phys. Rev. Spec. Top.-Accel. Beams* **2015**, *18*, 071303. [CrossRef]
53. Lu, W.; Huang, C.; Zhou, M.; Mori, W.B.; Katsouleas, T. Nonlinear theory for relativistic plasma wakefields in the blowout regime. *Phys. Rev. Lett.* **2006**, *96*, 165002. [CrossRef] [PubMed]
54. Corde, S.; Thaury, C.; Lifschitz, A.; Lambert, G.; Phuoc, K.T.; Davoine, X.; Lehe, R.; Douillet, D.; Rousse, A.; Malka, V. Observation of longitudinal and transverse self-injections in laser-plasma accelerators. *Nat. Commun.* **2013**, *4*, 1501. [CrossRef] [PubMed]
55. Antipov, S.; Baturin, S.; Jing, C.; Fedurin, M.; Kanareykin, A.; Swinson, C.; Schoessow, P.; Gai, W.; Zholents, A. Experimental Demonstration of Energy-Chirp Compensation by a Tunable Dielectric-Based Structure. *Phys. Rev. Lett.* **2014**, *112*, 114801. [CrossRef] [PubMed]
56. Emma, P.; Venturini, M.; Bane, K.L.F.; Stupakov, G.; Kang, H.S.; Chae, M.S.; Hong, J.; Min, C.K.; Yang, H.; Ha, T.; et al. Experimental Demonstration of Energy-Chirp Control in Relativistic Electron Bunches Using a Corrugated Pipe. *Phys. Rev. Lett.* **2014**, *112*, 034801. [CrossRef]
57. Chen, P.; Dawson, J.M.; Huff, R.W.; Katsouleas, T. Acceleration of electrons by the interaction of a bunched electron-beam with a plasma. *Phys. Rev. Lett.* **1985**, *54*, 693–696. [CrossRef]
58. Litos, M.; Adli, E.; An, W.; Clarke, C.I.; Clayton, C.E.; Corde, S.; Delahaye, J.P.; England, R.J.; Fisher, A.S.; Frederico, J.; et al. High-efficiency acceleration of an electron beam in a plasma wakefield accelerator. *Nature* **2014**, *515*, 92–95. [CrossRef]
59. D'Arcy, R.; Wesch, S.; Aschikhin, A.; Bohlen, S.; Behrens, C.; Garland, M.J.; Goldberg, L.; Gonzalez, P.; Knetsch, A.; Libov, V.; et al. Tunable Plasma-Based Energy Dechirper. *Phys. Rev. Lett.* **2019**, *122*, 034801. [CrossRef]
60. Shpakov, V.; Anania, M.P.; Bellaveglia, M.; Biagioni, A.; Bisesto, F.; Cardelli, F.; Cesarini, M.; Chiadroni, E.; Cianchi, A.; Costa, G.; et al. Longitudinal Phase-Space Manipulation with Beam-Driven Plasma Wakefields. *Phys. Rev. Lett.* **2019**, *122*, 114801. [CrossRef]
61. Wu, Y.P.; Hua, J.F.; Zhou, Z.; Zhang, J.; Liu, S.; Peng, B.; Fang, Y.; Nie, Z.; Ning, X.N.; Pai, C.H.; et al. Phase Space Dynamics of a Plasma Wakefield Dechirper for Energy Spread Reduction. *Phys. Rev. Lett.* **2019**, *122*, 204804. [CrossRef] [PubMed]
62. Dopp, A.; Thaury, C.; Guillaume, E.; Massimo, F.; Lifschitz, A.; Andriyash, I.; Goddet, J.P.; Tazfi, A.; Phuoc, K.T.; Malka, V. Energy-Chirp Compensation in a Laser Wakefield Accelerator. *Phys. Rev. Lett.* **2018**, *121*, 074802. [CrossRef] [PubMed]
63. Ke, L.T.; Feng, K.; Wang, W.T.; Qin, Z.Y.; Yu, C.H.; Wu, Y.; Chen, Y.; Qi, R.; Zhang, Z.J.; Xu, Y.; et al. Near-GeV Electron Beams at a Few Per-Mille Level from a Laser Wakefield Accelerator via Density-Tailored Plasma. *Phys. Rev. Lett.* **2021**, *126*, 214801. [CrossRef] [PubMed]
64. Gotzfried, J.; Dopp, A.; Gilljohann, M.F.; Foerster, F.M.; Ding, H.; Schindler, S.; Schilling, G.; Buck, A.; Veisz, L.; Karsch, S. Physics of High-Charge Electron Beams in Laser-Plasma Wakefields. *Phys. Rev. X* **2020**, *10*, 041015. [CrossRef]
65. Gordienko, S.; Pukhov, A. Scalings for ultrarelativistic laser plasmas and quasimonoenergetic electrons. *Phys. Plasmas* **2005**, *12*, 3109. [CrossRef]
66. Lu, W.; Tzoufras, M.; Joshi, C.; Tsung, F.S.; Mori, W.B.; Vieira, J.; Fonseca, R.A.; Silva, L.O. Generating multi-GeV electron bunches using single stage laser wakefield acceleration in a 3D nonlinear regime. *Phys. Rev. Spec. Top.-Accel. Beams* **2007**, *10*, 061301. [CrossRef]
67. Kuschel, S.; Schwab, M.B.; Yeung, M.; Hollatz, D.; Seidel, A.; Ziegler, W.; Savert, A.; Kaluza, M.C.; Zepf, M. Controlling the Self-Injection Threshold in Laser Wakefield Accelerators. *Phys. Rev. Lett.* **2018**, *121*, 154801. [CrossRef]

68. Li, Y.F.; Li, D.Z.; Huang, K.; Tao, M.Z.; Li, M.H.; Zhao, J.R.; Ma, Y.; Guo, X.; Wang, J.G.; Chen, M.; et al. Generation of 20 kA electron beam from a laser wakefield accelerator. *Phys. Plasmas* **2017**, *24*, 023108. [CrossRef]
69. Couperus, J.P.; Pausch, R.; Kohler, A.; Zarini, O.; Kramer, J.M.; Garten, M.; Huebl, A.; Gebhardt, R.; Helbig, U.; Bock, S.; et al. Demonstration of a beam loaded nanocoulombclass laser wakefield accelerator. *Nat. Commun.* **2017**, *8*, 487. [CrossRef]
70. Wang, W.T.; Feng, K.; Ke, L.T.; Yu, C.H.; Xu, Y.; Qi, R.; Chen, Y.; Qin, Z.Y.; Zhang, Z.J.; Fang, M.; et al. Free-electron lasing at 27 nanometres based on a laser wakefield accelerator. *Nature* **2021**, *595*, 516–520. [CrossRef]
71. Rousse, A.; Phuoc, K.T.; Shah, R.; Pukhov, A.; Lefebvre, E.; Malka, V.; Kiselev, S.; Burgy, F.; Rousseau, J.P.; Umstadter, D.; et al. Production of a keV X-ray beam from synchrotron radiation in relativistic laser-plasma interaction. *Phys. Rev. Lett.* **2004**, *93*, 135005. [CrossRef] [PubMed]
72. Corde, S.; Phuoc, K.T.; Lambert, G.; Fitour, R.; Malka, V.; Rousse, A.; Beck, A.; Lefebvre, E. Femtosecond X rays from laser-plasma accelerators. *Rev. Mod. Phys.* **2013**, *85*, 1–48. [CrossRef]
73. Yu, C.H.; Qi, R.; Wang, W.T.; Liu, J.S.; Li, W.T.; Wang, C.; Zhang, Z.J.; Liu, J.Q.; Qin, Z.Y.; Fang, M.; et al. Ultrahigh brilliance quasi-monochromatic MeV gamma-rays based on self-synchronized all-optical Compton scattering. *Sci. Rep.* **2016**, *6*, 29518. [CrossRef] [PubMed]
74. Phuoc, K.T.; Corde, S.; Thaury, C.; Malka, V.; Tafzi, A.; Goddet, J.P.; Shah, R.C.; Sebban, S.; Rousse, A. All-optical Compton gamma-ray source. *Nat. Photonics* **2012**, *6*, 308–311. [CrossRef]
75. Dopp, A.; Mahieu, B.; Lifschitz, A.; Thaury, C.; Doche, A.; Guillaume, E.; Grittani, G.; Lundh, O.; Hansson, M.; Gautier, J.; et al. Stable femtosecond X-rays with tunable polarization from a laser-driven accelerator. *Light-Sci. Appl.* **2017**, *6*, e17086. [CrossRef]
76. Wenz, J.; Dopp, A.; Khrennikov, K.; Schindler, S.; Gilljohann, M.F.; Ding, H.; Gotzfried, J.; Buck, A.; Xu, J.; Heigoldt, M.; et al. Dual-energy electron beams from a compact laser-driven accelerator. *Nat. Photonics* **2019**, *13*, 263–269. [CrossRef]
77. Nalkajima, K. Towards a table-top free-electron laser. *Nat. Phys.* **2008**, *4*, 92–93. [CrossRef]
78. Pompili, R.; Alesini, D.; Anania, M.P.; Arjmand, S.; Behtouei, M.; Bellaveglia, M.; Biagioni, A.; Buonomo, B.; Cardelli, F.; Carpanese, M.; et al. Free-electron lasing with compact beam-driven plasma wakefield accelerator. *Nature* **2022**, *605*, 659–662. [CrossRef]
79. Sarri, G.; Corvan, D.J.; Schumaker, W.; Cole, J.M.; Di Piazza, A.; Ahmed, H.; Harvey, C.; Keitel, C.H.; Krushelnick, K.; Mangles, S.P.D.; et al. Ultrahigh Brilliance Multi-MeV gamma-Ray Beams from Nonlinear Relativistic Thomson Scattering. *Phys. Rev. Lett.* **2014**, *113*, 224801. [CrossRef]
80. Schlenvoigt, H.P.; Haupt, K.; Debus, A.; Budde, F.; Jackel, O.; Pfotenhauer, S.; Schwoerer, H.; Rohwer, E.; Gallacher, J.G.; Brunetti, E.; et al. A compact synchrotron radiation source driven by a laser-plasma wakefield accelerator. *Nat. Phys.* **2008**, *4*, 130–133. [CrossRef]
81. Svensson, J.B.; Guenot, D.; Ferri, J.; Ekerfelt, H.; Gonzalez, I.G.; Persson, A.; Svendsen, K.; Veisz, L.; Lundh, O. Low-divergence femtosecond X-ray pulses from a passive plasma lens. *Nat. Phys.* **2021**, *17*, 639–645. [CrossRef]

Article

Laser Beat-Wave Acceleration near Critical Density

Ernesto Barraza-Valdez [1,*], Toshiki Tajima [1], Donna Strickland [2] and Dante E. Roa [3]

1. Department of Physics and Astronomy, University of California, Irvine, CA 92697, USA; ttajima@uci.edu
2. Department of Physics and Astronomy, University of Waterloo, Waterloo, ON N2L 3G1, Canada; strickla@uwaterloo.ca
3. Department of Radiation Oncology, University of California, Irvine, CA 92697, USA; droa@uci.edu
* Correspondence: ernestob@uci.edu

Abstract: We consider high-density laser wakefield acceleration (LWFA) in the nonrelativistic regime of the laser. In place of an ultrashort laser pulse, we can excite wakefields via the Laser Beat Wave (BW) that accesses this near-critical density regime. Here, we use 1D Particle-in-Cell (PIC) simulations to study BW acceleration using two co-propagating lasers in a near-critical density material. We show that BW acceleration near the critical density allows for acceleration of electrons to greater than keV energies at far smaller intensities, such as 10^{14} W/cm^2, through the low phase velocity dynamics of wakefields that are excited in this scheme. Near-critical density laser BW acceleration has many potential applications including high-dose radiation therapy.

Keywords: laser wakefield acceleration; beat wave; near-critical acceleration; fiber laser; endoscopic radiotherapy

1. Introduction

Laser wakefield acceleration (LWFA) allows us to make high energy acceleration of electrons [1–4]. Tajima and Dawson proposed using high-intensity pulsed laser (such as 10^{18} W/cm^2) to accelerate electrons with an accelerating gradient on the order of GeV/cm [1]. Their paper launched the laser wakefield acceleration (LWFA) branch of plasma physics, which was further aided by the advent of Chirped Pulse Amplification (CPA) and its advent also enabled LWFA realization [5]. The main allure and applications of LWFA has been to explore the energies that may not be covered easily by the conventional accelerator approaches, either in principle or by the ever-increasing cost and size of these. The energies of electrons accelerated by LWFA increase inversely proportional to the plasma density [1,3]. Thus, most of the explorations of LWFA so far have been in a density of plasma relatively far away from the critical density, the underdense regime (for a typical optical laser, the critical density is on the order of 10^{21}/cm^3), so that the typical operating plasma density has been densities of 10^{17}–10^{19}/cm^3. This is a gaseous plasma regime.

Despite LWFA having nearly half a century of history, there has yet to be sufficient exploration of laser-plasma acceleration near the critical density. Valenta et al. determined that electron densities of roughly $0.1 n_c$ were necessary for high repetition rate, low energy, and short pulse lasers [6]. More recently, Nicks et al. further explored how one can achieve bulk acceleration of electrons by exploring the maximum energy achieved for different near-critical densities, laser intensities, and laser pulse widths [4,7]. We note that in the near-critical densities the gas plasma is replaced by other materials such as nanomaterials [8]. In such materials, by choosing the radius of nanotubes, for example, we can raise or reduce the average electron density that laser electromagnetic fields see. The outer shell electrons in such materials behave as if they are in a plasma state [9].

The purpose of this paper is to theoretically and computationally explore the near-critical density regime using laser beat-wave (BW) acceleration simulations. We will give a brief introduction to the theory of LWFA in the underdense, relativistic, high-intensity regime. Then we investigate the use of laser BW near the critical density with

Citation: Barraza-Valdez, E.; Tajima, T.; Strickland, D.; Roa, D.E. Laser Beat-Wave Acceleration near Critical Density. *Photonics* **2022**, *9*, 476. https://doi.org/10.3390/photonics9070476

Received: 3 April 2022
Accepted: 28 June 2022
Published: 8 July 2022

Publisher's Note: MDPI stays neutral with regard to jurisdictional claims in published maps and institutional affiliations.

Copyright: © 2022 by the authors. Licensee MDPI, Basel, Switzerland. This article is an open access article distributed under the terms and conditions of the Creative Commons Attribution (CC BY) license (https://creativecommons.org/licenses/by/4.0/).

low-intensity lasers, by using the well-benchmarked EPOCH 1D3V (1D and 3D in spatial and velocity calculations, respectively) and collisionless and relativistic Particle-in-Cell code with stationary ions [10]. We will show that in this near-critical density regime, electron energies up to 10 keV are obtained using intensities $\leq 10^{14}$ W/cm^2. These low laser intensities allow for the use of novel fiber technology described by Sha et al. [11], along with many applications such as for radiation therapy treatment, as described by Roa et al. [12].

This paper is structured in the following way: Section 2 will describe the theory of conventional underdense LWFA and beat-wave acceleration (BWA). Section 3 will describe BWA at near-critical densities and show results of PIC simulations with low-intensity lasers and near-critical density plasma targets. Section 4 will discuss applications to medicine. Section 5 will summarize and conclude this paper.

2. Underdense LWFA and BWA

LWFA in underdense plasma operates where the plasma density is much lower than the critical density $n_e \ll n_c$. Through the Stimulated Raman Scattering (SRS) process [13,14], an electromagnetic wave excites a plasma wave with ω_p following the frequency or energy conservation of:

$$\omega_p = \omega_0 - \omega_1 \qquad (1)$$

where $\omega_p = \sqrt{4\pi n_e e^2/m}$ and the 'p' subscript denotes electron plasma, n_e is the electron plasma density, 'e' is the electron charge, and m is the electron mass. Following the above frequency equation where ω_0 is the incident wave and ω_1 is the scattered wave, the wave number (or momentum) must also be conserved such that $k_p = k_0 - k_1$.

Similarly, Rosenbluth and Liu derived the process of exciting plasma waves using the beat wave of two lasers such that frequency difference was equal to the plasma frequency following Equation (1) [15,16]. This is beat wave (BW) excitation of plasma waves. When the two lasers are co-propagating, the Forward Raman Scattering (FRS) mechanism becomes significant and electrons can then be accelerated by the plasma waves [2,13,16–18]. We classify this as Beat Wave Acceleration (BWA). If laser fields for the pump E_0 (higher frequency) and seed E_1 (lower frequency) are near the relativistic range of $\propto m\omega_0 c/e$ then the ponderomotive force created by the beatwave of the two lasers drives an electrostatic longitudinal plasma wave E_L such that:

$$eE_L = \nabla\left(\frac{eE_0 \cdot E_1}{m\omega_0\omega_1}\right) = e\left(\frac{m\omega_p c}{e}\right)e^{i\,k_p x} \qquad (2)$$

The phase velocity of this electrostatic wave (wake or plasmon) is driven by the group velocity of the lasers. For a plasma with density below the seed laser critical density (n_{crit}), the dispersion is given by $\omega = ck/\sqrt{1 - \omega_p^2/\omega^2}$ and the group velocity of the lasers is $v_g = \partial\omega/\partial k = c\sqrt{1 - n_e/n_{crit}}$ [19].

Therefore, in a highly underdense plasma the laser frequency $\omega_0, \omega_1 \gg \omega_p$ and both the laser phase velocity and plasmon group velocity reduce to $v_{ph} \approx v_g \approx c$. This is shown in Figure 1, where the 2D Fast Fourier Transform (FFT) of the transverse and longitudinal electric field of the laser beat wave PIC simulation in an underdense plasma ($n_e = 0.005 \times n_{crit}$) is plotted and shows the dispersion.

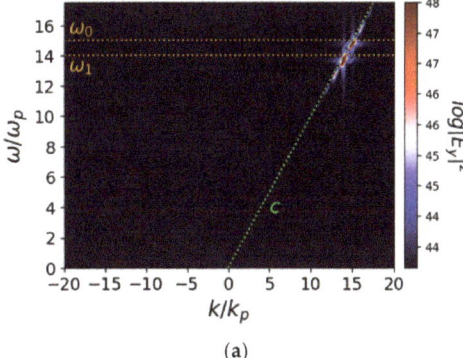 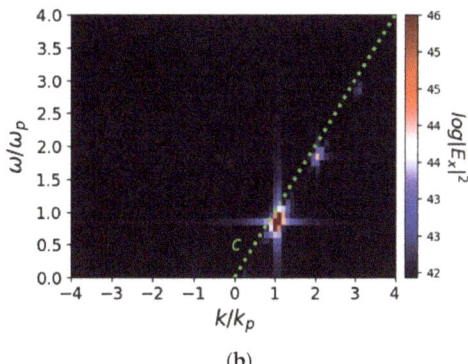

Figure 1. The 2D Fast Fourier Transform (FFT) of the (**a**) transverse (E_y) and (**b**) longitudinal (E_x) electric field in a 1D PIC simulation of highly underdense laser BW acceleration normalized to the plasma frequency (ω_p) and plasma wave number ($k_p = \omega_p/c$). ω_0 and ω_1 are the two copropagating laser frequencies of the beatwave, indicated by the orange dotted lines in (**a**). The diverging color indicates the intensity of the fields in logscale. The speed of light dispersion (slope) is indicated by the lime green dotted line. This simulation used an equivalent of $a_0 \approx 0.5$ and $a_1 \approx 0.5$, beatwave lasers both with Gaussian shapes, wavelengths of 0.5 μm and 1 μm with 100 fs pulsewidth and $n_e = 0.005 \times n_{crit}$.

A high phase velocity, much larger than the thermal velocity, allows the plasma wave to be stable and coherent against thermal plasma instabilities and allows the lasers to drive the plasma wave until saturation. In the relativistic regime, the wakefield amplitude saturates due to relativistic mass and detuning effects. The detuning time and length is defined as the length it takes for the laser beat wave and plasma wave to become more than $\pi/2$ out of phase such as described by Rosenbluth and Liu, Esarey et al. [3,15], and is typically very long. Thus, the saturated electrostatic wakefield is [2,15]:

$$E_L = \frac{m\omega_p c}{e}\left(\frac{16}{3}a_0 a_1\right)^{\frac{1}{3}} \quad (3)$$

where $a_{0,1} = \frac{e|E_{0,1}|}{m\omega_{0,1}c}$ is the normalized laser vector potentials for the pump, indicated by the 0 subscript, and the seed, the 1 subscript.

With the wake waves' high phase velocity, far away from the bulk thermal velocity of the plasma, the strength of these wakes will have to grow large enough, near the wave breaking limit [4,16], to be able to trap electrons from the fringes of the thermal distribution and accelerate them. If the amplitude of the wake waves is not strong enough, electrons will need to be externally injected at the high enough energies in order to be trapped. The range of velocities (energies) that the excited wake waves can trap and accelerate electrons is described by the trapping width velocity [20]:

$$v_{trap} = \sqrt{eE_L/mk} \quad (4)$$

where E_L is the amplitude of the wake (longitudinal) wave and k is its wave number. Thus, because $v_{ph} \gg v_{th}$ the wave number k is small, making the trapping width small. Wakes cannot functionally trap and accelerate electrons from the bulk plasma thermal distribution. This again reinforces that the laser and wakes are stable from thermal plasma instabilities. Figure 2 shows the electric field and phase space of the highly underdense BW simulation in Figure 1. One can see that only at relativistic laser intensities ($a_0 \geq 1$) is the electrostatic wake amplitude driven large enough to trap a small population of electrons from the tail end of the thermal distribution and accelerate them to relativistic energies. Additionally, Figure 2 shows that the observed wakefield amplitude (blue) matches Equation (3).

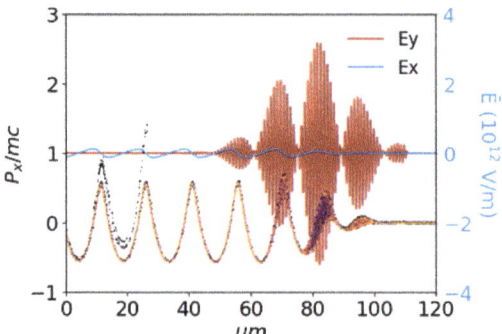

Figure 2. Electron phase space plot with electric fields of a 1D PIC simulation at 150 fs. The momentum is normalized to electron mass times the speed of light (c) on the left most y-axis (P_x/mc) vs. the position in the horizontal axis. The sequential color scale indicates the population density of electrons in that particular phase space point where bright orange indicates a large amount and purple or dark colors indicate small populations. The electric fields are indicated by the transverse (red) and longitudinal (blue) lines representing the laser and plasmon fields respectively, scaled to the right most y-axis (E 10^{12} V/m). This simulation used an equivalent of $a_0 \approx 0.5$ and $a_1 \approx 0.5$, beatwave lasers both with Gaussian shapes, wavelengths of 0.5 µm and 1 µm with 100 fs pulse width and $n_e = 0.005 \times n_{crit}$.

Once electrons with high enough velocities are trapped in the wakes, they can be accelerated. The maximum acceleration energy of trapped electrons is limited by the electron dephasing length and thus is proportional to a_0 and the Lorentz factor squared: $W_{max} = 2a_0\gamma^2 mc^2$ or $\propto a_0^2(\omega_0/\omega_p)^2$. For non-relativistic (nr), low intensities ($a_0 < 1$), in an underdense plasma we have no factor $2\gamma^2$ (due to the fact that relativistic dynamics of the phase velocity of the wake affects the extended dephasing length). If we assume in this case that the electron dephasing length is simply $\pi c/2\omega_p$, we obtain the low-intensity maximum electron energy which may lead to an expression such as $W_{max,nr} = \pi/2 \cdot mc^2 a_0^2(\omega_0/\omega_p)$. This type of energy would apply if the wakefield with nonrelativistic amplitude is excited but remains as a single wave. As we will see below, however, in the high-density regime of wakefields (near the critical density), we observe that a series of wakefields with different phase velocities tends to be excited.

As mentioned above, it is conventional wisdom that the maximum electron acceleration energy achieved using laser wakefield schemes is proportional to $(\omega_0/\omega_p)^2$ (due to the relativistic dynamics in underdense plasma). For this reason, we sought to see the limitations of the BWA with respect to density, similar to what was done by Nicks et al. [7]. We ran eight BWA simulations like those shown in Figure 2, with a pump and seed intensity given by $a_0, a_1 = 0.1$ and Gaussian pulse width of 100 fs, just below the non-relativistic regime. The kinetic energy distribution and maximum kinetic energies achieved after 1 ps are shown in Figure 3. Each simulation had uniform plasma density that is proportional to the critical density of the seed laser (λ_1 = 1 µm), as shown in the legend of Figure 3a.

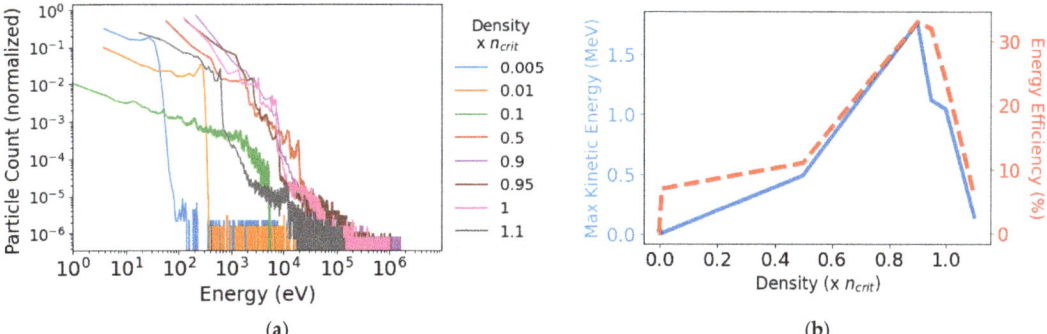

Figure 3. Energy distributions, maximum kinetic energies, and laser to total particle energy efficiency with respect to plasma density for BWA simulations after 1 ps using Gaussian lasers with intensities of $a_0, a_1 = 0.1$, and pulse width of 100 fs. The seed laser wavelength was held at $\lambda = 1$ μm while the pump wavelength was changed in order to satisfy Equation (1). (**a**) Normalized energy distributions (log-log scale) of eight different simulations with uniform plasma density from 0.005 n_{crit} to 1.1 n_{crit}. (**b**) The maximum electron energies achieved after 1 ps with respect to plasma density (left y-axis, blue), and the efficiency of the total laser energy converted to total particle kinetic energy (right y-axis, red).

For low densities (<$0.1 n_c$), Figure 3a shows that the excited plasma waves are barely able to trap and accelerate electrons from the fringes of the thermal distribution up to around 10 keV. However, at $0.1 n_c$ we see that the plasma waves (with a low phase velocity at high densities which we will show in the next section) begin to push the thermal distribution out to higher energies. Above this density, a large tail of the distribution is formed and accelerated beyond 10 keV.

Figure 3b shows the maximum kinetic energy achieved after 1 ps (left y-axis, blue). Figure 3b also shows the energy efficiency or total particle kinetic energy of the plasma with respect to the total lasers' energy. As mentioned in this section, the low-density regime does not allow for the high phase velocity ($v_{ph} \approx c$) plasma waves to efficiently trap particles. Thus, external injection mechanisms would be needed for high energy acceleration. In contrast, near the critical density, particle trapping from the bulk thermal distribution becomes significant until around $0.9 n_{crit}$. These particles can then be accelerated by the main wakefield to high energies. Additionally, one can see that the laser energy to total particle energy, efficiency, also increases with density which corresponds to the widening of the energy distributions in Figure 3a. Both the maximum kinetic energy and efficiency drops after $0.9 n_c$, although it is unclear why. With this, the next section will focus on lower intensities in order to achieve electron energies of 10 keV for applications such as radiation therapy.

3. Near-Critical Density BWA

For low laser intensities ($a_0 < 0.1$) in highly underdense plasma, the plasmon wave amplitudes are not strong enough to trap electrons from the bulk thermal distribution and accelerate them to high energies as described above, in Figures 2 and 3a. However, when n_e is approaches the critical density, additional physics must come into play. Nicks et al. showed electron energy scaling with respect to laser intensity ($1 > a_0 \geq 0.1$) for $0.1 n_{crit}$ and $0.3 n_{crit}$ in their Figure 5a,b [7]. Nicks et al. also showed that a somewhat discontinuous maximum energy gain of electrons as a function of a_0 (around 1) is observed. This arises from the transition between the nonrelativistic wakefields dynamics ($a_0 < 1$) and the relativistic one ($a_0 \geq 1$). Additionally, Figure 3 shows the electrons can be accelerated without external injection mechanisms near the critical densities.

Here, we show that using near-critical densities (of the seed laser) allows for low-intensity lasers to excite low phase velocity plasmons. This introduces the opportunity to pick up electrons in the bulk, which would not be possible in the conventional underdense operation of LWFA. This high-density, low-intensity BWA scheme makes it suitable for many applications.

For many industrial and medical applications, electron energies of greater than keV are required with low laser intensities of $\leq 10^{14}$ W/cm^2 (corresponding to $a_0 < 0.01$ for a 1 µm laser). For a 1 µm laser, the critical density is approximately 10^{21} cm^3, which is about one order of magnitude less than a conventional solid. This high density allows the BW accelerator to be done in atmospheric pressure rather than vacuum. Thus, our study will focus on using a 1 µm laser with plasma densities of approximately $n_e \approx 0.9 \times n_{crit} \approx 0.9 \cdot 10^{21}$ cm^{-3}. This density was chosen because it seems to provide the highest maximum acceleration energies along with maximum efficiency, as shown in Figure 3.

The excitation of low phase velocity plasmons with much lower laser intensities lends itself to the Enhanced Raman Forward Scattering (ERFS) method [21]. In the ERFS method, the laser intensities need not be equal as in the conventional BW case. Fisher and Tajima showed that ERFS allows for the lower frequency seed (ω_1) laser's intensity to be 10% of the higher frequency pump (ω_0) laser's intensity. In this case, the lower frequency laser seeds the growth of the plasma wave but there are also other seeding methods such as pulse shaping and electrostatic plasmon seeding. The smaller seed intensity further allows the usage of modern tabletop laser technology.

We now turn to the exploration of low-intensity, non-relativistic BW acceleration using the EFRS method. To represent a thin target of density 0.9×10^{21} cm^3 in the simulation, the plasma is set to be between 1–20 µm thick (with ions left to be infinitely heavier and stationary). Figure 4 shows the transverse and longitudinal field spectrum for 20 µm-thick plasma. Figure 4a is similar to Figure 1a except that the seed frequency is now just above the plasma frequency ($\omega_1 \approx 1.1\, \omega_p$). Additionally, the lasers propagate freely in vacuum before hitting the target. The free space propagation is clearly shown by the spectrum points that align with the speed of light in vacuum (lime green). In Figure 4b, one can see that there is excitation at ω_p with a broad range of wavenumber. This is due to nonlinear parametric processes and is allowed by the high-density plasma (near-critical) so that their phase velocities are low. The allowed group velocity of the photons (seed) is small (≈ 0.3 c) and so the ponderomotive force can excite plasma waves with small phase velocity which can trap and accelerate electrons from a cold thermal distribution with a temperature on the order of 10 eV. This allowed wide range of the phase velocities in nonrelativistic wakefields is the reason why we see this wide spectrum of plasma waves with frequency ω_p. Additionally, in the relativistic regime the detuning length between the laser beat wave and plasma wave phases leads to saturation of the longitudinal plasma waves. However, from the resonant detuning length given by Esarey et al. [3], we see that for an $a_0 = 0.007$ and $a_1 = 0.004$, the detuning length is approximately 1 mm and much larger than our target length.

Figure 5 shows the phase space and electric field components for this simulation using a laser intensity of 2.5×10^{14} W/cm^2 ($a_0 = 0.007$) with a pulse width of 2 ps. One can see that at 2 ps, the tail end of the laser pulses, and the longitudinal plasma wave amplitude (blue curve) has grown larger than the pump laser's amplitude (red curve). At 2.5 ps, the laser has left the simulation and one can see the strong plasma waves continue unimpeded and are able to accelerate electrons to keV energies.

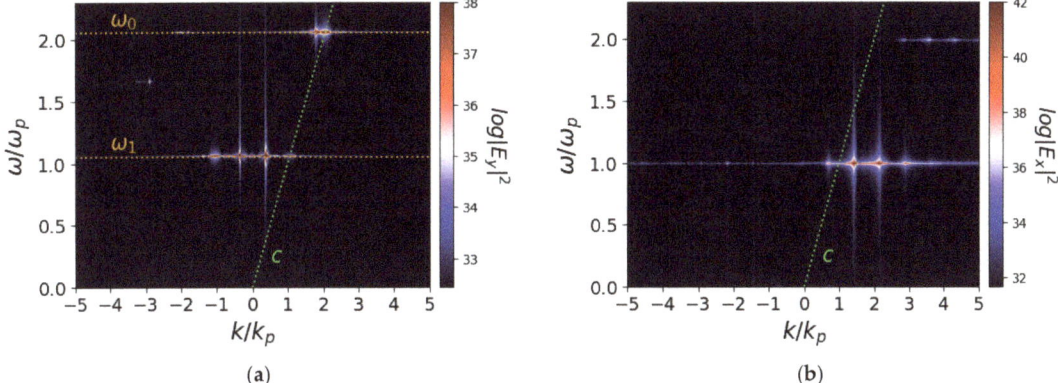

Figure 4. The 2D Fast Fourier Transform (FFT) of the (**a**) transverse (E_y) and (**b**) longitudinal (E_x) electric field in a 1D PIC simulation of near-critical density laser BW acceleration normalized to the plasma frequency (ω_p) and plasma wave number ($k_p = \omega_p/c$). ω_0 and ω_1 are the two copropagating laser frequencies of the beatwave, indicated by the orange dotted lines in (**a**). The diverging color indicates the intensity of the fields in logscale. The speed of light dispersion (slope) is indicated by the lime green dotted line. The EFRS method is used with two Gaussian lasers with intensities of approximately $a_0 = 0.007$ (2.5×10^{14} W/cm^2) and $a_1 = 0.004$ (9.7×10^{13} W/cm^2), $n_e = 0.9 \times n_{crit}$, $\lambda_0 \approx 0.5$ μm and $\lambda_1 = 1.0$ μm, and the pulse width is 2 ps.

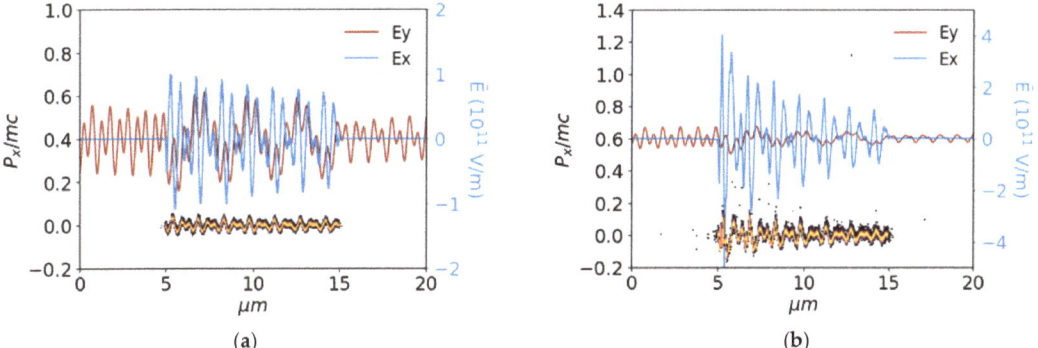

Figure 5. The phase space distribution and transverse and longitudinal electric fields for a 1D 10 μm plasma target at (**a**) 2 ps and (**b**) 2.5 ps. The momentum is normalized to electron mass times the speed of light (c) on the leftmost y-axis (P_x/mc) vs. the position in the horizontal axis. The sequential color scale indicates the population density of electrons in that particular phase space point where bright orange indicates a large amount and purple or dark colors indicate small populations. The EFRS method is used with $a_0 = 0.007$ (2.5×10^{14} W/cm^2) and $a_1 = 0.004$ (9.7×10^{13} W/cm^2) and $n_e = 0.9 \times n_{crit}$, $\lambda_0 \approx 0.5$ μm and $\lambda_1 = 1.0$ μm, and the pulse width is 2 ps.

Figure 6 shows the electron energies with respect to different simulations parameters. Figure 6a shows the electron energy distribution after 2.5 ps for varying thicknesses of the plasma target using laser intensities of $a_0 = 0.007$ (2.5×10^{14} W/cm^2) and $a_1 = 0.004$ (9.7×10^{13} W/cm^2). One can see that that below 5 μm, electrons are just barely accelerated above keV energies. This is most likely because the main plasma wave in the mix of wakefields is the one with a phase velocity near c so that the main plasma wavelength corresponds to approximately 1 μm; this is confirmed by Figure 5. Thus, for small thicknesses there is not enough wake waves to accelerate electrons. However, there does not seem to be more enhancement in the electron energy spectrum as the plasma thickness is increased.

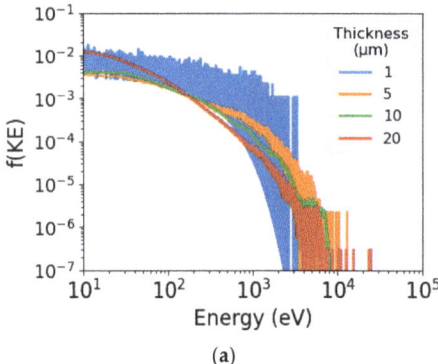
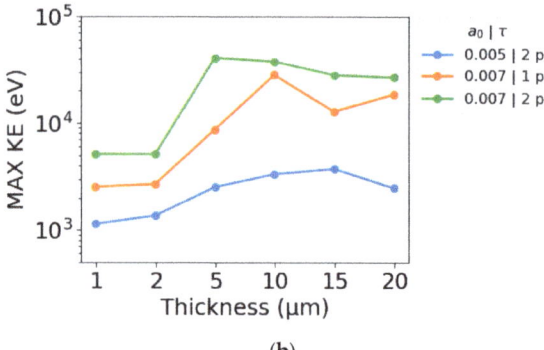

Figure 6. The electron energy gain with varying parameters: target length, pulse width, and intensity. (a) The energy distribution (log-log scale) of thin plasma target simulation after 2.5 ps with change of thickness. The intensity of the pump wave 2.5×10^{14} W/cm^{-2} and the seed intensity was one-tenth of that ($a_0 = \sqrt{10} \cdot a_1$). Pulsewidth of 2 ps. (b) Maximum kinetic energy (y-axis, log scale) of an electron found in simulation after 2.5 ps with respect to thickness (x-axis) given different laser parameters: (blue) 1.3×10^{14} W/cm^{-2} pump ($a_0 = 0.005$) with a pulse width of 2 ps, (yellow) 2.5×10^{14} W/cm^{-2} pump ($a_0 = 0.007$) with a pulse width of 1 ps, (green) 2.5×10^{14} W/cm^{-2} pump ($a_0 = 0.007$) with a pulse width of 2 ps.

In order to make this acceleration scheme more applicable, lower laser intensities than 2.5×10^{14} W/cm^2 are chosen. Figure 6b shows the maximum kinetic energy found in the simulation after 2.5 ps for three different laser parameters: 1.3×10^{14} W/cm^2 with 2 ps pulse width, 2.5×10^{14} W/cm^2 with 1 ps, and 2.5×10^{14} W/cm^2 with 2 ps pulse width. One can see that the intensity allows for higher electron energies, which is expected. In addition, increasing the pulse width to deliver more energy also increases the maximum kinetic energy that the electrons can achieve. Below 1.3×10^{14} W/cm^2 ($a_0 < 0.005$), we saw that the plasma waves continued to grow beyond 2.5 ps.

4. Applications to Medicine

As we have found, the high-density operation (near the critical density) LWFA opens an avenue to make very compact electron acceleration (though electron energies are modest, such as 10's keV) with modest laser intensity. The near-critical density exceeds the usual gaseous plasma density without external injection mechanisms. The opportunity of using carbon nanotubes (and possibly other nanomaterials) to match this regime of density with changing its occupation ratio (such as the tube diameter) introduces an added flexibility and value of this regime operation [8,22]. Also, this brings in a flexible density ramping, if desired or necessary, for additional control in the acceleration process. The size of the target in this high-density LWFA further reduces the size of the accelerator from even the gaseous LWFA, which is already far smaller than the conventional accelerators. Additionally, near-critical density LWFA lends itself to low-intensity schemes such as EFRS. This allows the seed laser intensity to be 10% of the pump laser's and still achieve 10's keV electron energies.

Meanwhile, if and when we can use an electron accelerator so tiny that it can sit in front of the tumor of a patient (such as at the tip of an endoscope), the electrons for radiotherapy purposes need not have MeV of energies, as they do not have to penetrate a patient's body. In this case, the needed electron energies may be as low as 10's keV. The penetration depth of such electrons is short and reaches only the tissues facing the accelerator at the tip of a device such as an endoscope. As an example, the penetration depth of a 10 keV electron can be estimated using the modified relativistic Bethe formula for electrons in water and gives a mean penetration depth on the order of 10 µm [23]. Assuming a laser spot size of 10 µm, we estimate the dose of this electron beam per pulse is approximately 10^2 Gy.

This study shows that our present regime of laser intensity and operation are within the reach of the fiber laser technology, see [11]. In addition, a new fiber grating technique [24] may help to create appropriate beat-wave resonance. Accordingly, this introduces a new possible way to operate an endoscopic electron radiotherapy using fiber laser. That is, an endoscopic radiation therapy. The surgeon would enter an internal part of a patient with an endoscope that has the HD LWFA attached at its tip. When he/she sees a tumor, he/she can turn on the HD LWFA at the suspected tumor. It could also be used to spray electrons after the surgical removal of a macroscopic tumor by endoscope, to make sure the remaining tissue can be devoid of active tumors (it may also be delivered as part of an acupuncture needle).

Such electrons may be used to address other therapy such as allowing for a handheld radiation therapy device that can directly target superficial skin cancers such as melanoma [25–28]. Further, we could also employ a vector medicine (with high Z) that can guide itself toward the targeted tissue (such as cancer cells) that attracts and absorbs electrons preferentially to the vector molecules with its high Z distinction [29].

5. Conclusions

To summarize, we used the well-benchmarked 1D3V relativistic PIC code EPOCH and showed the dynamics of LWFA and BWA in underdense plasmas and near-critical density plasmas. In Section 2, conventional LWFA was discussed. Conventional LWFA relies on high laser intensities and underdense plasmas so that the group velocity of the laser ($\approx c$) can excite longitudinal plasma waves with similar phase velocity. Thus, a robust and coherent plasma wave train is excited with immunity from thermal plasma instabilities. It is conventional wisdom that lower plasma density allows for more stable wake waves and therefore larger electron energy accelerations [4]. However, we showed in Figure 3 that near-critical densities allow for low phase velocity plasma waves to trap electrons deep inside the thermal distribution and accelerate them to high energies.

In Section 3, we studied a low-intensity EFRS scheme to accelerate electrons to keV energies using low-intensity lasers (approximately 10^{15} W/cm^2) near the critical density. At the near-critical densities, we have shown that using laser BW with the ERFS method, nonlinear processes are excited. One of these processes is the growth of multiple small phase velocity plasma waves rather than the single large phase velocity wakefield, shown in Figure 5. This ensemble of plasmon waves with low phase velocities allows for efficient trapping of electrons from the bulk thermal distribution.

The EFRS scheme in a thin target has two advantages: the use of low-intensity lasers and microscopic acceleration length. The microscopic acceleration length is beneficial in many industrial and medical applications as discussed in Section 4.

Author Contributions: Conceptualization, T.T.; Data curation, E.B.-V.; Formal analysis, E.B.-V.; Funding acquisition, T.T.; Investigation, E.B.-V.; Methodology, E.B.-V.; Software, E.B.-V.; Supervision, T.T.; Validation, E.B.-V.; Visualization, E.B.-V.; Writing—original draft, E.B.-V. and T.T.; Writing—review & editing, T.T., D.S. and D.E.R. All authors have read and agreed to the published version of the manuscript.

Funding: The work was in part supported by the Rostoker Fund.

Institutional Review Board Statement: Not applicable.

Informed Consent Statement: Not applicable.

Data Availability Statement: The data presented in this study are available on request from the corresponding author.

Acknowledgments: We benefitted a great deal of advice and inspirations specifically on this or in general over the years from W. J. Sha, J. C. Chanteloup, G. Mourou, S. Iijima, and F. Tamanoi. For these we are very grateful.

Conflicts of Interest: The authors declare no conflict of interest.

References

1. Tajima, T.; Dawson, J.M. Laser Electron Accelerator. *Phys. Rev. Lett.* **1979**, *43*, 267–270. [CrossRef]
2. Tajima, T. High Energy Laser Plasma Accelerators. *Laser Part. Beams* **1985**, *3*, 351–413. [CrossRef]
3. Esarey, E.; Schroeder, C.B.; Leemans, W.P. Physics of Laser-Driven Plasma-Based Electron Accelerators. *Rev. Mod. Phys.* **2009**, *81*, 1229–1285. [CrossRef]
4. Tajima, T.; Yan, X.Q.; Ebisuzaki, T. Wakefield Acceleration. *Rev. Mod. Plasma Phys.* **2020**, *4*, 7. [CrossRef]
5. Strickland, D.; Mourou, G. Compression of Amplified Chirped Optical Pulses. *Opt. Commun.* **1985**, *55*, 447–449. [CrossRef]
6. Valenta, P.; Klimo, O.; Grittani, G.M.; Esirkepov, T.Z.; Korn, G.; Bulanov, S.V. Wakefield Excited by Ultrashort Laser Pulses in Near-Critical Density Plasmas. In Proceedings of the Laser Acceleration of Electrons, Protons, and Ions V, Prague, Czech Republic, 1–3 April 2019; SPIE: Bellingham, WA, USA, 2019; Volume 11037, pp. 57–65.
7. Nicks, B.S.; Barraza-Valdez, E.; Hakimi, S.; Chesnut, K.; DeGrandchamp, G.; Gage, K.; Housley, D.; Huxtable, G.; Lawler, G.; Lin, D.; et al. High-Density Dynamics of Laser Wakefield Acceleration from Gas Plasmas to Nanotubes. *Photonics* **2021**, *8*, 216. [CrossRef]
8. Iijima, S. Helical Microtubules of Graphitic Carbon. *Nature* **1991**, *354*, 56–58. [CrossRef]
9. Zhang, X.; Tajima, T.; Farinella, D.; Shin, Y.; Mourou, G.; Wheeler, J.; Taborek, P.; Chen, P.; Dollar, F.; Shen, B. Particle-in-Cell Simulation of x-Ray Wakefield Acceleration and Betatron Radiation in Nanotubes. *Phys. Rev. Accel. Beams* **2016**, *19*, 101004. [CrossRef]
10. Arber, T.D.; Bennett, K.; Brady, C.S.; Lawrence-Douglas, A.; Ramsay, M.G.; Sircombe, N.J.; Gillies, P.; Evans, R.G.; Schmitz, H.; Bell, A.R.; et al. Contemporary Particle-in-Cell Approach to Laser-Plasma Modelling. *Plasma Phys. Control. Fusion* **2015**, *57*, 113001. [CrossRef]
11. Sha, W.J.; Chanteloup, J.C.; Mourou, G. Ultrafast Fiber Technologies for Compact Laser Wake Field in Medical Application. *Photonics* **2022**, *9*, 423.
12. Roa, D.; Kuo, J.; Moyses, H.; Taborek, P.; Tajima, T.; Mourou, G.; Tamanoi, F. Fiber-Optic Based Laser Wakefield Accelerated Electron Beams and Potential Applications in Radiotherapy Cancer Treatments. *Photonics* **2022**, *9*, 403. [CrossRef]
13. Shen, Y.R.; Bloembergen, N. Theory of Stimulated Brillouin and Raman Scattering. *Phys. Rev.* **1965**, *137*, A1787–A1805. [CrossRef]
14. Liu, C.S.; Rosenbluth, M.N.; White, R.B. Raman and Brillouin Scattering of Electromagnetic Waves in Inhomogeneous Plasmas. *Phys. Fluids* **1974**, *17*, 1211–1219. [CrossRef]
15. Rosenbluth, M.N.; Liu, C.S. Excitation of Plasma Waves by Two Laser Beams. *Phys. Rev. Lett.* **1972**, *29*, 701–705. [CrossRef]
16. Tajima, T.; Dawson, J.M. Laser Beat Accelerator. *IEEE Trans. Nucl. Sci.* **1981**, *28*, 3416–3417. [CrossRef]
17. Joshi, C.; Tajima, T.; Dawson, J.M.; Baldis, H.A.; Ebrahim, N.A. Forward Raman Instability and Electron Acceleration. *Phys. Rev. Lett.* **1981**, *47*, 1285–1288. [CrossRef]
18. Horton, W.; Tajima, T. Laser Beat-Wave Accelerator and Plasma Noise. *Phys. Rev. A* **1985**, *31*, 3937–3946. [CrossRef]
19. Ginzburg, V.L. *The Propagation of Electromagnetic Waves in Plasmas*, 2nd ed.; International Series of Monographs on Electromagnetic Waves; Pergamon Press: Oxford, UK; New York, NY, USA, 1970; Volume 7, ISBN 978-0-08-015569-2.
20. O'Neil, T. Collisionless Damping of Nonlinear Plasma Oscillations. *Phys. Fluids* **1965**, *8*, 2255–2262. [CrossRef]
21. Fisher, D.L.; Tajima, T. Enhanced Raman Forward Scattering. *Phys. Rev. E* **1996**, *53*, 1844–1851. [CrossRef]
22. Chattopadhyay, S.; Mourou, G.; Shiltsev, V.D.; Tajima, T. (Eds.) *Beam Acceleration in Crystals and Nanostructures*; World Scientific: Singapore, 2020; ISBN 9789811217135.
23. Podgoršak, E.B. (Ed.) *Radiation Oncology Physics: A Handbook for Teachers and Students*; International Atomic Energy Agency: Vienna, Austria, 2005; ISBN 978-92-0-107304-4.
24. Caucheteur, C.; Guo, T.; Albert, J. Multiresonant Fiber Gratings. *Opt. Photonics News OPN* **2022**, *33*, 42–49. [CrossRef]
25. Nicks, B.S.; Tajima, T.; Roa, D.; Nečas, A.; Mourou, G. Laser-Wakefield Application to Oncology. In *Beam Acceleration in Crystals and Nanostructures, Proceedings of the Workshop on Beam Acceleration in Crystals and Nanostructures, Batavia, IL, USA, 24–25 June 2019*; World Scientific: Singapore, 2020; pp. 223–236. ISBN 9789811217128.
26. Roa, D.; Leon, S.; Paucar, O.; Gonzales, A.; Schwarz, B.; Olguin, E.; Moskvin, V.; Alva-Sanchez, M.; Glassell, M.; Correa, N.; et al. Monte Carlo Simulations and Phantom Validation of Low-Dose Radiotherapy to the Lungs Using an Interventional Radiology C-Arm Fluoroscope. *Phys. Med.* **2022**, *94*, 24–34. [CrossRef]
27. Veness, M.; Richards, S. Role of Modern Radiotherapy in Treating Skin Cancer. *Australas. J. Dermatol.* **2003**, *44*, 159–168. [CrossRef] [PubMed]
28. Mierzwa, M.L. Radiotherapy for Skin Cancers of the Face, Head, and Neck. *Facial Plast. Surg. Clin.* **2019**, *27*, 131–138. [CrossRef] [PubMed]
29. Matsumoto, K.; Saitoh, H.; Doan, T.L.H.; Shiro, A.; Nakai, K.; Komatsu, A.; Tsujimoto, M.; Yasuda, R.; Kawachi, T.; Tajima, T.; et al. Destruction of Tumor Mass by Gadolinium-Loaded Nanoparticles Irradiated with Monochromatic X-Rays: Implications for the Auger Therapy. *Sci. Rep.* **2019**, *9*, 13275. [CrossRef] [PubMed]

Article
Laser Ion Acceleration in a Near Critical Density Trap

Ales Necas [1,*], Toshiki Tajima [2], Gerard Mourou [3] and Karoly Osvay [4]

[1] TAE Technologies, 19631 Pauling, Foothill Ranch, CA 92610, USA
[2] Department of Physics and Astronomy, University of California, Irvine, CA 92697, USA; ttajima@uci.edu
[3] Ecole Polytechnique, Route de Saclay, 91128 Palaiseau, France; gerard.mourou@polytechnique.edu
[4] National Laser-Initiated Transmutation Laboratory, University of Szeged, 6720 Szeged, Hungary; osvay@physx.u-szeged.hu
* Correspondence: anecas@tae.com

Abstract: In order to accelerate ions by a laser, we go back to the original and the fundamental idea of how longitudinal field structure generation can be carried out in an ionized media and how particles may be trapped by the created wakefield. The latter condition is characterized by the phase velocity of the longitudinal structure v_{ph} be equal to the particle trapping width v_{tr}. Since the trapping width is inversely proportional to the square-root of the mass of the accelerated particles, this width is much shorter for ions than for electrons. Thus, our dictum for laser ion acceleration is to impose a near critical density trap to decelerate laser group velocity, v_g and subsequently to generate longitudinal wakefield to be able to trap ions under the condition of $v_{tr} = v_{ph}$. We demonstrate this concept by PIC simulation and find that this method is effective, and the efficiency of laser ion acceleration is enhanced by a couple of orders of magnitude toward unity.

Keywords: laser; ion acceleration; laser wakefield; PIC simulation; phase velocity; group velocity; near critical density plasma

1. Introduction and History

The utilization of the collective force that resides in plasma was first put forward by V. Veksler in 1956 [1]. The plasma was chosen for two reasons: (A) plasma does not break down as it is already ionized; (B) the forces mediated by plasma are long-range and can interact with many particles. Norman Rostoker was a pioneer who started to utilize an electron beam to accelerate ions (e.g., [2–4]). Another early experiment [5] had a relatively thick metallic foil causing the sheath formation that did not propagate with ions, which limited ion acceleration process. In Habs's team work [6,7] the target thickness has been designed sufficiently thin so that the irradiating laser can form penetration enough to (a) cause the ponderomotive fields and (b) that ponderomotive fields propagate with the ions. The condition to realize this (a) and (b) have been established, which is called the coherent acceleration of ions by laser (CAIL) condition:

$$\sigma = a_0 \qquad (1)$$

where a_0 is the normalized vector potential of the laser while the normalization of the target thickness is $\sigma = \frac{n_e}{n_c}\frac{d}{\lambda_L}$, where n_e is the target density, n_c is the critical density, d is the target thickness, and laser wavelength, λ_L.

Habs's group likened the CAIL regime to a bullet train "Shinkansen". In order to pick up the much heavier ions (likened to "passengers"), it was argued that the laser (or its ponderomotive force) induced electrostatic accelerating structure or wake ("Shinkansen locomotive") must become nearly stationary as it approaches the "station" before to pick up the "passengers". Thus, we formulate the target in such a way so as to slow down the group velocity of the laser pulse to near 0 ($v_{gr} \to 0$) before the laser interacts with the thin foil.

The goal of this paper is to establish the laser group velocity $v_{gr} \to 0$ in front of the target. The photon group velocity in plasma is governed by

$$v_g = c\sqrt{1 - \frac{\omega_{pe}^2}{\omega^2}} = c\sqrt{1 - \frac{n_e}{\gamma n_c}}, \qquad (2)$$

where, ω_{pe} and ω are the plasma and the laser frequency respectively, $\gamma = \sqrt{1 + \frac{a_0^2}{2}}$ is relativistic factor. In this paper we assume the weakly relativistic case $a_0 \approx 1$. The phase velocity of the accelerating structure speed also equal to the group velocity of the photons [8]. Two regimes are defined in Equation (1) by the ratio of the plasma and critical density: over-dense regime ($n_e > n_c$) with laser not propagating and under-dense regime ($n_e < n_c$) with laser propagating. Thus, the plasma density can be adjusted to slow down the laser group velocity. This technique has been suggested [9] to slow down the laser group velocity to enhance proton acceleration.

In this paper we propose and show a scheme whereas the laser pulse is trapped in a region of less than or close to the critical density, this region is followed by the usual over dense target. It is important to resurrect the concept of trapping velocity and its role in accelerating ions with the laser-driven waves. The trapping velocity was first introduced by O'Neil (1965), among a series of nonlinear wave interaction studies of large (or finite amplitude) plasma waves [10,11]. The trapping velocity is given [12] by

$$v_{tr} = \sqrt{\frac{eE}{mk}}, \qquad (3)$$

where E is the electrostatic field in the plasma, m is the mass of the particles that are to be trapped, and k is the wavenumber of the electrostatic wave. If the particle velocity v is less than v_{tr}, that particle is trapped in a closed elliptical orbit of the equipotential contour orbit of the phase space [12]. If $v > v_{tr}$, on the other hand, particles execute untrapped open (and nearly straight) orbit. Thus, in order for a particle to gain substantial energy, it is must be trapped, i.e., $v < v_{tr}$. Laser excites a growing wakefield which drives increasing trapping velocity, v_{tr}. Particles with velocity, v, that satisfy the condition

$$|v_\phi - v| < v_{tr} \qquad (4)$$

can be trapped, where v_ϕ is the electrostatic wave phase velocity. At saturation, Equation (4) can be written as

$$v_\phi = v_{tr}, \qquad (5)$$

indicating the wakefield became large to trap bulk particles with $v \approx 0$ (or v much smaller compared with speed of light). With $v_\phi \sim c$ and $k = \omega_p/c$, Equation (5) can be used to obtain the Tajima-Dawson field $E_{TD} = m\omega_p c/e$ [13] with v_{tr} given in Equation (3). This also tells us that for effective ion acceleration, we have to make the phase velocity of the electrostatic wave (or thus the group velocity of the laser) 50 times smaller than the case for electrons. This is the motivation that for effective ion acceleration (and trapping), we need to choose the electron density near (or at) the critical density, reflective of Equation (2).

Because of the near critical density, the wake (or the plasma electrostatic accelerating structure) can now be able to trap ions and begin to increase their velocities. This allows ions to be moving with the often much faster electronic wake eventually. In this configuration trapped laser pulse converts almost all of its energy into particle energy.

In this paper we suggest a strategy to design the density of the pre-target plasma to decelerate and trap the laser photon to achieve a high efficiency laser-to-ion conversion. This is achieved by a laser-created resonator with a high reflectivity inside the pre-target region. The resulting trap-mirror configuration is akin to a to the flying mirror [14–16].

We perform parameter scan using 1D3V simulations to arrive at an optimized parameter regime; this is the main goal of Section 2. In Section 3 we examine the detailed evolution of the laser and plasma under this condition. Section 4 extends the 1D study to 2D by simulation the 1D best case scenario in 2D.

2. Far Increased Efficiency of Ion Acceleration by the Trap

We explore the above concept and theoretical expectation by carrying a series of particle in cell (PIC) simulations using the explicit 1D3V EPOCH code [17]. An extensive campaign (several hundred runs) to determine the optimal target yielded results shown in Table 1 for a fixed laser $a_0 = 1$. The density profile to provide the laser pulse trapping prior to the target and their designations are shown in Figure 1 with the pre-foil region divided into 3 segments with varying density. Each run in the campaign has been simulated using a domain $[-20, 20]$ μm resolved with 10,000 grids resulting with a skin depth c/ω_{pe} resolved with 25 grids, where we assumed electron density, $n_e = 10n_c$. To reduce noise, we used the fifth order particle weighing and 5000 particles per grid.

Table 1. Summary of the most successful runs based on laser-to-proton energy efficiency conversion. Parameter varied are in columns 2–8 are shown in Figure 1. The last two rows display the extreme cases of tailor region only and foil-only.

Run #	L_1	L_2	L_3	n_{e1}	n_{e2}	n_{e3}	Foil Thickness [nm]	Pulse Length [T_L]	Sigma	Effi. [%]
35	0.7	1.4	0.3	0.9	0.8	0.95	320	5	3.2	75
	0.7	1.4	0.3	0.45	0.4	0.43	320	5	3.2	6.2
	0.8	2.8	0.3	0.9	0.8	0.95	320	5	3.2	65
	0.5	0.5	0.15	0.9	0.8	0.95	320	5		4.5
	0.8	1.0	0.3	0.9	0.8	0.95	320	5		57
186	0.7	1.4	0.3	0.9	0.8	0.95	320	16		5.1
184	0.7	1.4	0.3	0.9	0.8	0.95	320	4		71.0
	0.7	1.4	0.3	0.9	0.8	0.95	320	8		42
233	0.2	1.4	0.6	0.9	0.8	0.95	320	8		4.4
34	0.7	1.4	0.3	0.9	0.8	0.95	160	5	1.6	70.1
48	0.7	1.4	0.3	0.95	0.8	0.9	640	5	6.4	59.9
Tailor only	0.7	1.4	0.3	0.95	0.8	0.9	0	5	0	38
Foil only	-	-	-	-	-	-	320	5	3.2	0.5

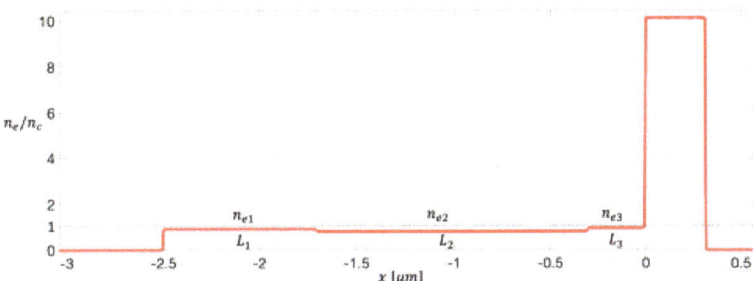

Figure 1. Density profile showing the shape of the tailor region and the foil. Inset shows the 6 free parameters to vary in addition to the foil density and thickness. The value of parameters shown is for the best-case scenario.

The first row in Table 1 shows the most successful run, yielding the highest proton conversion efficiency of 75%. In contrast, for the foil target alone—without the photon slowdown in the pre-foil—the efficiency is 0.5% (the bottom row of the Table 1). This case shows that the thickness of the typical thin foil 320 nm (we model here the electrons are pre-ionized) is far too greater than the thickness of the collisionless skin depth c/ω_{pe}. This makes the lack of laser field penetration into the thin foil. This leads to poor acceleration efficiency. (We note that more realistic cases lead to some alternative developments. For example, the laser may have a pre-pulse, which pre-ionizes part of the electrons in the thin foil.) Under this idealized thin foil laser-foil interaction, we show the most of the laser power is reflected due to the condition of $c/\omega_{pe} \ll d$ (Figure 2).

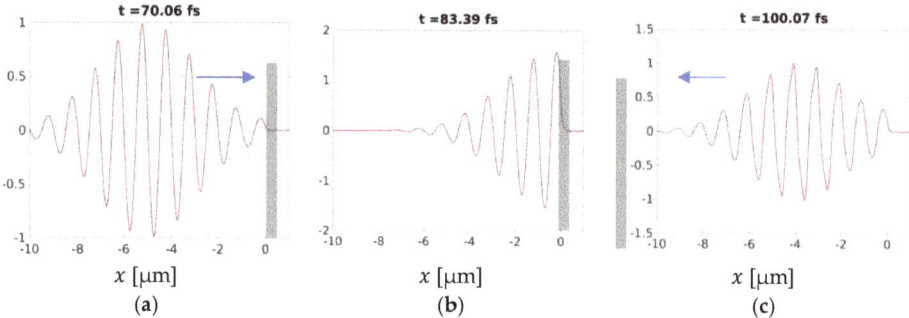

Figure 2. The evolution of the laser transverse electric field, E_y, upon interaction with an overdense foil. The field is normalized to the Tajima-Dawson field, $E_{TD} = m_e c \omega_L / e$, where ω_L is the laser frequency. The laser pulse is reflected and thus minimizing the interaction with the foil and subsequently the conversion efficiency is 0.5%. Laser pulse is injected from the left boundary and at t = 70.06 fs arrives at the foil (**a**), the maximum intensity reaches foil at t = 83.39 fs with the field penetration exhibiting exponential decay into the foil up to a few the skin depth lengths (**b**). Reflected laser pulse shape is slightly modified travelling to the left boundary (**c**).

Another run may be the case where we have no thin foil and institute only the pre-foil density tailoring (PFDT) alone. In this case, we observe the efficiency at 38% in the second from the last line in Table 1. In Table 1 we show various numerical combinations of the PFDT and the thin foil. Upon combination of the foil and PFDT, the proton conversion efficiency increases to 75%.

3. Excited Trapped Waves

In Figure 2 we track the evolution of the laser pulse interaction with the foil only; the laser transverse field is black, longitudinal electric field is blue, electron and proton densities are red and green respectively. The laser enters the computational domain at t = 0 from the left, and reaches the foil at a normal incidence at 33.4 fs, as shown in Figure 1. Figure 1 shows the full laser wave packet as a Gaussian irradiating 320 nm thick foil composed of hydrogen plasma at density $n_e = 10 n_c$. In Figure 2b, at 53.4 fs, half of the laser wave packet interacted with the foil compressing the electrons (red) into the foil up to the skin depth (c/ω_{pe}). Lastly, Figure 2c, at 70.1 fs, shows the full wave packet reflect and reverse the direction of propagation. Since the thickness of the foil is much greater than the skin depth, very little of the laser field has transmitted. However, we can see the longitudinal electric field (blue) set up at the backside of the foil indicating electrons have penetrated the foil and created the accelerating field. Overall, since the laser-plasma interaction duration is short, the conversion efficiency from the laser to the particles is very low ~0.5%. The photon group velocity, $v_g = 0$, has achieved our objective, however, immediately reaccelerated to the speed of light.

Lengthening of the laser-plasma interaction is accomplished by introduction of a subcritical region ($n_e < n_c$) in front of the over dense foil as shown in Figure 1 which reduces the photon group velocity well below the speed of light. The density is specifically tailored to allow the laser pulse trapping by dividing the region into 3 segments, i.e., without the over dense foil. In this scenario, the laser pulse impinges from left and the peak intensity arrives at 75.1 fs. The evolution of the laser pulse and the electron and proton density in the underdense tailor region is shown in Figure 3. The laser dispersion relation in vacuum for the laser carrier (i.e., the central frequency of the laser) is, of course, the well-known $\omega = k c$, where ω is the frequency of the carrier of the laser, k is the wavenumber. When the laser pulse enters the near critical density trap, the dispersion relation changes to accommodate the plasma frequency ω_p that is close to the laser frequency ω. In the trap region the dispersion relation of the photon is $\omega^2 = \omega_p^2 + k_t^2 c^2$, since the laser frequency is conserved, we obtain

$$k_t = \sqrt{k^2 - \frac{\omega_p^2}{c^2}}. \tag{6}$$

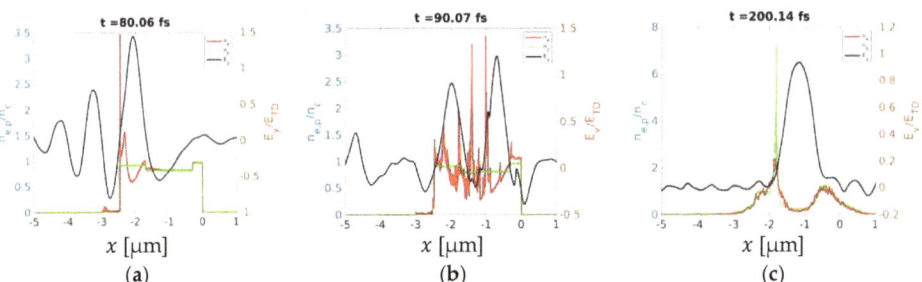

Figure 3. Snapshots of the spatial profiles of the electron density (red), proton density (green), and transverse electric field (black) at 80 fs, 90 fs, and 200 fs, respectively, for a_0 = 1 laser for the case of the tailor region only. The laser pulse enters the trapping region and strongly modifies the local electron density while ion density remains unperturbed (**a**) and penetrates the trapping region and is partially trapped (**b**) while only the electron density is perturbed. Ion density is strongly perturbed later in the evolution (**c**) with the laser pulse converted into a half cycle pulse; however, part of the laser energy is transmitted to the right.

Because the trap density is near critical by our design, the wavenumber of the trap k_t is much smaller than the vacuum laser wavelength, i.e., the wavelength is expanded as it can. The description leading to Equation (6) provides a credible explanation of the laser entering stationary underdense target, however, it fails to capture the long-time laser behavior within the trapped region.

Figure 3a shows the target after the laser pulse entrance. The laser pulse pondero-motive force strongly modifies the local electron density while the ion density remains unperturbed since proton respond on ~$1/\omega_{pi}$ times. Indeed, this first stage is akin to laser wakefield acceleration. However, in the next stage the strongly perturbed electron density exceeds the critical density and forms a flying mirror [14–16] that causes the laser pulse breaking up and trapping as shown in Figure 3b. At this stage the laser pulse entered the plasma region, however, the proton density remains unperturbed. The laser pulse trapping is achieved within a resonator with a high reflectivity that has an over-critical density on both ends and a sub-critical density in the middle shown in Figure 3c together with the highly perturbed proton density. Overall, the efficiency conversion is 38%. However, a large portion of the laser energy is transmitted.

To suppress the laser energy transmission through the target, we introduce the over-dense foil behind segment 3 shown in Figure 1. The laser-plasma evolution is similar to the case with tailor region only but with very little transmission shown in Figure 4a. Due to this unique configuration of laser pulse trapping, a half-cycle pulse is created in front of the foil for long times; Figure 4b shows the pulse at 1 ps with 20% of the peak transverse electric retained, and Figure 4c shows retention of almost 10% at 2 ps. Once such a long wavelength mode (even a subcyclic mode) is established, it exerts ponderomotive forces on the plasma. Because the group velocity is very small, as required in Equation (5), the ponderomotive force is effective in establishing an electrostatic longitudinal wave with small phase velocity that is equal to or less than the trapping width even for ions, i.e., accelerating not only electrons but also ions. This explains the enhanced efficiency of laser energy conversion into ions, once ions catch up with electron acceleration, most of the electron energy is now converted into ions (because they acquire the similar velocities and the large ion-to-electron mass ratio). Furthermore, this is accompanied by the trapped laser pulse expelling plasma electrons and ions, thus forming a depressed plasma density where the large amplitude laser is located with small k_t conveyed in Figure 4. The eigenmode is not only trapped but also modifies the trapping region by ejecting plasma to provide a deeper well and guide for trapping. The mode period preserves the initial laser pulse period $T_L = 3.3$ fs.

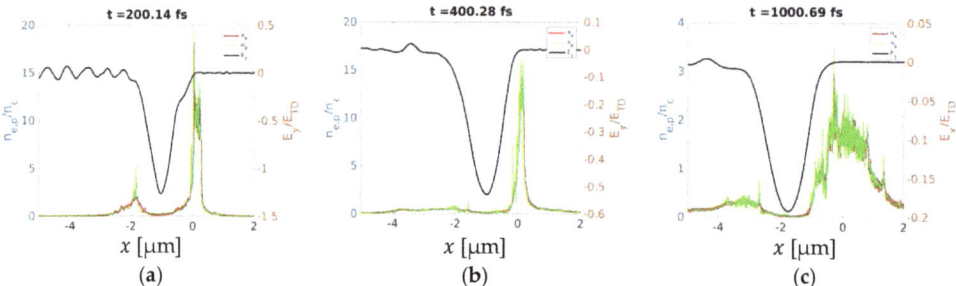

Figure 4. Snapshots of the spatial profiles of the electron density (red), proton density (green) and transverse electric field (black) at 200 fs, 400 fs, and 1000 fs respectively for $a_0 = 1$ laser for the case of the over-dense foil and tailor region. The laser pulse penetration of the trapping region is similar to Figure 3 with Figure 3c taken at same time as (**a**) shows the electrons and the ions are expelled from the region of the maximum trapping. The evolution of the half-cycle proceeds (**b**) with no laser field penetration beyond the foil. The overdense foil prevents the transmission and thus enhances and facilitates the laser pulse trapping for long times (**c**).

The proton energy spectrum is shown in Figure 5a for three different times corresponding to time slices shown in Figure 4. The earlier time spectra exhibit quasi-monoenergetic features at t = 400 fs protons with energy around 0.6 MeV coalesce into a beam indicating trapped protons. This feature is also depicted (red ellipse) in the phase space plot of Figure 5b is located at the leading edge of the plasma expanding to the left.

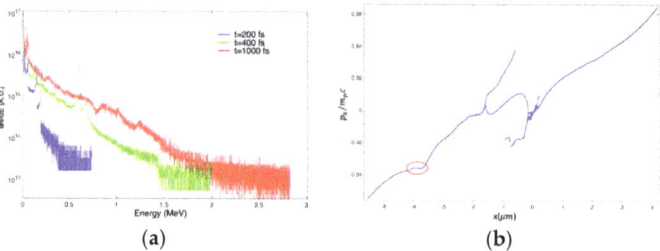

Figure 5. (**a**) Proton energy spectrum for the tailor plus foil at 200 fs, 400 fs, and 1000 fs respectively corresponding to snapshots in Figure 4. The quasi—monoenergetic feature in energy spectrum at 400 fs is explored in the phase plot (**b**) with the region highlighted in red ellipse indicating trapped region.

However, proton trapping is observed in the later stages as well. e.g., Figure 6 shows the proton phase plot at t = 1668 fs with the electrostatic potential color map plotted on the bottom. The potential exhibits many peaks and valleys with the trapping region located around -4 μm, the inset shows the zoomed in portion of the trapped region demonstrating the protons are confined and accelerated by the potential. The electrostatic potential has been derived from the electron and proton density and Poisson equation. The centroid of the trapped region is moving to the left with energy 47 keV which compares well to $p_x = -0.01\ m_p c$.

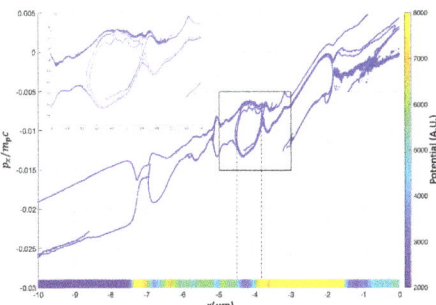

Figure 6. Plot of the proton phase space and electrostatic potential shown as a color plot on the bottom at 1700 fs. The potential displays a dip in the region where protons are trapped. The trapped region magnified in the inset.

To obtain a comparison between the various cases, we plot the total electromagnetic energy in the computational domain (solid) and the number of protons exceeding 10 keV normalized to laser energy, Y_p, (dash-dot) vs. time in Figure 7. We can observe that for the case of foil only the electromagnetic energy in the computational domain disappears on a time scale of the laser pulse return trip upon reflection from the overdense foil. Interestingly, for the case of 6 times longer pulse (magenta) the Y_p is the same as for the shorter laser pulse ($\tau_L = 5T_L$) cases and foil only. In contrast, for the cases of tailor only (blue) and tailor + foil (green) the stored energy in the electromagnetic fields is retained for much longer duration, consequently Y_p is greatly enhanced.

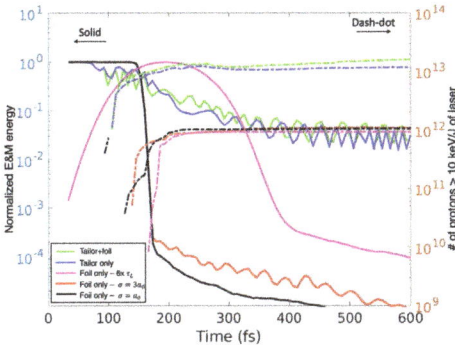

Figure 7. Normalized total electromagnetic energy in the computation domain (solid) and number of protons above 10 keV per input laser energy (dot-dash) vs. time. The case of tailor + foil (green) displays an elevated E&M energy for a long duration and subsequently high number of energetic protons. The case of 6× longer pulse (magenta) produces the same number of energetic protons per laser energy.

The trapping region allows the laser pulse to enter into a unique entity of half cycled pulse for a long time. The amplitude of this half cycle laser is very high, as the laser pulse is now collapsed on top of each other to form the narrow condensation of the laser trapping. Features of coherent sub-cyclic photon formation by itself must be of interest to the ultrafast photonics in general and attosecond laser science in particular [18]. There might be additional nonlinear plasma interaction when the stationary trap of a large amplitude plasma waves in the density trap [19].

We believe that the enhanced (or acquired) high level of coherent phase space structure (which we call in a general language as "structure formation" and coherent structure at it) of electrons and in particular that of ions are quite remarkable. In earlier works [20,21], Rau et al. remarked that sub-cyclic laser can make more coherent particle acceleration and its phase space structure. We, in fact, observe such a highly coherent phase space structures in our simulations. We have yet to learn how significant such highly coherent structural formation might result into new phenomena and physics.

4. Filamentation in 2D

We have carried out a 2D3V PIC simulation studies, guided by the extensive 1D simulation insights. A linearly polarized laser with $\tau_L = 5\ T_L$ pulse length is injected through the left boundary onto the target of special tailored ionized hydrogen plasma (again pre-ionized plasma is a rough but good approximation to the high intensity laser irradiation with $a_0 = 1$, which necessitates immediate above-field ionization). The longitudinal density profile cross section is same as shown in Figure 1 for the 1D case with transverse extend of ± 15 μm. The computational domain of 40×40 μm^2 is used and grid of 4000×2000 is applied with 40 particles per species per cell with 17 million particles per species. The laser focal length is 19 μm thus the laser is focused 1 μm in front of the foil, i.e., in the middle of the tailor region. The beam has a Gaussian profile $\exp(-y^2/w_0^2)$ with $w_0 = 4$ μm focal spot.

The 2D energy spectrum is shown in Figure 8 at t = 1000 fs with the evolution of the proton and electron density highlighted in Figure 9. A proton conversion efficiency of 38% is achieved for this tailor profile, and furthermore an efficiency of 55% is reached for the electrons. This is somewhat a reduction from the more ideal 1D results we cited above. We will follow with further studies and optimizations in future, however for the purpose of this paper, the foil only case with $3a_0 = \sigma$ results in efficiency of 0.5% and maximum proton energy of 0.05 MeV.

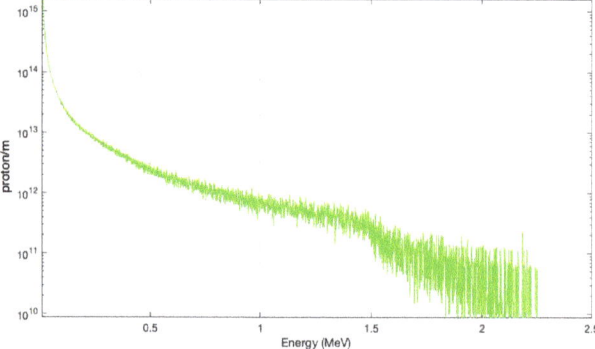

Figure 8. Spectrum of proton energy acceleration obtained from 2D PIC simulation with the density trap and foil at t = 1000 fs and efficiency of 55%. In contrast the foil only case results with maximum proton energy of 0.05 MeV and efficiency of 0.5%.

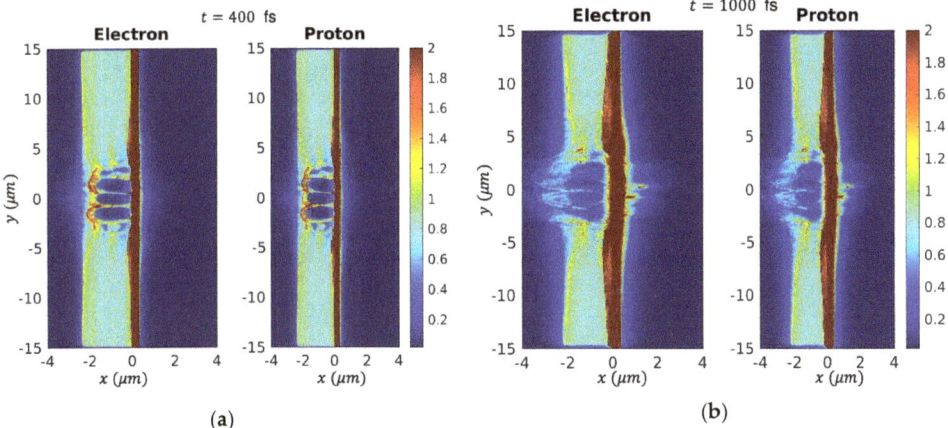

Figure 9. Evolution of electron and proton density at 400 fs and 1000 fs respectively for 2D simulation. Highly organized vortices emerge from the non-linear interaction of the laser pulse with the near critical foil (**a**). As in the 1D simulation, the vortices are maintained for extended period of time (**b**) compared to the case of laser foil-only.

The transverse electric field applies the ponderomotive force in 2D and is thus somewhat diminished from the 1D case as shown in Figure 10 at t = 400 fs. The maximum E_y in the 1D case was 0.5, in contrast the maximum field for the 2D case is 0.2.

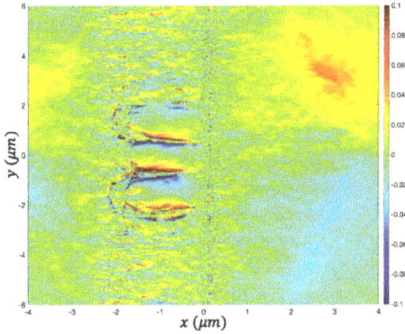

Figure 10. Transverse electric field normalized to the Tajima-Dawson field, $E_{TD} = m_e c \omega_L / e$, at 400 fs exhibits high degree of coherence and large amplitude ($0.2 \times E_{TD}$) later in time.

The electron and proton densities are shown in Figure 9. At t = 400 fs both electron and proton densities develop a density bubble similar to the density depression in the 1D case. This bubble is an indication of laser pulse trapping in the near critical density tailor region. Since both the proton and the electron exhibit the bubble, we can conclude that the protons are following electrons closely even at the later stages as shown in Figure 9b at t = 1000 fs. The laser pulse upon interaction with the tailor region undergoes strongly non-linear interaction similar to Figure 3b, thus it is remarkable that out of this chaos the plasma develops a well-organized structure shown in Figure 9.

5. Discussions

With the development of nanomaterial [22–25] and their adoption into many fields, we believe that the near-critical region proposed in this paper can be artificially grown using carbon nanotubes (CNT), carbon nano foams or other carbon allotropes. Indeed, this idea has been simulated [9,26,27]. Nanomaterials can be grown to precisely tailor density by setting the substrate structure, for example, the design of the precise profile of the critical or near critical density is within our capabilities.

We also observe that the laser that is trapped shows a marked coherence. In particular, as shown in Figure 4, we observe subcyclic laser pulse generated in side of the trap. We could design to make subcyclic laser pulse and condensation of entrant non-subcyclic laser pulse may be done by adopting out density trap strategy. Such a scheme may also help as a technique to generate subcyclic laser pulses. Rau et al. also mentioned that the use of subcyclic laser pulse is helpful to create more coherent wakefield acceleration than the case with longer laser pulse length [20,21]. Also, such creation of an intense laser subcyclic fields may be a useful technique to lend a path of intense subcyclic laser pulse generation field [18,28].

A potential application of the ion acceleration with a weakly relativistic laser presented here is a neutron generation through the deuterium and tritium fusion. Such neutrons have a large scope of applications ranging from neutron imaging to the incineration of spent nuclear fuel [29]. We thus look forward to the application of the present laser ion acceleration with the density trap to the transmutation of the spent nuclear waste by having efficient and effective ion acceleration and its driven neutrons may be of interest [30–36]. Since the present acceleration technique is (relatively) simple, compact, and controllable (via the laser operation), its application to the purpose of transmutator may be promising and operationally attractive [36]. It may be multiple of small ion accelerators that are attached to the vessel of the transmutator. This may be far different from a large and high energy (several 100 MeV or even GeV) accelerator [31]. We now have a candidate for high efficiency ion acceleration in a tiny accelerator for such a purpose.

In addition, low energy application (compared with high energy physics) of such a trap to nuclear physics may be of interest. For example, in a nuclear physics domain ions from our method may explore by simple and abundant ions from the present method, to help increase luminosity or other issues in possible experiments to test recent topic in nuclear physics experiments such as the one by [37,38].

6. Conclusions

We have demonstrated by simulations the concept of near critical density trap to effectively trap laser pulse and accelerate ions with efficiency of up to 75%. The mechanism is to make the laser group velocity sufficiently small so that the phase velocity of the induced electrostatic wave (wakefield) is also made substantially reduced. The smallness of the group velocity ("Shinkansen (bullet) train" (laser pulse)) is to pick up heavy ions ("passengers"). Once laser pulse is trapped, this process continues till most of the trapped laser pulse energy is used up to convert its energy into ion energy. This is the reason why ion acceleration is made very efficient. The increase of the efficiency from the cases without the density trap to the ones with it is a spectacular jump from sub 1% efficiency to over 70%. Further investigation will include laser irradiation of a mixture of carbon and hydrogen, as well as a more realistic portrayal of CNT.

Author Contributions: Conceptualization, A.N. and T.T.; methodology, A.N. and T.T.; software, A.N.; investigation, A.N., T.T., K.O. and G.M.; writing—review and editing, A.N., T.T., K.O. and G.M.; funding acquisition, K.O. All authors have read and agreed to the published version of the manuscript. please add this part.

Funding: We thank the support of the Hungarian National Research, Development, and Innovation Office through the National Laboratory program (contract # NKFIH-476-4/2021) and the Norman Rostoker Fund, etc., for the research study.

Institutional Review Board Statement: Not applicable.

Informed Consent Statement: Not applicable.

Data Availability Statement: Input decks for PIC simulation can be obtained upon a reasonable request.

Acknowledgments: We are deeply indebted to TAE Technologies and TAE investors for their trust and computational resources and to our colleagues S. Gales, T. Massard, P. Taborek, S. Iijima, K. Novoselov, D. Shiltsev, S. Hakimi, S. Nicks, E. Barraza, Y. Brechet, X. Q. Yan, T. Esirkepov, S. Bulanov, T. Kawachi, the late N. Rostoker, and the late J. Dawson for their collaboration, advices, and inspiration. We would like to dedicate this paper to the pioneers, the late V. Veksler and the late N. Rostoker, of the collective acceleration in plasma, whose works we were inspired by and tried to follow. They may be delighted that we came thus far.

Conflicts of Interest: The authors declare no conflict of interest.

References

1. Veksler, V.I. *CERN Symposium on High Energy Accelerators and Pion Physics*; CERN: Geneva, Switzerland, 1956; Volume 1, p. 80.
2. Rostoker, N.; Reiser, M. *Collective Methods of Acceleration. Papers Presented at the Third International Conference on Collective Methods of Acceleration, Dedicated to the Late Gersh Itskovich (André) Budker, University of California, Irvine, CA, USA, 22–25 May 1978*; CRC Press: Irvine, CA, USA, 1979; Volume 2.
3. Mako, F.; Tajima, T. Collective Ion Acceleration by a Reflexing Electron Beam: Model and Scaling. *Phys. Fluids* **1984**, *27*, 1815–1820. [CrossRef]
4. Tajima, T.; Mako, F. Self-Consistent Potential for a Relativistic Magnetized Electron Beam through a Metallic Boundary. *Phys. Fluids* **1978**, *21*, 1459–1460. [CrossRef]
5. Snavely, R.A.; Key, M.H.; Hatchett, S.P.; Cowan, T.E.; Roth, M.; Phillips, T.W.; Stoyer, M.A.; Henry, E.A.; Sangster, T.C.; Singh, M.S.; et al. Intense High-Energy Proton Beams from Petawatt-Laser Irradiation of Solids. *Phys. Rev. Lett.* **2000**, *85*, 2945. [CrossRef]
6. Henig, A.; Steinke, S.; Schnürer, M.; Sokollik, T.; Hörlein, R.; Kiefer, D.; Jung, D.; Schreiber, J.; Hegelich, B.M.; Yan, X.Q.; et al. Radiation-Pressure Acceleration of Ion Beams Driven by Circularly Polarized Laser Pulses. *Phys. Rev. Lett.* **2009**, *103*, 245003. [CrossRef]
7. Yan, X.Q.; Tajima, T.; Hegelich, M.; Yin, L.; Habs, D. Theory of Laser Ion Acceleration from a Foil Target of Nanometer Thickness. *Appl. Phys. B Lasers Opt.* **2010**, *98*, 711–721. [CrossRef]
8. Tajima, T.; Dawson, J.M. Laser Electron Accelerator. *Phys. Rev. Lett.* **1979**, *43*, 267. [CrossRef]
9. Yazdani, E.; Sadighi-Bonabi, R.; Afarideh, H.; Yazdanpanah, J.; Hora, H. Enhanced Laser Ion Acceleration with a Multi-Layer Foam Target Assembly. *Laser Part. Beams* **2014**, *32*, 509–515. [CrossRef]
10. Al'Tshul, L.M.; Karpman, V.I. Theory of Nonlinear Oscillations in a Collisionless Plasma. *Sov. Phys. JETP* **1966**, *22*, 361–369.
11. Bernstein, I.B.; Greene, J.M.; Kruskal, M.D. Exact Nonlinear Plasma Oscillations. *Phys. Rev.* **1957**, *108*, 546. [CrossRef]
12. O'neil, T. Collisionless Damping of Nonlinear Plasma Oscillations. *Phys. Fluids* **1965**, *8*, 2255–2262. [CrossRef]
13. Tajima, T.; Yan, X.Q.; Ebisuzaki, T. Wakefield Acceleration. *Rev. Mod. Plasma Phys.* **2020**, *4*, 7. [CrossRef]
14. Lefebvre, E.; Bonnaud, G. Transparency/Opacity of a Solid Target Illuminated by an Ultrahigh-Intensity Laser Pulse. *Phys. Rev. Lett.* **1995**, *74*, 2002. [CrossRef] [PubMed]
15. Iwawaki, T.; Habara, H.; Yabuuchi, T.; Hata, M.; Sakagami, H.; Tanaka, K.A. Slowdown Mechanisms of Ultraintense Laser Propagation in Critical Density Plasma. *Phys. Rev. E* **2015**, *92*, 13106. [CrossRef] [PubMed]
16. Bulanov, S.v.; Esirkepov, T.; Tajima, T. Light Intensification towards the Schwinger Limit. *Phys. Rev. Lett.* **2003**, *91*, 85001. [CrossRef] [PubMed]
17. Arber, T.D.; Bennett, K.; Brady, C.S.; Lawrence-Douglas, A.; Ramsay, M.G.; Sircombe, N.J.; Gillies, P.; Evans, R.G.; Schmitz, H.; Bell, A.R.; et al. Contemporary Particle-in-Cell Approach to Laser-Plasma Modelling. *Plasma Phys. Control. Fusion* **2015**, *57*, 1–26. [CrossRef]
18. Shou, Y.; Hu, R.; Gong, Z.; Yu, J.; Mourou, G.; Yan, X.; Ma, W. Others Cascaded Generation of a Sub-10-Attosecond Half-Cycle Pulse. *arXiv* **2020**, arXiv:2010.05724.
19. Zakharov, V.E. Collapse of Langmuir Waves. *Sov. Phys. JETP* **1972**, *35*, 908–914.
20. Hojo, H.; Rau, B.; Tajima, T. Particle Acceleration and Coherent Radiation by Subcycle Laser Pulses. *Nucl. Instrum. Methods Phys. Res. Sect. A Accel. Spectrometers Detect. Assoc. Equip.* **1998**, *410*, 509–513. [CrossRef]
21. Rau, B.; Tajima, T.; Hojo, H. Coherent Electron Acceleration by Subcycle Laser Pulses. *Phys. Rev. Lett.* **1997**, *78*, 3310. [CrossRef]
22. Kubo, R. Electronic Properties of Metallic Fine Particles. I. *J. Phys. Soc. Jpn.* **1962**, *17*, 975–986. [CrossRef]
23. Chattopadhyay, S.; Mourou, G.; Shiltsev, V.D.; Tajima, T. *Beam Acceleration in Crystals and Nanostructures-Proceedings of the Workshop*; World Scientific: Singapore, 2020.
24. Iijima, S. Helical Microtubules of Graphitic Carbon. *Nature* **1991**, *354*, 56–58. [CrossRef]
25. Geim, A.K.; Novoselov, K.S. The Rise of Graphene. *Nat. Mater.* **2007**, *6*, 183–191. [CrossRef] [PubMed]
26. Cristoforetti, G.; Baffigi, F.; Brandi, F.; D'Arrigo, G.; Fazzi, A.; Fulgentini, L.; Giove, D.; Koester, P.; Labate, L.; Maero, G.; et al. Laser-Driven Proton Acceleration via Excitation of Surface Plasmon Polaritons into TiO_2 Nanotube Array Targets. *Plasma Phys. Control. Fusion* **2020**, *62*, 114001. [CrossRef]

27. Chao, Y.; Cao, L.; Zheng, C.; Liu, Z.; He, X. Enhanced Proton Acceleration from Laser Interaction with a Tailored Nanowire Target. *Appl. Sci.* **2022**, *12*, 1153. [CrossRef]
28. Hassan, M.T.; Luu, T.T.; Moulet, A.; Raskazovskaya, O.; Zhokhov, P.; Garg, M.; Karpowicz, N.; Zheltikov, A.M.; Pervak, V.; Krausz, F.; et al. Optical Attosecond Pulses and Tracking the Nonlinear Response of Bound Electrons. *Nature* **2016**, *530*, 66–70. [CrossRef]
29. Tajima, T.; Necas, A.; Mourou, G.; Gales, S.; Leroy, M. Spent Nuclear Fuel Incineration by Fusion-Driven Liquid Transmutator Operated in Real Time by Laser. *Fusion Sci. Technol.* **2021**, *77*, 251–265. [CrossRef]
30. Tajima, T.; Necas, A. Report 2 TAE Technologies: Laser Ion Acceleration in a near Critical Density Trap. 2021; *unpublished*.
31. Rubbia, C.; Rubio, J.; Buono, S.; Carminati, F.; Fiétier, N.; Galvez, J.; Geles, C.; Kadi, Y.; Klapisch, R.; Mandrillon, P.; et al. *Conceptual Design of a Fast Neutron Operated High Power Energy Amplifier*; CERN/AT/95-44; CERN: Geneva, Switzerland, 1995; pp. 187–312.
32. Parish, T.A.; Davidson, J.W. Reduction in the Toxicity of Fission Product Wastes through Transmutation with Deuterium-Tritium Fusion Neutrons. *Nucl. Technol.* **1980**, *47*, 324–342. [CrossRef]
33. Feiveson, H.; Mian, Z.; Ramana, M.V.; von Hippel, F. Managing Spent Fuel from Nuclear Power Reactors: Experience and Lessons from around the World. International Panel on Fissile Materials 2011. Available online: https://fissilematerials.org/library/rr10.pdf (accessed on 27 January 2022).
34. Gales, S. Nuclear Energy and Waste Transmutation with High Power Accelerator and Laser Systems. Available online: https://indico.cern.ch/event/617648/contributions/2517094/attachments/1442136/2220662/18_GALES_IZEST-Talk-Nuclear-Transmutation-040417.pdf (accessed on 21 April 2018).
35. Tajima, T.; Necas, A.; Massard, T.; Gales, S. East Meets West again Now to Tackle the Global Energy Crises. *Phys. Uspekhi*, **2022**; *to be published*.
36. Tanner, J.; Necas, A.; Gales, S.; Tajima, T. Study of Neutronic Transmutation of Transuranics in a Molten Salt. *Nucl. Instrum. Methods Phys. Res. A*, 2021; *submitted*.
37. Feng, J.L.; Fornal, B.; Galon, I.; Gardner, S.; Smolinsky, J.; Tait, T.M.P.; Tanedo, P. Protophobic Fifth-Force Interpretation of the Observed Anomaly in Be 8 Nuclear Transitions. *Phys. Rev. Lett.* **2016**, *117*, 71803. [CrossRef]
38. Krasznahorkay, A.J.; Csatlós, M.; Csige, L.; Gácsi, Z.; Gulyás, J.; Hunyadi, M.; Kuti, I.; Nyakó, B.M.; Stuhl, L.; Timár, J.; et al. Observation of Anomalous Internal Pair Creation in Be 8: A Possible Indication of a Light, Neutral Boson. *Phys. Rev. Lett.* **2016**, *116*, 42501. [CrossRef]

Communication

Investigation of the Way of Phase Synchronization of a Self-Injected Bunch and an Accelerating Wakefield in Solid-State Plasma

Vasyl I. Maslov [1,2,*], Denys S. Bondar [1,2] and Ivan N. Onishchenko [1]

1. National Science Centre Kharkov Institute of Physics and Technology, 61108 Kharkov, Ukraine; bondar@kipt.kharkov.ua (D.S.B.); onish@kipt.kharkov.ua (I.N.O.)
2. Department of Plasma Physics, V. N. Karazin Kharkiv National University, 61022 Kharkiv, Ukraine
* Correspondence: vmaslov@kipt.kharkov.ua

Abstract: The electron acceleration, in a laser wakefield accelerator, controlled through plasma density inhomogeneity is studied on a basis of 2.5-dimensional particle-in-cell simulation. The acceleration requires a concordance of the density scale length and shift of the accelerated electron bunch relative to wake bubble during electron acceleration. This paper considers the excitation of a wakefield in plasma with a density equal to the density of free electrons in metals, solid-state plasma (the original idea of Prof. T. Tajima), in the context of studying the wakefield process. As is known in the wake process, as the wake bubble moves through the plasma, the self-injected electron bunch shifts along the wake bubble. Then, the self-injected bunch falls into the phase of deceleration of the wake wave. In this paper, support of the acceleration process by maintaining the position of the self-injected electron bunch using an inhomogeneous plasma is proposed. It is confirmed that the method of maintaining phase synchronization proposed in the article by using a nonuniform plasma leads to an increase in the accelerating gradient and energy of the accelerated electron bunch in comparison with the case of self-injection and acceleration in a homogeneous plasma.

Keywords: laser; wakefield; inhomogeneous plasma; acceleration; high energy

Citation: Maslov, V.I.; Bondar, D.S.; Onishchenko, I.N. Investigation of the Way of Phase Synchronization of a Self-Injected Bunch and an Accelerating Wakefield in Solid-State Plasma. *Photonics* **2022**, *9*, 174. https://doi.org/10.3390/photonics9030174

Received: 21 November 2021
Accepted: 4 March 2022
Published: 11 March 2022

Publisher's Note: MDPI stays neutral with regard to jurisdictional claims in published maps and institutional affiliations.

Copyright: © 2022 by the authors. Licensee MDPI, Basel, Switzerland. This article is an open access article distributed under the terms and conditions of the Creative Commons Attribution (CC BY) license (https:// creativecommons.org/licenses/by/ 4.0/).

1. Introduction

According to the general principles of wakefield acceleration, when a laser pulse is injected into a plasma, a charge separation is formed and a longitudinal accelerating field is excited. The formation of self-injected bunches in regions of increased electron density is also observed (see [1–6]). The plasma electrons are spontaneously injected into the wakefield due to a wave-breaking (see [4–6]). When a wakefield is excited in a solid-state density plasma by an X-ray laser pulse, both an increase in the accelerating gradient and an increase in the density of self-injected bunches are observed. Previously, the process of wakefield acceleration in high-density plasma by X-ray laser pulses was investigated [7,8]. It was shown that self-injected bunches are formed, and the amplitude of the longitudinal acceleration field reaches several teravolts per meter [9] in accordance with analytical estimates, obtained with the formula (see [10,11]). In this paper, the process of wakefield excitation in plasma is investigated by numerical simulation using the UMKA code [12]. Wake acceleration is a powerful tool for achieving high accelerating gradients, but often requires specific conditions—for example, significant acceleration rates are possible in a capillary at laser powers of 0.5 PW. Moreover, the excitation of the wakefield in capillaries was investigated [13,14]. It was shown that in a solid-state plasma, it is possible to excite fields whose amplitude reaches teravolts per centimeter [15]. It is possible to excite the wakefield in other environments, for example, by a beam in a dielectric, in which the accelerating gradient 13.8 GV/m is achieved [16]. To implement the wakefield acceleration method in a solid-density plasma, new types of lasers are required, which, in many respects, remain a promising idea [17,18]. The excitation of a wakefield in a dielectric was also previously investigated (see [19,20]). When the wakefield is excited by a beam driver, it is possible to effectively excite the wakefield even in the non-resonant case [21–23] and provide a high transformer ratio value, which can be approximately defined as the ratio of the maximum accelerating field after the driver to the maximum decelerating field inside the driver (see [24,25]). Thus, the wakefield excitation and acceleration bears great potential for the ability to customize the application for each specific case.

This paper deals with the support of the phase synchronization of the self-injected and accelerated electron bunch and the wake wave through the plasma density inhomogeneity. Two cases are considered. In the first case, the plasma is homogeneous. The wakefield is excited by a single laser pulse. The picture is standard for the wake process: the formation of a wake bubble and a self-injected bunch. The self-injected bunch moves along the wake bubble. At the beginning of its movement (Figure 1) the self-injected bunch is in the acceleration phase, moving to the opposite edge of the wake bubble (Figure 2). Thus, the phase synchronization of the self-injected bunch and the wake wave is violated, leading to the termination of acceleration and subsequent deceleration of the self-injected bunch. The main purpose of this work is to maintain phase synchronization as the self-injected bunch moves. The electron bunch acceleration is considered in solid-state plasma.

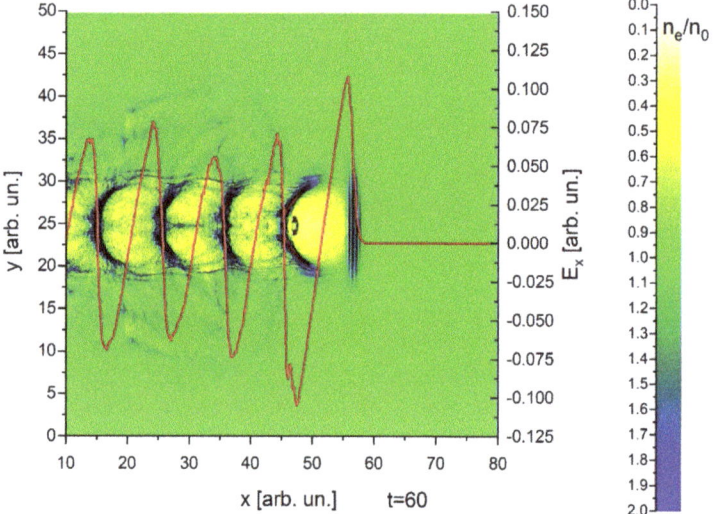

Figure 1. Excitation of a wakefield by a laser pulse in homogeneous plasma $t = 60T_0$. The self-injected bunch is close to the area of maximum accelerating gradient. Separate areas in which the ratio of electron densities reaches a value of 9 are highlighted in red. Plasma electron density and longitudinal accelerating field distributions. x, y are normalized to λ, E_x is normalized to $E_0 = m_e c \omega_\ell / 2\pi e$.

At the moment the self-injected bunch reaches approximately middle of the wake bubble, the acceleration ceases. Now let us take into account that in a denser plasma the plasma wavelength is lower and that the leading edge of the wake bubble is associated with the driver. Then, if the driver moves into a denser plasma, the trailing edge of the wake bubble shifts towards the leading edge. Now let us take into account that the maximum accelerating gradient is on the trailing edge of the wake bubble. Then, with a certain choice of plasma density inhomogeneity, the trailing edge moves synchronously with the accelerated bunch, and the accelerated bunch during acceleration is in the area of maximum accelerating gradient. In [1] plasma density inhomogeneity was used to control electron injection into the wake wave. In [2] a negative density gradient with respect to the laser pulse propagation direction and in [3] a positive density gradient were employed at the electron injection into the wake wave. In this paper a density gradient is used to support a synchronization of accelerated electrons with the maximum wakefield phase. Thus, the acceleration requires a concordance of the density scale length and shift of accelerated bunch relative to the wake bubble during electron acceleration. By timely reducing the length of the wake bubble (the length of the wake bubble is equal to the length of the nonlinear plasma wave loaded by driver and witness) one will be able to maintain the self-injected bunch at the trailing edge of the wake bubble in the area of the highest accelerating gradient of the wake bubble. The reduction of the length of the wake bubble occurs owing to a reduction in the length of the plasma wave. This is possible in inhomogeneous plasma. Namely, the plasma density must be increased approximately by a factor of four during the time (at a distance) until the self-injected bunch reaches the middle of the wake bubble.

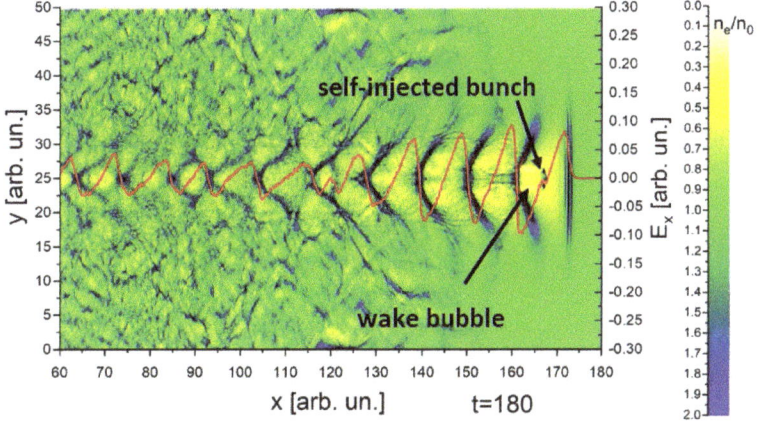

Figure 2. Excitation of a wakefield by a laser pulse in homogeneous plasma $t = 180T_0$. The self-injected bunch is close to the middle of the bubble. Separate areas in which the ratio of electron densities reaches a value of 9 are highlighted in red. Plasma electron density and longitudinal accelerating field distributions. x, y are normalized to λ, E_x is normalized to $E_0 = m_e c \omega_\ell / 2\pi e$.

2. Results of Simulation

The study was carried out through numerical simulation using the UMKA code. The simulation was performed by the PIC method. The electron density of a homogeneous plasma was $n_0 = 10^{23}$ cm^{-3}. All density values are normalized to n_0. The length of the system in the longitudinal direction is 300λ and the width of the system is 50λ in the transverse direction. All lengths and distances are normalized to the laser wavelength $\lambda = 10.65$ nm. Laser period is $T_0 = c^{-1}\lambda = 35.3$ as.

Wakefield amplitude $E = aE_0$ is normalized to $E_0 = m_e c \omega_\ell/2\pi e = 48.08$ TV/m, ω_l represents the laser frequency. We use frequency ratio approximately equal $\omega_{pe}\omega_l^{-1} = 0.1008$. Excitation of the wakefield by a single laser pulse with an amplitude of $a = 3$ is considered. FLHM (full length at half maximum) of laser pulse equals 2λ and FWHM (full width at half maximum) equals 8λ. We consider a homogeneous plasma near the injection boundary of a laser pulse in the formation interval of self-injected bunch. When a self-injected bunch is formed, it, together with the driver and bubble, approaches the point of plasma density growth (Figure 3). Moving along the system in an inhomogeneous plasma with increasing density, the self-injected bunch is held in one position at the area of maximum accelerating gradient. As a result, the self-injected bunch is constantly under the action of the accelerating field, without entering the deceleration phase (Figure 4). In the considered homogeneous case, at the moment the self-injected bunch reaches the point $x_1 = 47\lambda$, the self-injected bunch detaches from the wake bubble trailing edge. The bunch reaches the middle of the wake bubble at point $x_2 = 167\lambda$. In the interval from $x_1 = 47\lambda$ to the bottom of the system $x = 300\lambda$, the plasma density is inhomogeneous and varies according to the longitudinal distribution $n_e = n_0((x - 47\lambda)/40\lambda + 1)$. Consequently, it is possible to reach the plasma density value $n_e = 4n_0$ at the point $x_2 = 167\lambda$. Due to this, it is possible to achieve at the point $x_2 = 167\lambda$ a two-fold decrease of the plasma wavelength. At the same time, a decrease in the wake bubble length to approximately 60% of the initial length is observed.

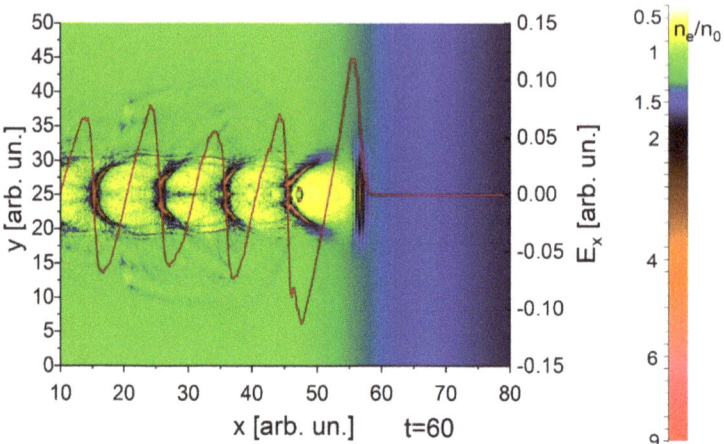

Figure 3. Excitation of a wakefield by a laser pulse in inhomogeneous plasma $t = 60T_0$. The self-injected bunch is close to the area of maximum accelerating gradient. Plasma electron density and longitudinal accelerating field distributions. x, y are normalized to λ, E_x is normalized to $E_0 = m_e c \omega_\ell / 2\pi e$.

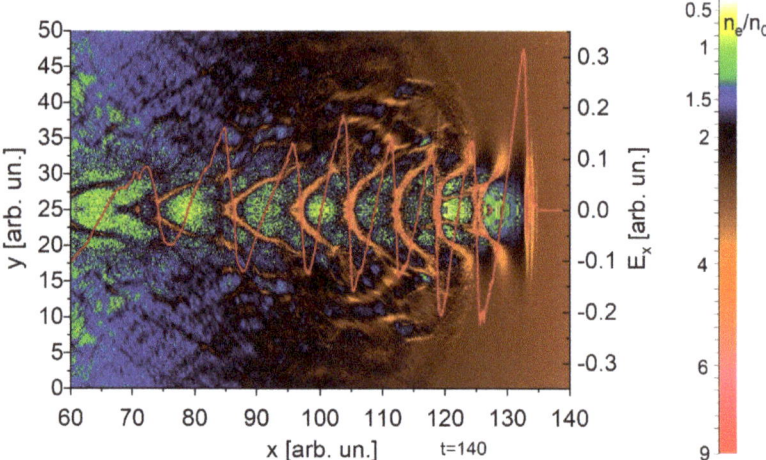

Figure 4. Excitation of a wakefield by a laser pulse in inhomogeneous plasma $t = 140T_0$. The self-injected bunch is close to the area of maximum accelerating gradient. Plasma electron density and longitudinal accelerating field distributions. x, y are normalized to λ, E_x is normalized to $E_0 = m_e c \omega_\ell / 2\pi e$.

The deviation is explained by the fact that the bubble is nonlinear and its length is greater than the linear plasma wavelength. A comparison of Figures 2 and 5 shows that the amplitude of the accelerating wakefield in the case of an inhomogeneous plasma is 2 times higher than the amplitude in the case of a homogeneous one.

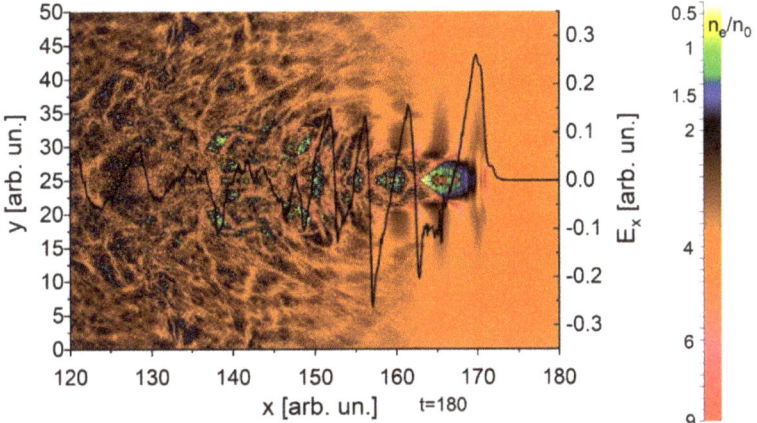

Figure 5. Excitation of a wakefield by a laser pulse in inhomogeneous plasma $t = 180T_0$. Plasma electron density distribution and longitudinal accelerating field. x, y are normalized to λ, E_x is normalized to $E_0 = m_e c \omega_\ell / 2\pi e$.

In Figure 2, it can be seen that at the moment when the acceleration process of the self-injected bunch has ceased in the homogeneous case, in the inhomogeneous case (see Figure 5) a significant part of the bunch is accelerated by field of 0.1, which is equal to the initial acceleration field in the homogeneous case. The proposed method for restoring phase synchronization in a laboratory experiment can be implemented, for example, when using multilayer sputtering with different metals. Similar technologies have been widely researched [26].

In Figure 6, one can observe self-injected bunches after about 140 laser periods after the beginning of acceleration in inhomogeneous (a) and homogeneous (b) plasmas. The maximum energy of accelerated electrons in inhomogeneous plasma is 1.7 times higher than in homogeneous plasma. Comparison of Figure 6a,b shows the efficiency of phase synchronization and confinement of the self-injected bunch in the area of high accelerating gradient. Namely, the self-injected and accelerated electron bunch is in the area of high accelerating gradient and is of a higher energy in the case of phase synchronization.

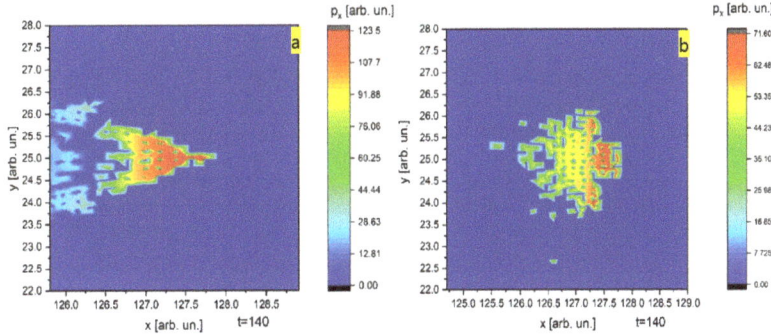

Figure 6. Distribution of the longitudinal momentum of self-injected bunch in inhomogeneous (**a**) and homogeneous (**b**) plasma $t = 140T_0$. p_x is normalized to $m_e c$.

3. Conclusions

During the study, it was shown that the use of a longitudinally inhomogeneous plasma renders it possible to provide phase synchronization of a self-injected bunch and an accelerating longitudinal wakefield, maintaining the self-injected bunch in the area of high accelerating gradient.

The longitudinal distribution according to which the plasma density changes must be developed with the condition, that at the distance that the self-injected bunch shifts, for example, to the middle of the wake bubble in the homogeneous plasma, in the inhomogeneous plasma, the plasma density should increase by a factor of 4.

The proposed method improves the efficiency of acceleration of the self-injected bunch and leads to an increase in the bunch electron energy.

Author Contributions: Conceptualization, V.I.M., I.N.O.; methodology, V.I.M., D.S.B., I.N.O.; software, D.S.B.; validation, V.I.M., D.S.B., I.N.O.; formal analysis, V.I.M., D.S.B., I.N.O.; investigation, V.I.M., D.S.B.; resources, V.I.M., D.S.B., I.N.O.; data curation, V.I.M., D.S.B., I.N.O.; writing—original draft preparation, V.I.M., D.S.B., I.N.O.; writing—review and editing, V.I.M., D.S.B., I.N.O.; visualization, D.S.B.; project administration, I.N.O.; funding acquisition, V.I.M., D.S.B., I.N.O. All authors have read and agreed to the published version of the manuscript.

Funding: This research received no external funding.

Institutional Review Board Statement: Not applicable.

Informed Consent Statement: Not applicable.

Data Availability Statement: Not applicable.

Acknowledgments: This work is supported by National Research Foundation of Ukraine "Leading and Young Scientists Research Support", grant agreement # 2020.02/0299.

Conflicts of Interest: The authors declare no conflict of interest.

References

1. Brantov, A.V.; Esirkepov, T.Z.; Kando, M.; Kotaki, H.; Bychenkov, V.Y.; Bulanov, S.V. Controlled electron injection into the wake wave using plasma density inhomogeneity. *Phys. Plasmas* **2008**, *15*, 073111. [CrossRef]
2. Bulanov, S.V.; Naumova, N.; Pegoraro, F.; Sakai, J. Particle injection into the wave acceleration phase due to nonlinear wake wave breaking. *Phys. Rev. E* **1998**, *58*, R5257. [CrossRef]
3. Ohkubo, T.; Zhidkov, A.; Hosokai, T.; Kinoshita, K.; Uesaka, M. Effects of density gradient on short-bunch injection by wave breaking in the laser wake field acceleration. *Phys. Plasmas* **2006**, *13*, 033110. [CrossRef]
4. Bulanov, S.V.; Inovenkov, I.N.; Kirsanov, V.I.; Naumova, N.M.; Sakharov, A.S. Nonlinear depletion of ultrashort and relativistically strong laser pulses in an underdense plasma. *Phys. Fluids B Plasma Phys.* **1992**, *4*, 1935–1942. [CrossRef]
5. Bulanov, S.V.; Pegoraro, F.; Pukhov, A.M.; Sakharov, A.S. Transverse-Wake Wave Breaking. *Phys. Rev. Lett.* **1997**, *78*, 4205. [CrossRef]
6. Liseikina, T.V.; Califano, F.; Vshivkov, V.A.; Pegoraro, F.; Bulanov, S.V. Small-scale electron density and magnetic-field structures in the wake of an ultraintense laser pulse. *Phys. Rev. E* **1999**, *60*, 5991. [CrossRef] [PubMed]
7. Tajima, T. Laser acceleration in novel media. *Eur. Phys. J. Spec. Top.* **2014**, *223*, 1037–1044. [CrossRef]
8. Tajima, T.; Nakajima, K.; Mourou, G. Laser acceleration. *La Riv. Nuovo Cim.* **2017**, *40*, 33–133.
9. Bondar, D.S.; Maslov, V.I.; Levchuk, I.P.; Onishchenko, I.N. Excitation of wakefield by a laser pulse in a metallicdensity electron plasma. *Probl. At. Sci. Technol.* **2018**, *6*, 156–159.
10. Albert, F.; Couprie, M.E.; Debus, A.; Downer, M.C.; Faure, J.; Flacco, A.; Gizzi, L.A.; Grismayer, T.; Huebl, A.; Joshi, C.; et al. 2020 roadmap on plasma accelerators. *New J. Phys.* **2021**, *23*, 031101. [CrossRef]
11. Assmann, R.W.; Weikum, M.K.; Akhter, T.; Alesini, D.; Alexandrova, A.S.; Anania, M.P.; Andreev, N.E.; Andriyash, I.; Artioli, M.; Aschikhin, A.; et al. Eupraxia conceptual design report. *Eur. Phys. J. Spec. Top.* **2020**, *229*, 3675–4284. [CrossRef]
12. Dudnikova, G.I.; Liseykina, T.V.; Bychenkov, V.Y. Parallel algorithms for numerical simulation of propagation of an electromagnetic radiation in plasma. *Comp. Techn.* **2005**, *10*, 37.
13. Leemans, W.P.; Gonsalves, A.J.; Mao, H.S.; Nakamura, K.; Benedetti, C.; Schroeder, C.B.; Tóth, C.; Daniels, J.; Mittelberger, D.E.; Bulanov, S.S.; et al. Multi-GeV electron beams from capillary-discharge-guided subpetawatt laser pulses in the self-trapping regime. *Phys. Rev. Lett.* **2014**, *113*, 245002. [CrossRef] [PubMed]

14. Pieronek, C.V.; Gonsalves, A.J.; Benedetti, C.; Bulanov, S.S.; Van Tilborg, J.; Bin, J.H.; Swanson, K.K.; Daniels, J.; Bagdasarov, G.A.; Bobrova, N.A.; et al. Laser-heated capillary discharge waveguides as tunable structures for laser-plasma acceleration. *Phys. Plasmas* **2020**, *27*, 093101. [CrossRef]
15. Hakimi, S.; Nguyen, T.; Farinella, D.; Lau, C.K.; Wang, H.Y.; Taborek, P.; Dollar, F.; Tajima, T. Wakefield in solid state plasma with the ionic lattice force. *Phys. Plasmas* **2018**, *25*, 023112. [CrossRef]
16. Thompson, M.C.; Badakov, H.; Cook, A.M.; Rosenzweig, J.B.; Tikhoplav, R.; Travish, G.; Blumenfeld, I.; Hogan, M.J.; Ischebeck, R.; Kirby, N.; et al. Breakdown limits on gigavolt-per-meter electron-beam-driven wakefields in dielectric structures. *Phys. Rev. Lett.* **2008**, *100*, 214801. [CrossRef] [PubMed]
17. Danson, C.N.; Haefner, C.; Bromage, J.; Butcher, T.; Chanteloup, J.-C.F.; Chowdhury, E.A.; Galvanauskas, A.; Gizzi, L.A.; Hein, J.; Hillier, D.I. Petawatt and exawatt class lasers worldwide. *High Power Laser Sci. Eng.* **2019**, *7*, e54. [CrossRef]
18. Kim, T.H.; Pathak, V.B.; Hojbota, C.L.; Mirzaie, M.; Pae, K.H.; Kim, C.M.; Yoon, J.W.; Sung, J.H.; Lee, S.K. Multi-GeV Laser Wakefield Electron Acceleration with PW Lasers. *Appl. Sci.* **2021**, *11*, 5831. [CrossRef]
19. Onishchenko, I.N.; Kiselev, V.A.; Linnik, A.F.; Sotnikov, G.V. Concept of dielectric wakefield accelerator driven by a long sequence of electron bunches. In Proceedings of the IPAC, Shanghai, China, 12–17 May 2013; p. 1259, ISBN 978-3-95450-122-9.
20. Onishchenko, I.N.; Kiseljob, V.A.; Berezin, A.K.; Sotnikov, G.V.; Uskov, V.V.; Linnik, A.F.; Fainberg, Y.B. The wake-field excitation in plasma-dielectric structure by sequence of short bunches of relativistic electrons. In Proceedings of the Particle Accelerator Conference, Dallas, TX, USA, 1–5 May 1995; p. 2782.
21. Lotov, K.V.; Maslov, V.I.; Onishchenko, I.N.; Yarovaya, I.P. Mechanisms of synchronization of relativistic electron bunches at wakefield excitation in plasma. *Probl. At. Sci. Technol.* **2013**, *4*, 73–76.
22. Lotov, K.V.; Maslov, V.I.; Onishchenko, I.N. Long sequence of relativistic electron bunches as a driver in wakefield method of charged particles acceleration in plasma. *Probl. At. Sci. Technol.* **2010**, *6*, 103–107.
23. Bondar, D.S.; Maslov, V.I.; Boychenko, A.P.; Ovsiannikov, R.T.; Onishchenko, I.N. Dependence of wakefield excitation in plasma by non-resonant sequence of electron bunches on their lengths. *Probl. At. Sci. Technol.* **2021**, *4*, 65–69. [CrossRef]
24. Lotov, K.V.; Maslov, V.I.; Onishchenko, I.N. Transformation ratio in wake-field method of acceleration for sequence of relativistic electron bunches. *Probl. At. Sci. Technol.* **2010**, *4*, 85–89.
25. Baturin, S.S.; Zholents, A. Upper limit for the accelerating gradient in the collinear wakefield accelerator as a function of the transformer ratio. *Phys. Rev. Accel. Beams* **2017**, *20*, 061302. [CrossRef]
26. Marzbanrad, B.; Toyserkani, E.; Jahed, H. Characterization of single-and multilayer cold-spray coating of Zn on AZ31B. *Surf. Coat. Technol.* **2021**, *416*, 127155. [CrossRef]

Perspective

Fiber-Optic Based Laser Wakefield Accelerated Electron Beams and Potential Applications in Radiotherapy Cancer Treatments

Dante Roa [1,*], Jeffrey Kuo [1], Harry Moyses [1], Peter Taborek [2], Toshiki Tajima [2], Gerard Mourou [3] and Fuyuhiko Tamanoi [4,5]

1. Department of Radiation Oncology, Chao Family Comprehensive Cancer Center, University of California, Irvine-Medical Center, 101 The City Drive, B-23, Orange, CA 92868, USA; jvkuo@hs.uci.edu (J.K.); mikemoyses@hotmail.com (H.M.)
2. Department of Physics and Astronomy, University of California, Irvine, CA 92697, USA; ptaborek@uci.edu (P.T.); ttajima@uci.edu (T.T.)
3. Ecole Polytechnique, 91128 Paliseau, France; gerard.mourou@polytechnique.edu
4. Institute for Integrated Cell-Materials Science, Institute for Advanced Study, Kyoto University, Kyoto 606-8501, Japan; tamanoi.fuyuhiko.2c@kyoto-u.ac.jp
5. Department of Microbiology, Immunology and Molecular Genetics, University of California, Los Angeles, CA 90095, USA
* Correspondence: droa@hs.uci.edu

Abstract: Ultra-compact electron beam technology based on laser wakefield acceleration (LWFA) could have a significant impact on radiotherapy treatments. Recent developments in LWFA high-density regime (HD-LWFA) and low-intensity fiber optically transmitted laser beams could allow for cancer treatments with electron beams from a miniature electronic source. Moreover, an electron beam emitted from a tip of a fiber optic channel could lead to new endoscopy-based radiotherapy, which is not currently available. Low-energy (10 keV–1 MeV) LWFA electron beams can be produced by irradiating high-density nano-materials with a low-intensity laser in the range of ~10^{14} W/cm^2. This energy range could be useful in radiotherapy and, specifically, brachytherapy for treating superficial, interstitial, intravascular, and intracavitary tumors. Furthermore, it could unveil the next generation of high-dose-rate brachytherapy systems that are not dependent on radioactive sources, do not require specially designed radiation-shielded rooms for treatment, could be portable, could provide a selection of treatment energies, and would significantly reduce operating costs to a radiation oncology clinic.

Keywords: LWFA; fiber optics; medicine; brachytherapy; cancer

1. Introduction

Laser wakefield acceleration (LWFA) was initially proposed by Tajima and Dawson in 1979 as a method to accelerate charged particles from a low-density plasma using wave-like oscillations induced by electromagnetic pulses from a laser beam targeting the plasma [1]. They calculated that a high-intensity laser of 1 µm wavelength and 10^{18} W/cm^2 of power irradiating a plasma density of 10^{18} cm^{-3} could accelerate electrons to GeV energies over a 1 cm distance.

Experimental verification of LWFA came to light with the advent of high-intensity short-pulse lasers (e.g., Nd: glass laser; 10^{17}–10^{18} W cm^{-2}; 1 ps pulse width) and chirped pulse amplification (CPA) technology described by Strickland and Mourou in 1985 [2]. Soon after, several groups reported electron accelerations to energies in the MeV to GeV range [3,4]. However, the electron beam current, attributed to pulse repetition rate, was significantly lower compared to conventional linear accelerators (linacs), and beam quality, reproducibility, and stability were not consistent in most cases [4].

Subsequent experiments demonstrated the production of monoenergetic electron beams of 25–170 MeV energies [5–9] using compact laser-plasma acceleration systems, which ignited the interest in a potential replacement of radiotherapy linacs with this technology. Since then, the use of LWFA in radiotherapy has focused on the production of external and clinically useful high-energy X-ray, electron [10–13], and proton [13–17] beams, but to date, there is still no commercially available device with this technology.

Conversely, limited attention has been devoted to the production of low-energy LWFA electron beams in the keV to MeV range. Production of these beams can be achieved by increasing the plasma density, thereby reducing the electron energy gain. Furthermore, the technology can be compact. Therefore, an LWFA electron beam could be produced from the tip of micron thick flexible fiber-optic channel that could transport a laser beam, as demonstrated by Nicks et al. [18] and, in a companion paper, by Barraza-Valdez et al. [19].

This could have a significant impact in radiation therapy and especially brachytherapy, which is a cancer treatment technique that delivers a high radiation dose in close proximity (≤ 1 cm) and/or inside a tumor volume in a patient's body [20,21].

This paper provides an overview of the production, medical applications, benefits, and cost reduction that an LWFA electron beam emitted from thin and flexible fiber-optic channels could have in radiotherapy.

2. Rationale

The interaction of a laser beam with plasma resembles that of a tsunami wave traveling through a body of water. If the tsunami travels in deep waters, its phase velocity can be very fast, and very few elements can get trapped and accelerated to these velocities. Likewise, when a laser interacts with a low-density plasma, the laser wake phase velocity can approach the speed of light, and a few electrons are captured by the laser wake and accelerated to very high energies.

On the other hand, if the tsunami travels in shallow waters, its phase velocity is very slow, but its amplitude is very high, trapping a significant amount of sediment in the process. Similarly, when a laser interacts with a high-density plasma, its phase velocity is significantly reduced ($v_g \sim 0$), and a strong coupling of the laser to the plasma motion occurs. In essence, this is what occurs in the production of low-energy LWFA electrons.

In these interactions, the LWFA electron energy gain changes from a relativistic (Tajima-Dawson [1]) to a non-relativistic interaction, as described by Barraza-Valdez et al. [19], with a sharp reduction of maximum electron energy as a function of the normalized laser intensity, a_0, which in this case approaches unity, as demonstrated by Nicks et al. [18]. Moreover, the ratio of the laser critical density, n_c, and the plasma density, n_e, also approaches unity at a given a_0, resulting in excited and broad plasma waves [19], and with virtually complete absorption and/or conversion of the laser energy to an electron beam energy.

The combination of multiple plasma waves produces consecutive electron trappings (and thus acceleration) over a wider range of plasma waves. This allows for occasional electron energy increases when the electron density increases, as opposed to the standard laser wakefield theory scaling described by Tajima and Dawson [1]. Increasing the laser pulse length leads to more electrons accelerated which yields a larger dose deposition, as shown in Figure 1.

For this application, the electron beam is produced by a laser beam traveling through a fiber optic channel until it reaches a lens located near the tip of the channel. The lens compresses the laser pulse and directs it to a micron-sized cavity filled with nano-tube fabric near critical density. The electrons in the cavity are separated by the electromagnetic field induced by the laser and accelerated to keV–MeV energies through LWFA, which produces the electron beam to be used for treatment (Figure 2).

Theoretical and computational studies by Barraza-Valdez et al. [19] have demonstrated that the proposed laser-matter interactions, with laser intensities of $\sim 10^{14}$ W/cm^2 and 10–100 micron target(s) at critical density, can yield a 10 keV electron beam via LWFA. Furthermore, Sha et al. [22] have described that fiber laser technology for this regime is feasible.

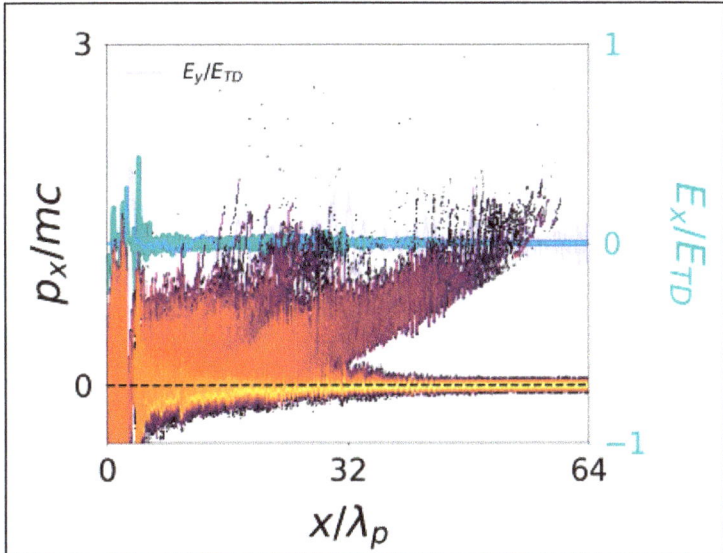

Figure 1. Electron phase space and field structure for a critical density case $n_c/n_e = 1$ and a laser pulse of length $8\lambda_p$ at a laser intensity $a_0 = 1$. Data shows the buildup of a large population of low-energy accelerated electrons for a high-density plasma (from Nicks et al. [18]).

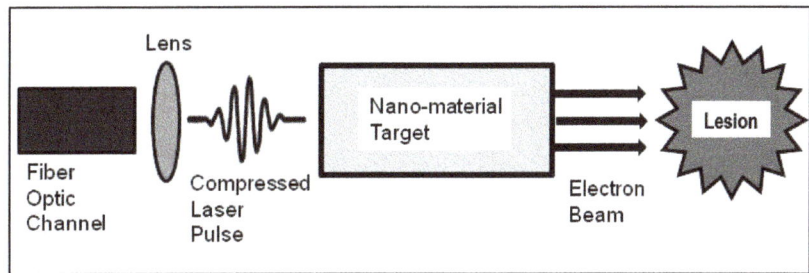

Figure 2. Schematic of a fiber optic channel and laser beam traveling through the fiber. At the end of the fiber, the laser enters a micro-lens which compresses the laser pulse prior to entering a high-density nano-tube fabric target. The target is near its critical density materials, which is the result of a nano-tube fabric spanned from a set of struts. An electron beam, produced from the LWFA interaction of the laser with a high-density target, is used for treatment. It is envisioned that the fiber optic channel, lens, and target cavity setup to be in the ~100 micron scale, and the electron beam could be aimed directly at a lesion volume.

3. Significance

3.1. Applications to Brachytherapy

Brachytherapy is a radiotherapy technique that delivers a large radiation dose adjacent to or inside a tumor in a patient's body [20,21]. The dose is delivered in one or more sessions and effectively conforms to the tumor volume due to its treatment proximity while minimizing collateral radiation dose to healthy organs nearby [21]. Superficial, intracavitary, interstitial, intravascular, and endoscopic brachytherapy techniques are available for treatment. Interstitial brachytherapy may require the patient to stay in the hospital overnight, while the others, for the most part, are outpatient procedures [21].

Gamma-emitting sources (e.g., ^{226}Ra, ^{137}Cs, ^{60}Co, ^{198}Au, ^{192}Ir, ^{103}Pd, and ^{131}Cs) with energies ranging from 0.2–0.8 MeV have been used for decades in needles, seeds, and ribbons for gynecological and prostate brachytherapy [23]. Further, electron-emitting sources (e.g., ^{90}Y, 0.9–2.3 MeV) in the form of microspheres are used in solutions to treat intrahepatic cancers [24–28].

Currently, high-dose-rate (HDR) brachytherapy units equipped with either a 10 Curie (Ci) ^{192}Ir (half-life of 73.8 days) or a 2.4 Ci ^{60}Co (half-life of 5.3 years) gamma-ray source inside a capsule, the size of a grain of rice and welded to the tip of a flexible wire, are routinely used in brachytherapy [23,28–30]. Even though kilovoltage X-rays from electronic generators have become available [31], HDR brachytherapy with gamma-ray sources remains the prevalent treatment modality.

HDR brachytherapy can deliver effective superficial, intracavitary, and interstitial treatments. However, source decay that leads to progressively longer treatment times, source replacement costs, and shielding costs are major drawbacks. For instance, an interstitial gynecological brachytherapy treatment with 20 implanted hollow needles treating a patient's cervix to a dose of 6 Gy in one fraction could take 5 min. (300 s) treatment time with a new (10 Ci) ^{192}Ir source (3000 Ci × seconds). A similar treatment (3000 Ci × seconds) delivered 4 months later (~3 Ci) would take 17 min. treatment time.

An HDR system based on LWFA (LWFA-HDR) could eliminate these disadvantages by removing the radioactive source and, instead, produce electron beams that can be easily shielded. Furthermore, it could eliminate the threat of stolen radioactive material that could be used as a dirty bomb, as stated by the United States Department of Homeland Security, and eliminate radiation safety accidents due to damage and/or mishandling of a radioactive source [32]. Further, radiation oncology clinics in the United States would not be bound by the Nuclear Regulatory Commission (NRC) for HDR clinical operations since a radioactive source would not be needed.

3.2. Current HDR and Potential LWFA-HDR Treatment

Delivery of an HDR brachytherapy treatment consists of sending a radioactive source attached to the tip of a flexible wire through a catheter connected to a brachytherapy applicator inside or adjacent to a tumor (lesion) volume. Some examples of brachytherapy applicators include surface applicators for skin cancer treatments (Figure 3a), cylindrical applicators of different diameters for vaginal or rectal treatments (Figure 3b), tandem-and-ovoids applicators for cervical and uterine treatments (Figure 3c), and hollow needles for interstitial treatments (e.g., gynecological and prostate) (Figure 3d).

Each applicator has a channel where the source stops at multiple predetermined locations for specific times to deliver a portion of the prescribed radiation dose. These locations are known as dwell positions and the times as dwell times (Figure 3e). An applicator may have more than one insertion channel, each connected to a corresponding catheter and with specific dwell positions/times per channel. Figure 3f-top shows 7 out of 8 catheters of a SAVI breast applicator (Cianna Medical, Aliso Viejo, CA, USA) connected to an HDR unit. Figure 3f-bottom shows a coronal radiograph of the SAVI applicator inside a patient. This applicator is inserted in a breast cavity left after surgical removal of a tumor (lumpectomy). Brachytherapy treatment is administered to eliminate any residual microscopic malignancies.

A computer simulation of the brachytherapy treatment delivery is performed before a patient receives their treatment. For this purpose, a computer tomography (CT) scan, encompassing the treatment region and the brachytherapy applicator, is used in the simulation to determine the dwell positions and dwell times needed to achieve a conformal radiation dose distribution around the tumor volume (Figure 4) while minimizing dose to nearby healthy organs.

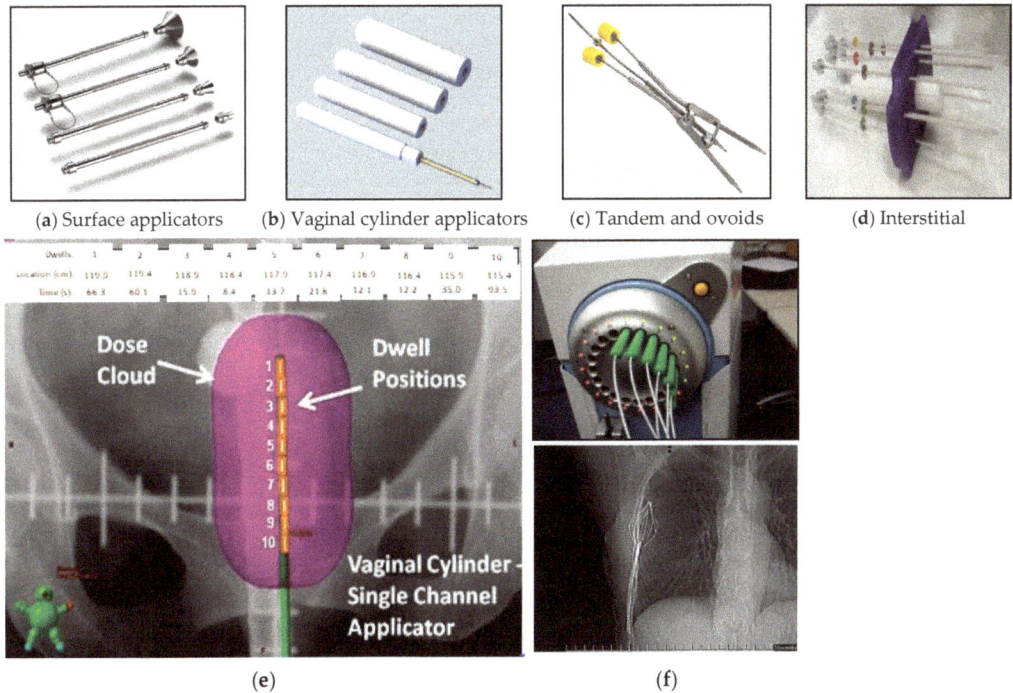

Figure 3. Surface applicators for skin cancer treatments (**a**), cylindrical applicators for vaginal and rectal cancer treatments (**b**), tandem and ovoids (Fletcher Suit) for cervical and uterine cancer treatments (**c**), interstitial needle array for interstitial gynecological or prostate treatments (**d**), number of dwells (1–10), dwell positions (locations in cm), dwell times (s), and dose distributions for a brachytherapy treatment using a cylindrical applicator [33]. (**e**). SAVI applicator catheters connected to a ^{192}Ir HDR source (**f-top**) and coronal radiograph of the SAVI applicator inside a patient (**f-bottom**).

The computer simulation provides a calculated dose distribution in three dimensions (3D) that can be adjusted by increasing/decreasing dwell times for optimal dose conformity to the tumor volume and minimal collateral dose elsewhere. The final dose is calculated by summing the dose contribution from each dwell position in each applicator channel.

A similar process could be used with an LWFA-HDR system. A catheter connected to an applicator is replaced by a fiber-optic channel where a laser beam could travel and irradiate a nano-particle cavity to produce an electron beam that can be emitted from the channel's tip. A computer simulation performed prior to treatment could determine the appropriate electron beam energy or mixed energies (for greater treatment depth), beam directionality, optimal dose distribution to the target volume, and collateral dose to healthy organs nearby. Further, a new LWFA-HDR applicator could be made of material to minimize electron beam attenuation and facilitate fiber-optic channel connectivity for treatment delivery.

The simplest clinical application of an LWFA-HDR could be in the treatment of skin cancers [34–38]. At present, 50 kV X-ray beams from electronic generators (e.g., Xoft Axxent, iCAD Inc., San Jose, CA, USA) and 6–12 MeV linac-based electron beams (e.g., Mobetron, IntraOp Medical Corporation, Sunnyvale, CA, USA), in addition to conventional HDR brachytherapy, are available for skin cancer treatment. From these technologies, only the 50 kV X-ray generator for electronic brachytherapy is portable, and one energy is available. An LWFA-HDR system could offer portability and a selection of electron beam energies suitable for superficial and deep-seated skin cancers. Moreover, electron beams emitted from fiber-optic channel tips could facilitate treating skin cancers near or at the nasal ridge, eyes, and ears, to name a few, where irregular anatomical surfaces are encountered.

In addition to comparable capabilities to current HDR systems, an LWFA-HDR could be used in theranostic and intraoperative radiation therapy (IORT). For instance, some liver cancers are treated with radioembolization, which involves injecting a radioactive solution containing ^{90}Y into the cancer(s) through its (their) blood supply. Perhaps, rather than using a radioactive solution for treatment, the LWFA-HDR could be used instead. A specially-designed fiber-optic channel(s) with a miniature camera for endoscopy and for LWFA electron beam irradiation could be sent to the liver cancer through the femoral artery near the groin. Real-time imaging of the treatment site could be used to aim the electron beam (or beams) and deliver a radiation dose. The development of a miniature endoscope that can travel through a blood vessel and provide essential imaging is in progress and could be available in the near future [39]. Hence, LWFA-HDR could provide a theranostic capability that, at present, is not available in radiation therapy.

Furthermore, the LWFA-HDR theranostic capability combined with vector-medicine, which identifies and tags cancer cells [40,41], could be a high-precision treatment against cancer. High-Z materials such as gadolinium and iodine could be attached to vector molecules. These molecules seek and bind to cancer cells identifying them as targets that, subsequently, could be aimed with the LWFA-HDR electron beam(s). In this way, the electron beam(s) aims not only to rely on real-time endoscopic imaging but also on specific cell biomarkers. Such biomarking can enhance treatment accuracy and reduce collateral damage.

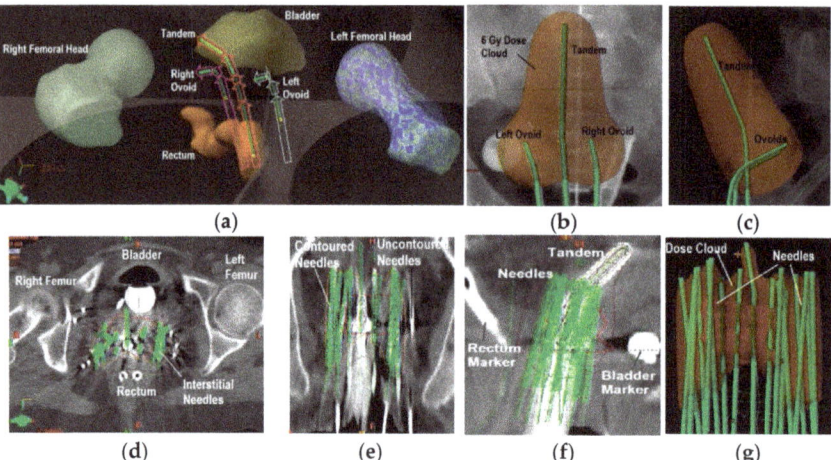

Figure 4. Three-dimensional computer rendering of a tandem-and-ovoids brachytherapy treatment generated from a patient's CT scan. Femoral heads, bladder, and rectum structures are depicted. The arrows in the green structures indicate the radiation treatment is administered with the source at the most distal dwell position (or farthest inside the applicator) first per applicator channel (a). A calculated 6 Gy prescription dose distribution (pear shape) for a tandem-and-ovoids (green structures) is shown in a coronal (b) and sagittal views (c). Axial CT image depicting interstitial brachytherapy needles for cervical cancer treatment (d). Coronal (e) and sagittal images (f) are also shown. Depiction of a 6 Gy prescription dose calculated from the dose contribution of all the interstitial needle channels (g).

3.3. Potential for FLASH Brachytherapy

FLASH is a proposed treatment modality under investigation for external beam radiotherapy (not brachytherapy) that is gaining interest in radiation oncology [42]. The significant difference between FLASH and conventional radiotherapy is the dose rate used. FLASH dose rate ranges from 50–400 Gy/s compared to 0.1–0.4 Gy/s for standard treatments. Ongoing radiobiological studies suggest that, at these dose rates, FLASH can spare healthy tissues by depleting them from their oxygen content and making them radioresistant. Further, it is theorized that FLASH could take advantage of a tumor's iron content, which is higher than healthy tissues, to inflict lethal damage to malignant cells and trigger apoptosis [42]. However, more basic (laboratory/animal) research and technology development (e.g., new linacs with FLASH dose rates) followed by human clinical trials remains to be done to fully elucidate a FLASH treatment capability [42,43].

Most of the hardware development for FLASH has been focused on external beam radiotherapy and not on brachytherapy delivery systems. Although work has been done in the production of sub-MeV LWFA electrons with ultrahigh instantaneous dose rates (~10 Gy/s), the average dose is still below what is required for FLASH [44]. It could be speculated that a sufficiently powerful laser source irradiating an optimized plasma/nano-particle medium could produce electron beams with dose rates that approximate FLASH. If that is possible, LWFA-HDR brachytherapy could be further revolutionized with this enhanced capability.

4. Cost Benefits and Market Size

As previously mentioned, minimal radiation shielding would be required to operate an LWFA-HDR system which can lead to significant savings for radiation oncology clinics due to a reduction in construction and shielding material costs. Any room could be easily retrofitted for treatment at a fraction of the price of an existing HDR treatment room. Moreover, it would eliminate the replacement and purchase of new radioactive sources due to source decay every 4–6 months for ^{192}Ir and 2–3 years for ^{60}Co, which results in further savings for the clinic.

It is expected that radiation oncology centers may be enticed to replace their existing HDR units with an LWFA-HDR system, primarily for the cost savings that it would provide. Moreover, not using a radioactive source in brachytherapy treatments eliminates the security risks that a source implies, which could be further persuasive reasons for adopting this technology. Table 1 provides a cost estimate comparison between existing HDR units and the proposed LWFA-HDR system. The estimated cost for an LWFA-HDR system accounts for laser source, and fiber-optic channel setup (see Figure 2) costs [22,44]. Costs for ^{192}Ir and ^{60}Co HDR units, room shielding construction, and source replacement are based on current market prices [45–48].

Table 1. Estimated purchase and maintenance cost comparisons for LWFA-HDR and conventional HDR systems.

Item	LWFA–HDR	^{192}Ir–HDR	^{60}Co–HDR
Purchase Estimate (one-time expense)	$100K–$300K	$200K–$350K	~$300K
Room Shielding (one-time expense)	None	$200K–$500K *	$300K–$500K **
Source Replacement	None	~$10K every 4–6 months	~130K every 60 months
Downtime due to Source Replacement	None	1–2 days	1–2 days
5-year Estimated Total	$300K	$910K	$930K

* US cost estimates [46,47]. ** Latin America cost estimates [48].

Table 2 provides information on radiotherapy linacs available worldwide in 2013 according to the 2015 Lancet Oncology Commission report [49], and Table 3 shows the number of radiotherapy linacs that were available in the United States in 2004 [50]. Although this number may be greater in 2022, the 2004 data was used to provide a conservative market size illustration for a LWFA-HDR system.

Table 2. Total number of radiotherapy linacs that were available worldwide in 2015 and reported in Lancet stratified by high, upper-middle, and low-income countries.

HI	UMI	LMI	LI	Total
8911 (68%)	3115 (24%)	1014 (8%)	32 (0%)	13,072 (100%)

HI = High-Income countries; UMI = Upper-Middle-Income countries; LMI = Lower-Middle-Income countries; LI = Low-Income countries.

Table 3. Radiation oncology clinics and radiotherapy linacs were available in the United States in 2004.

Rad. Onc. Clinics in the US in 2004	Radiotherapy Linacs
2246	5166

On average, the number of available HDR brachytherapy units in HI and UMI countries is ~20% of the number of radiotherapy linacs [51]. Therefore, from Table 2, these correspond to 1782 and 623 HDR units in HI and UMI countries, respectively. No published data was found on HDR units in LMI and LI countries. Based on this information and assuming a $300K cost (see Table 1) for an LWFA-HDR unit, the total addressable market (TAM) revenue estimate from HI and UMI countries could be $722M. Narrowing the market to HI countries, the serviceable available market (SAM) revenue estimate reduces to $534M. For the US market and using the data in Table 3, 1033 HDR units were available in the US in 2004. Therefore, the serviceable obtainable market (SOM) revenue estimate in the US market could be $310M. Figure 5 provides a market size depiction for the LWFA-HDR system.

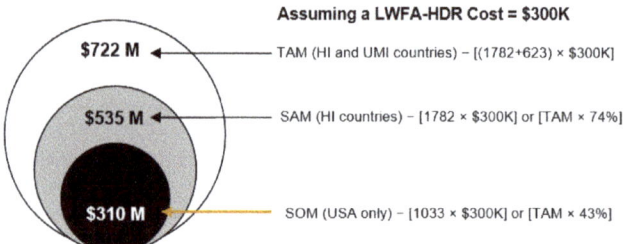

Figure 5. Estimated revenue from the LWFA-HDR brachytherapy system in HI & UMI, HI only, and US (based on Table 2 data) markets. Market size is depicted in terms of the total addressable market (TAM), serviceable available market (SAM), and serviceable obtainable market (SOM).

As indicated, this analysis does not include potential revenue from LMI and LI countries. However, it can be speculated that this technology could be of significant interest to those regions and, likely, within their financial means to afford it.

5. Conclusions

The aim of this paper was to present a vision of what could be achievable with electron beams produced via LWFA and their use in cancer treatments with brachytherapy. Furthermore, to describe the cost savings that an LWFA-HDR system could provide to a radiation oncology clinic since it eliminates the use of radioactive sources and radiation-shielded rooms for treatment. Although an in-depth analysis of the LWFA electron beam dosimetry applied to brachytherapy is not included, it will be forthcoming as the technology develops further.

An LWFA-HDR system with its capabilities described in this paper could significantly transform the delivery of brachytherapy treatments while making them more accessible and cost-effective to radiation oncology clinics, particularly in low- to middle-income countries.

Funding: This research received no external funding.

Institutional Review Board Statement: Not applicable.

Informed Consent Statement: Not applicable.

Data Availability Statement: Not applicable.

Acknowledgments: We are much indebted to Donna Strickland, W. J. Sha, J-C. Chanteloup for the fiber laser technology. We are grateful for discussions on LWFA with nano-materials with E. Barraza-Valdez, S. Nicks.

Conflicts of Interest: The authors declare no conflict of interest.

References

1. Tajima, T.; Dawson, J.M. Laser electron accelerator. *Phys. Rev. Lett.* **1979**, *43*, 267–270. [CrossRef]
2. Strickland, D.; Mourou, G. Compression of amplified chirped optical pulses. *Opt. Comm.* **1985**, *56*, 219–221. [CrossRef]
3. Nakajima, K.; Nakanishi, H.; Kawakubo, T.; Ogata, A.; Kitagawa, Y.; Shiraga, H.; Zhang, T.; Suzuki, K.; Kato, Y.; Sakawa, Y.; et al. Laser wakefield accelerator experiments using 1ps 30 TW Nd:glass laser. In Proceedings of the International Conference on Particle Accelerators, Washington, DC, USA, 17–20 May 1993; IEEE: Piscataway, NJ, USA, 1993; pp. 2556–2558.
4. Modena, A.; Najmudin, Z.; Dangor, A.E.; Clayton, C.E.; Marsh, K.A.; Joshi, C.; Malka, V.; Darrow, C.B.; Danson, C.; Neely, D.; et al. Electron acceleration from the breaking of relativistic plasma waves. *Nature* **1995**, *377*, 606–608. [CrossRef]
5. Mangles, S.P.D.; Murphy, C.D.; Najmudin, Z.; Thomas, A.G.R.; Collier, J.L.; Dangor, A.E.; Divall, E.J.; Foster, P.S.; Gallacher, J.G.; Hooker, C.J.; et al. Monoenergetic beams of relativistic electrons from intense laser-plasma interactions. *Nature* **2004**, *431*, 535–538. [CrossRef] [PubMed]
6. Geddes, C.G.R.; Toth, C.S.; van Tilborg, J.; Esarey, E.; Schroeder, C.B.; Bruhwiler, D.; Nieter, C.; Cary, J.; Leemans, W.P. High-quality electron beams from a laser wakefield accelerator using plasma-channel guiding. *Nature* **2004**, *431*, 538–541. [CrossRef] [PubMed]
7. Faure, J.; Glinec, Y.; Pukhov, A.; Kiselev, S.; Gordienko, S.; Lefebvre, E.; Rousseau, J.P.; Burgy, F.; Malka, V. A laser-plasma accelerator producing monoenergetic electron beams. *Nature* **2004**, *431*, 541–544. [CrossRef] [PubMed]
8. Leemans, W.P.; Nagler, B.; Gonsalves, A.J.; Toth, C.S.; Nakamura, K.; Geddes, C.G.R.; Esarey, E.; Schroeder, C.B.; Hooker, S.M. GeV electron beams from a centimetre-scale accelerator. *Nat. Phys.* **2006**, *2*, 696–699. [CrossRef]
9. Hafz, N.A.M.; Jeong, T.M.; Choi, I.W.; Lee, S.K.; Pae, K.H.; Kulagin, V.V.; Sung, J.H.; Yu, T.J.; Hong, K.-H.; Hosokai, T.; et al. Stable generation of GeV-class electron beams from self-guided laser-plasmas channels. *Nat. Photonics* **2008**, *2*, 571–577. [CrossRef]
10. Gonsalves, A.J.; Nakamura, K.; Daniels, J.; Benedetti, C.; Pieronek, C.; de Raadt, T.C.H.; Steinke, S.; Bin, J.H.; Bulanov, S.S.; van Tilborg, J.; et al. Petawatt Laser Guiding and Electron Beam Acceleration to 8 GeV in a Laser-Heated Capillary Discharge Waveguide. *Phys. Rev. Lett.* **2019**, *122*, 084801. [CrossRef]
11. Giulietti, A.; Bourgeois, N.; Ceccotti, T.; Davoine, X.; Dobosz, S.; Oliveira, P.D.; Galimberti, M.; Galy, J.; Gamucci, A.; Giulietti, D.; et al. Intense g-ray source in the giant-dipole-resonance range driven by 10-TW laser pulses. *Phys. Rev. Lett.* **2008**, *101*, 105005. [CrossRef]
12. Nakajima, K.; Yuan, J.; Chen, L.; Sheng, Z. Laser-driven very high energy electron/photon beam radiation therapy in conjunction with a robotic system. *Appl. Sci.* **2015**, *5*, 1–20. [CrossRef]
13. Nakajima, K. Laser-driven electron beam and radiation sources for basic, medical and industrial sciences. *Proc. Jpn. Acad. Ser. B* **2015**, *91*, 223–245. [CrossRef] [PubMed]
14. Giulietti, A. *Laser-Driven Particle Acceleration towards Radiobiology and Medicine*; Biological and Medical Physics, Biomedical Engineering; Springer: Berlin, Germany, 2016; ISSN 2197-5647.
15. Fourkal, E.; Shahine, B.; Ding, M.; Li, J.S.; Tajima, T.; Ma, C.M. Particle in cell simulation of laser-accelerated proton beams for radiation therapy. *Med. Phys* **2002**, *29*, 2788–2798. [CrossRef] [PubMed]
16. Fourkal, E.; Li, J.S.; Ding, M.; Tajima, T.; Ma, C.M. Particle selection for laser-accelerated proton therapy feasibility study. *Med. Phys.* **2003**, *30*, 1660–1670. [CrossRef]
17. Macchi, A. A review of laser-plasma ion acceleration. *arXiv* **2017**, arXiv:1712.06443v1.
18. Nicks, B.S.; Hakimi, S.; Barraza-Vadez, E.; Chesnut, K.D.; DeGrandchamp, G.H.; Gage, K.R.; Housley, D.B.; Huxtable, G.; Lawler, G.; Lin, D.J.; et al. Electron dynamics in the high-density laser-wakefield acceleration regime. *Photonics* **2021**, *8*, 216. [CrossRef]
19. Barraza-Valdez, E.; Tajima, T.; Strickland, D.; Roa, D. Laser beat wave acceleration near critical density. *Photonics* **2022**. submitted.
20. National Cancer Institute—Radiation Therapy to Treat Cancer. Available online: https://www.cancer.gov/aboutcancer/treatment/types/radiation-therapy/brachytherapy (accessed on 25 March 2022).
21. Khan, F.M. *The Physics of Radiation Therapy*, 4th ed.; Lippincott Williams & Wilkins: New York, NY, USA, 2010.
22. Shah, W.; Chanteloup, J.C.; Mourou, G. Ultrafast fiber technologies for compact laser wake-field in medical applications. *Photonics* **2022**. submitted.
23. Renner, W.D.; O'Connor, T.P.; Bermudez, N.M. An algorithm for generation of implant plans for high-dose-rate irradiators. *Med. Phys.* **1990**, *17*, 35–40. [CrossRef]

24. Arnold, C.A.; Pezhouh, M.K.; Lam-Himlin, D.; Pittman, M.E.; VandenBussche, C.; Voltaggio, L. 90Y-TheraSpheres: The new look of Yttrium-90. *Am. J. Surg. Pathol.* **2019**, *43*, 688–694. [CrossRef]
25. Salem, R.; Lewandowski, R.J.; Mulcahy, M.F.; Riaz, A.; Ryu, R.K.; Ibrahim, S.; Atassi, B.; Baker, T.; Gates, V.; Miller, F.H.; et al. Radioembolization for Hepatocellular Carcinoma Using Yttrium-90 Microspheres: A Comprehensive Report of Long-term Outcomes. *Gastroenterology* **2010**, *138*, 52–64. [CrossRef] [PubMed]
26. Salem, R.; Johnson, G.E.; Kim, E.; Riaz, A.; Bishay, V.; Boucher, E.; Fowers, K.; Lewandowski, R.; Padia, S.A. Yttrium-90 Radioembolization for the treatment of solitary, unresectable HCC: The legacy study. *Hepatology* **2021**, *74*, 2342–2352. [CrossRef] [PubMed]
27. Kennedy, A.S.; Coldwell, D.; Nutting, C.; Murthy, R.; Wertman, D.E., Jr.; Loehr, S.P.; Overton, C.; Meranze, S.; Niedzwiecki, J.; Sailer, S. 90Y-microsphere brachytherapy for unresectable colorectal liver metastases: Modern USA experience. *Int. J. Radiat. Oncol. Biol. Phys.* **2006**, *65*, 412. [CrossRef] [PubMed]
28. Van der Laars, R.; Prius, T.P.E. Introduction to HDR brachytherapy optimization. In *Brachytherapy from Radium to Optimization*; Nucletron Corporation: Veenendaal, The Netherlands, 1994.
29. Ezzel, G.A.; Luthermann, R.W. Clinical implementation of dwell time optimization techniques for single stepping-source remote applicators. In *Brachytherapy Physics*; Medical Physics Publishing: Madison, WI, USA, 1994.
30. Kubo, H.D.; Glasgow, G.P.; Pethel, T.D.; Thomadsen, B.R.; Williamson, J.F. High dose-rate brachytherapy treatment delivery: Report of the AAPM Radiation Therapy Committee Task Group No. 59. *Med Phys.* **1998**, *25*, 375–403. [CrossRef]
31. Ramachandran, P. New era of electronic brachytherapy. *World J. Radiol.* **2017**, *9*, 148–154. [CrossRef]
32. Valentin, J. Preface, Main Points, Introduction, Chapters 2 and 3. *Ann. ICRP* **2005**, *35*, 1–9. [CrossRef]
33. IAEA. 3D Brachytherapy Treatment Planning. Available online: https://inis.iaea.org/collection/NCLCollectionStore/_Public/49/093/49093364.pdf (accessed on 25 March 2022).
34. IAEA. *The Transition from 2-D Brachytherapy to 3-D High Dose Rate Brachytherapy*; Human Health Report No. 12.; IAEA: Vienna, Austria, 2015.
35. Chua, B.; Jackson, J.E.; Lin, C.; Veness, M.J. Radiotherapy for early non-melanoma skin cancer. *Oral Oncol.* **2019**, *98*, 96–101. [CrossRef]
36. Garbutcheon-Singh, K.B.; Veness, M.J. The role of radiotherapy in the management of non-melanoma skin cancer. *Australas. J. Dermatol.* **2019**, *60*, 265–272. [CrossRef]
37. Ota, K.; Adar, T.; Dover, L.; Khachemoune, A. Review: The reemergence of brachytherapy as treatment for non-melanoma skin cancer. *J. Dermatol. Treat.* **2018**, *29*, 170–175. [CrossRef]
38. Veness, M.; Delishaj, D.; Barnes, E.; Bezugly, A.; Rembielak, A. Current Role of Radiotherapy in Non-melanoma Skin Cancer. *Clin. Oncol.* **2019**, *31*, 749–758. [CrossRef]
39. Li, J.; Thiele, S.; Quirk, B.C.; Kirk, R.W.; Verjans, J.W.; Akers, E.; Bursill, C.A.; Nicholls, S.J.; Herkommer, A.M.; Giessen, H.; et al. Ultrathin monolithic 3D printed optical coherence tomography endoscopy for preclinical and clinical use. *Light Sci. Appl.* **2020**, *9*, 124. [CrossRef] [PubMed]
40. Matsumoto, K.; Saitoh, H.; Doan, T.L.H.; Shiro, A.; Nakai, K.; Komatsu, A.; Tsujimoto, M.; Yasuda, R.; Kawachi, T.; Tajima, T.; et al. Destruction of tumor mass by gadolinium-loaded nanoparticles irradiated with monochromatic X-rays: Implications for the Auger therapy. *Sci. Rep.* **2019**, *9*, 13705. [CrossRef] [PubMed]
41. Higashi, Y.; Matsumoto, K.; Saitoh, H.; Shiro, A.; Ma, Y.; Laird, M.; Chinnathambi, S.; Birault, A.; Doan, T.L.H.; Yasuda, R.; et al. Iodine containing porous organosilica nanoparticles trigger destruction of tumor spheroids upon irradiation with monochromatic X-ray: DNA double strand breaks and preferential effect of K-edge energy X-ray. *Sci. Rep.* **2021**, *11*, 14192. [CrossRef] [PubMed]
42. Wilson, J.D.; Hammond, E.M.; Higgins, G.S.; Petersson, K. Ultra-High dose rate (FLASH) radiotherapy: Silver bullet or fool's gold? *Front. Oncol.* **2020**, *9*, 1563. [CrossRef]
43. Ashraf, M.R.; Rahman, M.; Zhang, R.; Williams, B.B.; Gladstone, D.J.; Pogue, B.W.; Bruza, P. Dosimetry for FLASH Radiotherapy: A Review of Tools and the Role of Radioluminescence and Cherenkov Emission. *Front. Phys.* **2020**, *8*, 328. [CrossRef]
44. Labate, L.; Andreassi, M.G.; Baffigi, F.; Bizzarri, R.; Borghini, A.; Bussolino, G.C.; Fulgentini, L.; Ghetti, F.; Giulietti, A.; Koster, P. LESM: A laser driven sub-MeV electron source delivering ultra-high dose rate on thin biological samples. *J. Appl. Phys. D Appl. Phys.* **2016**, *49*, 275401. [CrossRef]
45. Sha, W.; CommScope Access Technologies Advanced Research, Santa Clara, CA, USA. Private communication, 2022.
46. Varian Medical Systems Sales Representative; Varian Medical Systems, Palo Alto, CA, USA. Private communication, 2022.
47. Scanderbeg, D.J.; Yashar, C.; Ouhib, Z.; Jhingran, A.; Einck, J. Development, implementation and associated challenges of a new HDR brachytherapy program. *Brachytherapy* **2020**, *19*, 874–880. [CrossRef]
48. Mailhot Vega, R.B.; Barbee, D.; Talcott, W.; Duckworth, T.; Shah, B.A.; Ishaq, O.F.; Small, C.; Yeung, A.R.; Perez, C.A.; Schiff, P.B.; et al. Cost in perspective: Direct assessment of American market acceptability of Co-60 in gynecologic high-dose-rate brachytherapy and contrast with experience abroad. *J. Contemp. Brachyther.* **2018**, *10*, 503–509. [CrossRef]
49. Atun, R.; Jaffray, D.A.; Barton, M.B.; Bray, F.; Baumann, M.; Vikram, B.; Hanna, T.P.; Knaul, F.M.; Lievens, Y.; Lui, T.Y.; et al. Expanding global access to radiotherapy. *Lancet* **2015**, *16*, 1153–1186. [CrossRef]
50. Ballas, L.K.; Elkin, E.B.; Schrag, D.; Minsky, B.D.; Bach, P.B. Radiation therapy facilities in the United States. *Int. J. Radiat. Oncol. Biol. Phys.* **2006**, *66*, 1204–1211. [CrossRef] [PubMed]
51. IROC; University of Texas—MD Anderson Cancer Center, Houston, TX, USA. Private communication, 2022.

Article

Laser Wakefield Photoneutron Generation with Few-Cycle High-Repetition-Rate Laser Systems

Daniel Papp [1], Ales Necas [2,*], Nasr Hafz [1,3], Toshiki Tajima [2], Sydney Gales [4], Gerard Mourou [5], Gabor Szabo [1,6] and Christos Kamperidis [1]

1. ELI-ALPS, ELI-HU Non-Profit Ltd., H-6728 Szeged, Hungary
2. TAE Technologies, 19631 Pauling, Foothill Ranch, CA 92610, USA
3. Doctoral School of Physics, Faculty of Science and Informatics, University of Szeged, 9 Dóm tér, H-6720 Szeged, Hungary
4. IJCLab, IN2P3/CNRS, University Paris-Saclay, 91405 Orsay, France
5. Ecole Polytechnique, Route de Saclay, 91128 Palaiseau, France
6. Department of Optics and Quantum Electronics, University of Szeged, H-6720 Szeged, Hungary
* Correspondence: anecas@tae.com

Abstract: Simulations of photoneutron generation are presented for the anticipated experimental campaign at ELI-ALPS using the under-commissioning e-SYLOS beamline. Photoneutron generation is a three-step process starting with the creation of a relativistic electron beam which is converted to gamma radiation, which in turn generates neutrons via the (γ, n) interaction in high-Z material. Electrons are accelerated to relativistic energies using the laser wakefield acceleration (LWFA) mechanism. The LWFA process is simulated with a three-dimensional particle in cell code to generate an electron bunch of 100s pC charge from a 100 mJ, 9 fs laser interaction with a helium gas jet target. The resultant electron spectrum is transported through a lead sphere with the Monte Carlo N-Particle (MCNP) code to convert electrons to gammas and gammas to neutrons in a single simulation. A neutron yield of 3×10^7 per shot over 4π is achieved, with a corresponding neutron yield per kW of 6×10^{11} n/s/kW. The paper concludes with a discussion on the attractiveness of LWFA-driven photoneutron generation on high impact, and societal applications.

Keywords: laser wakefield acceleration; electron; photoneutron; high-repetition laser; few-cycle laser

1. Introduction

Neutron sources are used in a wide array of applications, ranging from transmutation and incineration of spent nuclear fuel [1,2], neutron imaging [3], radioisotope production for medicine [4], cancer treatment [5], oil-well logging [6], gem colorization [7], driving subcritical nuclear fission reactors [8], security applications [9] and many others.

Neutron sources can be divided into three broad categories depending on their size: small, medium and large. A small size source generates a neutron intensity less than 10^9 n/s and is based on a natural decay of a radioisotopes. Few prominent examples are the AmBe source based on natural alpha emitters (Am) which induce (alpha, n) reactions on the Be9 target to generate neutrons; another source is Cf-252 based on a spontaneous fission. Medium-sized sources generate neutron intensity in the range of 10^9–10^{13} n/s. They are based on hadron and electron accelerators. In case of hadrons, either a low energy proton or deuteron irradiate a low-Z target such as beryllium or lithium to generate neutrons via stripping or a knock-out process; in contrast, a relativistic proton beam irradiates a high-Z target, e.g., lead, to initiate the spallation process. In case of electrons, a relativistic electron beam impinges on a high-Z material, e.g., lead, tungsten, etc., to convert to gammas via the bremsstrahlung process; generated gamma interacts with an atomic nucleus via the giant dipole resonance mechanism to eject neutrons. Large-size neutron sources are capable for producing large intensity, far exceeding 10^{16} n/s, and are associated with nuclear fission reactors.

One method of generating high-current (beyond 10^{12} n/s) neutron sources is using an RF LINAC electron accelerator, where the electron beam is absorbed in a high-Z target, and the generated bremsstrahlung interacts with the same target, generating photoneutrons. Experimental demonstrations and characterizations have been carried out earlier at the nELBE facility [10], utilizing a 1 mA 40 MeV electron beam. In an alternative configuration, electrons are converted to gamma in a first-stage converter and transported to a neutron generator. This configuration has been employed in the PARRNe experiment [11,12] with a W-converter and uranium carbide (UC_x) neutron generator that can produce 10^{13} fissions/s using a 100 kW beam of 30 MeV electrons as part of the ALTO project. Another facility [13] is already under implementation, using a 100 MeV, 100 kW electron beam driver, with a maximum-predicted neutron current of 1–4×10^{14} n/s. The high-Z target can be liquid lead [10], tungsten, or even enriched uranium [14,15]. High-intensity electron beams with currents exceeding 10 A can generate a peak neutron yield of 10^{10} n/pulse, as demonstrated at the GELINA facility [16], and 10^{12} neutron/pulse at ORELA [17], with both facilities able to achieve a repetition rate of 100 Hz. An overview of the present and upcoming neutron generator facilities leveraging particle beams was presented in [18].

Advances in laser technology also led to the demonstration of laser-driven photoneutron sources by several groups. One scheme generates electrons using the interaction of a strongly focused laser pulse on a solid (or close to solid) density target [19–21]. However, these sources, utilizing solid targets, are suffering from the limited, low-repetition rate on the solid-state targetry design [22].

Another laser-based neutron generation method relies on electron acceleration via laser wakefield acceleration (LWFA) in plasma [23]. Here, a short-laser pulse is focused on a gas target (gas jet or gas cell); this generates relativistic electrons in an acceleration length of a few mm, then is directed into a high-Z converter. In this scheme, the RF accelerators are essential and are replaced with a laser-driven plasma accelerator, potentially allowing a compact, tabletop-size experimental setup. The laser target itself is a gas jet or gas cell, which allows for operations at repetition rates of 1 kHz [24,25]. The viability of this method has already been demonstrated in the single-shot mode [26], where a tungsten converter was inserted in a 37 MeV-average-energy electron beam, generating few MeV neutrons.

In this paper, we investigate photoneutron generation using a laser wakefield acceleration (LWFA) electron source driven by a high-repetition-rate laser. Simulations have shown that 100 MeV of electron energy can be efficiently reached by relatively modest laser parameters (100 mJ pulse energy) [27], and ultrashort-pulse lasers with a similar pulse energy are available working at a 1 kHz repetition rate [28]. The laser plasma interaction generating and accelerating the electrons is simulated using a multidimensional (3d3v) particle-in-cell (PIC) code, EPOCH [29]. The subsequent electron interaction with matter—including gamma generation and neutron production—is simulated using the Monte Carlo N-Particle (MCNP) code [30].

The paper is organized in the following structure: Section 2 describes the principles of laser wakefield acceleration and presents the simulation results, including the electron energy spectrum. In Section 3, the electron spectrum is used to generate photons and photoneutrons. Additionally, in Section 3, a detailed study of photoneutron generation by a monoenergetic electron beam is given. In Section 4, we will discuss applications and the utilization of the generated neutrons, and we will concentrate on the transmutation of the spent nuclear fuel; radioisotope production, namely, the molybdenum-99 as a precursor to Tc-99; and neutron imaging.

2. Laser Electron Acceleration

The principle of LWFA is to send a short laser pulse through an under-dense gas (usually He, or N), where the laser leading edge also ionizes the gas, turning it into plasma. The mechanism that follows utilizes the laser's radiation pressure (ponderomotive force) to push aside plasma. At sufficiently high laser intensities, the electrons are removed from the axis of propagation of the laser, and a nonlinear plasma wake forms with close-to-spherical "bubbles" that contain no electrons inside [31–33], with a characteristic size of the plasma wavelength $\lambda_p = 2\pi c/\omega_p$—this is the so-called bubble or blow-out regime where $\omega_p = \sqrt{n_0 e^2/m_e \epsilon_0}$ is the plasma frequency and n_0 is the plasma electron density. This regime requires that the laser pulse length $c\tau_L$ is not larger than the plasma bubble. Note that the plasma wavelength decreases with density as $\sim n_0^{-1/2}$, so a shorter laser pulse length is required to permit the blow-out regime at higher densities.

This laser wake travels with the group velocity of the laser in the plasma (which equals the group velocity of light) $v_p = v_g = c\sqrt{1 - \omega_p^2/\omega_L^2}$. In this ion cavity, the charge distribution produces a longitudinal electric field. Here, τ_L is the laser pulse duration and ω_L is the laser frequency. The diameter of the laser focal spot must also be of similar magnitude, in the order of 10 µm.

The acceleration process is also helped by relativistic plasma self-focusing [34], which keeps the laser focus from diverging, helping it to propagate further in the plasma, preserving its high intensity, and the conditions necessary for the blow-out regime.

If electrons are injected at the back end of the bubble, they will be accelerated until they reach the mid-point of the plasma bubble, where the acceleration field is zero. As the bubble itself moves close to the speed of light, the electrons are eventually accelerated to relativistic velocities. Depending on the density of the plasma, the electron acceleration is generally limited by dephasing (the electrons reach the midpoint of the bubble) or the depletion of the laser pulse, with the latter being dominant at shorter laser-pulse lengths [33].

In this paper, we analyze photoneutron generation, assuming a state-of-the-art laser system, similar to the one described in [28], with the assumed parameters of 100 mJ (nominal) pulse energy, 8 fs FWHM pulse duration, 6 µm FWHM focal spot, and 900 nm central wavelength. The energy content of the laser electric field in the simulation was 112 mJ. These figures correspond to the expected laser parameters of the SYLOS3 laser (currently under development) at ELI-ALPS.

The simulation of the laser wakefield acceleration follows the same approach as described in Papp et al. [27]. Simulations have been carried out using the EPOCH3D [29] particle in the cell code. A moving window reference frame was applied, moving with the phase velocity of the laser pulse. The dimensions of the simulation domain are $x \times y \times z = 24 \times 24 \times 24$ µm and are subdivided by $480 \times 120 \times 120$ cells with 4 macroparticles per cell, applying a fourth-order electromagnetic solver which limits the numerical dispersion effects.

The longitudinal plasma profile had half(semi)-gaussian entrance and exit ramps of 100 µm length (between 10% and 90% density values), with a flat density in between, at 400 µm length (between 90% densities of the entrance and exit ramps). This plasma length was optimized, and was longer than the nominal depletion length of 218 µm. The electron density in the flat region was 1.5×10^{19} cm^{-3}, which is optimal based on preliminary simulations. The plasma was a pure He gas.

The electron density can be seen in Figure 1a. The electron distribution function and spectrum is shown in Figure 1b,c, respectively. The spectrum is broad, with a well-defined quasi-monoenergetic peak at 110 MeV. The spectrum also has an exponential tail past 180 MeV—the high-space charge causes the electron bunch to expand, and it accelerates the front end of the bunch further. The average energy of the electron bunch is 70 MeV with a bunch charge of 453 pC (3×10^9 electrons). While the broadband nature of the electron spectrum might not be suitable for some applications, in the generation of photoneutrons, the spectral quality of the beam is of secondary importance.

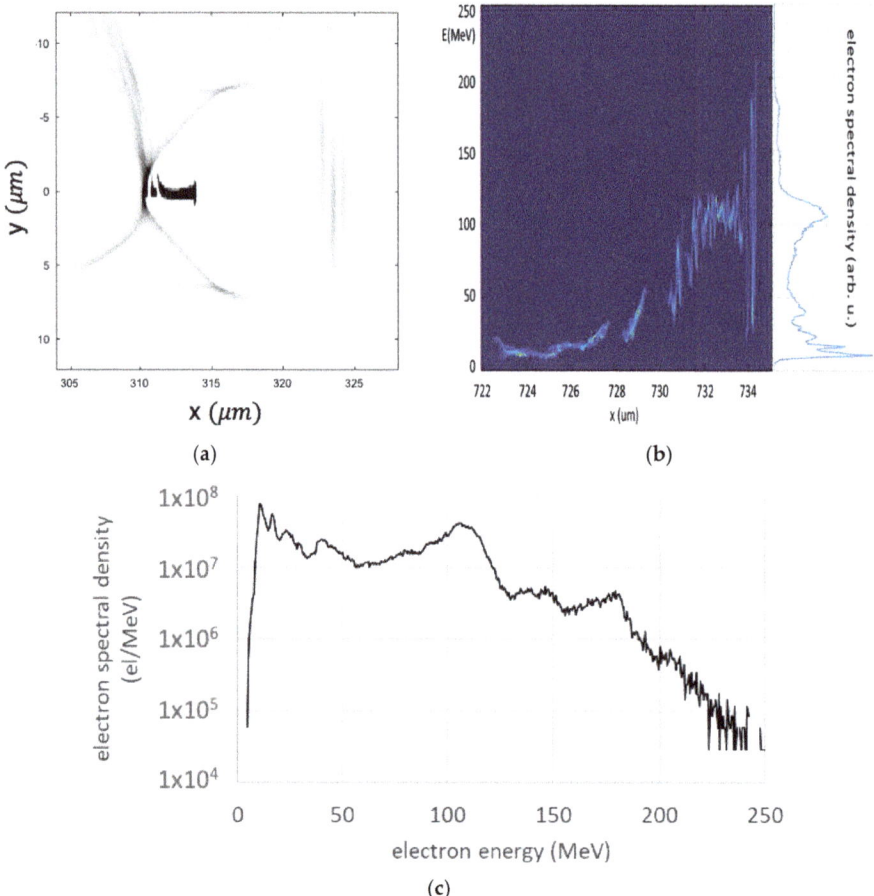

Figure 1. Electron density at the center of the density plateau (a), electron distribution function and spectrum after the plasma (b), spectrum on a log-lin plot (c).

The efficiency of the electron acceleration at these laser pulse parameters is very high; the accelerated electron bunch has a total energy of 32 mJ, which corresponds to a 29% laser-to-electron conversion efficiency. The cause of this high conversion efficiency is the strong coupling between the laser and the plasma and the high bunch charge (number of accelerated electrons). As discussed above, the short laser pulse duration allows for higher plasma densities. The higher plasma density permits the self-focusing of the laser for the whole length of the plasma accelerator, keeping the laser pulse intensity sufficiently high for the blow-out regime. The short pulse duration also shortens the depletion length [33], allowing for the transfer of the majority of the laser energy into the plasma. After 500 μm of propagation, at the end of the plasma plateau, 61% of the laser energy is spent, mostly exciting the plasma wake (some of it also diffracted out of the domain). The energy into the plasma wake then goes into accelerating the electron bunch. The high density provides a sufficient number of electrons to be accelerated. It must be noted that conversion efficiencies of 3% are demonstrated in LWFA experiments with TW-class lasers [25], and with higher laser energies, conversion efficiencies above 10% are expected [35].

3. Photoneutron Generation

Photons usually interact with atomic electrons or with the nuclear field, leaving the nucleus unaffected; however, a sufficiently large energy gamma photon may overcome the neutron binding energy to cause a (γ, n) reaction to eject a neutron from the nucleus as a result of the giant dipole resonance (GDR) mechanism. Photon energy is transferred to the nucleus by the oscillating electric field of the photon, which induces oscillation among the nucleons. Photoneutron production is more probable than proton ejection, since the latter requires the need to overcome the Coulomb barrier.

Intense photoneutron production can thus be realized via a bremsstrahlung converter, with the neutron energy spectra extending to 10 MeV and peaking around 1 MeV. The process is initiated via an energetic-electron bombard high-Z material (e.g., lead, tungsten or uranium) to generate energetic gamma rays with an energy spectrum extending up to the most energetic electron. The cross-section of the (γ, n) reaction increases with photon energy, reaching a maximum over a broad energy range of approximately 12 to 16 MeV for medium and heavy nuclei. The peak energy of the GDR can be approximated [36] by 80 $A^{-1/3}$ MeV for A > 40, where A is the atomic mass number, e.g., 208 for lead, which corresponds to 13.5 MeV. The width of the resonance is 3 MeV for lead, as shown in Figure 2. The neutron binding energy for Pb-208 is 7.8 MeV, indicating a threshold energy for the photon. This fact is also reflected in Figure 2 as the threshold energy.

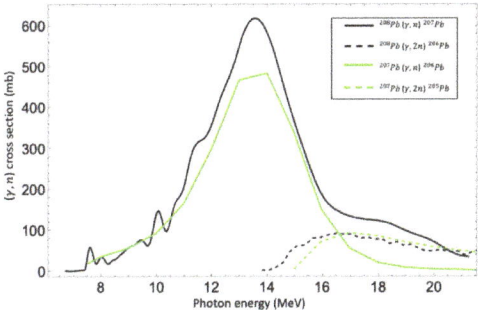

Figure 2. Photonuclear cross-section for two isotopes of lead, obtained from the END-F and TENDL cross-sectional libraries.

Above the photon energy of 35 MeV, the photoneutron production is mainly due to the quasi-deuteron (QD) effects. In this process, the photon interacts with the dipole moment of the proton–neutron pair rather than the nucleus as a whole.

The electron–matter interaction is collision-dominated for electron energy lower than 10 MeV and a radiative interaction process that dominates high-energy electrons. The collisional interaction is described by the Bloch–Bethe formulae proportional to Z (atomic number), whereas the radiation process is described by the bremsstrahlung process proportional to Z^2. Thus, to increase the electron–matter interaction, energetic electrons and a choice of high-Z converter material are needed. For the study presented in this paper, we select the naturally occurring lead. Although complex geometries are readily modelled using the MCNP code, we have chosen the simple geometry of a lead sphere with a density of ρ = 11.35 g/cm^3, and an isotropic electron source at its origin. The MCNP code samples from the electron distribution and utilizes END-F cross-sections and models to convert them to photons, and subsequently, from photons to neutrons. Thus, a comprehensive electron, photon and neutron transport is realized. A total of 10^8 histories are run to maintain an error below 3% for all the energy bins. Furthermore, since the (γ, n) reaction has a threshold of 7 MeV, we remove all electrons and photons with energy less than 5 MeV from the simulation which speeds up computation, but as a consequence, suppresses all positron annihilation processes.

The pertinent metric for the photoneutron generation is the yield of neutrons generated per electron. We investigated the yield of a mono-energetic electron source located at the center of a natural lead sphere by varying the sphere radius and electron energy. The results are presented in Figure 3 for various electron energies. The LWFA-accelerated electron energy gain is given by the expression $W_e = \frac{2}{3} a_0 m_e c^2 n_c/n_e$, with $a_0 = 3-5$, $m_e c^2 = 0.511$ MeV, $n_c/n_e = 100$. Thus, electron energy of 100 MeV is readily achieved. The radiative stopping power in lead for a 100 MeV electron is 150 MeV/cm and the mass attenuation coefficient for 1–100 MeV photon in lead is 0.1 cm^2/g or 1 cm, thus, a lead sphere of 6–8 cm is needed to sufficiently covert electrons to photons and photons to neutrons. For a 100 MeV electron beam, the neutron yield saturates for a sphere radius of 6 cm at around 0.03 n/e, with a yield efficiency of 3×10^{-4} n/e/MeV. In contrast the DT fusion yield is 1×10^{-5} n/d. The yield improves for spallation to 30 n/p; however, a proton with energy over 1 GeV is needed.

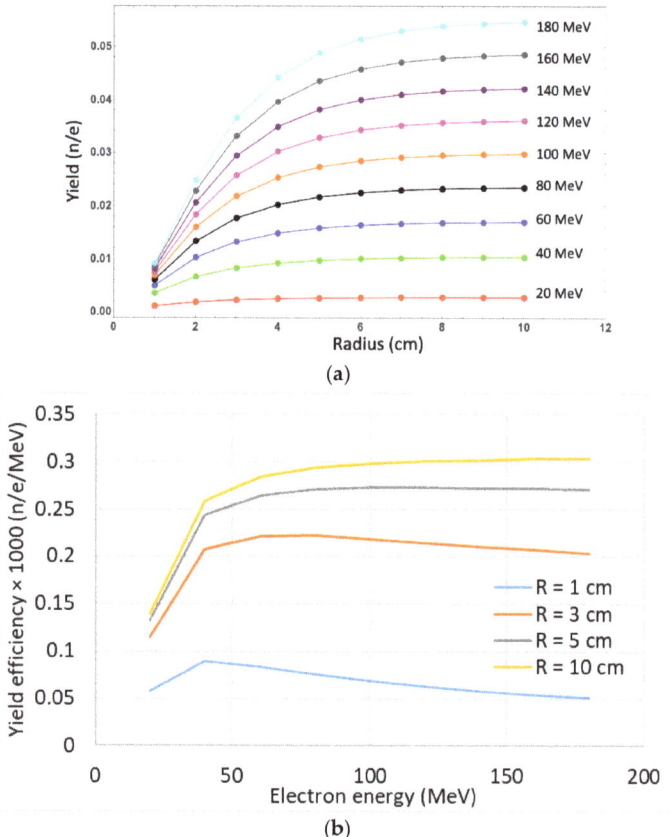

Figure 3. Neutron yield per electron for various electron energies and radius of a lead sphere (**a**), with electrons that are sourced at the sphere origin. The efficiency of neutron generation as a function of electron energy (**b**), for selected lead sphere radii.

Figure 3b also shows the energy dependence of the conversion efficiency. Even for larger spheres, the conversion efficiency does not increase significantly beyond 100 MeV. As a consequence, the requirements on the electron beam quality are relaxed—the electron spectrum should have a significant component above 50 MeV. Since the LWFA electron energy spectrum is complex, it is instructive to study the photoneutron generation using monoenergetic electrons. In this example, 20 MeV and 50 MeV isotropic electron sources are introduced at the center of a 10 cm natural lead sphere. The generated photon energy spectrum is shown in Figure 4, which extends to the highest energy electron. For the 20 MeV case, the average photon energy is 2.8 MeV and yield of 5 photons per electrons. In contrast, the 50 MeV case generates an average photon energy of 4.9 MeV, with a yield of 15 photons per electron. The neutron energy spectra are shown in Figure 5 with a yield of 0.0028 n/e and 0.014 n/e for 20 MeV and 50 MeV electron sources, respectively.

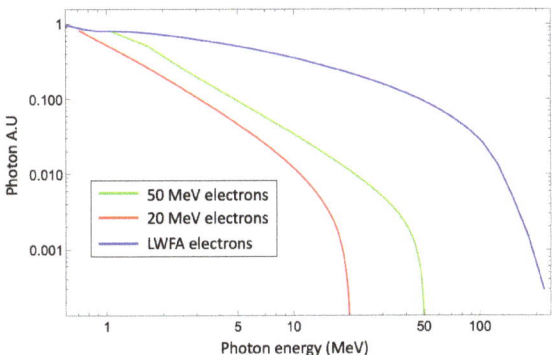

Figure 4. Photon energy spectrum resulting from injecting mono-energetic 20 MeV (red), 50 MeV (green) electrons and LWFA electrons (blue) at a center of a 10 cm lead sphere.

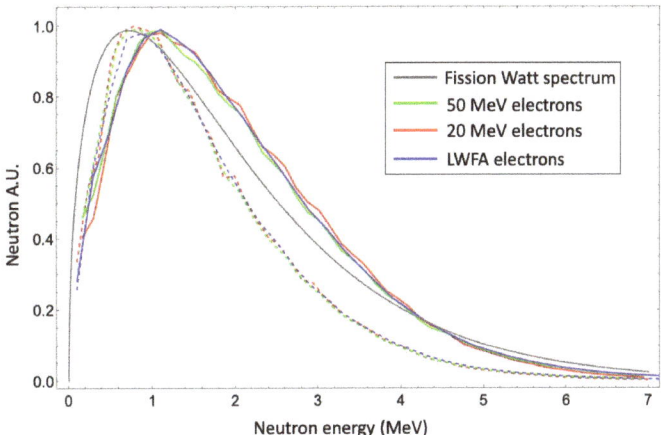

Figure 5. Neutron energy spectra for 20 MeV (red), 50 MeV (green) electron beams and LWFA electrons (blue) sampled at r = 0.5 cm (solid), r = 10 cm (dashed) and Watt fission spectrum (gray) for U-235.

The conversion of electrons to photoneutrons is now studied, utilizing the electron spectrum, as shown in Figure 1. For this study, we increased the number of electrons to transport to 10^9 to have a sufficient sampling of the high-energy electron tail. The highest energy electron bin is 250 MeV, and Figure 4 confirms that the highest energy photon is also 250 MeV. The neutron spectrum from the LWFA electrons is shown in Figure 5.

The summary of results of photoneutron generation from the monoenergetic and LWFA electrons are presented in Table 1. The LWFA electrons' average energy $\langle E_e \rangle$ = 71 MeV. The average photon energy for the monoenergetic cases, 2.6 MeV and 4.9 MeV, respectively, is not only below the peak of the (γ, n) reaction cross-section, but also below the photoneutron generation threshold energy of 7 MeV. For the electron of the 20 MeV case, 4% of photons contribute to photoneutron generation, this increases to 17% for the electron source of 50 MeV case and 28% for the LWFA electrons. The neutron spectra are shown in Figure 5 along with Watt fission spectrum for comparison. The average neutron energy is same for all cases; however, a moderation is observed when sampling neutrons at r = 0.5 cm and r = 5 cm; i.e., the average energy decreases from 2.0 MeV to 1.7 MeV for all cases. The electron yield, Y_e, can be obtained from the electron creation table in the MCNP output. Besides the original electrons, electrons are generated via pair production, Compton recoil, photo-electric and knock-on effects; for this analysis, we lowered the cut-off energy to 0.5 MeV. In contrast, the photons are predominantly generated via bremsstrahlung and positron annihilation with a yield shown in Table 1. Lastly, the neutron yield, Y_n, is shown in the last column.

Table 1. Yields and average energies for the monoenergetic and LWFA electron sources.

Energy (MeV)	$\langle E_\gamma \rangle$ (MeV)	<E_n>(MeV)		Y_e	Y_γ	Y_n
		0.5 cm	5 cm			
20	2.6	2.0	1.7	6.3	5	0.003
50	4.9	2.0	1.7	16	15	0.01
LWFA (<E_e> = 71 MeV)	11.3	2.0	1.7	23	23	0.02

In Section 2, we reported 3×10^9 electrons in the bunch at the laser exit, which generates 6×10^7 neutrons using the yield $Y_n = 0.02$ n/e. Since the 100 mJ laser has been used, an efficiency of 6×10^{11} n/s/kW is obtained. This neutron yield is similar to the experimental work of Gu et al. [37], however, with a 120 J laser. The efficiency is in line with electron linac generators [38] and exceeds 140 neutrons per shot reported in [39] for d(d, n)^{3}He fusion reactions using 200 mJ and a 160 fs laser.

4. Photoneutron Applications

In the introduction, we highlighted a wide spectrum of neutron applications of global importance. In this section, we will focus on such applications and we will quantify the attractiveness of our proposed LWFA-driven neutron generation approach:

(a) Medical radio-isotope production (Moly-99 to Tc-99 precursor);
(b) Incineration of spent nuclear fuel;
(c) Neutron radiography/imaging.

4.1. Medical Radioisotope Production

Over 40 million medical imaging procedures are performed with the radioisotope technetium-99m per year. Tc-99m can be generated from the decay of the parent molybdenum-99 nuclei with a half-life of 66 h. Mo-99 is generated in a nuclear reactor as a result of the fission products with a 6.1% yield, as shown in Figure 6.

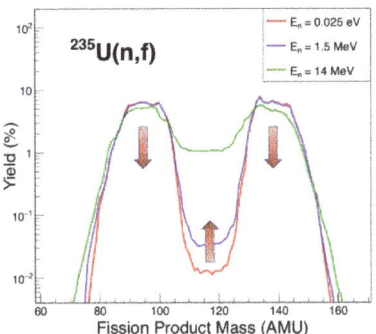

Figure 6. Fission product yield for various neutron energy bombardment. ^{99}Mo yield from fission is 6% of all the fission products. Adapted from data from T.R. England and B.F. Rider, LA-UR-94-3106 (1994).

However, and mainly due to the overall controversy around the future of nuclear power, there is a severe shortage of Tc-99m, and thus, many imaging procedures are postponed or cancelled. An alternative to a nuclear reactor is a sub-critical assembly irradiated by, e.g., DT fusion neutrons, which is a path that Shine Medical [10] is following. Their approach is to utilize a ~100s keV electrostatically accelerated deuteron beam impinging on a tritium target (gas or solid) to produce 14 MeV neutrons, with the neutrons subsequently interacting with 20% of enriched U-235 to produce Mo-99. Shine Medical's approach is constrained by tritium, which by itself imposes certain constraints in production, delivery logistics and handling.

In this report, we propose to generate laser-driven LWFA electrons to produce Mo-99 by photoneutrons, where high-energy electrons interact with high-Z material (as described in the introduction)—e.g., lead, tantalum or uranium, to convert to gamma—via bremsstrahlung, which in turn, interacts with a nucleus through the (γ, n) reaction. However, a direct pathway for irradiating a uranium assembly directly with laser-generated electrons is also an option (photofission).

Average single imaging or treatment with Tc-99m utilizes 30 mCi, assuming 5.2×10^6 Ci/g, which translates to a single treatment requiring 5.4 ng of Tc-99m. A high average-power laser can generate a sufficient amount of Mo-99. (From Section 3, we estimate that we can obtain 6×10^7 n per laser shot, for a Mo-99 yield of 6.1 %. Using these numbers, we can estimate to generate the required Mo-99 amount in 10 s using a 1 MHz laser or 10^4 s for a 1 kHz laser. An improvement factor of 10 could be achieved if we use electron irradiation of an enriched U-235 assembly directly together with a double-stage multiplier, a possibility we intend to explore in our proposed experiment. Considerations of such duty-cycle were not taken into account in this study).

4.2. Transmutation of Spent Nuclear Fuel

Conventional nuclear power plants, whether run in a critical or a sub-critical operation, will generate spent nuclear fuel (SNF) as a waste product. The waste can be split into two main components:

(1) Fission products such as iodine, strontium, molybdenum, etc.
(2) Actinides such as plutonium and isotopes of uranium and thorium and minor actinides (americium, curium and neptunium).

The management of SNF is usually carried out by partitioning and transmutation (P&T), whereas uranium and plutonium (partially) are removed by the PUREX process, and the P&T proceeds with sending the MA and long-lived fission products to transmutation. Transmutation is accomplished by irradiation of the partitioned SNF with neutrons. One example of transmutation by fission is shown here:

$$n + {}^{240}Pu\ (24{,}000\ years) \rightarrow {}^{134}Cs\ (2\ years) + {}^{104}Ru\ (stable) + 2\ n + energy$$

Pu-240 has a half-life of 24,000 years; however, when bombarded by neutrons, Pu-240 fissions into Cs-134 and Ru-104 plus neutrons and energy. Thus, in this particular example, we have reduced the required storage duration by 10,000-fold. The motivation for the transmutation of nuclear waste is shown in Figure 7 by comparing the overall SNF radiotoxicity to the reference of naturally occurring uranium (green line) necessary to fabricate 1 ton of enriched uranium fuel. The reference is radiotoxicity associated with uranium and its radioactive progenies. The reference radiotoxicity is reached after a period of 130,000 years for nuclear waste if left untreated, which is also called the open cycle. In contrast, a complete partitioning and transmutation without any losses can shorten the duration to 270 years (brown curve—fission products) and decrease the storage volume by a factor of 10, which is also called a fully-closed cycle. At this point, only fission product's radiotoxicity contributes. The long-term radiotoxicity is mainly dominated by transuranic elements, in particular the Am-241 and several isotopes of plutonium (Pu-239, Pu-240, Pu-241) and their descendants. However, several long-lived fission products contribute to long-term radiotoxicity with Tc-99, I-129, Cs-135, Zr-93 and Pd-107 as the prominent examples. Iodine and cesium are the most problematic as they readily diffuse out of geological repositories and reach the biosphere.

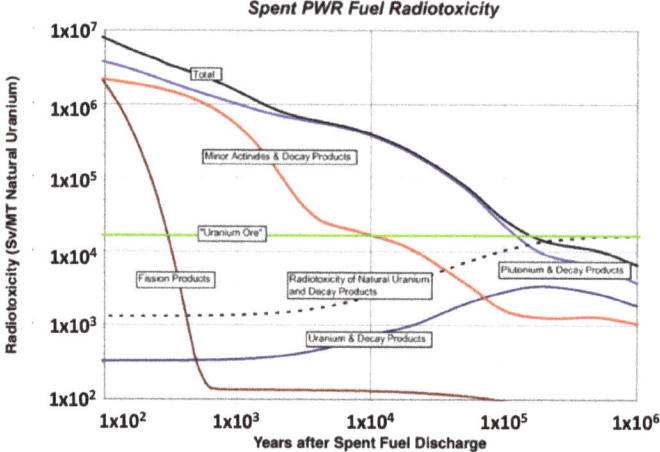

Figure 7. Motivation for transmutation adapted from [40]. Comparison of the radiotoxicity of nuclear waste from uranium-based PWR to that produced by the naturally occurring uranium needed to generate 1 metric ton of enriched uranium. Permission to reuse figure granted from Elsevier.

The transmutation of the MA must be performed in a sub-critical assembly ($k_{eff} < 1$) due to their neutron-rich isotopes, i.e., it is difficult to maintain criticality with a large MA present. Thus, we propose to utilize laser-generated photoneutrons to drive the transmutation of MA and long-lived fission products.

4.3. Neutron Radiography/Imaging and Neutron Spectroscopy

Neutrons, through their high interaction with light elements and a weak interaction with the heavy elements, are ideal to non-destructively penetrate and imagine the content of metal containers, e.g., shipping containers or car spark plugs, as shown in Figure 8. The laser-generated photoneutrons are ideally suited for this application. However, it is required to collimate and create a quasi-monoenergetic neutron beam that is optimized for various imaging applications. Using neutrons helps to locate rare-earth metals, can analyze whether a canister with fuel is filled, check whether O-rings fit snuggly after assembly (space rocket where further corrections are impractical), etc. Neutron spectroscopy, which utilizes laser-generated neutrons, has been proposed [41,42].

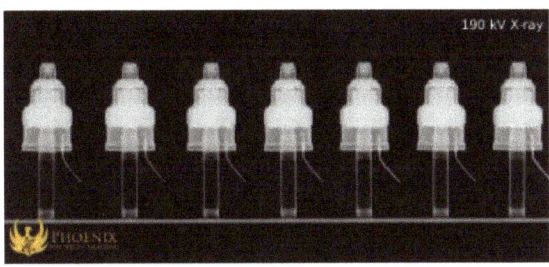

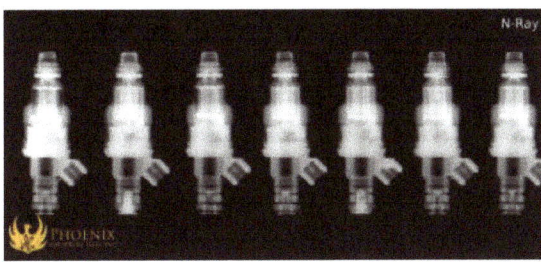

Figure 8. Comparison of imaging using X-rays (**top**) and neutrons (**bottom**). Used with permission.

5. Conclusions

We present computational estimates on photo-neutron generation, using laser-driven LWFA electron sources as the neutron drivers. Due to the rapid progress in high-average power, high-repetition-rate laser technology, such as electron sources, are in a development phase within the laser plasma acceleration community. Specifically, and pertinent to the present work, all calculations have been performed with the eSYLOS electron beamline at ELI-ALPS, Hungary [43], with which we propose to utilize (once commissioned) for the purposes of demonstrating a novel neutron generation scheme, with comparable or better yields to other laser-driven neutron sources. Our goal is to perform proof-of-principle experiments which we later intend to optimize as the neutron source with the abovementioned laser and electron source infrastructure.

The applications targeted are of high societal importance, with the added benefit of being forgiving to the required initial electron beam quality and specifications, something that laser-driven LWFA electron sources can nowadays routinely deliver. With the advent of 1 kHz few TW laser systems, we envision our proposal as the first stepping stone for introducing these laser/LWFA-driven neutron sources to these important societal applications, and as the first necessary step to ramp up to even higher repetition rates (1 MHz range) once the future generation of laser systems manifests.

The photoneutron generation presented is largely unoptimized. As a future work, we propose to optimize the electron density and electron profiles to achieve higher efficiency based on the curves in Figure 3a,b. We can observe that beyond the electron energy of 100 MeV, the yield of n/e/MeV is improved only marginally. Further, we propose to modify the converter with other materials, e.g., tungsten, tantalum, or even fissile material such as low-enriched uranium. An additional conversion of ^{9}Be is proposed to leverage the (n, 2n) reaction.

Particle accelerators have, approximately, a 100-year history (1924 Gustav Ising) of development, and although they have come a long way since then, they are still bulky and costly machines. The laser driven electron sources must compete with the state-of-the-art industrial electron beam (IBA [44], KIPT [13]) regarding energy and current. A laser-generated electron beam current is scalable with an increasing repetition rate and number of beam lines; however, in contrast to the RF sources, they are neither well-collimated nor mono-energetic. These are disadvantages if the beam is required to be transported, but the proposed application relies on in situ electron generation.

Author Contributions: Conceptualization, D.P., A.N., N.H., T.T., S.G., G.M., G.S. and C.K. Formal analysis, D.P.; Writing—original draft, A.N.; Writing—review & editing, D.P. and S.G. All authors have read and agreed to the published version of the manuscript.

Funding: We are thankful for the support of the Hungarian National Research, Development, and Innovation Office through the Hungarian National Laser-Initiated Transmutation Laboratory (NLTL) (contract # NKFIH-877-2/2020), the Norman Rostoker Fund for the research. National Research, Development and Innovation Office of Hungary, Project No. 2020-1.2.4-TÉT-IPARI-2021-00018.

Institutional Review Board Statement: Not applicable.

Informed Consent Statement: Not applicable.

Data Availability Statement: Not applicable.

Acknowledgments: We are deeply indebted to our colleagues Thierry Massard, Peter Taborek, Sumio Iijima, Konstantin Novoselov, Vladimir Shiltsev, Sahel Hakimi, Scott Nicks, Ernesto Barraza, Yves Brechet, Xueqing Yan, Timur Esirkepov, Sergei Bulanov, Tetsuya Kawachi, the late Norman Rostoker, and the late John Dawson for their collaboration, advice, and inspiration.

Conflicts of Interest: The authors declare no conflict of interest.

Dedication: We would like to dedicate this paper to the pioneers, the late V. Veksler and the late N. Rostoker, of the collective acceleration in plasma, whose works we were inspired by and tried to follow. They may be delighted that we came thus far.

References

1. Rubbia, C.; Rubio, J.; Buono, S.; Carminati, F.; Fiétier, N.; Galvez, J.; Geles, C.; Kadi, Y.; Klapisch, R.; Mandrillon, P.; et al. Conceptual Design of a Fast Neutron Operated High Power Energy Amplifier. In *Proceedings of the CERN/AT/95-44, 1995*; CERN: Geneva, Switzerland, 1995; pp. 187–312.
2. Tajima, T.; Necas, A.; Mourou, G.; Gales, S.; Leroy, M. Spent Nuclear Fuel Incineration by Fusion-Driven Liquid Transmutator Operated in Real Time by Laser. *Fusion Sci. Technol.* **2021**, *77*, 251–265. [CrossRef]
3. Woracek, R.; Santisteban, J.; Fedrigo, A.; Strobl, M. Diffraction in Neutron Imaging—A Review. *Nucl. Instrum. Methods Phys. Res. A* **2018**, *878*, 141–158. [CrossRef]
4. Pudjorahardjo, D.S.; Wahyono, P.I.; Syarip. Compact Neutron Generator as External Neutron Source of Subcritical Assembly for Mo-99 Production (SAMOP). *AIP Conf. Proceed.* **2020**, *2296*, 20115.
5. Moss, R.L. Critical Review, with an Optimistic Outlook, on Boron Neutron Capture Therapy (BNCT). *Appl. Radiat. Isot.* **2014**, *88*, 2–11.
6. Frankle, C.M.; Dale, G.E. Unconventional Neutron Sources for Oil Well Logging. *Nucl. Instrum. Methods Phys. Res. A* **2013**, *723*, 24–29.
7. Krambrock, K.; Ribeiro, L.G.M.; Pinheiro, M.V.B.; Leal, A.S.; de BC Menezes, M.Â.; Spaeth, J.-M. Color Centers in Topaz: Comparison between Neutron and Gamma Irradiation. *Phys. Chem. Min.* **2007**, *34*, 437–444. [CrossRef]
8. Gulik, V.; Tkaczyk, A.H. Cost Optimization of ADS Design: Comparative Study of Externally Driven Heterogeneous and Homogeneous Two-Zone Subcritical Reactor Systems. *Nucl. Eng. Des.* **2014**, *270*, 133–142. [CrossRef]
9. Gozani, T.; Morgado, R.E.; Seher, C.C. Nuclear-Based Techniques for Explosive Detection. *J. Energetic Mater.* **1986**, *4*, 377–414.
10. Beyer, R.; Birgersson, E.; Elekes, Z.; Ferrari, A.; Grosse, E.; Hannaske, R.; Junghans, A.R.; Kögler, T.; Massarczyk, R.; Matić, A.; et al. Characterization of the Neutron Beam at NELBE. *Nucl. Instrum. Methods Phys. Res. A* **2013**, *723*, 151–162.
11. Ibrahim, F.; Obert, J.; Bajeat, O.; Buhour, J.M.; Carminati, D.; Clapier, F.; Donzaud, C.; Ducourtieux, M.; Dufour, J.M.; Essabaa, S.; et al. Photofission for the Production of Radioactive Beams: Experimental Data from an on-Line Measurement. *Eur. Phys. J. A-Hadron. Nucl.* **2002**, *15*, 357–360. [CrossRef]

12. Essabaa, S.; Arianer, J.; Ausset, P.; Bajeat, O.; Baronick, J.P.; Clapier, F.; Coacolo, L.; Donzaud, C.; Ducourtieux, M.; Galès, S.; et al. Photo-Fission for the Production of Radioactive Beams ALTO Project. *Nucl. Instrum. Methods Phys. Res. B* **2003**, *204*, 780–784. [CrossRef]
13. Bezditko, A.P.; Gordienko, A.N.; Gladkikh, P.I.; Gvozd, A.M.; Kapliy, D.A.; Karnaukhov, I.M.; Karnaukhov, I.I.; Lyashchenko, V.N.; Mytsykov, A.O.; Moisieienko, M.P.; et al. 100 MeV/100 KW Accelerator Adjustment for the NSC KIPT Neutron Source Physical Start Up. *Probl. At. Sci. Technol.* **2020**, *129*, 135–142.
14. Bezditko, O.; Karnaukhov, I.; Mytsykov, A.; Zelinsky, A.; Tarasov, D. Status of the NSC KIPT Neutron Source. *Energy* **2017**, *2*, 1013.
15. Zelinsky, A.Y.; Bezditko, O.; Demchenko, P.O.; Karnaukhov, I.; Oleinik, V.; Peev, F.; Ushakov, I.; Vodin, O.; Gohar, Y. NSC KIPT Neutron Source on the Base of Subcritical Assembly Driven with Electron Linear Accelerator. In Proceedings of the IPAC 2013, Shanghai, China, 13–17 May 2013.
16. Flaska, M.; Borella, A.; Lathouwers, D.; Mihailescu, L.C.; Mondelaers, W.; Plompen, A.J.M.; van Dam, H.; van der Hagen, T.H.J.J. Modeling of the GELINA Neutron Target Using Coupled Electron–Photon–Neutron Transport with the MCNP4C3 Code. *Nucl. Instrum. Methods Phys. Res. A* **2004**, *531*, 392–406. [CrossRef]
17. Coceva, C.; Simonini, R.; Olsen, D.K. Calculation of the ORELA Neutron Moderator Spectrum and Resolution Function. *Nucl. Instrum. Methods Phys. Res.* **1983**, *211*, 459–467. [CrossRef]
18. Colonna, N.; Gunsing, F.; Käppeler, F. Neutron Physics with Accelerators. *Prog. Part Nucl. Phys.* **2018**, *101*, 177–203. [CrossRef]
19. Pomerantz, I.; Mccary, E.; Meadows, A.R.; Arefiev, A.; Bernstein, A.C.; Chester, C.; Cortez, J.; Donovan, M.E.; Dyer, G.; Gaul, E.W.; et al. Ultrashort Pulsed Neutron Source. *Phys. Rev. Lett.* **2014**, *113*, 184801. [CrossRef] [PubMed]
20. Kleinschmidt, A.; Aumüller, S.; Bagnoud, V.; Jahn, D.; Schanz, V.A.; Zimmer, M.; Roth, M. Moderation of a Laser-Generated Neutron Beam at PHELIX. *Helmholtz Inst. Jena Annu. Rep.* **2018**, *2017*, 37.
21. Günther, M.M.; Rosmej, O.N.; Tavana, P.; Gyrdymov, M.; Skobliakov, A.; Kantsyrev, A.; Zähter, S.; Borisenko, N.G.; Pukhov, A.; Andreev, N.E. Forward-Looking Insights in Laser-Generated Ultra-Intense γ-Ray and Neutron Sources for Nuclear Application and Science. *Nat. Commun.* **2022**, *13*, 170. [CrossRef]
22. Prencipe, I.; Sgattoni, A.; Dellasega, D.; Fedeli, L.; Cialfi, L.; Choi, I.W.; Kim, I.J.; Janulewicz, K.A.; Kakolee, K.F.; Lee, H.W.; et al. Development of Foam-Based Layered Targets for Laser-Driven Ion Beam Production. *Plasma Phys. Control Fusion* **2016**, *58*, 34019.
23. Tajima, T.; Dawson, J.M. Laser Electron Accelerator. *Phys. Rev. Lett.* **1979**, *43*, 267. [CrossRef]
24. Guénot, D.; Gustas, D.; Vernier, A.; Beaurepaire, B.; Böhle, F.; Bocoum, M.; Lozano, M.; Jullien, A.; Lopez-Martens, R.; Lifschitz, A.; et al. Relativistic Electron Beams Driven by KHz Single-Cycle Light Pulses. *Nat. Photonics* **2017**, *11*, 293–296. [CrossRef]
25. Gustas, D.; Guénot, D.; Vernier, A.; Dutt, S.; Böhle, F.; Lopez-Martens, R.; Lifschitz, A.; Faure, J. High-Charge Relativistic Electron Bunches from a KHz Laser-Plasma Accelerator. *Phys. Rev. Accel. Beams* **2018**, *21*, 13401. [CrossRef]
26. Jiao, X.J.; Shaw, J.M.; Wang, T.; Wang, X.M.; Tsai, H.; Poth, P.; Pomerantz, I.; Labun, L.A.; Toncian, T.; Downer, M.C.; et al. A Tabletop, Ultrashort Pulse Photoneutron Source Driven by Electrons from Laser Wakefield Acceleration. *Matter. Radiat. Extrem.* **2017**, *2*, 296–302. [CrossRef]
27. Papp, D.; Lécz, Z.; Kamperidis, C.; Hafz, N.A.M. Highly Efficient Few-Cycle Laser Wakefield Electron Accelerator. *Plasma Phys. Control Fusion* **2021**, *63*, 65019.
28. Toth, S.; Stanislauskas, T.; Balciunas, I.; Budriunas, R.; Adamonis, J.; Danilevicius, R.; Viskontas, K.; Lengvinas, D.; Veitas, G.; Gadonas, D.; et al. SYLOS Lasers–the Frontier of Few-Cycle, Multi-TW, KHz Lasers for Ultrafast Applications at Extreme Light Infrastructure Attosecond Light Pulse Source. *J. Phys. Photonics* **2020**, *2*, 45003.
29. Arber, T.D.; Bennett, K.; Brady, C.S.; Lawrence-Douglas, A.; Ramsay, M.G.; Sircombe, N.J.; Gillies, P.; Evans, R.G.; Schmitz, H.; Bell, A.R.; et al. Contemporary Particle-in-Cell Approach to Laser-Plasma Modelling. *Plasma Phys. Control Fusion* **2015**, *57*, 113001. [CrossRef]
30. Briesmeister, J.F. (Ed.) *MCNP^{TM}—A General Monte Carlo N-Particle Transport Code*; Code Version 4C, also Univ. of California Tech. Report UC-700; Los Alamos National Laboratory: Los Alamos, NM, USA, 2000.
31. Pukhov, A.; Meyer-ter-Vehn, J. Laser Wake Field Acceleration: The Highly Non-Linear Broken-Wave Regime. *Appl. Phys. B* **2002**, *74*, 355–361. [CrossRef]
32. Pukhov, A.; Gordienko, S.; Kiselev, S.; Kostyukov, I. The Bubble Regime of Laser–Plasma Acceleration: Monoenergetic Electrons and the Scalability. *Plasma Phys Control Fusion* **2004**, *46*, B179. [CrossRef]
33. Lu, W.; Tzoufras, M.; Joshi, C.; Tsung, F.S.; Mori, W.B.; Vieira, J.; Fonseca, R.A.; Silva, L.O. Generating Multi-GeV Electron Bunches Using Single Stage Laser Wakefield Acceleration in a 3D Nonlinear Regime. *Phys. Rev. Spec. Top.-Accel. Beams* **2007**, *10*, 61301. [CrossRef]
34. Sprangle, P.; Ting, A.; Tang, C.M. Radiation Focusing and Guiding with Application to the Free Electron Laser. *Phys. Rev. Lett.* **1987**, *59*, 202. [CrossRef] [PubMed]
35. Götzfried, J.; Döpp, A.; Gilljohann, M.F.; Foerster, F.M.; Ding, H.; Schindler, S.; Schilling, G.; Buck, A.; Veisz, L.; Karsch, S. Physics of High-Charge Electron Beams in Laser-Plasma Wakefields. *Phys. Rev. X* **2020**, *10*, 41015. [CrossRef]
36. Meyers, R.A. *Encyclopedia of Physical Science and Technology*; Academic Press: Cambridge, MA, USA, 2002. Available online: http://113.161.190.196:8080/thuvienso/handle/123456789/668 (accessed on 11 February 2022).
37. Qi, W.; Zhang, X.; Zhang, B.; He, S.; Zhang, F.; Cui, B.; Yu, M.; Dai, Z.; Peng, X.; Gu, Y. Enhanced Photoneutron Production by Intense Picoseconds Laser Interacting with Gas-Solid Hybrid Targets. *Phys. Plasmas* **2019**, *26*, 43103.

38. Chao, Y.; Cao, L.; Zheng, C.; Liu, Z.; He, X. Enhanced Proton Acceleration from Laser Interaction with a Tailored Nanowire Target. *Appl. Sci.* **2022**, *12*, 1153. [CrossRef]
39. Pretzler, G.; Saemann, A.; Pukhov, A.; Rudolph, D.; Schätz, T.; Schramm, U.; Thirolf, P.; Habs, D.; Eidmann, K.; Tsakiris, G.D.; et al. Neutron Production by 200 MJ Ultrashort Laser Pulses. *Phys. Rev. E Stat. Phys. Plasmas Fluids Relat. Interdiscip. Top.* **1998**, *58*, 1165. [CrossRef]
40. Salvatores, M.; Palmiotti, G. Radioactive Waste Partitioning and Transmutation within Advanced Fuel Cycles: Achievements and Challenges. *Prog. Part. Nucl. Phys.* **2011**, *66*, 144–166. [CrossRef]
41. Kishon, I.; Kleinschmidt, A.; Schanz, V.A.; Tebartz, A.; Noam, O.; Fernandez, J.C.; Gautier, D.C.; Johnson, R.P.; Shimada, T.; Wurden, G.A.; et al. Laser Based Neutron Spectroscopy. *Nucl. Instrum. Methods Phys. Res. A* **2019**, *932*, 27–30.
42. Zimmer, M.; Scheuren, S.; Kleinschmidt, A.; Mitura, N.; Tebartz, A.; Schaumann, G.; Abel, T.; Ebert, T.; Hesse, M.; Zähter, Ş.; et al. Demonstration of Non-Destructive and Isotope-Sensitive Material Analysis Using a Short-Pulsed Laser-Driven Epi-Thermal Neutron Source. *Nat. Commun.* **2022**, *13*, 1173.
43. Shalloo, R.; Najmudin, Z.; Hafz, N.; Li, S.; Papp, D.; Kamperidis, C. E-SYLOS: A KHz Laser Wakefield Driven Beamline for Radiobiological and Imaging Applications at ELI-ALPS. Available online: https://agenda.infn.it/event/17304/contributions/99022/ (accessed on 10 May 2022).
44. IBA. Available online: https://www.iba-industrial.com/accelerators (accessed on 10 January 2022).

Review

Prospects of Relativistic Flying Mirrors for Ultra-High-Field Science

Masaki Kando [1,*,†], Alexander S. Pirozhkov [1,†], James K. Koga [1,†], Timur Zh. Esirkepov [1,†] and Sergei V. Bulanov [1,2,†]

[1] Kansai Photon Science Institute, National Institutes for Quantum Science and Technology, 8-1-7 Umemidai, Kizugawa, Kyoto 619-215, Japan
[2] Institute of Physics of the ASCR, ELI-Beamlines, Na Slovance 2, 18221 Prague, Czech Republic
* Correspondence: kando.masaki@qst.go.jp
† These authors contributed equally to this work.

Abstract: Recent progress of high-peak-power lasers makes researchers envisage ultra-high-field science; however, the current or near future facilities will not be strong enough to reach the vacuum breakdown intensity, i.e., the Schwinger field. To address this difficulty, a relativistic flying mirror (RFM) technology is proposed to boost the focused intensity by double the Doppler effect of an incoming laser pulse. We review the principle, theoretical, and experimental progress of the RFM, as well as its prospects.

Keywords: intense laser; high-field science; laser plasma; laser wake wave; QED critical field

1. Introduction

Recent progress of high-peak-power lasers such as chirped pulse amplification [1] opens a new multidisciplinary field in ultra-high-field science (UHFS), in which the plasma, laser, beam, and quantum electrodynamics are employed. One of the scientific goals of UHFS is to observe vacuum breakdown under the conditions of terrestrial laboratories by electromagnetic waves such as lasers [2,3]. Currently, multi-petawatt laser facilities are being operated, and the record focused intensity is 1.1×10^{23} W/cm^2 [4], of which the electric (magnetic) field is 9.1×10^{14} V/m (3.0×10^6 T). The forthcoming 10 PW laser facilities may reach higher intensity, or the planned 100 PW laser facility might boost 10–100-fold focused intensity. However, this electric field is still far below the Schwinger field, which is known as the quantum electrodynamics (QED) critical field $E_s = m^2c^3/(e\hbar)$ = 1.3×10^{18} V/m, where m, e, c, and $\hbar$ are the electron mass, the elementary charge, the speed of light, and the reduced Planck constant, respectively.

Several approaches have been proposed to overcome this difficulty, such as the collision of an intense laser pulse with a high-energy electron beam [5,6], a multiple laser beam focusing [7], a superposition of high- and low-frequency electromagnetic waves [8], and so on. With the help of the Lorentz boost for high-energy electron beams, the field seen by the electron in the rest frame is enhanced by twice the Lorentz factor $\gamma = E/(mc^2)$, where E is the electron energy. The multi-beam focus effectively increases the interaction volume, thus increasing the probability of electron–positron pairs under a fixed laser energy condition. The high-frequency radiation can be used as a catastrophe singularity to be formed. As another technique, a relativistic flying mirror, was proposed for the pulse intensification due to the double-Doppler effect of reflected laser pulses from a moving focusing mirror [9]. Such mirrors are formed as electron density cusps in intense laser interaction with underdense plasma.

This review paper discusses the relativistic flying mirror model, experimental verifications, related topics, applications to UHFS, and the prospects.

2. Theoretical Model

Here, we review a simple theoretical model for relativistic flying mirrors (RFMs) [9–11]. As shown later, a wake wave is excited in tenuous plasma when an intense, ultrashort laser pulse propagates in the plasma by pushing plasma electrons outwards from the center of the laser due to a strong ponderomotive force. First, we start with an ideal moving mirror whose velocity is close to the speed of light in vacuum.

2.1. Ideal Moving Mirror

Let us derive the relationship between the reflection angle and the reflected light frequency [12]. The mirror propagates along the positive direction with the velocity of $V = \beta c$, where c is the speed of light in vacuum. Light with a frequency ω is incident on the mirror at an angle of α, as seen in Figure 1.

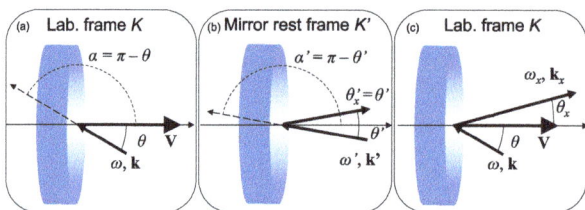

Figure 1. The light reflection by a flying mirror propagating perpendicular to its surface, an oblique incidence case. (**a**,**c**) are shown in the laboratory frame of reference, and (**b**) is in the mirror rest frame. From [13].

Then, consider in the mirror rest frame by performing a Lorentz transformation $x' = \gamma_m(x - \beta ct), y' = y, z' = z, t' = \gamma_m(t - \beta x/c)$, where primes (') denote the variables in the rest frame and $\gamma_m = (1 - \beta^2)^{-1/2}$ is the relativistic factor of the mirror. The light phase $\phi = \omega t - \mathbf{k} \cdot \mathbf{r}$ is Lorentz invariant. We obtain

$$\omega t - \frac{\omega}{c}(x \cos \alpha + y \sin \alpha) = \omega' t' - \frac{\omega'}{c}(x' \cos \alpha' + y' \sin \alpha') \qquad (1)$$

and equations

$$\omega' = \omega \gamma_m (1 - \beta \cos \alpha), \qquad (2)$$

$$\cos \alpha' = \frac{\cos \alpha - \beta}{1 - \beta \cos \alpha}. \qquad (3)$$

In the mirror rest frame, the angle of reflection is the same as that of incidence, and the frequency does not change; thus, we obtain $\alpha' = \pi - \theta'$ and $\omega'_r = \omega'$. Finally, we return to the laboratory frame of reference by the inverse Lorentz transformation and obtain

$$\cos \theta_x = \frac{2\beta + (1 + \beta^2) \cos \theta}{1 + \beta^2 + 2\beta \cos \theta}, \qquad (4)$$

and

$$\omega_x = \omega \frac{1 + \beta \cos \theta}{1 - \beta \cos \theta_x} \approx \left(4\gamma_m^2 \cos^2 \frac{\theta}{2} \right) \omega. \qquad (5)$$

The approximation at the end of Equation (5) is the case when the velocity of the mirror is ultra-relativistic ($\gamma_m \gg 1$). The pulse duration of the reflected pulse is shortened by the same factor $\approx 4\gamma_m^2 \cos^2(\theta/2)$ as the frequency upshift because the number of light cycles is Lorentz invariant.

2.2. Practical Moving (Flying) Mirror Implementation

As we saw in the previous subsection, a relativistically moving mirror has several interesting features in a thought experiment. Several methods are proposed to realize such moving mirrors, as in [13]. Here, we review a case of relativistic flying mirrors formed by the breaking plasma waves in the interaction of an intense laser pulse with underdense, gaseous plasma [9] (see Figure 2). Plasma waves are excited by the ponderomotive force of the intense laser pulse (driver), called wake waves. Such plasma waves tend to break when the laser intensity is high enough that a plasma density profile is not uniform due to phase mixing. Another laser pulse (source) is incident to the breaking wave (relativistic flying mirror) and is partially reflected by the mirror.

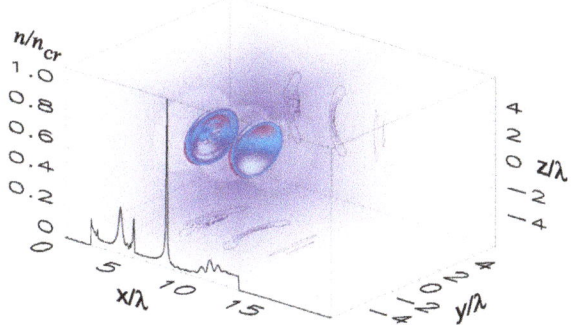

Figure 2. Relativistic flying mirrors formed in underdense plasma. From [9].

Several reflectivities of RFMs are given in [10] depending on the kind of the formed singularity. Here, we show the reflectivities for the cases of the Dirac Delta function and Cusp structure, respectively:

$$R_\delta \approx \left(\frac{\omega_p}{\omega_s \cos^2(\theta/2)}\right)^2 \frac{1}{2\gamma_{ph}}, \tag{6}$$

$$R_{cusp} \approx \frac{\Gamma^2(2/3)}{2^2 3^{4/3}} \left(\frac{\omega_p}{\omega_s \cos^2(\theta/2)}\right)^{8/3} \frac{1}{\gamma_{ph}^{4/3}}, \tag{7}$$

where $\omega_p = \sqrt{n_e e^2/(\epsilon_0 m)}^{1/2}$ is the electron plasma frequency, n_e is the electron plasma density, ϵ_0 is the permittivity of free space, θ is the incidence angle of the source pulse (Figure 1), γ_{ph} is the Lorentz factor associated with the group velocity of the driver in plasma, ω_s is the angular frequency of the source pulse, and $\Gamma(x)$ is the Euler gamma function [14]. Here, the reflectivities R_δ and R_{cusp} are in terms of the photon number; therefore, they are Lorentz invariants. Recently, Liu et al. calculated the reflectivity formula for a square-root Lorentzian distribution [15]:

$$n(x) = \frac{C_{lsrd}}{L} \frac{c}{\omega_p} \sqrt{\frac{L^2}{x^2 + L^2}}, \tag{8}$$

where $C_{srld} = \sqrt{1 + a_0^2/2} \sinh^{-1}(\lambda_{NP}/4L)$, and $\lambda_{NL} \approx (2\sqrt{1 + a_0^2/2}/\pi)\lambda_p$, $a_0 = eE/(mc\omega_d)$ is the normalized driver laser amplitude, ω_d is the angular frequency of the driver, λ_p is the plasma wavelength, and L is a characteristic length. The reflectivity for the SRLD case is

$$R_{srld} = \left[\frac{\omega_p C_{srld}}{2\gamma_{ph}\omega_s} K_0(4\gamma^2 L\omega_s/c)\right]^2, \quad (9)$$

where $K_0(x)$ is the modified Bessel function of the second kind. Liu et al. also presented the modified reflectivity formula for a Gaussian temporal source beam. One-dimensional PIC simulations reproduce these new formulas well.

2.3. Limitations of Relativistic Flying Mirrors

The temperature of the plasma is essential for how densely the plasma electrons form. The higher temperature typically results in lower cusp density. Nonetheless, the reflectivity is reduced, but the above-breaking limit regime can increase the reflectivity because the higher-order singularities are formed in such a case [16].

The reflected source pulse gains energy from the electron singularity, and its energy comes from the driver laser energy. Thus, the reflected source energy has a certain limit determined by the driver laser energy.

The other limitation comes from the mirror's recoil effect during the reflection of the source laser pulse. The recoil effect degrades the upshifting factor and, thus, the performance of the RFM. Considering energy and momentum conservation, the modified formula for the upshift factor is given in [14,17].

In addition, to minimize the recoil effect, Valenta et al. proposed a characteristic time τ_c using a one-dimensional PIC simulation [14]:

$$\tau_c = \kappa \frac{3^{4/3} mc^2}{2\Gamma^2(2/3)} \left(\frac{\omega_s}{\omega_p}\right)^{8/3} \gamma^{1/3} \frac{n_e \lambda_p}{I_s}, \quad (10)$$

where κ is a parameter that may be obtained from the simulation and I_s is the source pulse irradiance. The source pulse duration should be smaller than τ_c. An example estimate for κ of 1.5×10^{-4}, an electron density of $0.01 n_c$, and a normalized source laser intensity of $a_s = 0.1$ gives a duration of 9 fs.

The modified frequency upshift factor for taking this recoil effect is described as [14,17]

$$\omega_r \approx 4\gamma_{ph}^2 \omega_s \left(\frac{1}{1 + 4\gamma_{ph} R P_s \tau_s/(N_e mc^2)}\right) \approx 4\gamma_{ph}^2 \omega_s \left(1 - \frac{4\gamma_{ph} R P_s \tau_s}{N_e mc^2}\right) \quad (11)$$

where N_e is the number of electrons in the cusp, R is the reflectivity of the RFM, P_s is the power of the incident source pulse, and τ is the source pulse duration. The last expression is obtained by approximating the second term in the bracket in the last expression smaller than unity, which is typical for the RFM. Thus, we can recover Equation (5) in the limit using $\theta = 0$.

3. Experimental Demonstration

This section introduces experimental demonstrations of the relativistic flying mirror concepts and related ones. The broader experiments, including the reflection of electromagnetic radiation from moving objects, were listed in the previous review [13].

3.1. Relativistic Flying Mirrors

The relativistic flying mirror experiment was conducted with the setup [18,19] as shown in Figure 3a. The target was a gas-jet target, and the wakes were excited by irradiating a 2-TW, 76-fs Ti: sapphire laser pulse (referred to as "Driver") onto it. The onset of the wake breaking or flying mirrors formed was the generation of energetic electrons up to 30 MeV. Another laser pulse split from the driver pulse was focused onto the gas-jet to collide with the driver pulse in plasma with a counter-crossing angle of 135° with respect to the driver propagation axis. The reason for not using the 180° colliding angle was to avoid possible damage to the laser system by the returning pulse. After the spatial and temporal overlapping high-frequency radiation was observed in the forward direction of the driver pulse. With careful statistical analysis, they concluded that the observed signals were around 13 nm.

The same group conducted the second experiment. The setup was similar to the first experiment, except for the head-on colliding configuration thanks to the countermeasures for the returning pulse problem [20,21] (see Figure 3b). In this experiment, reflected light into $(13 \pm 4)°$ was detected with an imaging spectrometer, and the photon number was half the theoretical estimate (see Figure 4). Furthermore, the timing scan shows that the reflection from the flying mirrors occurred at some proper timing range.

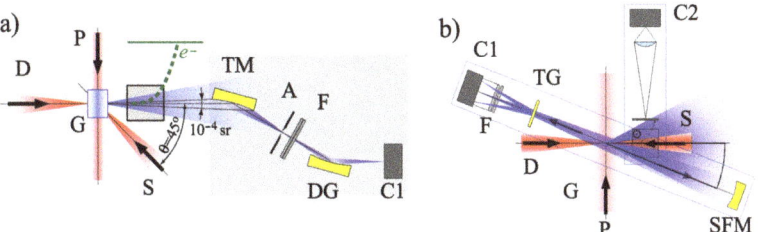

Figure 3. Experimental setups for the RFM. (**a**) A counter-crossing setup where the source beam is directed to the driver at 135°. (**b**) A head-on colliding setup. D: driver pulse, S: source pulse, P: probe laser, G: gas-jet target, TM: toroidal mirror, DG: diffraction grating, A: aperture slit, F: filters, SFM: spherical focusing mirror, TG: transmission grating, C1: X-ray charge-coupled device (CCD), C2: image intensified camera, e: electron beam.

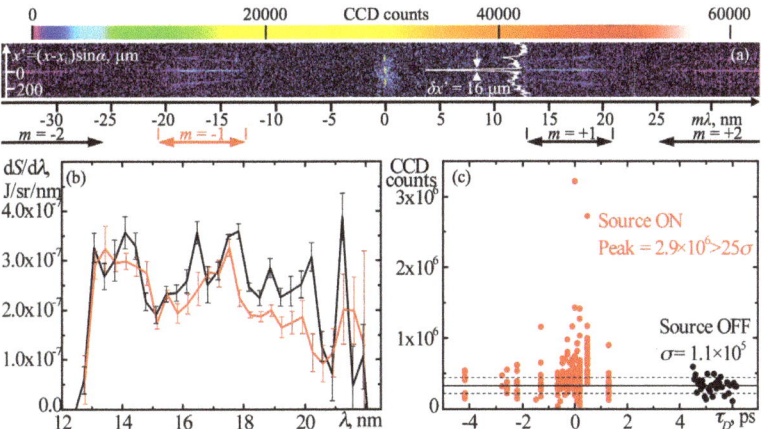

Figure 4. Reflected signals from [20]. (**a**) Raw CCD image of the reflected light after the transmission grating in the spectrometer. (**b**) Reflected light spectra with the diffraction orders of +1 and −1. (**c**) The reflected light intensity (CCD counts within the 1st diffraction order) vs. time delay between the driver and source pulses with the source-off shots (time is assigned arbitrarily).

3.2. Burst Intensification of Stimulated Emission of Radiation

RFMs utilize the electron density cusps as a moving mirror. We can see other singularities in the nonlinear interaction in Figure 5. Experimentally, the intense XUV light was observed in an experiment similar to that of the flying mirror without a source laser pulse. The emission contained harmonics of the fundamental driver laser wavelength with even and odd numbers in the forward direction [22–24]. The emission was considered a result of collective synchrotron radiation in density singularities. This is called burst intensification by singularity emitting radiation (BISER) [25]. The duration of the XUV harmonics is calculated to be sub-fs. This regime of coherent X-ray radiation is very sensitive to the driving laser quality [26].

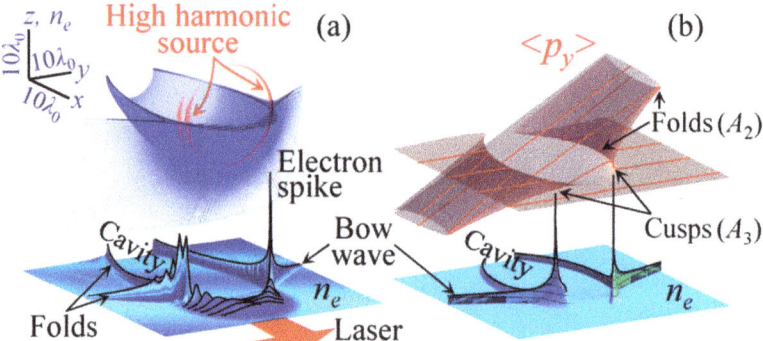

Figure 5. (**a**) The 3D PIC simulation of the BISER. The electron density and its cross-section are shown together with the electromagnetic energy (shown in red). (**b**) Electron density and phase space distribution with the catastrophe model. (From [22]).

3.3. Measurement of Plasma Waves

We have seen in the previous subsections that the radiation of shorter wavelengths in the XUV region has been demonstrated in the flying mirror experiments and in the experiments on high-order harmonic generation in underdense plasma [22]. In both experiments, the electron density singularities play an essential role in generating the shorter-wavelength radiation. However, the direct measurement of such density cusps has not been demonstrated. Here, we describe potential methods to measure electron density singularities in future experiments.

The regular wake waves were measured with the frequency domain interferometer (FDI), which utilizes two temporally separated probe pulses to co-propagate with a driving laser of the wakes [27,28]. The timing of the two pulses is set so that one sits on the higher density region of the wake or plasma electron density oscillation and the other on the lower part. By scanning the timing between the driving laser and the two probe lasers and keeping the probes' separation time the same, the probe pulses can map the electron density distribution as a function of time. The readout of the density is performed by the phase retrieval algorithm as in standard interferometers. The difference is that an interferogram is formed in the frequency domain. The FDI is suited for a relatively longer plasma wavelength or a lower-density plasma. The drawback of this method is that several scans are necessary to map the distributions.

The modified scheme was proposed where chirped probe pulses are used instead of short (usually, the shortest in the given experimental conditions) probe pulses. The method is referred to as frequency domain holography (FDH) [29]. The technique was demonstrated to map electron density distribution in a weakly nonlinear regime in a single shot. The feature of the curved wake structure was successfully observed, as is seen in the numerical simulations.

Another method is also used for characterizing wake waves, and the shorter probe pulse is introduced in a shadowgraphy configuration [30,31]. In a standard shadowgraph setup, a moderate pulse duration (same as the driving laser duration such as 30 fs) cannot resolve the fast oscillation of the wakes because the wake time scale is very fast, in tens of femtoseconds, driven by typical Ti: sapphire laser pulses. The shorter pulses are created by spectral broadening due to the self-phase modulation in a gas-filled, hollow capillary. Negative chirped mirrors recompress the broadened pulse. The measured images are very similar to those obtained with numerical codes showing the electron density modulations (see Figure 6). However, the RFMs or high-density singularities of electron densities are not apparent. Measuring density singularities with improved spatial and temporal resolutions may be possible [32,33].

Instead of the optical probe, laser-accelerated electron beams are also used to probe plasma density modulations. The electron beam has a similar pulse duration to the laser pulse duration because the accelerating phase of the wake is somewhat limited to a shorter wake cycle that is on the order of femtoseconds. The probe electron beams are sensitive to the wake's electromagnetic field; thus, the initially uniform distribution is modified after passing through the probing region. The measured profiles are referred to as the first measurement of breaking wakes [34].

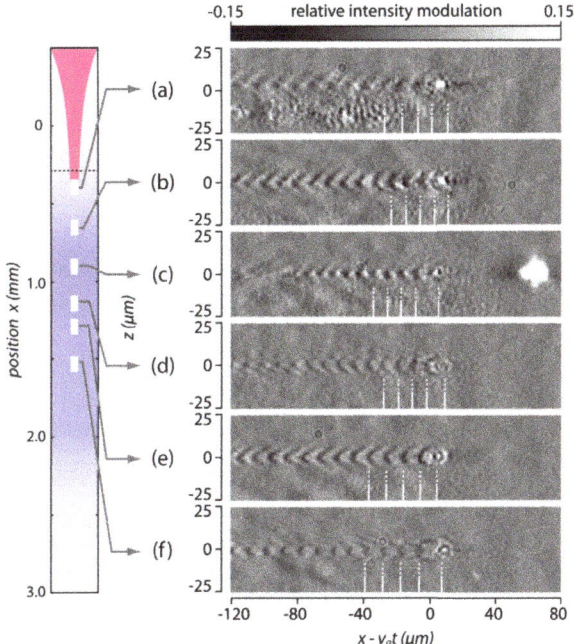

Figure 6. Shadowgrams measured with a 5.9 fs probe laser pulse. (a–f) Measured at different longitudinal positions described in the left figure. (From [31]).

4. Applications

In this section, applications to ultra-high field science using RFMs are discussed.

4.1. Intensification

Intensification of an incoming laser pulse is one of the favorable features of the RFM and was proposed in the original paper [9]. In the mirror rest frame, the density cusp distribution is parabolic, and the reflected light is focused to a diffraction-limited spot determined by the source wavelength in the boosted frame $\lambda'_s \approx \lambda_s/(2\gamma_{ph})$. The photon energy is finally multiplied as $\sim 4\gamma_{ph}^2$, and the pulse duration is also scaled as the same factor. A particle-in-cell (PIC) simulation demonstrates the intensification of the reflected light, as seen in Figure 7.

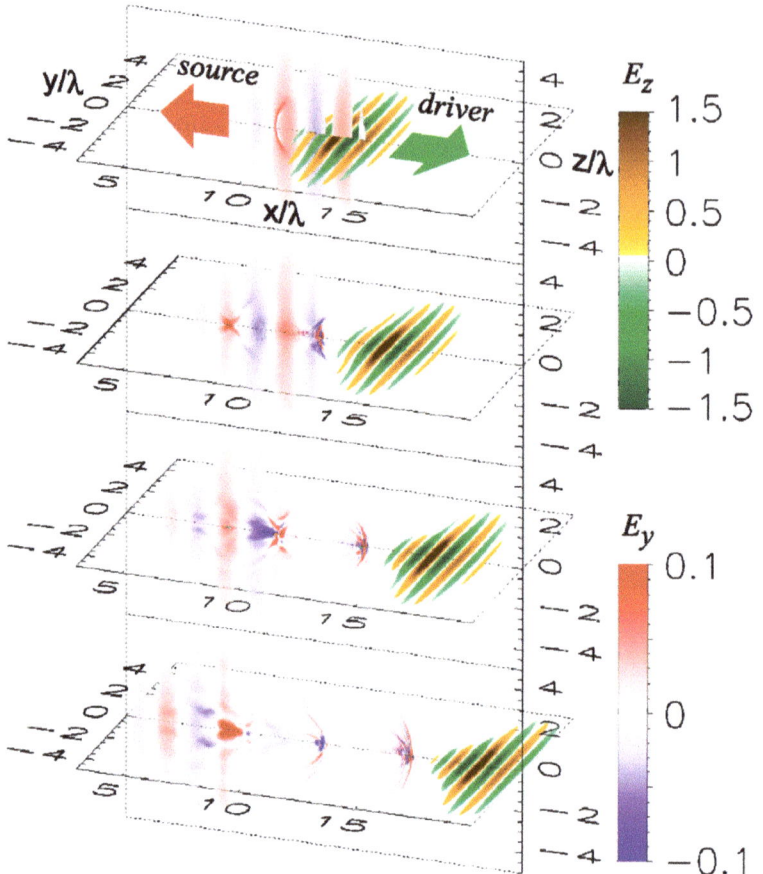

Figure 7. Reflection of laser light by the flying mirror seen in the three-dimensional PIC simulation. The cross-sections of the electric field components are shown at each time step of t = 16, 18, 20, and 22 × $2\pi/\omega_d$ (top-down). The reflection and focusing of the source pulse are seen in Frames 3 and 4 from the top (from [9]).

Thus, the reflected pulse is ideally intensified as $(4\gamma_{ph}^2)^2 \times (2\gamma_{ph})^2 R = 64\gamma_{ph}^6 R$. Here, R is the reflectivity of the RFM in terms of the photon number. If we use a delta-function-like cusp structure as Eq.(6) and $\omega_s = \omega_d$, i.e., $\omega_s \approx \gamma_{ph}\omega_p$, the focused source intensity is

$$I_r = 32\gamma_{ph}^3 I_s. \tag{12}$$

S. S. Bulanov et al. proposed to use a converging plasma wake by using a focusing beam to excite wake waves [35]. In the ideal case, the focused spot size of the reflected pulse is improved down to the diffraction limit, i.e., $\approx \lambda_r$ in the laboratory frame. The focused intensity may be

$$\begin{aligned} I_r^{conv} &= (4\gamma_{ph}^2)^2 \times (4\gamma_{ph}^2)^2 R = 256\gamma_{ph}^8 R I_s \\ &= 128\gamma_{ph}^5 I_s, \end{aligned} \tag{13}$$

where we use the reflectivity of a delta function distribution in the last expression.

Recently, Jeong et al. calculated a detailed electric field distribution focused by an RFM with the vector diffraction model [17]. Jeong et al. proposed to use a colliding setup to achieve a single electron–positron pair production under the focused electric field by the RFM in a vacuum by carefully considering the recoil effect. This is one of the fascinating goals of UHFS. Using a delta-function reflectivity Equation (6), the required laser and plasma parameters are a drive laser power of 250 TW, a driver spot radius of 158 µm, a source power of 180 TW at the fourth harmonic with a duration of 3.5 fs, and a γ factor of 12.2.

4.2. Photon–Photon Scattering

Koga et al. proposed to use RFMs to observe photon–photon scattering, which has not yet been detected in experiments [36]. The experimental difficulties mainly come from the extremely small cross-section ($\sim 10^{-30}$ pb at a photon energy of 1 eV). The cross-section increases as the photon energy increases; thus, using coherent X-rays is a possible solution of that problem. Of course, increasing the colliding number and energy of photons and decreasing the area are essential. As is seen in the RFMs' features, the RFMs can approach these two points. In addition, the stimulated scattering using three-photon beams is also employed to enhance the effect. Photon–photon scattering can be observed using the relativistic mirror concept and future powerful laser facilities.

4.3. Ultrashort X-ray Pulse Generation

Because the reflected pulse is compressed in time, the RFMs can offer a coherent, ultrashort X-ray pulse. If a mirror works ideally, the pulse shape of the X-ray pulse can be relatively easily modified by shaping a source laser temporal profile. Since the source pulse is generated by a near-infrared laser, several optics are available to manipulate a temporal profile, such as chirping, double-pulse, and so on. Probably, it is an upper limit for the pulse duration due to how long the cusp structure remains. Here, we give an example for an attosecond pulse duration. Assuming that $n_e = 1.7 \times 10^{19}$ cm^{-3}, $\gamma = 10$, the source energy of 180 µJ, $\tau_s = 20$ fs, and $I_s = 1 \times 10^{16}$ W/cm^2, the reflected pulse has a photon energy of 620 eV and a pulse energy of 0.8 µJ with a duration of 50 as. These parameters are chosen so that the source pulse does not affect the mirror due to the recoil effect.

As introduced in the previous section, the BISER can emit coherent electromagnetic radiation in the forward direction. This can be a simple mechanism to generate coherent, attosecond XUV to soft X-ray regions. The maximum harmonic number is estimated to be $n_H = \omega_c/\omega_f \approx a_0^3$, where ω_c and ω_f are the critical frequency and laser frequency, respectively, and a_0 is the normalized laser amplitude. In practical units,

$$n_H \approx 500 \left(\frac{P}{1 \text{ PW}}\right) \left(\frac{n_e}{10^{19} \text{ cm}^{-3}}\right) \left(\frac{\lambda}{1 \text{ µm}}\right)^2, \tag{14}$$

where P, λ, and n_e are the laser peak power, the laser wavelength, and the electron density, respectively. The total emitted photon energy ε in cgs units is approximately equal to

$$\varepsilon \approx \frac{e^2 N_e^2 a_0^4 \gamma \omega_f^2 \tau_H}{8c} \propto N_e^2 P^{4/3} n_e^{5/6} \omega^{1/3} \tau_h, \tag{15}$$

where N_e is the number of electrons in the singularity, γ is the Lorentz factor associated with the laser group velocity in plasma, and τ_H is the duration of the emission. Assuming practical parameters $P = 100$ TW, $n_e = 5 \times 10^{19}$ cm^{-3}, $a_0 = 12$, $\gamma = 5.8$, $\tau_H = 0.1$ fs, and $\lambda = 0.8$ µm, the maximum harmonic number is $n_H \sim 160$ (the photon energy of 250 eV) and the maximum energy ~ 0.6 mJ. This can be a very bright, soft X-ray source.

4.4. Analog Black Holes

Chen and Mourou proposed to use accelerating plasma mirrors for investigating the black hole information paradox in laboratories [37]. The current research on analog black holes is mainly theoretical because it seems impossible to address this paradox by direct astrophysical observations; typical stellar-sized black holes are too cold and young to see the paradox, which might be observed in the end-stage of black hole evaporation.

Among several proposals to investigate the Hawking effects in laboratories, an accelerating mirror is recognized that can mimic black holes and emit Hawking-like thermal radiation (Unruh radiation). According to the equivalence principle, the Hawking temperature of gravity g is expressed as $T_H = \hbar g/2\pi c k_B$, and the observer at the uniform acceleration of a feels radiation in a vacuum such as $T_U = \hbar a/2\pi c k_B$, where k_B is the Boltzmann constant.

The acceleration of the mirror is achieved by varying a plasma density along the laser propagation [37–39]. Assuming that the plasma density $n_e(x) = n_{p0}(1 + x/D)^{2(1-\eta_0)}$, the acceleration is

$$a(x) \approx \frac{(1-\eta_0)c^2}{D(1+x/D)^2} \exp\left(\frac{(1-\eta_0)x/D}{1} + x/D \right). \tag{16}$$

This is an extensive experiment, and much still needs to be considered and verified before the actual experiment is conducted. An international, Analog Black Hole Evaporation via Lasers (AnaBHEL), collaboration is currently pursuing an experimental realization of the Chen–Mourou proposal. The concept, design, and status of AnaBHEL are presented in [40].

5. Discussion

The relativistic flying mirror (RFM) concept was reviewed, and the potential applications of the RFMs were also presented. Here we give the necessary theoretical considerations and technological challenges to realize the proposed visions.

The detail of the realistic parameters is owed to numerical calculations such as PIC. In PIC calculations, resolving the upshifted frequency is problematic due to the high spatial and temporal resolutions necessary for shorter wavelengths. For example, in standard parameters, a spatial grid is determined by the laser wavelength to be 0.8 μm, which is shorter than the plasma wavelength. Treating shorter wavelengths of 10 nm requires finer spatial and temporal grids. Thus, a new scheme might be necessary for resolving shorter wavelengths and/or smaller spot sizes.

As is shown in theoretical consierations, the plasma temperature effect reduces the density of the electrons in a cusp, which limits the effectiveness of the RFMs. The initial plasma temperature is strongly affected by the prepulse condition of the driving laser. Ionized electrons can be heated by absorption of the laser's energy and transfer the energy via collisions. This effect in an actual situation has not yet been addressed in gaseous plasma.

Experimental challenges remain in many aspects. The focusability of the RFM to the theoretically estimated size has not yet been demonstrated. This is a crucial fundamental property of the RFM.. Another concept to be demonstrated is the pulse compression of the reflected pulse. According to the theory, the compression must happen as long as the upshift of the frequency happens. However, the effect must be measured experimentally to prove the concept. This is crucial for ultrashort X-ray generation.

Practically, the repeatability of the reflection must be improved. This is necessary for the applications and the precise characterization mentioned above. For example, the temporal characterization in the sub-femtosecond regime requires many shots. The detailed mechanism for forming a cusp structure or singularities in plasma has been addressed experimentally, mainly investigated numerically. Singularities or breaking waves should be monitored with an ultrashort pulse (optical light or an electron beam).

6. Conclusions

We reviewed the relativistic flying mirror concept highlighting the theoretical and experimental achievements. The flying mirror has several attractive properties, such as high-frequency and ultra-short pulse generation. In addition, the intensification can be expected due to the focusing mirror shape. Some of these features are to be demonstrated experimentally. In the near term, the ultra-short, coherent source can be realized. In the long term, the RFM might enable terrestrial laboratory experiments in quantum electrodynamics and astrophysics, which would be nearly unattainable without it.

Funding: This work was partly supported by JSPS Kakenhi JP 19KK0355 and 19H00669 and the QST Director Fund Creative Research No. 20, QST IRI. S.B. acknowledges the support by the project High Field Initiative (cz.02.1.01/0.0/15_003/0000449).

Institutional Review Board Statement: Not applicable.

Informed Consent Statement: Not applicable.

Data Availability Statement: Not applicable.

Conflicts of Interest: The authors declare no conflict of interest.

Abbreviations

The following abbreviations are used in this manuscript:

BISER	Burst intensification by singularity emitting radiation
CCD	Charge-coupled device
FDI	Frequency domain interferometry
FDH	Frequency domain holography
PIC	Particle-in-cell
RFM	Relativistic flying mirror
SRLD	Square-root Lorentzian distribution
UHFS	Ultra-high-field science
QED	Quantum electrodynamics

References

1. Strickland, D.; Mourou, G. Compression of Amplified Chirped Optical Pulses. *Opt. Commun.* **1985**, *55*, 447–449. [CrossRef]
2. Mourou, G.A.; Tajima, T.; Bulanov, S.V. Optics in the relativistic regime. *Rev. Mod. Phys.* **2006**, *78*, 309–371. [CrossRef]
3. Piazza, A.D.; Mueller, C.; Hatsagortsyan, K.Z.; Keitel, C.H. Extremely high-intensity laser interactions with fundamental quantum systems. *Rev. Mod. Phys.* **2012**, *84*, 1177–1228. [CrossRef]
4. Yoon, J.W.; Kim, Y.G.; Choi, I.W.; Sung, J.H.; Lee, H.W.; Lee, S.K.; Nam, C.H. Realization of laser intensity over 10^{23} W/cm^2. *Optica* **2021**, *8*, 630. [CrossRef]
5. Bulanov, S.V.; Esirkepov, T.Z.; Hayashi, Y.; Kando, M.; Kiriyama, H.; Koga, J.K.; Kondo, K.; Kotaki, H.; Pirozhkov, A.S.; Bulanov, S.S.; et al. Extreme field science. *Plasma Phys. Control. Fusion* **2011**, *53*, 124025. [CrossRef]
6. Bamber, C.; Boege, S.J.; Koffas, T.; Kotseroglou, T.; Melissinos, A.C.; Meyerhofer, D.D.; Reis, D.A.; Ragg, W.; Bula, C.; McDonald, K.T.; et al. Studies of nonlinear QED in collisions of 46.6 GeV electrons with intense laser pulses. *Phys. Rev. D* **1999**, *60*, 092004. [CrossRef]
7. Bulanov, S.S.; Mur, V.D.; Narozhny, N.B.; Nees, J.; Popov, V.S. Multiple Colliding Electromagnetic Pulses: A Way to Lower the Threshold of e^+e^- Pair Production from Vacuum. *Phys. Rev. Lett.* **2010**, *104*, 220404. [CrossRef]
8. Dunne, G.V.; Gies, H.; Schützhold, R. Catalysis of Schwinger vacuum pair production. *Phys. Rev. D* **2009**, *80*, 111301. [CrossRef]
9. Bulanov, S.; Esirkepov, T.Z.; Tajima, T. Light intensification towards the Schwinger limit. *Phys. Rev. Lett.* **2003**, *91*, 085001. [CrossRef]
10. Panchenko, A.V.; Esirkepov, T.Z.; Pirozhkov, A.S.; Kando, M.; Kamenets, F.F.; Bulanov, S.V. Interaction of electromagnetic waves with caustics in plasma flows. *Phys. Rev. E* **2008**, *78*, 056402. [CrossRef]
11. Bulanov, S.V.; Esirkepov, T.Z.; Kando, M.; Pirozhkov, A.S.; Rosanov, N.N. Relativistic mirrors in plasmas. Novel results and perspectives. *Physics-Uspekhi* **2013**, *56*, 429–464. [CrossRef]
12. Einstein, A. Zur Elektrodynamik bewegter Körper. *Ann. Der Phys.* **1905**, *322*, 891–921. [CrossRef]
13. Kando, M.; Esirkepov, T.; Koga, J.; Pirozhkov, A.; Bulanov, S. Coherent, Short-Pulse X-ray Generation via Relativistic Flying Mirrors. *Quantum Beam Sci.* **2018**, *2*, 9. [CrossRef]
14. Valenta, P.; Esirkepov, T.Z.; Koga, J.K.; Pirozhkov, A.S.; Kando, M.; Liu, Y.K.; Fang, P.; Chen, P.; Mu, J.; Korn, G.; et al. Recoil effects on reflection from relativistic mirrors in laser plasmas. *Phys. Plasmas* **2020**, *27*, 032109. [CrossRef]
15. Liu, Y.-K.; Chen, P;Fang, Y. Reflectivity and spectrum of relativistic flying plasma mirrors. *Phys. Plasmas* **2021**, *28*, 103301. [CrossRef]
16. Bulanov, S.V.; Esirkepov, T.Z.; Kando, M.; Koga, J.K.; Pirozhkov, A.S.; Nakamura, T.; Bulanov, S.S.; Schroeder, C.B.; Esarey, E.; Califano, F.; et al. On the breaking of a plasma wave in a thermal plasma. II. Electromagnetic wave interaction with the breaking plasma wave. *Phys. Plasmas* **2012**, *19*, 113103. [CrossRef]

17. Jeong, T.M.; Bulanov, S.V.; Valenta, P.; Korn, G.; Esirkepov, T.Z.; Koga, J.K.; Pirozhkov, A.S.; Kando, M.; Bulanov, S.S. Relativistic flying laser focus by a laser-produced parabolic plasma mirror. *Phys. Rev. A* **2021**, *104*, 053533. [CrossRef]
18. Kando, M.; Fukuda, Y.; Pirozhkov, A.S.; Ma, J.; Daito, I.; Chen, L.; Esirkepov, T.Z.; Ogura, K.; Homma, T.; Hayashi, Y.; et al. Demonstration of laser-frequency upshift by electron-density modulations in a plasma wakefield. *Phys. Rev. Lett.* **2007**, *99*, 135001. [CrossRef]
19. Pirozhkov, A.S.; Ma, J.; Kando, M.; Esirkepov, T.Z.; Fukuda, Y.; Chen, L.M.; Daito, I.; Ogura, K.; Homma, T.; Hayashi, Y.; et al. Frequency multiplication of light back-reflected from a relativistic wake wave. *Phys. Plasmas* **2007**, *14*, 123106. [CrossRef]
20. Kando, M.; Pirozhkov, A.S.; Kawase, K.; Esirkepov, T.Z.; Fukuda, Y.; Kiriyama, H.; Okada, H.; Daito, I.; Kameshima, T.; Hayashi, Y.; et al. Enhancement of Photon Number Reflected by the Relativistic Flying Mirror. *Phys. Rev. Lett.* **2009**, *103*, 235003. [CrossRef]
21. Kando, M.; Pirozhkov, A.S.; Fukuda, Y.; Esirkepov, T.Z.; Daito, I.; Kawase, K.; Ma, J.L.; Chen, L.M.; Hayashi, Y.; Mori, M.; et al. Experimental studies of the high and low frequency electromagnetic radiation produced from nonlinear laser-plasma interactions. *Eur. Phys. J. D* **2009**, *55*, 465–474. [CrossRef]
22. Pirozhkov, A.S.; Kando, M.; Esirkepov, T.Z.; Gallegos, P.; Ahmed, H.; Ragozin, E.N.; Faenov, A.Y.; Pikuz, T.A.; Kawachi, T.; Sagisaka, A.; et al. Soft-X-ray Harmonic Comb from Relativistic Electron Spikes. *Phys. Rev. Lett.* **2012**, *108*, 135004. [CrossRef]
23. Pirozhkov, A.S.; Kando, M.; Esirkepov, T.Z.; Gallegos, P.; Ahmed, H.; Ragozin, E.N.; Faenov, A.Y.; Pikuz, T.A.; Kawachi, T.; Sagisaka, A.; et al. High order harmonics from relativistic electron spikes. *New J. Phys.* **2014**, *16*, 093003. [CrossRef]
24. Sagisaka, A.; Ogura, K.; Esirkepov, T.; Neely, D.; Pikuz, T.; Koga, J.; Fukuda, Y.; Kotaki, H.; Hayashi, Y.; Gonzalez-Izquierdo, B.; et al. Observation of Burst Intensification by Singularity Emitting Radiation generated from relativistic plasma with a high-intensity laser. *High Energy Density Phys.* **2020**, *36*, 100751. [CrossRef]
25. Pirozhkov, A.S.; Esirkepov, T.Z.; Pikuz, T.A.; Faenov, A.Y.; Ogura, K.; Hayashi, Y.; Kotaki, H.; Ragozin, E.N.; Neely, D.; Kiriyama, H.; et al. Burst intensification by singularity emitting radiation in multi-stream flows. *Sci. Rep.* **2017**, *7*, 17968. [CrossRef] [PubMed]
26. Pirozhkov, A.S.; Esirkepov, T.Z.; Pikuz, T.A.; Faenov, A.Y.; Sagisaka, A.; Ogura, K.; Hayashi, Y.; Kotaki, H.; Ragozin, E.N.; Neely, D.; et al. Laser Requirements for High-Order Harmonic Generation by Relativistic Plasma Singularities. *Quantum Beam Sci.* **2018**, *2*, 7. [CrossRef]
27. Marquès, J.R.; Geindre, J.P.; Amiranoff, F.; Audebert, P.; Gauthier, J.C.; Antonetti, A.; Grillon, G. Temporal and Spatial Measurements of the Electron Density Perturbation Produced in the Wake of an Ultrashort Laser Pulse. *Phys. Rev. Lett.* **1996**, *76*, 3566–3569. [CrossRef]
28. Siders, C.W.; Blanc, S.P.L.; Fisher, D.; Tajima, T.; Downer, M.C.; Babine, A.; Stepanov, A.; Sergeev, A. Laser Wakefield Excitation and Measurement by Femtosecond Longitudinal Interferometry. *Phys. Rev. Lett.* **1996**, *76*, 3570–3573. [CrossRef]
29. Matlis, N.H.; Reed, S.; Bulanov, S.S.; Chvykov, V.; Kalintchenko, G.; Matsuoka, T.; Rousseau, P.; Yanovsky, V.; Maksimchuk, A.; Kalmykov, S.; et al. Snapshots of laser wakefields. *Nat. Phys.* **2006**, *2*, 749–753. [CrossRef]
30. Buck, A.; Nicolai, M.; Schmid, K.; Sears, C.M.S.; Sävert, A.; Mikhailova, J.M.; Krausz, F.; Kaluza, M.C.; Veisz, L. Real-time observation of laser-driven electron acceleration. *Nat. Phys.* **2011**, *7*, 543–548. [CrossRef]
31. Sävert, A.; Mangles, S.P.D.; Schnell, M.; Siminos, E.; Cole, J.M.; Leier, M.; Reuter, M.; Schwab, M.B.; Möller, M.; Poder, K.; et al. Direct Observation of the Injection Dynamics of a Laser Wakefield Accelerator Using Few-Femtosecond Shadowgraphy. *Phys. Rev. Lett.* **2015**, *115*, 055002. [CrossRef]
32. Esirkepov, T.Z.; Mu, J.; Gu, Y.; Jeong, T.M.; Valenta, P.; Klimo, O.; Koga, J.K.; Kando, M.; Neely, D.; Korn, G.; et al. Optical probing of relativistic plasma singularities. *Phys. Plasmas* **2020**, *27*, 052103. [CrossRef]
33. Kotov, A.; Esirkepov, T.; Soloviev, A.; Sagisaka, A.; Ogura, K.; Bierwage, A.; Kando, M.; Kiriyama, H.; Starodubtsev, M.; Khazanov, E.; et al. Enhanced diagnostics of radiating relativistic singularities and BISER by nonlinear post-compression of optical probe pulse. *J. Instrum.* **2022**, *17*, P07035. [CrossRef]
34. Wan, Y.; Seemann, O.; Tata, S.; Andriyash, I.A.; Smartsev, S.; Kroupp, E.; Malka, V. Direct observation of relativistic broken plasma waves. *Nat. Phys.* **2022**, *18*, 1186–1190. [CrossRef]
35. Bulanov, S.S.; Maksimchuk, A.; Schroeder, C.B.; Zhidkov, A.G.; Esarey, E.; Leemans, W.P. Relativistic spherical plasma waves. *Phys. Plasmas* **2012**, *19*, 020702. [CrossRef]
36. Koga, J.K.; Bulanov, S.V.; Esirkepov, T.Z.; Pirozhkov, A.S.; Kando, M.; Rosanov, N.N. Possibility of measuring photon–photon scattering via relativistic mirrors. *Phys. Rev. A* **2012**, *86*, 053823. [CrossRef]
37. Chen, P.; Mourou, G. Accelerating Plasma Mirrors to Investigate the Black Hole Information Loss Paradox. *Phys. Rev. Lett.* **2017**, *118*, 045001-5. [CrossRef]
38. Chen, P.; Mourou, G. Trajectory of a flying plasma mirror traversing a target with density gradient. *Phys. Plasmas* **2020**, *27*, 123106. [CrossRef]
39. Lobet, M.; Kando, M.; Koga, J.K.; Esirkepov, T.Z.; Nakamura, T.; Pirozhkov, A.S.; Bulanov, S.V. Controlling the generation of high frequency electromagnetic pulses with relativistic flying mirrors using an inhomogeneous plasma. *Phys. Lett. A* **2013**, *377*, 1114–1118. [CrossRef]
40. Collaboration, A.; Chen, P.; Mourou, G.; Besancon, M.; Fukuda, Y.; Glicenstein, J.F.; Nam, J.; Lin, C.E.; Lin, K.N.; Liu, S.X.; et al. AnaBHEL (Analog Black Hole Evaporation via Lasers) Experiment: Concept, Design, and Status. *arXiv* **2022**, arXiv:2205.12195.

Article

AnaBHEL (Analog Black Hole Evaporation via Lasers) Experiment: Concept, Design, and Status

Pisin Chen [1,2,3,*], Gerard Mourou [4], Marc Besancon [5], Yuji Fukuda [6], Jean-Francois Glicenstein [5], Jiwoo Nam [1,2,3], Ching-En Lin [1,2], Kuan-Nan Lin [1,2], Shu-Xiao Liu [1], Yung-Kun Liu [1,2], Masaki Kando [6], Kotaro Kondo [6], Stathes Paganis [1,2], Alexander Pirozhkov [6], Hideaki Takabe [1], Boris Tuchming [5], Wei-Po Wang [2], Naoki Watamura [1], Jonathan Wheeler [4] and Hsin-Yeh Wu [1,2] on behalf of the AnaBHEL Collaboration

1. Leung Center for Cosmology and Particle Astrophysics, National Taiwan University, Taipei 10617, Taiwan
2. Department of Physics, National Taiwan University, Taipei 10617, Taiwan
3. Graduate Institute of Astrophysics, National Taiwan University, Taipei 10617, Taiwan
4. IZEST, Ecole Polytechnique, 91128 Palaiseau, France
5. Irfu, CEA, Université Paris-Saclay, 91191 Gif sur Yvette, France
6. Kansai Photon Science Institute, National Institutes for Quantum Science and Technology, 8-1-7 Umemidai, Kizugawa 619-0215, Kyoto, Japan
* Correspondence: pisinchen@phys.ntu.edu.tw

Abstract: Accelerating relativistic mirrors have long been recognized as viable settings where the physics mimic those of the black hole Hawking radiation. In 2017, Chen and Mourou proposed a novel method to realize such a system by traversing an ultra-intense laser through a plasma target with a decreasing density. An international AnaBHEL (Analog Black Hole Evaporation via Lasers) collaboration was formed with the objectives of observing the analog Hawking radiation, shedding light on the information loss paradox. To reach these goals, we plan to first verify the dynamics of the flying plasma mirror and characterize the correspondence between the plasma density gradient and the trajectory of the accelerating plasma mirror. We will then attempt to detect the analog Hawking radiation photons and measure the entanglement between the Hawking photons and their "partner particles". In this paper, we describe our vision and strategy of AnaBHEL using the Apollon laser as a reference, and we report on the progress of our R&D concerning the key components in this experiment, including the supersonic gas jet with a graded density profile, and the superconducting nanowire single-photon Hawking detector. In parallel to these hardware efforts, we performed computer simulations to estimate the potential backgrounds, and derived analytic expressions for modifications to the blackbody spectrum of the Hawking radiation for a perfectly reflecting point mirror, due to the semi-transparency and finite-size effects specific to flying plasma mirrors. Based on this more realistic radiation spectrum, we estimate the Hawking photon yield to guide the design of the AnaBHEL experiment, which appears to be achievable.

Keywords: AnaBHEL (Analog Black Hole Evaporation via Lasers); Hawking radiation; information loss paradox; relativistic flying mirror

1. Introduction

The question of whether the Hawking evaporation [1] violates unitarity and, therefore, results in the loss of information [2], has remained unresolved since Hawking's seminal discovery. The proposed solutions include black hole complementarity [3], firewalls [4,5] (see, for example, [6,7], for a recent review and [7–9] for a counterargument), soft hairs [10], black hole remnants [11], islands [12,13], replica wormholes [14,15], and instanton tunneling between multiple histories of Euclidean path integrals [16]. So far, the investigations remain mostly theoretical since it is almost impossible to settle this paradox through direct astrophysical observations, as typical stellar-size black holes are cold and young; however, the solution to the paradox depends crucially on the end-stage of the black hole evaporation.

There have been proposals for laboratory investigations of the Hawking effect, including sound waves in moving fluids [17,18], electromagnetic waveguides [19], traveling index of refraction in media [20], ultra-short laser pulse filament [21], Bose–Einstein condensates [22], and electrons accelerated by intense lasers [23]. It should be emphasized that the Chen–Tajima proposal [23] differs from other concepts mentioned above in that it is based on the equivalence principle, which mimics the Hawking radiation of an *eternal* (non-dynamical) black hole. Experimentally, Reference [22] reported on the observation of a thermal spectrum of the Hawking radiation in the analog system and its entanglement. However, most of these are limited to verifying the thermal nature of the Hawking radiation.

It has long been recognized that accelerating mirrors can mimic black holes and emit Hawking-like thermal radiation [24]. In 2017, Chen and Mourou proposed a scheme to physically realize a relativistic mirror by using a state-of-the-art high-intensity laser to impinge a plasma target with a decreasing density [25,26]. The proposal follows the same philosophy as Reference [23], but differs in that it mimics the Hawking radiation from *gravitational collapse* and, therefore, from a dynamical black hole, which is a more direct analogy to the original Hawking evaporation. It is also unique in that it does not rely on a certain fluid to mimic the curved spacetime around a black hole, but rather a more direct quantum field theoretical analogy between the spacetime geometry defined by a black hole and a flying mirror.

Based on this concept, an international AnaBHEL collaboration has been formed to carry out the Chen–Mourou scheme, which is the only experimental proposal of its kind in the world. Our ultimate scientific objectives are to detect analog Hawking radiation for the first time in history and through the measurement of the quantum entanglement between the Hawking particles and their vacuum fluctuating pair partner particles, to shed some light on the unresolved information loss paradox. From this perspective, the AnaBHEL experiment may be regarded as a *flying* EPR (Einstein–Podolsky–Rosen) experiment [27].

The concept of a flying plasma mirror was proposed by Bulanov et al. [28–31]. It provides an alternative approach to the free electron laser (FEL) in generating high-frequency coherent radiation. The flying plasma mirror approach provides a great prospect for future applications. A series of proof-of-principle experiments led by Kando at KPSI in Japan [32–35] has validated the concept. However, the mirror reflectivity (as a function of frequency) as well as other physical properties, such as the reflection angular distribution, etc., have not been characterized in those two experiments.

In this paper, we first review the physics of a flying mirror as an analog black hole. We then reveal the concept of accelerating relativistic plasma mirrors as analog black holes, with the attention paid to the aspects pertinent to the investigation of the Hawking radiation and the information loss paradox, including the laser–plasma dynamics that give rise to the acceleration of the plasma mirror, the reflectivity, the frequency shift of the reflected spectrum, and corrections due to the finite-size and semi-transparency effects of a realistic plasma mirror to the blackbody spectrum of the analog Hawking radiation based on an idealized, perfectly reflecting, point mirror. We then report on the progress of our R&D, i.e., of the key components in the AnaBHEL experiment, including those of the supersonic gas jet and the superconducting nanowire single-photon Hawking detector. We conclude by projecting our experimental outlook.

2. Flying Mirror as Analog Black Hole

Figure 1 depicts the analogy between the Hawking radiation of a real BH (left) and that of an accelerating mirror (right). The fact that accelerating mirrors can also address the information loss paradox was first suggested by Wilczek [36]. As is well-known, the notion of black hole information loss is closely associated with quantum entanglement. In order to preserve the "black hole unitarity", Wilczek argued that, based on the moving mirror model, in vacuum fluctuations, the *partner modes* of the Hawking particles would be trapped by the horizon until the end of the evaporation, where they would be released and the initial pure state of a black hole would be recovered with essentially zero cost of energy. More recently, Hotta et al. [37] argued that the released partner modes are simply indistinguishable from the zero-point vacuum fluctuations. On the other hand, there is also the notion that these partner modes would be released in a burst of energy, for example, in the Bardeen model [38] (See Figure 2).

One common *drawback* in all analog black hole concepts involves setting up in a laboratory with flat spacetime (therefore, the standard quantum field theory is known to be valid); it is inevitable that any physical process, including analog black hole systems, must preserve the unitarity. Therefore, none of the proposed analog black holes can in principle *prove* the loss of information even if that is indeed so. The real issue is, therefore, not so much about whether the unitarity is preserved, but more about *how* it is preserved. That is, it is even more important to determine how the black hole information is retrieved. Does it follow the Page curve [39], a modified Page curve where the Page time is significantly shifted towards the late time [16], or alternative scenarios [40]? The measurement of the entanglement between the Hawking particles and the partner particles as well as the evolution of the entanglement entropy [41], should help to shed much light on the black hole information loss paradox. As pointed out by Chen and Yeom [41], different scenarios of black hole evolution can be tested by different mirror trajectories [42,43].

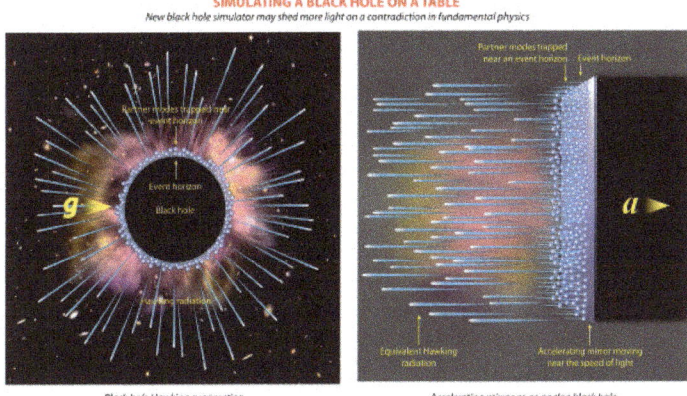

Figure 1. The analogy between the Hawking radiation from a true BH (**left**) and that from an accelerating mirror (**right**). One may intuitively appreciate the analogy based on Einstein's Equivalence Principle.

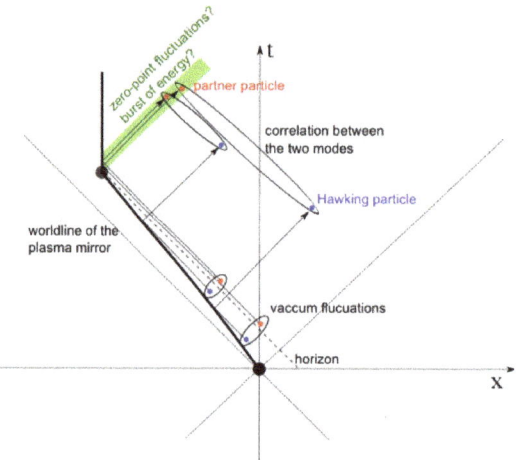

Figure 2. (Reproduced from Reference [25].) The 'worldline' of an accelerating relativistic plasma mirror and its relation with vacuum fluctuations around the horizon. In particular, the entanglements between the Hawking particles (blue) emitted at early times and their partner particles (red) collected at late times are illustrated. The green strip represents either a burst of energy or zero-point fluctuations emitted when the acceleration stops abruptly.

3. Accelerating Plasma Mirror via Density Gradient

As is well known, plasma wakefields [44,45] in the nonlinear regimes of plasma perturbations will blow out all intervening plasma electrons, leaving an "ion bubble" trailing behind the driving laser pulse or electron beam. Eventually, the expelled electrons will rush back and pile up with a singular density distribution. S. Bulanov et al. [28–31,34] suggested that such a highly nonlinear plasma wake could serve as a relativistically flying mirror where an optical frequency light, upon reflecting from the flying plasma mirror, would instantly blueshift to an X-ray. For a more in-depth understanding of the flying plasma mirror, please read [46,47] for an overview. To apply this flying plasma mirror concept to the investigation of black hole Hawking evaporation, one must make the plasma mirror accelerate.

In this regard, one important issue is the correspondence between the plasma density gradient and the mirror spacetime trajectory. In order to mimic the physics of the Hawking evaporation, the plasma mirror must undergo a non-trivial acceleration that gives rise to a spacetime trajectory that is black hole physics meaningful. Such black hole-relevant trajectories have been well studied theoretically in the past 40 years with a wealth of literature available. This, as proposed [25,26], can be realized by preparing the plasma target with a prescribed density gradient (See Figure 3 for a schematic drawing of the concept).

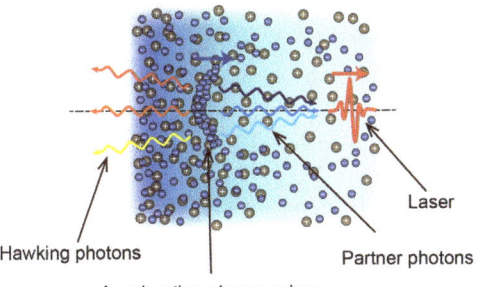

Figure 3. Schematic drawing of the concept of accelerating plasma mirror driven by an intense laser that traverses a plasma with a decreasing density. Due to the variation of the laser intensity in the transverse dimension, which is typically in Gaussian distribution, the flying plasma mirror induced by the laser is concave in the forward direction.

Mirror Trajectory and Plasma Density Correspondence

Two effects govern the acceleration of a plasma mirror [26]. One is the speeding up of the driving laser pulse as it traverses a plasma with a decreasing density, the so-called "down ramp", due to the increase of the laser refractive index. The other is the change of the local plasma wavelength and, therefore, the length of the ion bubble, which enlarges the distance of the plasma mirror from the laser. The acceleration and, thus, the trajectory of a plasma mirror as a function of the local plasma density and its gradient was derived in [26], where both effects mentioned above are included. For the detailed derivations of the flying plasma mirror trajectory, the reader should consult Reference [26]. We caution that our theoretical description of the plasma mirror trajectory should be experimentally verified. In general,

$$\frac{\ddot{x}_M}{c^2} = \frac{1 - (1/2)\omega_p^2/\omega_0^2}{[1 - (3\pi/2)c\omega_p'/\omega_p^2]^3} \times \left\{ -\frac{\omega_p^2}{\omega_0^2}\frac{\omega_p'}{\omega_p} + \frac{3\pi c}{2}\left[\frac{\omega_p''}{\omega_p^2} - 2\frac{\omega_p'^2}{\omega_p^3}\right]\right\}, \quad (1)$$

where x_M is the position of the plasma mirror, $\ddot{x}_M$ is its second time derivative, ω_0 the laser frequency, $\omega_p(x) = c\sqrt{4\pi r_e n_p(x)}$ us the local plasma frequency, $r_e = e^2/m_e c^2$ is the classical electron radius, and $\omega_p' \equiv \partial \omega_p(x)/\partial x$. Our desire is to achieve the highest acceleration possible. To accomplish that, one should design the system in such a way that the denominator of Equation (1) is minimized.

A simple but well-motivated plasma density profile is the one that corresponds to the exponential trajectory investigated by Davies and Fulling [24,48], which is of special geometrical interest because it corresponds to a well-defined horizon [49]. Inspired by that, we consider the following plasma density variation along the direction of the laser propagation inside the plasma target with thickness L:

$$n_p(x) = n_{p0}(a + be^{x/D})^2, \quad -L \leq x \leq 0, \quad (2)$$

where $n_{p0}(a+b)^2$ is the plasma density at $x = 0$, D is the characteristic length of density variation. Accordingly, the plasma frequency varies as

$$\omega_p(x) = \omega_{p0}(a + be^{x/D}), \quad -L \leq x \leq 0, \quad (3)$$

where $\omega_{p0} = c\sqrt{4\pi r_e n_{p0}}$. In our conception, the time derivatives of the plasma frequency are induced through the spatial variation of the plasma density via the relation $\omega_p(x) = c\sqrt{4\pi r_e n_p(x)}$. Thus,

$$\omega'_p(x) = \frac{b}{D} e^{x/D} \omega_{p0}, \tag{4}$$

$$\omega''_p(x) = \frac{b}{D^2} e^{x/D} \omega_{p0}. \tag{5}$$

Inserting these into Equation (1), we then have, for the constant-plus-exponential-squared distribution of Equation (2),

$$\begin{aligned}\frac{\ddot{x}_M}{c^2} &= -\frac{1-(\omega_{p0}^2/2\omega_0^2)(a+be^{x/D})^2}{[1+(3b/4)(\lambda_{p0}/D)e^{x/D}/(a+be^{x/D})^2]^3} \\ &\quad \times \frac{\lambda_{p0}}{D} \frac{be^{x/D}}{(a+be^{x/D})} \left\{ \frac{\omega_p^2}{\omega_0^2} \frac{1}{\lambda_{p0}} \right. \\ &\quad + \left. \frac{3}{4D}\left[\frac{1}{a+be^{x/D}} - \frac{2be^{x/D}}{(a+be^{x/D})^2}\right]\right\}. \end{aligned} \tag{6}$$

PIC simulations of the laser–plasma interactions were performed based on the above plasma density profile [50]. The acceleration of the plasma mirror agrees well with the formula (See Figure 4).

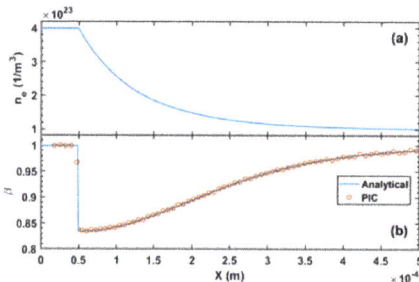

Figure 4. PIC simulation of plasma mirror acceleration [50]. (**a**) A plasma target with a constant-plus-exponential density gradient, $n_p(x) = n_{p0}(1+e^{-x/D})^2$, $n_p(x=0) = 1.0 \times 10^{17} \text{cm}^{-3}$. (**b**) Comparison of the plasma mirror speed, $\beta = \dot{x}_M/c$, between the analytic formula (solid blue curve) and the PIC simulations (orange circles). The two agree extremely well. Note that the convention of the laser propagation direction in this PIC simulation is from left to right, which is opposite to that in the typical theoretical treatment of flying mirrors as analog black holes.

4. Analog Hawking Temperature

There exists a wealth of literature on the vacuum fluctuating modes of quantum fields, their reflections from a flying mirror, and the analog "Hawking temperature" of such a flying mirror as an analog black hole [49]. In general, such analog Hawking temperature depends on the actual mirror trajectory. According to Reference [26],

$$\int_0^t \bar{c}\, dt = \int_{x_M}^0 dx \left[1 + \frac{3b\lambda_{p0}}{4D} \frac{e^{x/D}}{(a+be^{x/D})^2}\right], \quad x \leq 0, \tag{7}$$

where $\bar{c} = \eta c = (1-\omega_p^2/2\omega_0^2)c$ is the speed of light in the plasma medium, which is position dependent. In our conception [25], the plasma target thickness is supposed to be much larger than the characteristic scale of the density variation, i.e., $L \gg D$. In this situation, it is safe to extend the integration to $x_M \to -\infty$ (and $t \to \infty$). Taking this approximation, we find

$$x_M(t) = -\eta_a ct - A e^{-\eta_a ct/D} + A, \quad t \to \infty, \tag{8}$$

where $\eta_a = 1 - a^2 \omega_{p0}^2 / 2\omega_0^2$ and $A = \eta_a D[ab(\omega_{p0}^2/\omega_0^2) - (3b/4a^2)(\lambda_{p0}/D)]$. This is identical to the Davies–Fulling trajectory, i.e., Equation (4.51) of Reference [49],

$$z(t) \to -t - A e^{-2\kappa t} + B, \quad t \to \infty, \tag{9}$$

where A, B, κ are positive constants and $c \equiv 1$.

Transcribing the $x_M(t)$ coordinates to the (u, v) coordinates, where $u = \eta_a ct - x_M(t)$ and $v = \eta_a ct + x_M(t)$, we see that only null rays with $v < A$ can be reflected. All rays with $v > A$ will pass undisturbed. The ray $v = A$, therefore, acts as an effective horizon [49]. Following the standard recipe [49], we obtain the Wightman function as

$$D^+(u, v; u', v') = -\frac{1}{4\pi} \ln \left[2A e^{2\eta_a c(t+t')/2D} \right. \\ \times \left. \sinh(\eta_a c \Delta t / 2D) \right], \tag{10}$$

where $\Delta t = t - t' = \Delta u / 2\eta_a c$ in the $t \to \infty$ limit. The constant factors in the argument of the log function in the above equation do not contribute to the nontrivial part of the physics. Note that in our notation, t is the time when the ray hits the mirror. Let us denote the observation time and position by T and X. Then $u = \eta_a cT - X = \eta_a ct - x_M$. For large t, $u = \eta_a cT - X = 2\eta_a ct - A$. This leads to $\Delta u = 2\eta_a c \Delta t = \eta_a c \Delta T$ for a static mirror at $X = $ const. Integrating over T and T', we then have, in the asymptotic limit of $t, t' \to \infty$,

$$D^+(u, v; u', v') = -\frac{1}{4\pi} \ln \left[\sinh(\eta_a c \Delta t / 2D) \right]. \tag{11}$$

This leads to the response function (of the particle detector) per unit of time with the form

$$\mathcal{F}(E)/\text{unit time} = \frac{1}{E} \frac{1}{(e^{E/k_B T_H} - 1)}, \tag{12}$$

where the analog Hawking temperature of the mirror measured by a stationary particle detector is

$$k_B T_H = \frac{\hbar c}{4\pi} \frac{\eta_a}{D}. \tag{13}$$

Here, k_B is the Boltzmann constant. It is interesting to note that the analog Hawking temperature associated with our constant-plus-exponential-squared density profile depends strongly on the characteristic length D and only weakly on the plasma density (through η_a). This points to the possibility of employing gaseous instead of solid plasma targets, which would greatly simplify our proposed experiment.

5. Conceptual Design

The original experimental concept proposed by Chen and Mourou [25] invoked a two-plasma-target approach, where the first plasma target converts an optical laser into an X-ray pulse through the flying plasma mirror mechanism. The converted X-ray pulse then impinges on a nano-thin-film that is fabricated with a graded density in different layers. This design has the advantage of having a solid-state density, providing a higher plasma frequency, which is proportional to the square root of the plasma density and, therefore, a higher density gradient for maximizing the Hawking temperature. On the other hand, the drawbacks of this concept are multiple. First, the typical conversion efficiency of flying plasma mirrors is $\sim 10^{-5}$, rendering it difficult for the converted X-ray pulse to remain in the nonlinear regime. Second, the solid plasma target would induce extra backgrounds, which are linearly proportional to the target density.

In 2020, Chen and Mourou proposed a second design concept [26], where the conversion of optical laser to X-ray was no longer needed and, thus, the first plasma target was removed, and the nano-thin-film solid plasma target was replaced by a supersonic gas jet. This largely simplifies the design and the technical challenges. Figure 5 shows a schematic conceptual design of the single-target, optical laser approach. The key components now reduce to a supersonic gas jet with a graded density profile and a superconducting nanowire single-photon Hawking detector, the R&D progress of which will be described in later sections.

In our design of the AnaBHEL experiment, we assume the driving laser has the frequency $\omega_0 = 3.5 \times 10^{15}$ s^{-1} and the wavelength $\lambda_p = 540$ nm. For the plasma target, we set $a = b = 1$ in Equation (2) so that $n_p(x) = n_{p0}(1 + e^{x/D})^2$, and we assume $n_p(x = 0) = 1.0 \times 10^{17}$ cm^{-3} = $4n_{p0}$. The corresponding plasma frequency is $\omega_{p0} = 0.9 \times 10^{13}$ s^{-1} and the plasma wavelength $\lambda_{p0} = 200$ μm. Next, we design the plasma target density profile. Since our formula is not constrained by the adiabatic condition, we are allowed to choose a minute characteristic length $D = 0.5$ μm. Then we find

$$k_B T_H \sim 3.1 \times 10^{-2} \text{ eV}, \tag{14}$$

which corresponds to a characteristic Hawking radiation frequency $\omega_H \sim 4.8 \times 10^{13}$ s^{-1} > ω_{p0}. Thus, the Hawking photons can propagate through and out of the plasma for detection.

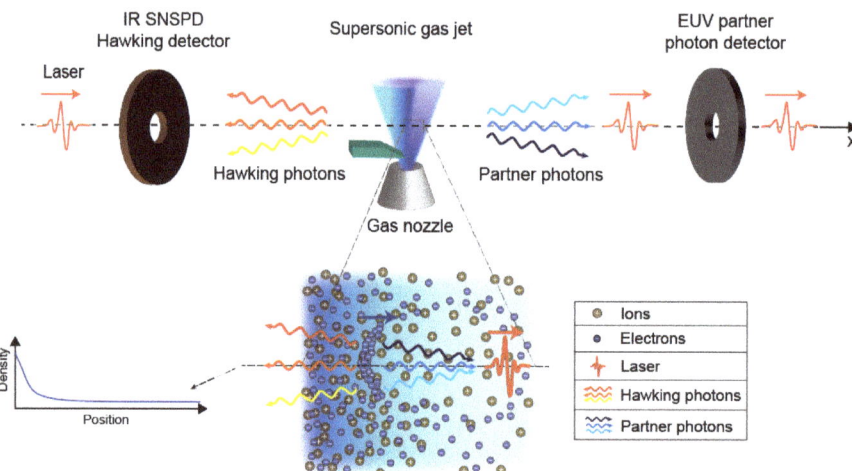

Figure 5. A conceptual design of the7 AnaBHEL experiment. The enlarged figure is a gaseous plasma target with a decreasing density profile where the penetrating optical laser pulse (red) would induce an accelerating flying plasma mirror (blue). Hawking photons would be emitted to the backside of the mirror, and would suffer from the Doppler redshift and be in the infrared range. The partner photons, on the other hand, would penetrate the semi-transparent plasma mirror and propagate in the same direction as that of the laser, which does not suffer from the Doppler redshift and would be in the EUV range.

6. Hawking Photon Yield

Among the proposed models, the physics of flying/moving mirrors is perhaps the one closest to that of real black holes, since in both cases the radiation originated from vacuum fluctuations. The essence of the Hawking radiation lies in the gravitational redshift of the field modes' phases. Since the key is the phase shift, various analog models or experimental proposals attempt to generate the same phase shift as that of the Hawking radiation but now in flat spacetime, i.e., laboratory. Indeed, in the flying mirror model, the gravitational redshift is mimicked by the Doppler redshift.

Due to the spherically symmetric nature of typical black hole spacetimes, the spherical coordinate origin is effectively a perfectly reflecting point mirror and the corresponding Hawking radiation is expected to be emitted radially, hence the situation is effectively (1+1)-dimensional and, thus, most of the flying mirror literature only considers a real perfectly reflecting point mirror in (1+1)-dimensional flat spacetime. Nevertheless, in the laboratory, the spacetime is (1+3)-dimensional. In addition, our proposed relativistic flying mirror generated through laser–plasma interaction has a low reflectivity [26] and a finite transverse/longitudinal size; therefore, it is necessary to take these practical effects into consideration to estimate the particle production yield.

The standard treatment in the flying mirror model [24,48,49,51] considers a real scalar field in (1+1)D flat spacetime subjected to a single, relativistic, time-dependent Dirichlet boundary condition in space to represent a relativistic perfectly reflecting point mirror. Since the boundary condition is externally provided, the breakdown of Poincaré invariance leads to the possibility of spontaneous particle creations following quantum field theory.

The generalization of this standard calculation to a flying plasma mirror with a finite reflectivity in n-dimensional flat spacetime can be made by starting with the action functional [52]:

$$S_\mu[\phi] = -\frac{1}{2}\int_{-\infty}^{\infty} d^n x \, \partial^\mu \phi(x) \partial_\mu \phi(x) \\ -\frac{\mu}{2}\int_{-\infty}^{\infty} d^n x \, V(x)\phi^2(x), \tag{15}$$

where natural units are employed, $\mu = 4\pi n_s \alpha / m_e$ is the coupling constant with dimension of mass, $\alpha = 1/137$ is the fine structure constant, n_s is the surface density of the electrons on the mirror, and

$$V(x) = \gamma^{-1}(t) H(\mathbf{x}_\perp) f(x - x_M(t)), \tag{16}$$

encodes the mirror's trajectory $x_M(t)$, longitudinal/transverse distribution H/f, and the Lorentz factor γ.

Solving the equation of motion for ϕ with the in-mode/out-mode boundary conditions in (1+1) dimensions, one finds (assuming the field to be in the in-vacuum state $|0; \text{in}\rangle$ with the mirror flying to the negative x-direction) the created particles (due to the field mode reflected to the mirror's right to have the frequency spectrum) [53–56]:

$$N = \int_0^\infty d\omega \int_0^\infty d\omega' |\beta_{\omega\omega'}|^2, \tag{17}$$

where

$$\beta_{\omega\omega'} = -\frac{\omega}{2\pi\sqrt{\omega\omega'}} \int_{-\infty}^{\infty} du \, \mathcal{R}_{\omega'}(u) e^{-i\omega' p(u) - i\omega u}, \tag{18}$$

and ω'/ω is the incident/emitted plane wave mode's frequency, $\mathcal{R}$ is the mirror's reflectivity, $u = t - x_M(t)$, and $p(u) = t + x_M(t)$ is the phase shift/ray-tracing function induced upon reflection off the receding mirror. From Equation (18), one sees that for a given trajectory x_M, the spectrum would be different depending on the reflectivity.

A simple model that mimics the formation and evaporation of a Schwarzschild black hole is the collapse of a spherical null shell. In this scenario, the relevant ray-tracing function is

$$u = p(u) - \frac{1}{\kappa}\ln[\kappa(v_H - p(u))], \tag{19}$$

where $\kappa > 0$ is the black hole's surface gravity, and v_H is the past event horizon, which is conventionally set to zero. For field modes propagating in the vicinity of v_H (late time), $u \approx -\kappa^{-1} \ln[-\kappa p(u)]$, and $\omega' \gg \omega$ (extreme gravitational/Doppler redshift), one obtains

$$|\beta_{\omega\omega'}|^2 \approx \frac{1}{2\pi\kappa\omega'} \frac{1}{e^{\omega/T_H} - 1}, \tag{20}$$

for a perfectly reflecting point mirror, and

$$|\beta_{\omega\omega'}|^2 \approx \frac{\mu^2}{8\pi\kappa\omega\omega'^2} \frac{1}{e^{\omega/T_H} + 1}, \tag{21}$$

for a semi-transparent point mirror, where $T_H = \kappa/(2\pi)$ is the analog Hawking temperature. In general, the accelerating mirror radiates along the entire worldline, but only those radiated in the late time are relevant to the analog Hawking radiation. In particular, the spectrum Equation (20) for a perfectly reflecting point mirror is in exact accordance with the Hawking radiation emitted by a Schwarzschild black hole. Although a semi-transparent point mirror possesses a different spectrum due to the time-dependent and frequency-dependent reflectivity, it nevertheless has the same temperature as that of a perfectly reflecting point mirror.

As previously mentioned, practical considerations in the laboratory force us to work in (1+3)-dimensional spacetime and a mirror with some kind of longitudinal/transverse distribution. In the case of a semi-transparent mirror, it is possible to find the corresponding analytic spectrum through a perturbative approach. The result is

$$\frac{dN}{d^3k} = \int d^3p |\beta_{\mathbf{k}\mathbf{p}}|^2, \tag{22}$$

where [56]

$$\begin{aligned}\beta_{\mathbf{k}\mathbf{p}} &\approx \frac{\langle \mathbf{k}, \mathbf{p}; \text{out}|0; \text{in}\rangle}{\langle 0; \text{out}|0; \text{in}\rangle} \\ &\approx F(\mathbf{k},\mathbf{p}) \times \frac{-i\mu}{16\pi^3 \sqrt{\omega_k \omega_p}} \\ &\times \int dt\, \gamma^{-1}(t) e^{i(\omega_k+\omega_p)t - i(k_x - p_x)x_M(t)},\end{aligned} \tag{23}$$

where ω_p/ω_k is the incident/emitted plane wave mode frequency, respectively, and

$$\begin{aligned}F(\mathbf{k},\mathbf{p}) &= \int d^2x_\perp H(\mathbf{x}_\perp) e^{-i(\mathbf{k}_\perp + \mathbf{p}_\perp)\cdot \mathbf{x}_\perp} \\ &\times \int d\zeta f(\zeta) e^{-i(k_x - p_x)\zeta}, \quad \zeta = x - x_M(t),\end{aligned} \tag{24}$$

is the form factor due to the mirror's longitudinal and transverse geometry, which is independent of the mirror's motion and reflectivity.

According to particle-in-cell (PIC) simulations [50], a mirror of square-root-Lorentzian density distribution and a finite transverse area can generate a good-quality mirror. Thus, we shall consider the case:

$$\begin{aligned}V(x) &= \frac{\gamma^{-1}(t)[\Theta(y+L/2) - \Theta(y-L/2)]}{\sqrt{(x - x_M(t))^2 + W^2}} \\ &\times [\Theta(z+L/2) - \Theta(z-L/2)],\end{aligned} \tag{25}$$

where W is the half-width at half maximum of the square-root-Lorentzian distribution and $L \times L$ is the transverse area. In addition, according to the plasma density profile designed in Reference [26], the mirror follows the trajectory:

$$t(x_M) = \begin{cases} -\frac{x_M}{v}, & v \to 1, \ 0 \le x_M < \infty, \\ -x_M + \frac{3\pi}{2\omega_{p0}(1+b)}\left[\frac{1+b}{1+be^{x_M/D}} - 1\right], & \text{else}, \end{cases} \qquad (26)$$

where $\{\omega_{p0}, b, D\}$ are positive plasma mirror parameters and time t is written as a function of the trajectory x_M. This trajectory is designed such that it approximates the black hole-relevant trajectory: $u \approx -\kappa^{-1}\ln[-\kappa p(u)]$ either (i) at the late-time ($t \to \infty$) for any value of b, or (ii) in a near-uniform plasma background ($b \ll 1$) during the entire accelerating phase. In either case, the spectrum relevant for the analog Hawking radiation is

$$\frac{dN}{d\omega_k d\Omega} \approx \frac{\mu^2}{8\pi\kappa}\frac{\omega_k}{e^{\omega_k/T_{\text{eff}}(\theta_k)}+1}\int dp_x \frac{\mathcal{F}_L(\mathbf{k}_\perp, P_\perp)\mathcal{F}_W(k_x, p_x)}{p_x^2}, \qquad (27)$$

where $T_{\text{eff}}(\theta_k) = \kappa/[(1+\cos\theta_k)\pi]$ is the effective temperature, $\kappa = 1/(2D)$, and $\mathcal{F}_{L/W}$ are complicated form factors due to the mirror's transverse/longitudinal distributions given in Reference [56]. Notice that the form factor $\mathcal{F}_L$ leads to diffraction, whereas $\mathcal{F}_W$ may enhance the production rate.

Using the PIC simulation parameter values: $\mu = 0.096$ eV, $\kappa = 0.2$ eV ($D = 0.5$ µm), $\omega_{p0} = 0.006$ eV, $W = 0.0074$ eV^{-1} (1.5 nm), $L = 254$ eV^{-1} (50 µm), and $b = 1$, the resulting analog Hawking temperature is $T_{\text{eff}} \sim 0.031$ eV (369 K) in the far infrared regime and the number of produced analog Hawking particles per laser crossing is

$$N \approx \int_0^\kappa d\omega_k \int d\Omega \, \frac{dN}{d\omega_k d\Omega} = (0.27 + 0.02),$$

where 0.27 and 0.02 correspond to the red and the blue areas in Figure 6, respectively.

Assuming a petawatt-class laser, such as that in the Apollon Laser Facility in Saclay, France, which can provide 1 laser shot per minute and 8 h of operation time per day, a 20-day experiment with a 100% detector efficiency would give the total yield of events as

$$N_{\text{detect}} = (1 \times 60 \times 8 \times 20) \times 1 \times N \approx 3000. \qquad (28)$$

It should be reminded that this value is highly idealized. Fluctuations of the physical parameters, especially that of the characteristic length of the density gradient, D, which we have not yet measured, would impact the expected Hawking photon yield.

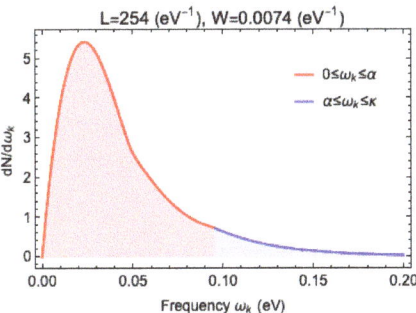

Figure 6. Frequency spectrum of analog Hawking particles [56]. The area shaded in red gives a total number of 0.27 while that shaded in blue gives 0.02.

7. Supersonic Gas Jet

As estimated in Reference [25], the gradient of the electron number density required for the experiment is $\sim 10^{20}/\text{cm}^3/\text{cm}$, which is attainable with a supersonic gas jet. There are several methods proposed in the literature, such as a shock wave generated induced by a laser that propagates perpendicular to the gas jet [57,58], and a supersonic gas flow impinged by a thin blade [59,60]. The estimated gradients of the electron number densities reached by different groups in [57,59,60] are summarized in Table 1. It is clear that, in principle, both methods can provide gradients that satisfy our requirement. As our first attempt, we chose the latter method for its simplicity.

Table 1. The maximum gradients of the electron number densities obtained from different groups. Our target value is also shown.

Method	Laser-Induced Shock Wave		Blade-Induced Shock Wave	Our Target Value
Groups	Kagonovich et al. (2014) [57]	Schmid et al. (2010) [59]	Fang-Chiang et al. (2020) [60]	
$(\frac{\partial n_e}{\partial x})_{max}$ [cm^{-4}]	10^{22}	$\sim 4 \times 10^{22}$	$\sim 10^{20}$	2×10^{20}

The supersonic gas jet can be realized by passing high-pressure gas through the de Laval nozzle, which is also known as the converging-diverging nozzle. The gas flow will reach sonic speed at the throat of the nozzle and then be accelerated in the diverging section to reach supersonic speed. Based on the design of the nozzle in [61], we produce our own nozzle to generate supersonic gas flow. Figure 7 shows the inner geometry and the image of the nozzle we built. The nozzle is connected to the tank of an air compressor that can provide air with pressure up to 8 atm. An electrically controlled valve is placed between the nozzle and the tank to control the flow.

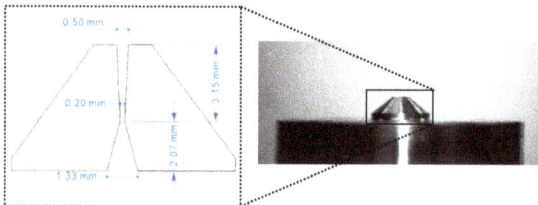

Figure 7. (**left**) Sketch of the nozzle used in our work. (**right**) The photo of our nozzle.

There are several techniques to quantitatively characterize the density of a supersonic gas jet, including interferometry and shadowgraphy [62–65], tomography [62,66,67], planar laser-induced fluorescence (PLIF) [60,68,69], Schlieren optics [70,71] (more references can be found in [71]). As the first step, we built a Schlieren imaging system in the lab for the jet characterization. Our Schlieren optics is equipped with a rainbow filter, which allows for the visualization of the gas jet as well as quantitative analysis of its refractive index. Figure 8 demonstrates the schematic diagram of our system.

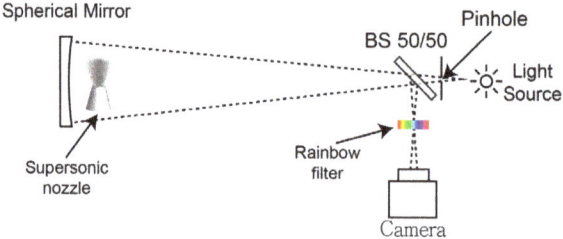

Figure 8. Schematic diagram of our Schlieren optics.

The principle behind the Schlieren optics is that the variation of the refractive index would diffract light. A rainbow filter that intercepts the diffracted light then provides information that would quantitatively determine the diffraction angle according to the color codes. The imaging system is calibrated with a plano-convex lens, whose refractive index is known. In this way, the map of the refractive index gradient, which is directly related to the gas density gradient, can be obtained.

Figure 9 shows the image using our Schlieren optics. The figure shows the supersonic jet produced by the nozzle. The so-called "shock diamonds" are clearly demonstrated, which is an indicator of the jet propagating with supersonic speed in the atmosphere.

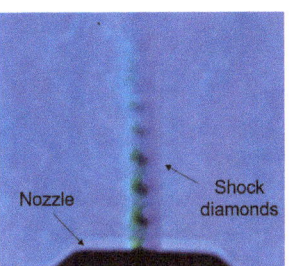

Figure 9. The obtained image with our Schlieren imaging system. Supersonic jet with shock diamonds are shown.

The design of the nozzle is verified by comparing the shock diamond structure from the data with the computational fluid dynamic (CFD) simulation result. The 3D fluid simulation was performed with OpenFOAM code. In the simulation, a compressible Navier–Stokes flow solver, rhoCentralFoam [72], is used to study the behavior of the supersonic jet.

With the conventional Abel inversion technique, the gradient of the refractive index was reconstructed and compared with the simulation result in Figure 10. Line profiles at different horizontal positions, y, relative to the axial center of the gas jet are shown in Figure 11. We found the positions of several peaks in the data agree reasonably with simulation results. This implies the behavior of our self-made supersonic nozzle is as expected and our Schlieren optics can characterize the profile of the supersonic jet. Further improvement is ongoing to obtain results with higher accuracy.

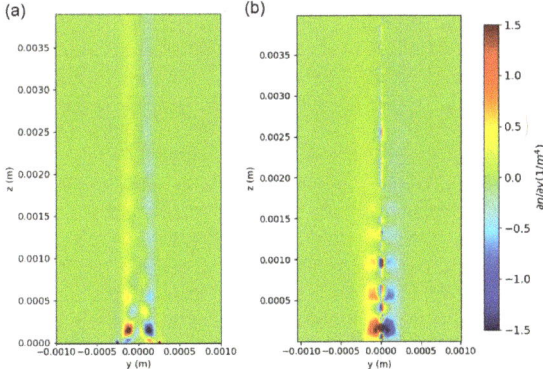

Figure 10. Two-dimensional map of the gradient of the refractive index, $\partial n / \partial y$, based on the (**a**) simulated result and (**b**) reconstructed data. Here, y and z are the horizontal and vertical coordinates, respectively.

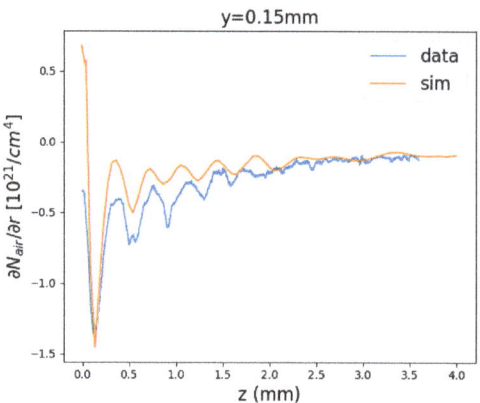

Figure 11. The line profile of $\partial n/\partial y$ as a function of the vertical position z. The data successfully captured the positions of the first few shock diamonds.

8. Superconducting Nanowire Single-Photon Hawking Detector

Observing the *Hawking* photons is the main goal and one of the major challenges of the planned AnaBHEL experiment. There is probably no single technology that satisfies all requirements. The detector must be a single photon detector, with efficiency close to 100%. The desired Hawking photon sensitivity wavelength range should be from 10 µm to 100 µm. A second detector design is required for the forward-moving *partner* photon with sensitivity at the UV (1–100 nm). The low expected signal yield and the potentially large asynchronous thermal and plasma-induced backgrounds set stringent detector timing requirements (to picosecond level or better). Since within the data acquisition timing window accidental coincidences may still be present, single photon pair polarization measurement will be required in order to unambiguously tag the pair as *Hawking* and *partner* photons. In addition to the above requirements, the detector should have a very fast recovery to avoid photon pile-up, a very low dark current rate (DCR), and the ability to cover relatively large areas.

Superconducting nanowire single-photon detectors (SNSPDs) satisfy most of the above requirements [73]. Thin superconducting films (∼10 nm) from materials such as NbN and WSi are sputtered on substrates. Subsequently, electron nanolithography is used to etch narrow wire structures (50–100 nm wide). The detector operates at a temperature below the Curie temperature T_C at an appropriate bias current that maximizes efficiency. Additional cavity structures are needed in order to bring the efficiency close to 100%.

The intrinsic time jitter of SNSPDs is ∼1 ps. Recently, time jitters using short straight nanowires and are found to be <3 ps for NbN [74] and 4.8 ps for WSi wires [75]. Thanks to their short reset time, these devices exhibit very high count rates at the level of hundreds of MHz. Although the expected Hawking photon yield is low, such a fast recovery detector reduces dramatically the probability of photon pileup (multiple counts in the same time window). The dark count rate (DCR) is extremely low at the level of one count for a period of hours, depending on the operating temperature and the bias current.

Typical SNSPD designs relevant to AnaBHEL are based on a superconducting nanowire patterned from a thin film of thickness between 5 and 10 nm. The most common nanowire design follows a meandering structure geometry. However, in our case, we need to consider specific structures that have sensitivity to polarization. SNSPDs are DC-biased with operation currents close to their critical currents so that efficiency is maximized. As discussed in [73], the detection process is divided into the following steps: (I) Photon absorption; (II) Creation of quasiparticles and phonons combined with their diffusion; (III) Emergence of a non-superconducting nanowire segment; (IV) Redirection of the bias current in readout circuitry, leading to a voltage pulse; and (V) detector recovery.

During step (II), the impinging near-IR photon photo-excites an electron (the relaxation of which leads to the formation of a cloud of quasiparticles and phonons). An instability of the superconducting state emerges due to the quasiparticle cloud, which results in the reduction of the effective critical current density and a part of the nanowire experiences a transition to the non-superconducting state (III). The occurrence of a normal-conducting hot spot in the nanowire can lead to the detection of the photon event as the current flowing through the bias resistor (bias current) is re-directed. Due to internal Joule heating, the resistive domain of the nanowire keeps growing, which leads to increased resistance at the level of kΩ. This significant non-zero resistivity causes the redirection of the bias current from the nanowire to the readout electronics (IV). Finally, the resistive domain is cooled down and the superconductivity is restored, bringing the nanowire back to its initial state (V).

Specific requirements of the AnaBHEL experiment photon sensors are summarized in Table 2 (first row). Realistic operational parameters and performance for typical SNSPD materials are also presented.

Table 2. SNSPD superconducting material properties and performance for specific designs summarized in [73]. Operating prototype WSi sensors for wavelengths close to 10 µm have been reported in [76].

Material	Curie T (K)	Operating T (K)	Wavelength (µm)	Efficiency [%]	t-Jitter (ps)
Requirements	<10	1–4	>10 (for UV: 1–100 ns)	>95	<10
NbN	10	0.8–2.1	1.55	92–98.2	40–106
NbTiN	14	2.5–2.8	1.55	92–99.5	14.8–34
WSi	3	0.12–2	1.55	93–98	150
MoSi	<3	0.8–1.2	1.55	80–87	26–76
MoSi (UV)	5	<4	0.250	85	60

In most applications, SNSPDs are coupled to fibers with a typical operation wavelength at the telecom window (1550 nm). AnaBHEL is an open-air experiment with a tight requirement of operation at mid to far infrared ($\lambda > 10$ µm) regime. As reported in [76,77], significant progress has been made for open-air longer wavelength operating SNSPDs. To achieve sensitivity for wavelengths longer than 10 µm, materials of lower Curie temperatures must be used. WSi is an example of such material. However, further R&D on other materials is needed.

In addition to efficiency, successful detection of the Hawking and partner photons in AnaBHEL requires good detector acceptance in both the forward and backward parts of the experimental apparatus. A single-pixel SNSPD covers a very small active area of the order of 10×10 µm^2. To maximize photon acceptance, a 1×1 mm^2 pixel array would be preferred. This kilopixel array has already been produced [78] and used in exoplanet transit spectroscopy in the mid-infrared regime.

Hawking Photon Sensor Fabrication and Characterization

In 2021, a R&D program was initiated in Taiwan to develop photon sensors for Hawking photon detection. Academia Sinica, NTU, and NCU groups are currently sharing equipment and laboratories for the fabrication and testing of prototype SNSPDs, the preferred technology for Hawking-photon sensors.

We have been producing NbN films of 10 nm thickness using the Academia Sinica magnetron sputtering machine shown in Figure 12 (Kao Duen Technology, Model: KD-UHV, N-11L17). The films grown on two different substrates, MgO and distributes Bragg reflector (DBR), were used. The films were sputtered at UHV pressure of 10^{-9} Torr. Sample NbN films on a sample holder are shown in Figure 13.

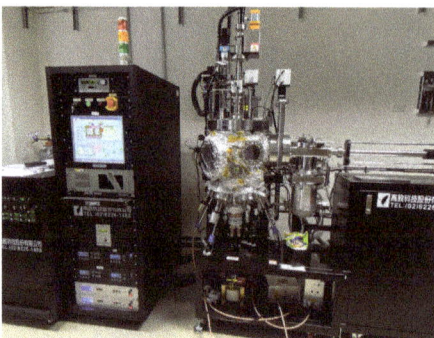

Figure 12. Sputtering machine for film production (Kao Duen Technology, Model: KD-UHV, N-11L17).

Figure 13. NbN films on a sample holder as they come out from the sputtering machine. The blue sample pieces are 10 nm-thick NbN on the DBR substrate. The gray sample piece shown in the middle is 10 nm-thick NbN grown on the MgO substrate. The difference in color is due to the fine NbN layer thickness.

The superconducting transition properties of the NbN films have been determined using magnetic susceptibility measurements with a SQUID, as well as electric resistivity measurements. In the left side of Figure 14, the MPMS3 SQUID magnetometer is used to measure the magnetic susceptibility of the NbN samples grown on MgO. On the right side of the same figure, the superconducting transition is shown as the material becomes diamagnetic. A 4 mm × 4 mm NbN sample was placed in the SQUID and its magnetic susceptibility was measured in the temperature range of 2–20K in steps as small as 0.1K per step as it approached the Curie temperature T_C.

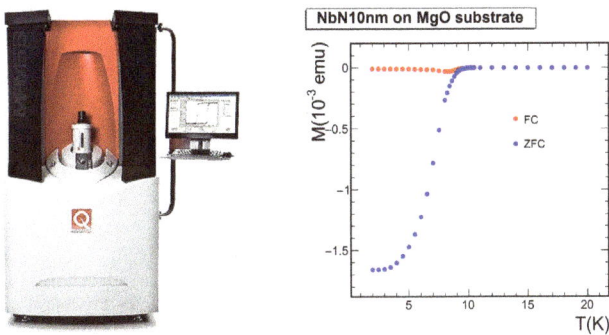

Figure 14. MPMS3 SQUID magnetometer.

Electric resistivity measurements were performed with the Triton 500 cryogenics system set up by the NTU-CCMS group, shown in Figure 15 (left). A superconducting transition measurement for a NbN film sample is shown in Figure 15 (right). Samples of 3×3 mm^2 sizes were prepared and glued on a sample holder with CMR-direct GE varnish. The sample was wire-bonded to readout pads on the sample holder using aluminum wires. The holder carried 20 readout pads, allowing us to perform more than the minimum requirement of 4 bonds. In this way, we ensured that we still had connectivity in case some bonds broke in very low operating temperatures. The resistivity was first measured at room temperature to check for possible oxidation or defects in the film growth process, and to test the connectivity of the wire bonds.

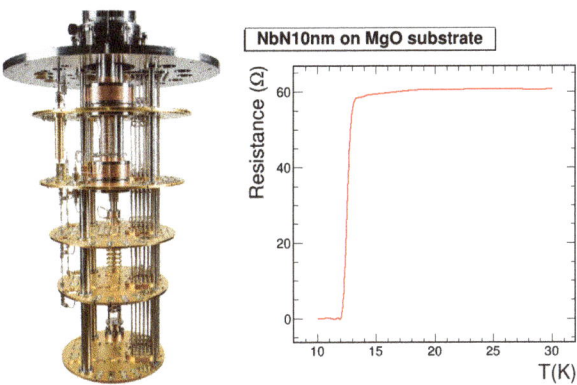

Figure 15. Triton 500 Cryogenics setup by the NTU-CCMS group (**left**). Resistance versus temperature measurement of a NbN film sample grown on MgO substrate (**right**).

After the successful characterization of the NbN-sample superconducting properties, we proceed with the production of prototype nanowire sensors. The performance requirements for the Hawking photon sensors necessitate the use of the electron beam lithography (EBL) for the etching of nanowires from the NbN films. Currently, nanowire prototypes of different widths and lengths are under design. The baseline design using an autoCAD drawing of a 20×20 µm^2 sensing area, with a nanowire with a width of 100 nm and a pitch of 100 nm, is shown in Figure 16 and the zoom-in is shown in Figure 17.

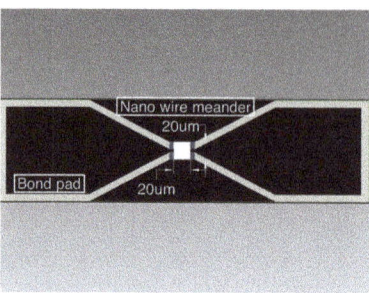

Figure 16. Baseline SNSPD sensor prototype autoCAD drawing.

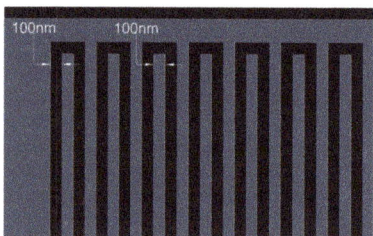

Figure 17. Nanowire prototype fabricated by the AnaBHEL Collaboration, shown here through the autoCAD zoom-in.

The SNSPD sensor prototypes are produced by the EBL, ELS-7000 ELIONIX, machine located in the Academia Sinica laboratories, as shown in Figure 18 (Left). Mean while, our AnaBHEL Collaboration has purchased a Junsun Tech MGS-500 sputtering machine installed at the NEMS center of NTU Figure 18 (Right), which will be fully utilized.

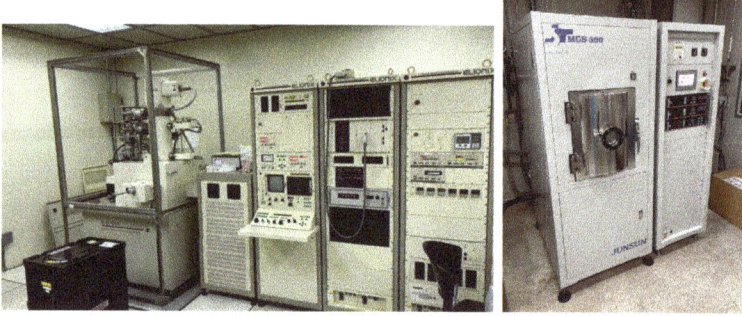

Figure 18. Electron beam lithography machine located in (**Left**) Academic Sinica laboratories (EBL, ELS-7000 ELIONIX); and (**Right**) Junsun Tech MGS-500 sputtering machine installed at the NEMS center of NTU.

In order to maximize the single photon detection efficiency, various structures such as cavities or Bragg reflectors can be utilized. As part of the ongoing R&D, distributed Bragg reflectors (DBR) have been grown in the NTU MEMS facility. The measured reflectivity of a DBR for a sensor sensitive at 1550 nm is shown in Figure 19. The good agreement with a finite-difference time-domain method (FDTD) simulation of the structure, gives us the confidence to proceed with new cavity designs optimal for longer wavelengths.

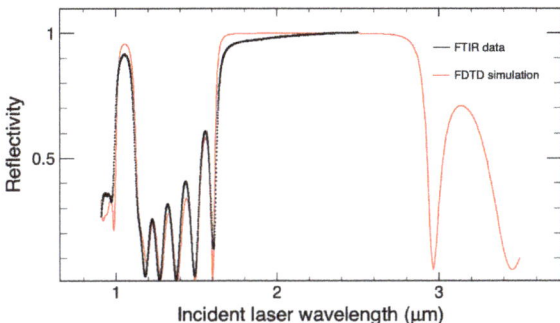

Figure 19. Reflectivity of a distributed Bragg reflector structure used to enhance the efficiency of sensors sensitive at 1550 nm. Data are shown in black and the FDTD simulation is in red.

We are currently in the process of setting up a system test bench to characterize the Hawking sensors, using single photons at the infrared. The setup includes a SPAD commercial sensor for single photon calibration shown in Figure 20. We plan to first verify the sensor operation at 1550 nm where most commercially available SNSPDs operate, as shown in Figure 21. Finally, the sensors will be tested at longer wavelengths relevant to the AnaBHEL experiment shown in Figure 22.

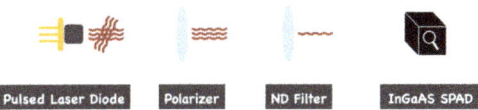

Figure 20. Single-photon calibration setup using SPAD.

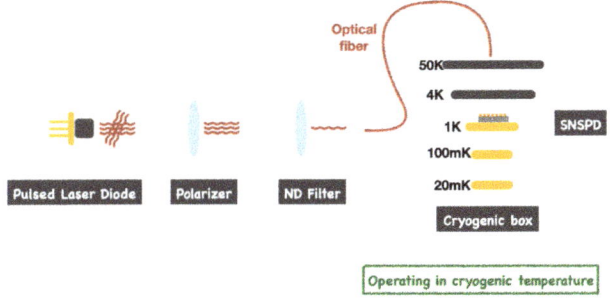

Figure 21. Test-bench setup for testing sensors at 1550 nm using fibers connected to sensors.

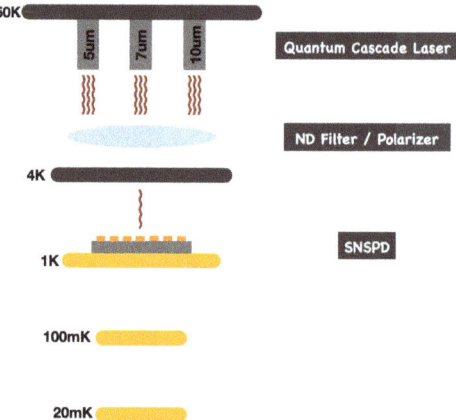

Figure 22. Test-bench setup for testing sensors in open-air transmission by bringing the lasers in the cryostat. In the actual AnaBHEL experiment, the entire experimental chamber would be embedded in a cryogenic system with a high vacuum.

9. Experimental Backgrounds

The propagation of the high-intensity laser through a plasma target would necessarily induce background photons that would compete against the rare Hawking signals. The plasma electrons perturbed by the propagating laser would execute non-trivial motions and can therefore emit photons. In addition, they can interact with the electromagnetic fields induced by the laser and charged particles, and also with the plasma ions through scatterings.

The radiations induced from interactions between the electrons and the background ions can be categorized into Thomson/Compton scattering and Bremsstrahlung. These processes have long been well studied and the radiation so induced can be estimated when the electron trajectories are given.

There is also the possibility of radiation caused by electron acceleration. The analytic solution for plasma accelerating in the blowout regime of plasma wakefield excitations has been studied by Stupakov [79], where it was shown that there are not only accelerated plasma inside the bubble but also charged particles that oscillate along the boundary of the plasma bubble. The work [79] was for the case of the plasma wakefield accelerator (PWFA) [45], but the method can also be applied to a laser wakefield accelerator (LWFA) [44], which is the basis of our flying plasma mirror. Thus we also expect to have the same type of electron motions that are oscillating around the plasma bubble. These electrons in the plasma wakefields perform a *figure-8 motion* in the plasma, and they can emit low-energy photons through synchrotron radiation. These photons are propagating in the direction parallel to the laser, which could affect the observation of the partner photons downstream. Therefore, we should study these electrons carefully.

In the following, we categorize the trajectories of the plasma electrons obtained from simulations by using a machine learning-based technique. We classify the electrons into several categories, according to their characteristic motions. After this classification, we are able to identify the leading radiation processes for the electrons and evaluate the radiation spectrum. We use SMILEI [80] for particle-in-cell (PIC) simulations and python and the scikit-learn library [81] for the clustering analysis.

9.1. Simulation Setup

The PIC simulations are in 2D and we refer to the coordinate as x and y. The simulation box size is 250 μm × 150 μm, i.e., $0 \leq x \leq 250$ μm, -75 μm $\leq y \leq 75$ μm, with 4000×400 grids. A Gaussian laser with 800nm wavelength and $a_0 = 5.0$ is applied at the boundary of $x = 0$ (left end of the simulation) and travels in the x-positive direction. We place helium gas in the simulation box that can be ionized by the impinging laser. The helium density ρ_{He} is given by

$$\rho_{\text{He}} = \begin{cases} \frac{n_0}{2}(1 + e^{-(x-\ell_0)/2})^2, & x \geq \ell_0, \\ 2n_0, & \text{else,} \end{cases} \quad (29)$$

where $n_0 = 1 \text{ mol}/\text{m}^3$ and $\ell_0 = 10 \text{ μm}$. We do the simulation for 265 time steps, where each step is 3.82 femtoseconds in real-time.

9.2. Categorization of Electron Motions

Following the categorization technique introduced in [82], we identify electron trajectories that would induce photons that dominate the background signals. The trajectory categorization introduced in [82] is essentially clustering in momentum space using k-mean clustering method.

Let us denote the i-th particle's trajectory by $p_i(t) = (x_i(t), y_i(t))$, where $x_i(t)$ and $y_i(t)$ are the x, y coordinate of the i-th particle at time t, respectively. The total time steps of the simulation are denoted as T. (In this case, T = 265). If we have N particles to track, then our data set $\mathcal{S}$ will be $\mathcal{S} = \{p_i | i \in 1 \ldots N\}$. Let us denote the Fourier coefficient of $x_i(t)$ and $y_i(t)$ as $\tilde{x}_i(k)$ and $\tilde{y}_i(k)$, respectively. The categorization will be done with the following steps.

1. Restrict the tracked particle data to those that have been simulated for more than 380 femtoseconds.
2. Prepare a data set,

$$\tilde{\mathcal{S}} = \{(\tilde{x}_i(k_1), \tilde{x}_i(k_2), \ldots, \tilde{x}_i(k_T), \tilde{y}_i(k_1), \ldots, \tilde{y}_i(k_T), \\ \bar{y}_i, \bar{p}_{ix}, \bar{p}_{iy}, a_y^{\max}, a_y^{\min}), \quad i \in 1, \ldots, N\}, \quad (30)$$

where $\bar{p}_{ix}$ and $\bar{p}_{iy}$ are the mean of momentum of the i-th particle in x and y direction, respectively, $\bar{y}_i$ is the mean of the y-coordinate of the i-th particle, $a_y^{\max}$ and $a_y^{\min}$ are the maximum and minimum of the acceleration in the y-direction, and k_t is the corresponding frequency of the t-th Fourier coefficient.

3. Calculate k principal component values (PCVs) from the data set. This reduces the space of clustering from $2T + 5$-dimensional vector space to k dimensional vector space.
4. Perform k-mean clustering in the k-dimensional space, for a given number of clusters K.

Our choice of data set at step 2 is different from the one used in [82], where we have additional value $\bar{y}_i$ and the information of its acceleration in the y-direction. We added these since the longitudinal behavior is quite important for the experimental purpose, and indeed, by adding these we were able to separate the modes into more reasonable categories.

9.3. Classification Results

We have used $k = 30$, $K = 12$ in the following, i.e., we classify the particles into 12 sets by using 30 PCs. Although we have classified them into 12 categories, since we have included the mean value of y coordinate, $\bar{y}_i$, into the data, we obtain pairs of categories that are almost symmetric along $y = 0$. In the following, we classify those two into the same category, since their physical processes are the same.

9.3.1. Wakefield Accelerated Electrons

The first kind is the electrons accelerated with the LWFA process. They are accelerated in the forward direction, to a highly relativistic regime $\beta \sim 1$. These are shown in Figure 23.

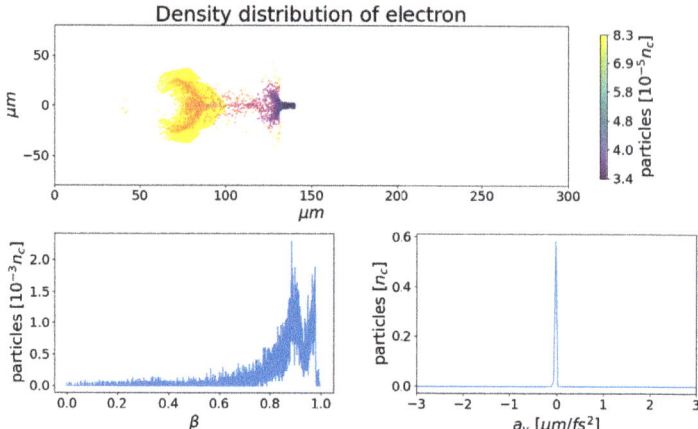

Figure 23. Electrons accelerated by the laser wakefield acceleration (LWFA) mechanism. The top figure is the electron density distribution shown by different colors The bottom left figure is the velocity distribution in $\beta = v/c$, where v is the velocity of the electron and c is the speed of light. bottom right of the figure shows the acceleration of the electron on the y-axis.

These electrons can radiate photons by interacting with the nuclei, i.e., through Thomson/Compton scattering or as Bremsstrahlung.

9.3.2. Snowplowed Electrons

Snowplowed electrons are the ones that are pushed forward by the laser's ponderomotive potential and are clustered at the front of the laser pulse.

Figure 24 is a snapshot of the snowplowed electrons.

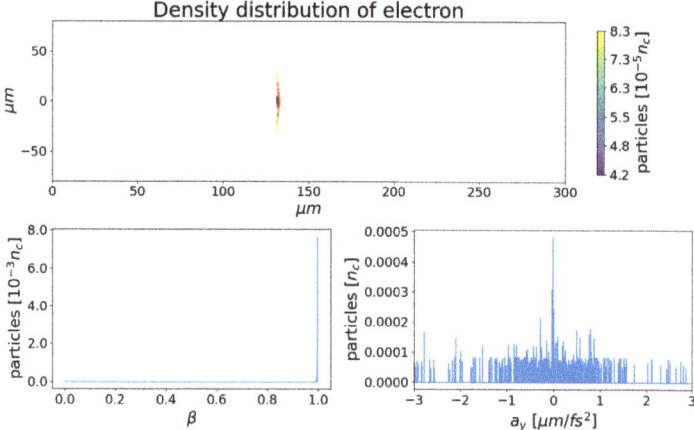

Figure 24. Snowplowed electrons. The top figure is the electron density distribution shown by color. The bottom left figure is the velocity distribution in $\beta = v/c$, where v is the velocity of the electron and c is the speed of light. The bottom right of the figure shows the acceleration of the electron on the y-axis.

9.3.3. Backward Scattered Electrons

These electrons typically have $\beta \sim 0.7$ and are shown in Figure 25.

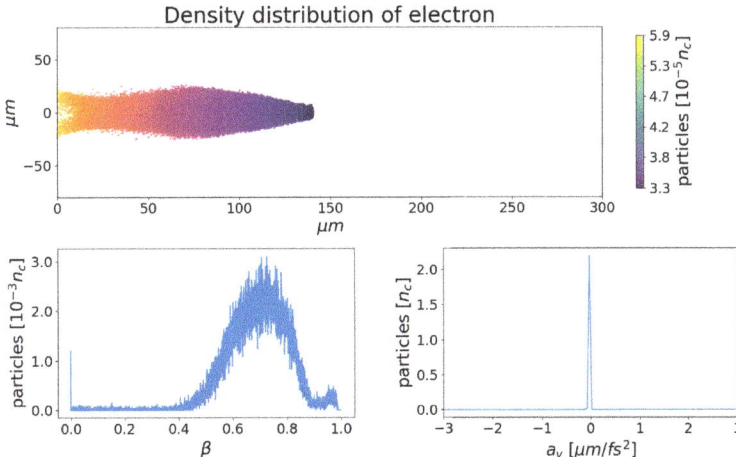

Figure 25. Backward accelerated electrons. The top figure is the electron density distribution shown by color. The bottom left figure is the velocity distribution in $\beta = v/c$, where v is the velocity of the electron and c is the speed of light. bottom right of the figure shows the acceleration of the electron on the y-axis.

They might contribute to the background radiation via Thomson/Compton scattering or Bremsstrahlung.

9.3.4. Slide-Away Electrons

There are certain fractions of plasma electrons that are pushed by the transverse plasma wakefields and propagate in the transverse direction. In practice, they would not affect the experiment since they are not moving toward the sensor, however, one would have to consider their hitting and reflection from the gas nozzle, which would induce background photon events.

Figure 26 is a snapshot of slide-away electrons. As pointed out previously, slide-away electrons slide toward the positive y direction, and are classified into a different category through the process.

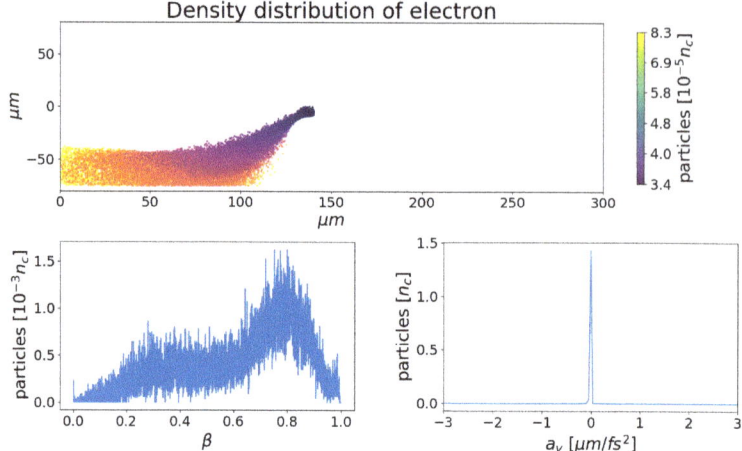

Figure 26. Slide-away electrons. The top figure is the electron density distribution shown by color. The bottom left figure is the velocity distribution in $\beta = v/c$, where v is the velocity of the electron and c is the speed of light. bottom right of the figure shows the acceleration of the electron on the y-axis.

9.3.5. Transverse Oscillating Electrons

The last ones are the oscillating electrons. These are the electrons that are attracted by the Coulomb force of the plasma ion bubble and they oscillate around the laser trajectory in the traverse direction. Figure 27 shows the density distribution, velocity, and acceleration in the y-direction of these electrons.

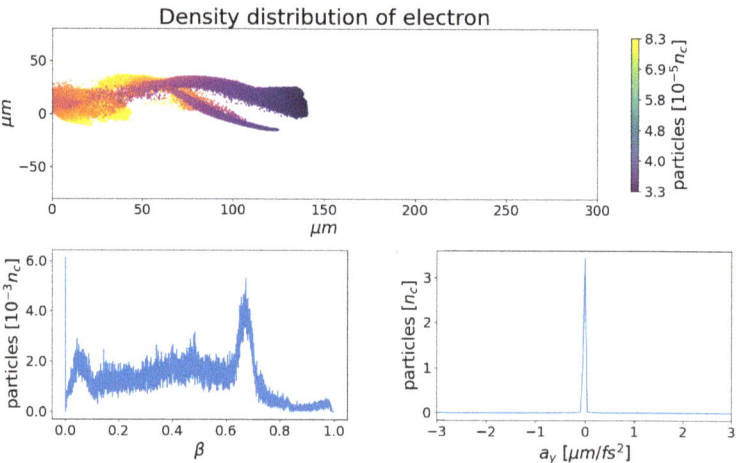

Figure 27. Oscillating electrons. The top figure is the electron density distribution shown by color. The bottom left figure is the velocity distribution in $\beta = v/c$, where v is the velocity of the electron and c is the speed of light. bottom right of the figure shows the acceleration of the electrons in the y-axis.

This distribution has a tail that extends into the non-relativistic region. We expect that they would emit photons through synchrotron radiation, which can affect the identification of the Hawking photon signals.

9.3.6. Low-Frequency Soliton Radiations

We note that laser–plasma interaction also induces additional low-frequency background photons emitted by collective effects such as solitons, which are not included in the above discussion. Such near-plasma-frequency radiation was first pointed out by Bulanov [83] and has been recorded experimentally [35]. The radiation released by the solitons propagates essentially in the forward direction, where the seek-after *partner photon* signals are expected to be in the EUV range. Thus such soliton-induced radiation signals may not render competing backgrounds to our experiment. Nevertheless, we will further investigate this collective soliton effect to determine whether some of such radiation might be reflected backward so as to confuse the Hawking photons, whose wavelengths are indeed close.

Our next step is to estimate the radiation with the corresponding process according to these categories, and compare the result with the radiation spectrum generated by the PIC simulation code and assess their impacts on the AnaBHEL experiment.

10. Strategy of AnaBHEL

We execute the AnaBHEL project based on the following strategy.

Stage-1

R&D of the key components, namely the superconducting nanowire single-photon Hawking detector and the supersonic gas jet with the designed density profile, are mainly carried out at the Leung Center for Cosmology and Particle Astrophysics (LeCosPA), National Taiwan University. These are going well, as reported in the previous sections.

Stage-2

Dynamics of the laser-induced plasma mirror trajectory and its correspondence with the plasma density profile. The first attempt was scheduled at Kansai Photon Science Institute (KPSI) in Kyoto, Japan, using its PW laser facility, in the summer of 2022. We expect that the iterative interplay between the gas jet design and the laser–plasma interaction data acquisition is indispensable.

Stage-3

The full-scale analog black hole experiment used to detect Hawking and partner photons will be pursued when the Hawking detector is fully developed and the plasma mirror trajectory is characterized. It is our desire that the Stage-3 experiment be carried out at the Apollon Laser Facility in Saclay, France.

11. Conclusions

The information loss paradox associated with the black hole Hawking evaporation is arguably one of the most challenging issues in fundamental physics because it touches on a potential conflict between the two pillars of modern physics, i.e., general relativity and quantum field theory. Unfortunately, typical astrophysical stellar-size black holes are too cold and too young to be able to shed light on this paradox. Laboratory investigation of analog black holes may help to shed some light on this critical issue.

There have been various proposals for analog black holes. Different from the approach of invoking fluids (ordinary and superfluid via the Bose–Einstein condensate) that tries to mimic the curved spacetime related to the black hole environment, our approach attempts to create an accelerating boundary condition to a flat spacetime while relying on its nontrivial interplay with the quantum vacuum fluctuations. We believe that these different approaches have their respective pros and cons, and are complementary to each other. Together, a more complete picture of black hole evaporation would hopefully emerge.

Since its launch in 2018, the AnaBHEL collaboration has shown progress (although, there was the COVID-19 pandemic). Although the R&D is not yet complete, we are confident that the end is in sight.

Author Contributions: Conceptualization, P.C. and G.M.; methodology, P.C.; theory, K.-N.L., P.C.; hardware, J.N., Y.-K.L., C.-E.L., S.-X.L., S.P., H.-Y.W., W.-P.W., M.B., J.-F.G., B.T. software, Y.-K.L., N.W.; validation, H.T.; investigation, A.P., M.K., Y.F., K.K., Y.-K.L., P.C., J.W.; writing—original draft preparation, P.C.; writing—review and editing, all authors; visualization, Y.-K.L., H.-Y.W., N.W.; project administration, P.C., S.P., B.T.; funding acquisition, P.C., S.P. All authors have read and agreed to the published version of the manuscript.

Funding: The Taiwan team and P.C. are supported by Taiwan's Ministry of Science and Technology (MOST) under project number 110-2112-M-002-031, and by the Leung Center for Cosmology and Particle Astrophysics (LeCosPA), National Taiwan University. S.P. is further supported by Taiwan's Ministry of Education (grant MoE/NTU grant number: 111L104013). M.K. and A.P. are supported by JSPS Kakenhi JP19H00669 and JP19KK0355 and Strategic Grant by the QST President: IRI. K.K. is supported by JSPS Kakenhi (grant number JP21H01103).

Data Availability Statement: Not applicable.

Acknowledgments: The authors are grateful to the Computer and Information Networking Center, National Taiwan University, for the support of the high-performance computing facilities.

Conflicts of Interest: The funders had no role in the design of the study; in the collection, analyses, or interpretation of data; in the writing of the manuscript, or in the decision to publish the results.

References

1. Hawking, S.W. Particle Creation by Black Holes. *Commun. Math. Phys.* **1975**, *43*, 199; Erratum in *Commun. Math. Phys.* **1976**, *46*, 206. [CrossRef]
2. Hawking, S.W. Breakdown of predictability in gravitational collapse. *Phys. Rev. D* **1976**, *14*, 2460–2473. [CrossRef]
3. Susskind, L.; Thorlacius, L.; Uglum, J. The stretched horizon and black hole complementarity. *Phys. Rev. D* **1993**, *48*, 3743–3761. [CrossRef] [PubMed]
4. Almheiri, A.; Marolf, D.; Polchinski, J.; Sully, J. Black Holes: Complementarity or Firewalls? *J. High Energy Phys.* **2013**, *2*, 62. [CrossRef]
5. Almheiri, A.; Marolf, D.; Polchinski, J.; Stanford, D.; Sully, J. An apologia for firewalls. *J. High Energy Phys.* **2013**, *9*, 18. [CrossRef]
6. Mathur, S.D. The information paradox: A pedagogical introduction. *Class. Quant. Grav.* **2009**, *26*, 224001. [CrossRef]
7. Chen, P.; Ong, Y.C.; Page, D.N.; Sasaki, M.; Yeom, D. Naked Black Hole Firewalls. *Phys. Rev. Lett.* **2016**, *116*, 161304. [CrossRef]
8. Bousso, R.; Porrati, M. Soft hair as a soft wig. *Class. Quant. Grav.* **2017**, *34*, 204001. [CrossRef]
9. Giddings, S.B. Gravitational dressing, soft charges, and perturbative gravitational splitting. *Phys. Rev. D* **2019**, *100*, 126001. [CrossRef]
10. Hawking, S.; Perry, M.; Strominger, A. Soft Hair on Black Holes. *Phys. Rev. Lett.* **2016**, *116*, 231301. [CrossRef]
11. Chen, P.; Ong, Y.C.; Yeom, D. Black Hole Remnants and the Information Loss Paradox. *Phys. Rep.* **2015**, *603*, 1–45. [CrossRef]
12. Almheiri, A.; Engelhardt, N.; Marolf, D.; Maxfield, H. The entropy of bulk quantum fields and the entanglement wedge of an evaporating black hole. *J. High Energy Phys.* **2019**, *12*, 063. [CrossRef]
13. Almheiri, A.; Mahajan, R.; Maldacena, J.; Zhao, Y. The Page curve of the Hawking radiation from semiclassical geometry. *J. High Energy Phys.* **2020**, *3*, 149. [CrossRef]
14. Penington, G.; Shenker, S.H.; Stanford, D.; Yang, Z. Replica wormholes and the black hole interior. *J. High Energy Phys.* **2022**, *3*, 205. [CrossRef]
15. Almheiri, A.; Hartman, T.; Maldacena, J.; Shaghoulian, E.; Tajdini, A. Replica Wormholes and the Entropy of the Hawking Radiation. *J. High Energy Phys.* **2020**, *5*, 13. [CrossRef]
16. Chen, P.; Sasaki, M.; Yeom, D.; Yoon, J. Solving information loss paradox via Euclidean path integral. *Int. J. Mod. Phys. D* **2022**, *8*, 14.
17. Unruh, W.G. Experimental Black-Hole Evaporation? *Phys. Rev. Lett.* **1981**, *46*, 1351. [CrossRef]
18. Unruh, W.G. Sonic analogue of black holes and the effects of high frequencies on black hole evaporation. *Phys. Rev. D* **1995**, *51*, 2827. [CrossRef]
19. Schützhold, R.; Unruh, W.G. Hawking Radiation in an Electromagnetic Waveguide? *Phys. Rev. Lett.* **2005**, *95*, 031301. [CrossRef]
20. Yablonovitch, E. Accelerating reference frame for electromagnetic waves in a rapidly growing plasma: Unruh-Davies-Fulling-DeWitt radiation and the nonadiabatic Casimir effect. *Phys. Rev. Lett.* **1989**, *62*, 1742. [CrossRef]
21. Belgiorno, F.; Cacciatori, S.L.; Clerici, M.; Gorini, V.; Ortenzi, G.; Rizzi, L.; Rubino, E.; Sala, V.G.; Faccio, D. Hawking Radiation from Ultrashort Laser Pulse Filaments. *Phys. Rev. Lett.* **2010**, *105*, 203901. [CrossRef] [PubMed]
22. De Nova, M.; Golubkov, J.R.; Kolobov, K.; Steinhauer, J. Observation of thermal Hawking radiation and its temperature in an analogue black hole. *Nature* **2019**, *569*, 688. [CrossRef] [PubMed]
23. Chen, P.; Tajima, T. Testing Unruh Radiation with Ultraintense Lasers. *Phys. Rev. Lett.* **1999**, *83*, 256. [CrossRef]
24. Fulling, S.A.; Davies, P. Radiation from a moving mirror in two dimensional space-time: Conformal anomaly. *Proc. R. Soc. Lond.* **1976**, *A348*, 393.

25. Chen, P.; Mourou, G. Accelerating Plasma Mirrors to Investigate the Black Hole Information Loss Paradox. *Phy. Rev. Lett.* **2017**, *118*, 045001. [CrossRef] [PubMed]
26. Chen, P.; Mourou, G. Trajectory of a flying plasma mirror traversing a target with density gradient. *Phys. Plasmas* **2020**, *27*, 123106. [CrossRef]
27. Aspect, A.; Grangier, P.; Roger, G. Experimental Realization of Einstein-Podolsky-Rosen-Bohm Gedankenexperiment: A New Violation of Bell's Inequalities. *Phys. Rev. Lett.* **1982**, *49*, 91. [CrossRef]
28. Bulanov, S.V.; Esirkepov, T.Z.; Tajima, T. Light Intensification towards the Schwinger Limit. *Phys. Rev. Lett.* **2003**, *91*, 085001. [CrossRef]
29. Naumova, N.M.; Nees, J.A.; Sokolov, I.V.; Hou, B.; Mourou, G.A. Relativistic Generation of Isolated Attosecond Pulses in a λ^3 Focal Volume. *Phys. Rev. Lett.* **2004**, *92*, 063902-1. [CrossRef]
30. Esirkepov, T.Z.; Bulanov, S.V.; Tajima, T. Flying Mirrors: Relativistic Plasma Wake Caustic Light Intensification. In *Quantum Aspects of Beam Physics*; Chen, P., Reil, K., Eds.; World Scientific: Singapore, 2004; p. 186.
31. Bulanov, S.V.; Esirkepov, T.Z.; Kando, M.; Pirozhkov, A.S.; Rosanov, N.N. Relativistic mirrors in plasmas. Novel results and perspectives. *Physics-Uspekhi* **2013**, *56*, 429. [CrossRef]
32. Pirozhkov, A.; Ma, J.; Kando, M.; Esirkepov, T.Z.; Fukuda, Y.; Chen, L.-M.; Daito, I.; Ogura, K.; Homma, T.; Hayashi, Y.; et al. Frequency multiplication of light back-reflected from a relativistic wake wave. *Phys. Plasmas* **2007**, *14*, 123106. [CrossRef]
33. Kando, M.; Fukuda, Y.; Pirozhkov, A.S.; Ma, J.; Daito, I.; Chen, L.-M.; Esirkepov, T.Z.; Ogura, K.; Homma, T.; Hayashi, Y.; et al. Demonstration of Laser-Frequency Upshift by Electron-Density Modulations in a Plasma Wakefield. *Phys. Rev. Lett.* **2007**, *99*, 135001. [CrossRef] [PubMed]
34. Pirozhkov, A.S.; Esirkepov, T.Z.; Kando, M.; Fukuda, Y.; Ma, J.; Chen, L.-M.; Daito, I.; Ogura, K.; Homma, T.; Hayashi, Y.; et al. Demonstration of light reflection from the relativistic mirror. *J. Phys. Conf. Ser.* **2008**, *112*, 042050. [CrossRef]
35. Kando, M.; Pirozhkov, A.S.; Kawase, K.; Esirkepov, T.Z.; Fukuda, Y.; Kiriyama, H.; Okada, H.; Daito, I.; Kameshima, T.; Hayashi, Y.; et al. Enhancement of Photon Number Reflected by the Relativistic Flying Mirror. *Phys. Rev. Lett.* **2009**, *103*, 235003. [CrossRef] [PubMed]
36. Wilczek, F. Quantum Purity at a Small Price: Easing a Black Hole Paradox. In Proceedings of the Houston Conference Black Holes, Houston, TX, USA, 16–18 January 1992.
37. Hotta, M.; Schutzhold, R.; Unruh, W.G. Partner particles for moving mirror radiation and black hole evaporation. *Phys. Rev. D* **2015**, *91*, 124060. [CrossRef]
38. Bardeen, J. Black hole evaporation without an event horizon. *arXiv* **2014**, arXiv:1406.4098.
39. Page, D.N. Information in black hole radiation. *Phys. Rev. Lett.* **1993**, *71*, 3743. [CrossRef]
40. Hotta, M.; Sugita, A. The Fall of Black Hole Firewall: Natural Nonmaximal Entanglement for Page Curve. *Prog. Theor. Exp. Phys.* **2015**, *2015*, 123B04. [CrossRef]
41. Chen, P.; Yeom, D.-H. Entropy evolution of moving mirrors and the information loss problem. *Phys. Rev. D* **2017**, *96*, 025016. [CrossRef]
42. Good, M.R.R.; Linder, E.V.; Wilczek, F. Moving mirror model for quasithermal radiation fields. *Phys. Rev. D* **2020**, *101*, 025012. [CrossRef]
43. Good, M.R.R.; Linder, E.V. Eternal and evanescent black holes and accelerating mirror analogs. *Phys. Rev. D* **2018**, *97*, 065006. [CrossRef]
44. Tajima, T.; Dawson, J.M. Laser Electron Accelerator. *Phys. Rev. Lett.* **1979**, *43*, 267. [CrossRef]
45. Chen, P.; Dawson, J.M.; Huff, R.; Katsouleas, T. Acceleration of Electrons by the Interaction of a Bunched Electron Beam with a Plasma. *Phys. Rev. Lett.* **1985**, *54*, 693. [CrossRef]
46. Chen, P.; Reil, K. (Eds.) *Quantum, Aspects of Beam Physics*; World Scientific: Singapore, 2004.
47. Mourou, G.; Tajima, T. Zetta-Exawatt Science and Technology. *Eur. Phys. J. Spec. Top.* **2014**, *223*. Available online: https://portail.polytechnique.edu/izest/en/en/science-techn/science (accessed on 7 December 2022).
48. Davies, P.C.W.; Fulling, S.A. Radiation from moving mirrors and from black holes. *Proc. R. Soc. A* **1977**, *356*, 237.
49. Birrell, N.D.; Davies, P.C.W. Quantum Fields in Curved Space. In *Cambridge Monographs on Mathematical Physics*; Cambridge University Press: Cambridge, UK, 1984.
50. Liu, Y.K.; Chen, P.; Fang, Y. Reflectivity and Spectrum of Relativistic Flying Plasma Mirrors. *Phys. Plasmas* **2021**, *10*, 103301. [CrossRef]
51. DeWitt, S. Quantum field theory in curved spacetime. *Phys. Rep.* **1975**, *19*, 295. [CrossRef]
52. Barton, G.; Calogeracos, A. On the quantum electrodynamics of a dispersive mirror.: I. mass shifts, radiation, and radiative reaction. *Ann. Phys. N. Y.* **1995**, *238*, 227. [CrossRef]
53. Nicolaevici, N. Quantum radiation from a partially reflecting moving mirror. *Class. Quant. Grav.* **2001**, *18*, 619. [CrossRef]
54. Nicolaevici, N. Semitransparency effects in the moving mirror model for Hawking radiation. *Phys. Rev. D* **2009**, *80*, 125003. [CrossRef]
55. Lin, K.-N.; Chou, C.-E.; Chen, P. Particle production by a relativistic semitransparent mirror in (1+3)D Minkowski spacetime. *Phys. Rev. D* **2021**, *103*, 025014. [CrossRef]
56. Lin, K.-N.; Chen, P. Particle production by a relativistic semitransparent mirror of finite transverse size. *arXiv* **2021**, arXiv:2107.09003.

57. Kaganovich, D.; Gordon, D.F.; Helle, H.; Ting, A. Shaping gas jet plasma density profile by laser generated shock waves. *J. Appl. Phys.* **2014**, *116*, 013304. [CrossRef]
58. Helle, M.H.; Gordon, D.F.; Kaganovich, D.; Chen, Y.; Palastro, J.P.; Ting, A. Laser-Accelerated Ions from a Shock-Compressed Gas Foil. *Phys. Rev. Lett.* **2016**, *117*, 165001. [CrossRef] [PubMed]
59. Schmid, K.; Buck, A.; Sears, C.M.S.; Mikhailova, J.M.; Tautz, R.; Herrmann, D.; Geissler, M.; Krausz, F.; Veisz, L. Density-transition based electron injector for laser driven wakefield accelerators. *Phys. Rev. ST Accel. Beams* **2010**, *13*, 091301. [CrossRef]
60. Fang-Chiang, L.; Mao, H.-S.; Tsai, H.-E.; Ostermayr, T.; Swanson, K.K.; Barber, S.K.; Steinke, S.; van Tilborg, J.; Geddes, C.G.R.; Leemans, W.P. Gas density structure of supersonic flows impinged on by thin blades for laser–plasma accelerator targets. *Phys. Fluids* **2020**, *32*, 066108. [CrossRef]
61. Hsu-hsin, C. Construction of a 10-TW Laser of High Coherence and Stability and Its Application in Laser-Cluster Interaction and X-ray Lasers. Ph.D. Thesis, National Taiwan University, Taipei, Taiwan, 2005.
62. Golovin, G.; Banerjee, S.; Chen, S.; Powers, N.; Liu, C.; Yan, W.; Zhang, J.; Zhang, P.; Zhao, B.; Umstadter, D. Control and optimization of a staged laser-wakefield accelerator. *Nucl. Instrum. Methods Phys. Res. Sect. A* **2016**, *830*, 375. [CrossRef]
63. Kim, K.N.; Hwangbo, Y.; Jeon, S.-G.; Kim, J. Characteristics of the Shock Structure for Transition Injection in Laser Wakefield Acceleration. *J. Korean Phys. Soc.* **2018**, *73*, 561. [CrossRef]
64. Fang, M.; Zhang, Z.; Wang, W.; Liu, J.; Li, R. Sharp plasma pinnacle structure based on shockwave for an improved laser wakefield accelerator. *Plasma Phys. Controlled Fusion* **2018**, *60*, 075008. [CrossRef]
65. Hansen, A.M.; Haberberger, D.; Katz, J.; Mastrosimone, D.; Follett, R.K.; Froula, D.H. Supersonic gas-jet characterization with interferometry and Thomson scattering on the OMEGA Laser System. *Rev. Sci. Instrum.* **2018**, *89*, 10C103. [CrossRef]
66. Couperus, J.P.; Köhler, A.; Wolterink, T.A.W.; Jochmann, A.; Zarini, O.; Bastiaens, H.M.J.; Boller, K.J.; Irman, A.; Schramm, U. Tomographic characterisation of gas-jet targets for laser wakefield acceleration. *Nucl. Instrum. Methods Phys. Res. Sect. A* **2016**, *830*, 504. [CrossRef]
67. Adelmann, A.; Hermann, B.; Ischebeck, R.; Kaluza, M.C.; Locans, U.; Sauerwein, N.; Tarkeshian, R. Real-Time Tomography of Gas-Jets with a Wollaston Interferometer. *Appl. Sci.* **2018**, *8*, 443. [CrossRef]
68. Epstein, A.H. MIT Gas Turbine Lab Report. 1974; p. 117. Available online: https://www.gas-turbine-lab.mit.edu/gtl-reports (accessed on 7 December 2022).
69. Hanson, R.K.; Seitzman, J.M. *Handbook of Flow Visualization*; Routledge: London, UK, 2018; pp. 225–237.
70. Settles, G.S. *Schlieren and Shadowgraph Techniques*; Spinger: Berlin, Germany, 2001.
71. Mariani, R.; Lim, H.D.; Zang, B.; Vevek, U.S.; New, T.H.; Cui, Y.D. On the application of non-standard rainbow schlieren technique upon supersonic jets. *J. Vis.* **2020**, *23*, 383–393. [CrossRef]
72. Greenshields, C.J.; Wellerm, H.G.; Gasparini, L.; Reese, J.M. Implementation of semi-discrete, non-staggered central schemes in a colocated, polyhedral, finite volume framework, for high-speed viscous flows. *Int. J. Number. Methods Fluids* **2010**, *63*, 1. [CrossRef]
73. Zadeh, I.E.; Chang, J.; Los, J.W.N.; Gyger, S.; Elshaari, A.W.; Steinhauer, S.; Dorenbos, S.N.; Zwiller, V. Superconducting nanowire single-photon detectors: A perspective on evolution, state-of-the-art, future developments, and applications. *Appl. Phys. Lett.* **2021**, *118*, 190502. [CrossRef]
74. Korzh, B.; Zhao, Q.-Y.; Allmaras, J.P.; Frasca, S.; Autry, T.M.; Bersin, E.A.; Beyer, A.D.; Briggs, R.M.; Bumble, B.; Conlangelo, M.; et al. Demonstration of sub-3 ps temporal resolution with a superconducting nanowire single-photon detector. *Nat. Photonics* **2020**, *14*, 250–255. [CrossRef]
75. Korzh, B.; Zhao, Q.-Y.; Frasca, S.; Zhu, D.; Ramirez, E.; Bersin, E.; Colangelo, M.; Dane, A.E.; Beyer, A.D.; Allmaras, J.; et al. Wsi superconducting nanowire single photon detector with a temporal resolution below 5 ps. In Proceedings of the Conference on Lasers and Electro-Optics, Hong Kong, China, 29 July–3 August 2018; p. FW3F.3.
76. Verma, V.B.; Korzh, B.; Walter, A.B.; Lita, A.E.; Briggs, R.M.; Colangelo, M.; Zhai, Y.; Wollman, E.E.; Beyer, A.D.; Allmaras, J.P.; et al. Single-Photon detection in the mid-infrared up to 10 micron wavelength using tungsten silicide superconducting nanowire detectors. *APL Photonics* **2021**, *6*, 056101. [CrossRef]
77. Wollman, E.; Verma, V.B.; Walter, A.B.; Chiles, J.; Korzh, B.; Allmaras, J.P.; Zhai, Y.; Lita, A.E.; McCaughan, A.N.; Schmidt, E.; et al. Recent advances in superconducting nanowire single-photon detector technology for exoplanet transit spectroscopy in the mid-infrared. *J. Astron. Telesc. Instruments Syst.* **2021**, *7*, 011004. [CrossRef]
78. Wollman, E.; Verma, V.B.; Lita, A.E.; Farr, W.H.; Shaw, M.D.; Mirin, R.P.; Nam, S.W. Kilopixel array of superconducting nanowire single-photon detectors. *Opt. Express* **2019**, *27*, 35279–35289. [CrossRef]
79. Stupakov, G. Short-range wakefields generated in the blowout regime of plasma-wakefield acceleration. *Phys. Rev. Accel. Beams* **2018**, *21*, 041301. [CrossRef]
80. Derouillat, J.; Beck, A.; Perez, F.; Vinci, T.; Chiaramello, M.; Grassi, A.; Fle, M.; Bouchard, G.; Plotnikov, I.; Aunai, N.; et al. SMILEI: A collaborative, open-source, multi-purpose particle-in-cell code for plasma simulation. *Comp. Phys. Comm.* **2018**, *222*, 351–373. [CrossRef]
81. Pedregosa, F.; Varoquaux, G.; Gramfort, A.; Michel, V.; Thirion, B.; Grisel, O.; Blondel, M.; Prettenhofer, P.; Weiss, R.; Dubourg, V.; et al. Scikit-learn: Machine Learning in Python. *J. Mach. Learn. Res.* **2011**, *12*, 2825.

82. Markidis, S.; Peng, I.B.; Podobas, A.; Jongsuebchoke, I.; Bengtsson, G.; Herman, P.A. Automatic Particle Trajectory Classification in Plasma Simulations. In Proceedings of the 2020 IEEE/ACM Workshop on Machine Learning in High Performance Computing Environments (MLHPC) and Workshop on Artificial Intelligence and Machine Learning for Scientific Applications (AI4S), Atlanta, GA, USA, 12 November 2020; pp. 64–71.
83. Bulanov, S.V.; Esirkepov, T.Z.; Naumova, N.M.; Pegoraro, F.; Vshivkov, V.A. Solitonlike Electromagnetic Waves behind a Superintense Laser Pulse in a Plasma. *Phys. Rev. Lett.* **1999**, *82*, 3440. [CrossRef]

MDPI
St. Alban-Anlage 66
4052 Basel
Switzerland
Tel. +41 61 683 77 34
Fax +41 61 302 89 18
www.mdpi.com

Photonics Editorial Office
E-mail: photonics@mdpi.com
www.mdpi.com/journal/photonics

www.ingramcontent.com/pod-product-compliance
Lightning Source LLC
LaVergne TN
LVHW070408100526
838202LV00014B/1415